Adventure Guide to Northern Florida & the Panhandle

Jim & Cynthia Tunstall

Hunter Publishing, Inc.
130 Campus Drive
Edison NJ 08818
(908) 225 1900 / (800) 255 0343
Fax (908) 417 0482
e-mail: hunterpub@emi.net
http://www.hunterpublishing.com

In Canada:
1220 Nicholson Road
Newmarket, Ontario
Canada L3Y 7V1
(800) 399 6858
Fax (800) 363 2665

ISBN 1-55650-769-0

© 1997 Jim & Cynthia Tunstall

All rights reserved. No part of this publication may be reproduced, stored in a retrieval system, or transmitted in any form, or by any means, electronic, mechanical, photocopying, recording, or otherwise, without the written permission of the publisher.

This guide focuses on recreational activities. As all such activities contain elements of risk, the publisher, authors, affiliated individuals and companies disclaim all responsibility for injury, harm, or illness that may occur to anyone through, or by use of, the information in this book. Every effort was made to insure the accuracy of information in this book, but the publisher and authors do not assume, and hereby disclaim, all liability for any loss or damage caused by errors, omissions, misleading information or potential travel problems caused by this guide, even if such errors or omissions result from negligence, accident or any other cause.

Cover photo and all interior photos: Cynthia Tunstall.

Maps: Kim André and Lissa K. Dailey.

ACKNOWLEDGMENTS

At the risk of sounding like Academy Award winners, please indulge us for a few moments of thanks. (STOP: Don't skip this part — there's going to be a pop quiz at the end of the book!)

The folks who bring adventuring to you in Florida have their stuff together as you'll discover, not only from these pages, but also the additional information that's available by calling or writing the sources listed throughout the guide.

We offer a great big "Thank You" to the US Forest Service, US Fish & Wildlife Service, Florida Department of Environmental Protection's Division of Recreation and Parks, Florida Marine Patrol, Florida Game & Fresh Water Fish Commission, Office of Greenways and Trails, Florida Forest Service and Florida Department of Transportation. Also, invaluable assistance was provided by the Florida Trail Association, Ned DeLoach's Diving Guide to Underwater Florida, Florida Association of Dive Operators, Florida Association of Canoe Liveries and Outfitters and the Northwest Florida, St. Johns River, Southwest Florida and Suwannee River water management districts. The chambers of commerce and tourist councils that aided in this guide are too numerous to list here, but you'll meet them under the "information sources" in each chapter.

Last, but not least, it would have been impossible to complete this guide without the enthusiasm and tireless work of the Tallahassee Lassies – Debbie, Lorraine, Traci, Shari, Cathy, Sharon, Kelly, Joanna, Jennifer and the rest of the crew at Geiger & Associates.

ABOUT THE AUTHORS

Jim Tunstall has been on the staff of The Tampa Tribune since 1978. He currently is a roving feature writer covering slices of life, back roads and country characters in North Florida. His freelance travel articles have appeared in Better Homes & Gardens, Colorado Homes & Lifestyles, the Chicago Sun-Times, the San Francisco Examiner, the Atlanta Journal-Constitution and dozens of other national and regional publications. This is his first book. He lives in a radar blip called Lecanto, Florida, with his wife and co-author, two horses, two dogs, two cats, one parrot and a lot of native wildlife. At times the ranch gets a bit crowded.

Cynthia Tunstall has been a freelance writer and photographer for 18 years, specializing in travel, equestrian sports and wildlife. Her stories and art have appeared in *Islands, Better Homes & Gardens, Country America, Seattle Homes & Lifestyles,* the *Miami Herald,* the *Chicago Sun-Times, Buffalo News,* the *San Francisco Examiner* and other national and regional publications. She has written two non-travel books, *Recipes for Love* (Bartlett Publishing) and *Training and Showing Your Miniature Horse* (Small Horse Press). She is to blame for the menagerie at the Rancho Tunstall.

Contents

INTRODUCTION	1
Geography & History	3
The Nature Of Adventure	5
How To Use This Book	8
Travel Strategies & Helpful Facts	13
WESTERN PANHANDLE	23
Geography & History	26
Getting Around	27
Touring	29
Pensacola/Escambia County	29
Adventures	40
On Foot	40
On Horseback	43
On Wheels	44
On Water	45
In The Air	51
Eco-Travel Excursions	52
Where To Stay & Eat	52
Pensacola/Escambia County	52
Milton/Santa Rosa County	53
Fort Walton Beach/Destin	54
South Walton	54
Campgrounds	56
CENTRAL PANHANDLE	57
Geography & History	59
Getting Around	60
Touring	62
Panama City Beach/Bay County	62
Washington County	65
Holmes County	67
Jackson County	68
Gulf County	69
Adventures	72
On Foot	72
On Horseback	75
On Wheels	76

On Water	77
In The Air	85
Eco-Travel Excursions	85
Where To Stay & Eat	85
Panama City/Bay County	86
Washington County	87
Holmes County	87
Jackson County	87
Calhoun County	88
Gulf County	88
Campgrounds	88
EASTERN PANHANDLE	**91**
Geography & History	93
Getting Around	95
Touring	96
Gadsden County	96
Liberty County	99
Franklin County	102
Wakulla County	106
Leon County	109
Jefferson County	113
Adventures	113
On Foot	113
On Horseback	116
On Wheels	116
On Water	118
Eco-Travel Excursions	123
Where To Stay & Eat	124
Gadsden County	124
Franklin County	124
Wakulla County	125
Leon County	125
Campgrounds	126
SUWANNEE REGION	**129**
Geography & History	131
Getting Around	132
Touring	133
Madison County	133
Hamilton County	135
Columbia County	137
Suwannee County	140
Adventures	142

On Foot	142
On Horseback	145
On Wheels	147
On Water	150
Where To Stay & Eat	156
Madison & Hamilton Counties	156
Suwannee County	156
Columbia & Lafayette Counties	158
Campgrounds	158

NORTHERN HEARTLAND	**161**
Geography & History	164
Getting Around	165
Touring	166
Gilchrist County	166
Alachua County	167
Bradford County	172
Union County	173
Baker County	174
Adventures	175
On Foot	175
On Horseback	179
On Wheels	181
On Wheels II	182
On Water	183
In The Air	187
Where To Stay & Eat	188
Gilchrist & Alachua Counties	188
Bradford County	190
Campgrounds	190

NORTHEAST FLORIDA	**193**
Geography & History	196
Getting Around	198
Touring	199
Nassau County	199
Jacksonville	202
Duval & Clay Counties	202
St. Augustine	207
St. Johns & Putnam Counties	207
Adventures	211
On Foot	211
On Horseback	216
On Wheels	217

On Water	218
In The Air	224
Where To Stay & Eat	224
Nassau County	224
Jacksonville/Duval County	226
Putnam County	226
St. Augustine/St. Johns County	226
Campgrounds	227

NORTH-CENTRAL FLORIDA — 229

Geography & History	231
Getting Around	232
Touring	234
Flagler County	234
Daytona Beach/Volusia County	236
Lake County	239
Marion County	241
Adventures	243
On Foot	243
On Horseback	251
On Wheels	253
On Water	256
On Water II	263
In The Air	263
Where To Stay & Eat	264
Flagler County	264
Volusia County	264
Lake County	265
Marion County	265
Campgrounds	266

THE NATURE COAST & BIG BEND — 269

Geography & History	272
Getting Around	274
Touring	276
Citrus County	276
Levy, Dixie & Taylor Counties	281
Adventures	285
On Foot	285
Golf Courses	287
On Horseback	287
On Wheels	289
On Water	291
In The Air	299

Where To Stay & Eat 300
Campgrounds 301

Maps

Counties of Northern Florida & the Panhandle	6
Northern Florida Trail Sections	7
Pensacola	30
Escambia County	31
Santa Rosa County	32
Okaloosa County	35
Walton County	38
Bay County	63
Washington County	65
Holmes County	67
Jackson County	68
Gulf County	70
Calhoun County	71
Gadsden County	98
Torreya State Park	100
Liberty County	101
Franklin County	103
Wakulha County	107
Tallahassee	109
Leon County	110
Jefferson County	112
Madison County	134
Hamilton County	135
Ichetucknee Springs State Park	138
Columbia County	139
Suwannee County	141
Suwannee River State Park	142
Lafayette County	157
Gainesville	163
Gilchrist County	167
Alachua County	168
Bradford County	173
Union County	174
Baker County	175
Nassau County	200
Duval County	202
Clay County	203

Jacksonville & Vicinity	204
St. Johns County	206
Putnam County	208
Gold Head Branch State Park	212
Flagler County	235
Volusia County	237
Lake County	240
Marion County	241
Withlacoochee State Trail	245
Citrus County	276
Sumter County	280
Levy County	282
Dixie County	283
Taylor County	284

Introduction

Welcome to the wild, wonderful and sometimes wacky "other" Florida. (That's the one far from the "Land of the Mouse" and "Miami Vice.")

The wild side of the equation: You're going on a safari into 39 counties in North and Northwest Florida that remain, for the most part, untamed. While there are isolated pockets of man's handiwork – burger barns, speed traps and time-share salesmen, for example – more than three-quarters of this region is owned by government or large private landholders. Much of this part of Florida remains as it was hundreds of years ago and most of it welcomes tourists. Of course, being wisened travelers and keen students of geography, you already recognize that snow and mountain sports are out in Florida (until the next ice age or volcanic awakening), but the north and northwest are rich playing fields for hikers, bicyclists, horseback riders, paddlers, divers, anglers and eco-travelers, among others. You're also going to find plenty of spots to spank a golf ball, as well as some launch pads for less conventional adventures. What about driving a dragster up to 200 mph down the quarter-mile or hurling yourself out of a perfectly safe airplane (two miles above the planet) with nothing between you and the ever after except a ripcord?

The wonderful side: Climate makes this region a year-round destination, though you'll find a few asterisks and precautions a little later in the introduction. Florida's geography makes its adventures within the stamina limits of just about everyone. It's flat with a capital "F" – the highest summit is a whopping 345 feet above sea level – but unspoiled land; interior waterways and some of the most beautiful beaches in the world make up for the lack of dramatic relief.

The blue-light special: During the next few hundred pages, you're going to run into some colorful characters who provide insights into what North and Northwest Florida, past and present, are all about. Speaking of colorful.

The wacky side: Well, make sure you pack an open mind and a sense of humor. You'll find all kinds of offbeat encounters while you're touring, from UFOs and ghostly tenants to a death-row museum and a road-kill gift shop. You'll meet an artistic elephant, learn how to measure a submerged alligator (without losing a

Introduction

Pelicans resting their wings.

finger) and get a crash-course in hippopotamus husbandry. You're even going to get, at no added charge, a guaranteed way to kill chiggers. (That's especially valuable for northerners who take home a handful of Spanish moss.) By the time you're finished reading, you're going to be a certified Marlin Perkins.

What other guide book makes you that offer?

A minor confession: Not every place is untamed. While much of this land is public and a large share of the private tracts are natural, you're going to visit a few of the big population centers – Pensacola, Jacksonville and Daytona Beach, among them. That means limited encounters with crowds, tourist trappings, hot-wired spring breakers and skylines distorted by smog. But there are some nifty adventure bases, too, and they're great landing zones for those coming here by air from faraway places. With the exception of brief excursions into the neon jungle, most of your time is going to be spent in sleepy burgs and fishing villages such as Steinhatchee and Cross Creek, vast forests and wildlife refuges, some of the most challenging canoe trails and dive sites in the Southeast and a wide assortment of other back-to-nature destinations the locals like to call paradise.

When you're finished, you may even believe they're right. These adventures are going to take you to hundreds of public and private sites – national forests, state parks and trails, water management district tracts and a variety of other staging areas that beg adventurers to have a good time.

If you want to taste the real Florida, this guide book is your meal ticket. It provides all of the information you need to plan an attack on the great outdoors. Ride a trail, paddle a river, peddle a path or hike a historic gateway, literally for days if you have the fortitude, and camp under the stars along the way. Go for a ride on a glider, bi-plane or seaplane; take an airboat and zip along a pristine river; dare to dive into water cold enough to keep your speared quarry fresh for days; or water-ski with some of the world's greatest acrobats. But don't worry yourself about frostbite. Unless you stay in a Motel 6 and turn the thermostat too low, there are only a dozen or so days when it gets that chilly.

There's enough adventure here to fill your dance card for months.

So call the boss, leave word that you're going to be late and dig in. But don't forget to front-end load – plan ahead, don't fly by the seat of your pants.

Geography & History

The Sunshine State goes from sea to shining sea in a mere matter of 70 miles or less in many places, though in some the path shows much more on the old odometer because of rural road systems.

While a handful of hot spots have become increasingly popular in the last decade or two, much of North and Northwest Florida remains undiscovered and therefore uncrowded. While there are no breathtaking panoramas such as those found in the mountain and canyon states, the canvas here is painted with subtler beauty. The terrain changes from coastal and cypress swamps to dry uplands in a handful of miles. You can experience idyllic barrier islands, such as St. George, Cape St. George, St. Vincent and Dog, off the Central Panhandle, where there are beautiful sunrises and sunsets. Many of the beaches here are decorated with 40-foot dunes, ghost-white sand and blue-green water. Some of them have been recognized by Stephen Leatherman, the University of Maryland researcher known as "Dr. Beach," as among the most beautiful sand slips in the world. Moving into the interior, there are vast wilderness areas such as the Blackwater River State Forest and the Osceola National Forest. And you'll get a chance to see a Florida-style waterfall at Falling Waters State Recreation Area and burn calories on a subterranean hiking trail at Florida Caverns State Park.

The changing habitats you're going to encounter include:

- ❏ Those cypress swamps, which, to some, are the calling cards of Florida. Twisted bald cypress trees rise from pristine rivers that are surrounded by plenty of wildlife, from white-tail deer and wild hogs to river otters, alligators and turtles.
- ❏ Salt and freshwater marshes, seas of grass that dot the coast and river fronts, respectively, provide a rich environment for sandhill cranes, ospreys, woodstorks, bald eagles and several other endangered or threatened species.

- Forest swamps that are populated with hickory, black and sweet gum, cabbage palms and water oaks, as well as bobcats, turkeys and tune-crooning songbirds.
- Prairies, such as Paynes Prairie near Gainesville, which has a diverse mix, from interior wetlands to vast grassy plains to upland forests that are home to native species (owls, raccoons, alligators and wading birds) and some non-native types (American bison and Spanish horses, whose ancestry stretches to the first European arrivals).
- Fertile hardwood hammocks thick with century-old trees, such as maple and live oaks, and residents such as red-tail and red-shoulder hawks, raccoons and flying squirrels.
- Pine flatwoods, where long-leaf pines grow in the higher, drier regions and slash pines settle in the transition zones between dry and wet. Black bears, deer, fox squirrels, bobcats and gray foxes are among the tenants.
- Sandhill areas, which are more arid and sparsely settled. Oaks, mainly turkey and red, are the most common trees, while critters that burrow to escape the heat (gopher tortoises and indigo snakes included) are among the ones you can expect to see.

History? Naturally, though it's not as deep as in some areas of the nation, primarily because peninsular Florida was covered by water long after the rest of the continent was born. Still, the state has a reasonably rich and, at times, colorful heritage. You're going to learn about it as you move around the circuit, but you're also going to have a little fun. After all, most of you graduated from some kind of school and have had enough lectures in "History to Bore You."

The first inhabitants (depending on whose class you attended) pitched a tent somewhere between 10,000 and 20,000 years ago. Two early Indian tribes settled North and Northwest Florida – the Apalachees, who were skillful fighters and hunters, and the peaceful Timucuans. While artifacts from both cultures are pretty much limited to museum exhibits, some of the area's rivers still cough up pottery shards and arrowpoints. The Timucuans left a more lasting clue of their existence, oyster-shell and burial mounds that are preserved at several historic sites you'll encounter on the tour. The Seminoles are among the more recent tribes and, despite three wars with federal troops and exile to reservations west of the Mississippi River, a small core who refused to surrender or be captured planted the seed for the 15,000 Seminoles who now live on three Florida reservations.

The Spanish, as you'll learn later in this book, had a great influence on the development of early Florida. They also were Florida's first punching bag, being alternately beaten to a pulp by the Apalachees, English, French and some of the indigenous wildlife.

On the history-can-be-fun side of the ledger, stay tuned for:

- ❏ The misadventures of Ponce de Leon, who got lost, shot and frustrated by his failure to find the mythical fountain of youth for merry King Ferdinand and his delightful daughter, Juana.
- ❏ The now-nameless sculptor who left out a few anatomical parts when he carved the king of beasts on a bridge in St. Augustine and did himself in to end the ridicule he was facing.
- ❏ Stephen Foster, the famous composer who immortalized the Suwannee River without setting eyes on it. Fortunately, he ignored his brother's suggestion, the Yazoo River. As everyone knows, the Yazoo wasn't entirely snubbed. It later was honored by a well-known lawnmower maker.

The Nature Of Adventure

Sure, your parents, some of your friends, even a few of you have spent an embarrassing number of vacations:

- ❏ Vegetating on beaches.
- ❏ Fighting the crowds in theme parks where humans dress as animals.
- ❏ Parking your keisters in a bus where a guy with a voice like Carlton the Doorman narrates highlights that flash by in a blur.

But more of you are choosing the adventure route. That doesn't mean you have to be Richard E. Byrd, Neil Armstrong, or Evil Knievel to get a natural buzz. Yes, you can push yourself to reasonable limits in North and Northwest Florida – whether it's trying a hiking or cycling marathon, squeezing into a shoulder-wide cave several fathoms below the surface or skydiving toward earth at something close to warp speed. If you want risk, the venues are here. But the activities that follow in this guide offer many more chances to get your cardiovascular system working at a reasonable rate – soft to moderate adventures, if you will – without necessarily playing Russian roulette.

Know your limits. Pay attention to climate, the remoteness of the regions and your physical abilities and limits. This guide has activities for everyone. You can canoe or kayak a jungle river, peddle rural highways that seem to be frozen in another time, hike a trail taken by ancient Indians, or dive the ghostly remains of a centuries-old ship. Many of the adventures can be experienced for an hour, a day, a week or a month. And beyond the physical side, this guide gives you a chance to taste Old Florida's cultures and aesthetics.

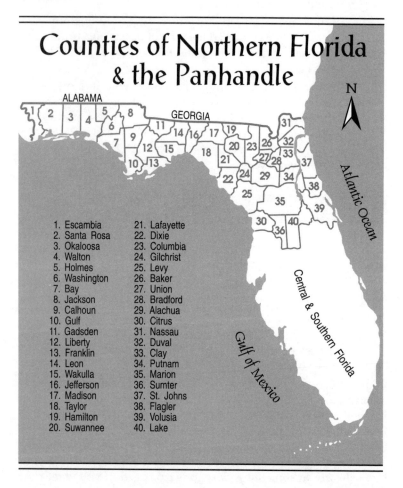

Counties of Northern Florida & the Panhandle

1. Escambia
2. Santa Rosa
3. Okaloosa
4. Walton
5. Holmes
6. Washington
7. Bay
8. Jackson
9. Calhoun
10. Gulf
11. Gadsden
12. Liberty
13. Franklin
14. Leon
15. Wakulla
16. Jefferson
17. Madison
18. Taylor
19. Hamilton
20. Suwannee
21. Lafayette
22. Dixie
23. Columbia
24. Gilchrist
25. Levy
26. Baker
27. Union
28. Bradford
29. Alachua
30. Citrus
31. Nassau
32. Duval
33. Clay
34. Putnam
35. Marion
36. Sumter
37. St. Johns
38. Flagler
39. Volusia
40. Lake

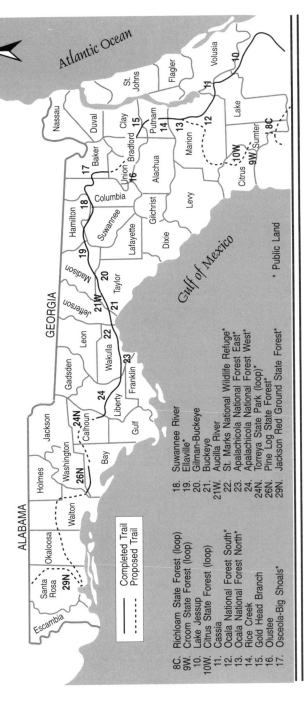

How To Use This Book

The chapters divide North and Northwest Florida into eight regions that, if you're fortunate enough to have a lot of discretionary time and income, allow you to march through the entire landing zone in clockwise fashion. If you're a working stiff with a heavy mortgage and a grouchy boss, choose the one that tickles your fancy most and plan a shorter itinerary. Many of the regions have major airports. Those that don't are close enough to one that you won't have to drive more than an hour or two to reach your destination.

Each chapter has a section on its geography and history where you get a closer look at the past and present. There is information on airports, highways and climate in the "getting around" entries. Since some of you want to get a look at the sights and sounds, the "touring" areas of the chapters have recommended cultural, historical and even some funky pit stops. At the end of the "touring" areas, you'll find some useful contact numbers, chambers of commerce and tourist-type offices, where you can get additional information about your destination.

The "adventure" areas provide specific information about the activities, guided tours where they're available, directions on getting there and what you'll encounter when you arrive. You'll find that many hiking, bicycling and horseback trails allow all three activities and some of the canoe trails are equally appealing to snorkelers. Most "adventure" sections are followed by information sources. These can be important because the directions to some venues are complicated and a few require advance permits or reservations.

Now, here are some general things to know about the adventures.

ON FOOT

While the flat land may make hiking in Florida relatively easy, the length of some of the trails requires a bit of advance warning. There are thousands of miles of trails in the 39 counties and, unless otherwise noted, trail lengths are one-way. If you don't have a road crew to pick you up at the other side, please remember that a 4.7-mile trail means a 9.4-mile hike back to the sedan if you walk the full course. There are several options: Designated trails that are paved or packed hard, wilderness routes that are similar to what the American Indians and early explorers hiked and hundreds of miles of beaches (Florida has more coastline than any state except Alaska). You can find slow-paced nature trails that take only an hour or two or marathon choices, such as the Florida National Scenic Trail, on which you can spend months. While there are too many trails to list them all, this guide offers a representative sample for all skill levels and information sources from which to get more information.

One other warning: While many of the trails are clearly marked, several are located in vast forests where it's very easy to get lost. Talk to the folks who are in charge of the site. Ask for detailed and current maps, special permits or gear you might need and ask about wildlife warnings. It's also smart not to hike alone, and never separate from your partner or group.

Finally, consider a few safeguards offered by the US Forest Service:

- ❑ Know the conditions. It's flat, but there is varied and sometimes rugged terrain; heat and humidity can rapidly cause dehydration. The southern areas in this guide are within the Lightning Capital of the United States.
- ❑ Start early, particularly in summer. Mornings are cooler and afternoons are not only hotter but prone to storms. If you're camping, the early birds have a camp set before weather becomes a factor.
- ❑ Don't exceed your physical limits.
- ❑ Pack fresh water. Florida has an abundance of springs and clear rivers, but many of the trails don't go near them. Even if they did, the water usually isn't safe to drink. A good rule of thumb is to bring one gallon per person per day.
- ❑ Pack food, such as granola bars, trail mix and jerky, in case something goes wrong and you're stuck out there for a while.

ON HORSEBACK

Several national and state forests, parks and conservation areas provide trails, and a few have stalls, for the toughened-fanny crowd. Most trails operated through the Rails to Trails program – which are converted railroad beds – offer a separate trail for riders. While pickings are pretty lean in some areas, none are entirely lacking trails, and those in the Ocala area (see page 251) are arguably the most diverse because Marion County is Florida's horse haven. There are some outfitters who rent or provide organized trail rides around the regions. There's even one resort in the Ocala area that caters to horse-and-carriage fanciers, and a stable south of Jacksonville (see page 216) allows you to ride on the beach.

Three warnings: Some multi-use trails don't separate riders from cyclists and hikers, so be prepared (if your horse is prone) for the flinch factor; there are some trails in areas where hunting is allowed, so steer clear during the season; and Florida requires a negative Coggins test if you bring your own mounts.

ON WHEELS

In-line skaters are allowed on just about any paved course included in this guide, but the focus under the "on wheels" section of these chapters is on bicyclists. This part of Florida has a wide assortment of options. Some cities, including Gainesville (see page 181), have curbed bicycle paths along their streets in addition to the other venues. Most of the areas that have designated hiking trails welcome peddlers and in several areas, especially those where the conventional options are limited, you'll find some improvised ones. Many of the forests, parks and management areas have on-road and/or off-road trails. And for the diehards there's the six-day, 283-mile Seven Hills to the Sea Bicycle Tour in the Panhandle or the six-day, 327-mile Florida Springs Bicycle Tour in north-central Florida. You can even climb Sugarloaf Mountain (see page 254) on a bike, though Everest it isn't.

Again, it's impossible to include all of the trails in this book, but in the "on wheels" sections you'll find lists of outfitters and additional information sources from whom everything is available. A few of the outfitters provide guided tours if you'd rather not go on your own and more will be happy to offer itineraries. Here are a few rules for the road or off-road, depending on your preference:

- ❑ Florida has a helmet law. While some counties have chosen not to make the use of them mandatory, don't take chances with your noggin. Bring one and wear it.
- ❑ Carry food, water, maps and rain gear. You may be glad you did.
- ❑ Ride on designated trails only, stay off private property and, should you choose an area where hunting is al-

lowed, don't come when it is. Generally, state and federal lands that permit hunting keep hunters and adventurers far apart, but don't take chances. Call or write in advance to be sure.
- ❏ Courtesy. Yield to hikers and horseback riders. Especially yield to cars. You don't want to become a hood ornament.
- ❏ Don't exceed your limits.
- ❏ Heat, humidity and lightning can be just as perilous to riders as cars.
- ❏ Plan ahead. Know your equipment and the area. Bring a repair kit and supplies (food, water and a change of gear for a change of weather).
- ❏ As with hiking, it's not smart to go solo.

ON WATER

Again, Florida has more coastline than any state except Alaska. Add the hundreds of rivers and lakes scattered across the north and northwest and, well, pilgrim, this is a destination where water sports rule.

Milton (see page 45) has earned a reputation as Florida's canoe capital for good reason: There are six designated canoe trails (five in the Blackwater River State Forest), including some of the most challenging in the state. But this region doesn't own the franchise. There are scores of designated and improvised trails throughout the 39 counties and plenty of sandbars and state lands on which you can pitch a tent for multi-day excursions. There's even a 91-miler that allows you to tackle the elements in the Gulf of Mexico, where a kayak is a better bet than a canoe. Some of the interior trails require higher skill levels, but there are several that are suitable in terms of length, current and obstacles for beginners. Most areas have outfitters who rent gear, and some offer guided tours and base camps. All of the chapters include a list of sites, sources and outfitters for additional information. Please pay attention to the length, skill levels, access points and additional sources so you don't get stuck up the creek without a paddle.

Diving? It's capital time again. The Branford area (page 152) could be considered the spring- and cave-diving capital of Florida, though the other regions have their share of attractive sites, too. If freshwater diving is your pleasure, you're going to find crystal clear springs and runs that yield fossils and ancient artifacts,

Dolphin in the Gulf of Mexico.

spacious caverns where even non-cave divers can get a taste of that adventure and narrow chimneys and tunnels where your skill and courage are tested. Some cave-diving sites won't let you bring a light with you unless you have cave-diving certification. This isn't a game for amateurs. Many cave divers, experienced ones, have died because they got lost and ran out of air. So make sure you know what you're doing and are cave-certified; otherwise, stick with the springs and caverns. On the saltwater side of the diving ledger, some of the Panhandle (page 48) and Northeast Florida (page 77) areas are second only to the Keys in the number of wrecks and reefs, where creatures great and small share the wet with you. You can dive a World War I battleship, spear a tasty snapper, collect tropicals or shoot photographs.

If you're an angler, there are thousands of rivers, lakes and saltwater sites where you can hook everything from largemouth bass, bream and black crappie to cobia, sharks and marlin. Each chapter includes a list of favorite fishing holes as well as guides, marinas, bait-and-tackle shops and piers. Each also packs a warning about getting a fishing license and size and bag limits.

IN THE AIR

The view of Florida from an eagle's perspective is incredible. On a clear day, at 3,000 feet, you can see both the Atlantic and Gulf coasts from the center of the state. You can tour in a fixed-wing craft, biplane or seaplane; take a ride in a helicopter, hot-air balloon or parasail. Or, if you really want to soar like an eagle, climb into a glider for a soundless flight.

ECO-TRAVEL EXCURSIONS

These entries include tours that are a little more out of the ordinary, such as a pair offered in and around the barrier islands off Apalachicola (page 123). Just to whet your appetite a little, Jeanni McMillan leads excursions where you can hunt feisty blue crabs by flashlight or learn to throw a cast net, while at Tom Gray's Baybottom University Fun School, adventures include dragging a shrimp trawl, tonging oysters and pulling crab pots.

WHERE TO STAY & EAT

In some areas, finding a good place to stay and eat is a matter of picking from an overwhelming menu. In other areas, it's a real challenge unless, of course, you're a back-to-nature type who only needs an MRE and a six-by-three-foot patch of land to spread a sleeping bag.

Even in the less developed areas, there are too many choices to print them all. Furthermore, some of those listed are subjective based on good value, service, food and atmosphere, while others are randomly selected. Rates range from cheap to those that nearly require a second mortgage. The lodging ranges from mom-and-pops and chain motels to exquisite bed-and-breakfasts and five-star (spell that $$$$$) resorts. When the dinner bell chimes, you can roll up your sleeves beside crusty locals at crab shacks, fill up your tank at casual or family-style restaurants or put on your fancy duds and head to an epicurean wonder. If you have questions, call the accommodations, restaurants or area chambers of commerce for additional information. Menus, prices and an establishment's existence change pretty rapidly in Florida.

Additionally, campgrounds are included as separate listings. You'll find everything from primitive sites in parks and on sandbars to posh resorts where you can park a six-figure stretch Winnebago. On the river, sandbars are a good choice because they have few, if any, annoying plants (poison ivy) and creatures (picnic-basket-sacking raccoons and bears) and they aren't on private property.

Travel Strategies & Helpful Facts

As mentioned earlier, this guide is organized in a clockwise fashion that allows the leisure set to attack everything in sequence. That doesn't mean those of you who have little leisure time should risk your future, not to mention the kids' inheritance, by keeping up with the Richie Riches. In some cases, such as those where

Alligator, Homosassa Springs.

you've booked a multi-day excursion through area outfitters, they may be willing to fetch you from the airport. But a rental, unless you're bringing your own sedan, is a better bet to cover the course. Rental agencies have set up shop in most cities with airports, even regional and sandlot strips.

In some areas, particularly near the more traveled cities like Daytona Beach, Jacksonville, Panama City and Pensacola, you might consider planning your trip away from the traditional summer and winter tourist seasons, the spring break fiasco (especially in Daytona and Panama City) or the legislative session (February-April) in Tallahassee. Otherwise, the crowds are moderate to minimal in most of these destinations.

Here are a few other precautions to keep this part of Florida the way it is:

1) Leave the wildflowers growing along roadsides and in pastures, the air plants that decorate the forests and the Spanish moss where you find them. The first two are illegal to pick. Moss ought to be illegal because of the chiggers, a blight you'll learn more about on page 17.

2) If you happen upon a beach with those beautiful dunes, please, please, PUHLEEZE don't walk on them. That's why they've disappeared in many places around Florida. Use the boardwalks where they're provided, or take the long way around where they're not. Who knows? If you do, your grandkids may see them.

3) Remember Smokey the Bear's warning? Only you can prevent forest fires. Put them out, avoid them in the dry season, whenever available, use a site that already was used for a fire (otherwise, clear the area of everything that isn't meant for the fire, such as lightweight burnable stuff that might blow in the wind) and don't play Paul Bunyon – don't chop down trees. Use downed firewood that is available throughout the forest. Dig a hole for your fire pit and, when you leave, douse it and cover the hole.

Finally, while touring and adventuring directions are complete to most of the landing zones, some – such as every turn in those marathoners' cycling tours – are far too complex to print here. So take advantage of the information sources.

WILDLIFE & INSECTS

The Sometimes Good, The Bad & The Ugly

Florida has more than its share of wildlife and the franchise on bugs. So, come prepared to keep a safe distance from (or outrun and outclimb) the former and Raid-soak the latter.

- ❏ Alligators. The best advice: Steer clear on land and in water – you can't outrun or outswim them. On land, the only hope is to run a zigzag pattern, and on water, well, there isn't a lot of hope. But most of them are shy. They're more than happy to run or swim away, unless you threaten a female's nest, threaten a bull during mating season or bump into one that's down on its luck and hasn't had a meal in a year or so. One other exception: Thanks to folks who insist on feeding them marshmallows, chicken and other alligator treats, some have little fear of humans, so keep your distance.
- ❏ Raccoons. Oh, how cute. And too often, oh, how rabid. Those that seem overly aggressive or have no fear of you ought to be avoided. The same applies to those that stumble – there's a far better chance they're rabid than drunk. You don't want to undergo the treatment for rabies.
- ❏ Black bears. They're usually not aggressive, but they are wild. They also pack a large appetite and love mischief. Keep your food and scraps away from them. That means locking coolers and food in your vehicle when you're not there and putting trash in dumpsters, making sure the lid is tightly shut. We don't have to tell you to avoid feeding them, right?
- ❏ Feral hogs. Brought here by the Spanish, these wild critters are more of a destructive nuisance than anything. They destroy native plants by chowing on their roots, and they also gobble native wildlife, from rodents, salamanders and frogs to young birds and turtle eggs. Like black bears, wild hogs usually aren't aggressive, but don't take chances. Boars can leave a nasty tattoo at shin level with their tusks.
- ❏ Snakes. Florida has several poisonous species that you may run into on the trail or water. **Coral snakes** are frequently confused with the harmless scarlet kingsnakes, because both are black,

red and yellow. If the black and red bands are separated by yellow, you've found a coral. It's the deadliest of those that are listed here, but it has a handicap: It has to gnaw on you to break the skin. Many of its victims believe it's pretty and pick it up. Dumb idea. The coral lives in pine woods, lake borders and hammocks. The **eastern diamondback rattlesnake** is identifiable by yellow-bordered, diamond-shaped markings on its body. It often coils before it strikes (you'll probably hear the rattle of its tail), and it can strike a distance of up to one-half of its body length. It likes palmettos, pine woods and grassy areas. The **canebrake rattlesnake** is grayish-brown or pinkish-buff with dark bands across its body, an orange or rusty-red stripe down the middle of its back and a brown or black tail that ends with a rattle. It's common in flatwoods, hammocks and, during the warm months, swampy areas. The **pygmy** or **ground rattlesnake** usually grows to no more than 24 inches and makes a sound like a buzzing insect if you get near enough. They're fat little suckers with a gray body marked by round, brown spots as well as reddish spots alternating with darker ones down the middle of the back. Habitats include palmettos, slash pine and flatwoods. The **cottonmouth moccasin** varies from an olive-brown to black and sometimes has dark crossbands. It usually has a dark horizontal band that runs from the corner of its eyes to the back of its jaws. The cottonmouth is a water snake with an often aggressive disposition. The **copperhead** is pinkish-tan with reddish-brown crossbands and a copper-colored head. Rare in Florida except the Panhandle, it's often confused with the young cottonmouth. All of these will be more than willing to bite or gnaw on you, and the results can be quite disastrous, so keep your distance from snakes, even if you're sure they're harmless.

❑ Mosquitoes. Found in shady, wooded and low-lying water areas, they're usually kept under control by off-the-shelf repellents or a well-aimed slap, but they can carry diseases, such as encephalitis, so be prepared for the army, which includes 60 or so saltwater and freshwater varieties. Those fog-spraying trucks don't help much. Mosquitoes follow them, laughing and getting high. Other than using repellents, the best deterrent is a matter of nature: Most of you adventure in the daytime. Mosquitoes prefer to attack at twilight, when even the most ardent outdoors-types are chilling out over a brewski or screw-cap wine. If you must be out at that hour, rely on good netting, a smoky fire or foot speed.

- Yellow flies, deer flies, brown bombers and various other names, which aren't suitable for print. You'll run into them in upland forests and around horses. Repellents work. So does a swift swat. If one lands on you, tighten the muscle in question. It locks the fly in place and you can smack it to smithereens. If you're quick enough, you won't even be left with an itch.
- No-see-ums. Years ago, natives called then sand gnats, but that wasn't a fitting name. They're the size of a microscopic fleck of black pepper (hence the name) and they attack like piranhas, causing a maddening itch. The best solution, other than staying the heck away from some of our best adventure zones, is a healthy coating of Avon Skin So Soft. (Sorry for the unabashed plug, but the stuff works wonders as a deterrent.)
- Chiggers look like granules of red pepper. They're usually encountered by moss-gathering Yankees and indiscriminating campers, and they can itch for days because they tunnel under the skin. If they do, execute them by smothering them with nail polish and stop the itch with Calamine lotion. The best advice, of course, is to prevent them by never sitting directly on the ground and by covering exposed flesh with repellent. (If you're a northerner who insists on taking some moss home, see page 230 for a sure-fire cure.)
- Fire ants. Their name says everything about their sting, a painful blister that causes supreme problems for anyone allergic to the venom. The mounds are easy to spot. They're dome-like, sometimes large enough to look similar to an English bobby's helmet. Fire ants don't attack one at a time, they swarm. Uh-oh.
- Ticks. They're common in uplands whenever the weather is warm. Ticks can cause Lyme disease, whose symptoms are much like the flu: muscle aches, fatigue and fever that, if left untreated, can lead to meningitis, swollen joints and irregular heartbeat. If one locks in on you, carefully remove it with a pair of tweezers. Don't leave any of the mouth in your skin (grip it close to your skin). A drop of kerosene or gasoline sometimes causes them to cry "uncle."
- Scorpions. Black death, they're not. But Florida's kind loves dry areas, pine trees and unattended boots, so shake out the latter if you shed them when you go to sleep at night. The bite? It's similar to a wasp or bee sting, but rarely serious unless you're allergic.
- Poisonous plants. **Poison ivy** and **poison sumac** are abundant in many uplands. Ivy stands upright or lies along the ground. It has three leaflets per leaf and berries that are white. Sumac has

similar berries and leaves with seven to 13 points. They produce small, itchy blisters that are best cured with Cortisone creams. Florida also has poisonous **oleander** trees and **mushrooms** (please – even if you're an old hippie – don't take a chance on the mushrooms).

CLIMATE

While this guide covers a lot of turf, the north and northwest don't have a wide fluctuation in climate. Coastal areas generally are a little cooler in summer and a little warmer in winter than the interiors. The winters generally are mild. In the northern interior regions, the thermometer may drop into single digits two to six days per year (seldom in the coastal areas), with the winter averages being 40 to 46° on the low side and 65 to 68° on the high. Coastal areas avoid some of the heat and humidity in summer, with averages ranging from 81 to 89°. The interiors usually get three to six days a year topping the century mark. The coldest months are January and February; the hottest are July, August and early September. The latter also are the worst sunburn seasons. Mid-January to mid-March is the main rainy season, with afternoon thunderstorms common in July and August.

There are two other weather worries – lightning and hurricanes.

Lightning is at its worst during the summer months. The north-central part of the state is one of the world's greatest lightning belts. When a thunderstorm is approaching, stay away from any type of water, avoid open fields and don't use trees for shelter, particularly pines and oaks, which are favorite lightning targets. It's also a good idea to shed any metal attractants, such as a backpack that has an aluminum frame.

Hurricanes can wreck a vacation anytime from June through November, though the most active months seem to be August, September and October. If you're getting ready to come to the region and one is approaching, cancel your reservations and reschedule. You don't want to tangle with them. If you're here already, listen to weather and civil-defense stations for evacuation orders and routes. Keep in mind, too, that a hurricane's devastation can be long-term, so if one recently has swept through an area you're planning to visit, call ahead to adventure operators or park and forest services to get a damage assessment.

CLOTHING & GEAR

Clothing. International Falls or Buffalo this isn't, but if you're planning on a winter visit, bring enough layered clothing (jackets, windbreakers, sweaters and sweatshirts) to beat any condition. Don't forget a poncho or raincoat, too. Those winter rains can dampen an adventure more than the summer ones. But you can leave the ski masks, heavy long johns (it's a good idea to pack a lightweight set) and ear muffs at home. Summer clothing is more of a concern due to heat and humidity. Keep it light, but also pack the kind of things that will keep the sun and ultraviolet rays off your skin. Sandals are fine for the beach and tennis shoes are OK for mild adventures but, if you're into the serious stuff, good hiking or horse-riding boots are a must. Shorts are a safe bet, particularly if you cover exposed areas with bug repellent or sunscreen; a better idea are those convertibles that allow you to zip on or off the lower legs depending on conditions. Lightweight shirts or T-shirts are essential, as is a hat, preferably one with a bill to keep the sun out of your eyes and off your delicate nose. Those who don't pay attention go home looking like Rudolph the Rednose – or worse. For the evenings, the dress code in Florida is pretty casual unless you're going to a fancy restaurant. Most have a sign saying "Shirts and Shoes Required," which summarizes the way of life here, though many places require long pants and shirts with collars. Coats and ties need only be packed if you're planning an upscale night out.

And don't forget an umbrella, winter or summer.

Gear. Bug repellent is essential. Apply it to exposed skin as well as your clothes, and avoid sweet-smelling cologne or perfume. Also pack some sort of bug-bite reliever, just in case. Sunscreen (25 or better) is another must to avoid sunburn or sun poison, and don't forget a pair of sunglasses. Liquids, snacks and vitamin supplements should be packed for the trail. As for your adventuring gear, it's always best to bring your favorites

A white heron on the Chassahoitzka River.

with you, but larger outfitters in the region usually have everything you'll need.

DRIVING & ROAD CONDITIONS

With few exceptions, most of the areas you'll visit in North and Northwest Florida have a good system of major and secondary highways. In the more rural areas, it may take a little longer to get there, but the less-than-direct route usually avoids, and therefore protects, an adventure, environmental or wildlife area.

Unless you're a serious backpacking cyclist, a car is going to be needed to tour and experience the adventures in the eight geographical regions contained in this guide. And, while most of your activities can be reached from a paved or hard-packed road, don't attempt to drive a Yugo along one marked for four-wheel-drive vehicles only. Skip it and find another adventure. Also be wary of using hard-packed dirt roads during the rainy season. There are few worse feelings than driving 20 miles on a forest road, getting stuck in mud and having to hoof it back. Even ardent hikers get their shorts in a knot when this happens.

Another good piece of advice is to fill your gas tank whenever possible. This is the "other" Florida, far from the land where there's a service station on every other corner. On some of these routes, you may drive 50 or 100 miles between gas points. If a cellular telephone or CB radio is an option, take the option. They could save your life and certainly your day.

There are two other essentials. A Florida state road map can be obtained from any AAA office (free to members or a nominal charge to non-members), and local maps can be obtained from chambers of commerce listed in each chapter.

SPECIAL CONCERNS

The smartest advice is: Leave it as you found it.

This part of Florida remains for the most part natural because locals and travelers who came before left it alone. Respect the wildlife. Respect the plants. Respect private property and protected public lands. If there's a fence or locked gate, it's a pretty clear indication you're not wanted inside.

If you camp, leave only what was there when you arrived. Take the trash and garbage with you. Bury human waste at least a foot deep and 100 or more feet from any water sources. Use biodegradable soap and wash from a bucket far from water sources. And don't drink from rivers or lakes. They may look safe, but bacteria from animal waste can cause diarrhea, cramps and a lot of other things that will wipe the smile from your face. Instead, carry drinking water with you. If that's impossible, boil water from local sources for 20 minutes or treat it with a water purification kit.

Finally, don't take a souvenir home.

Pack that old Brownie or Polaroid and take a photograph home instead

INFORMATION SOURCES

Under the "getting around" sections of each chapter, you'll find a long list of information sources that can make your adventures much more pleasurable and answer additional questions you may have about the region. More sources as well as outfitters follow some of the individual adventures. Advance planning is a sure-fire way to avoid unexpected surprises, whether that means a closed motel, a trail wrecked by a hurricane or any number of other potential snags. Some of these sources also can supply more detailed maps or directions for your activities.

Now, enough preparations and precautions. Let's strap in, suck a little oxygen and prepare for some G-force adventures.

Western Panhandle

Famous double-takes after a first-time UFO encounter:
1) "Lord, I'll never touch another drop."
2) "I didn't see it if you didn't see it."
3) "Billy Earl, I think I'm having a hot flash."

Time-out for a question from a reader in Atlanta. What the heck do UFOs have to do with adventure travel? That's a fair question, ma'am. Here's the fair-to-partly-cloudy answer: If you believe the believers, they may be an unexpected adventure during your visit. You see, Gulf Breeze, a little splinter of land sticking into the Gulf of Mexico, has one offbeat distinction – more UFO "sightings" than anywhere east of the Mississippi River. And sightings are just the tip of it. Folks in these parts say they've been beamed aboard flying saucers, forced to marry deformed beings from a parallel universe and subjected to all kinds of pokings and proddings. Maybe it's something in the water, but who's to say, right? Real or imagined, these "encounters" are the reason non-believers, and more than a couple of peninsular Floridians, are sure at least part of the Western Panhandle isn't just in a different time zone but a different dimension.

Extraterrestrial encounters or not, this dimension is filled with diversity.

You can explore beaches that are as they were 30 years ago and more – electric-blue water, wind-sculpted dunes and hardly a footprint, except for a tiny trail left by a sandpiper on her way to breakfast.

Before it was discovered, the Walton County beachfront had few tourists and little development. There were a sprinkling of mom-and-pop hideaways, an occasional fishing village and a core of faithful vacationers who wanted to keep it secret. Ultimately, they couldn't. As growth exploded to the east and west, the 26-mile patch known as the Beaches of South Walton changed, too. The saving grace: The 18 communities that make up the area, from well-publicized Seaside to relatively obscure Blue Mountain and Frangista Beach, have locked out most of the glitz that overwhelms some of their neighbors. There are no chain motels, fast-food joints or T-shirt shacks. Instead, there are posh resorts and beachside bungalows, rooftop cafés and five-star restaurants and more than a fair share of life-supporting ecosystems and wildlife sanctuaries.

But the Beaches of South Walton County are just part of the diversity.

Pensacola, a Navy town and mid-size city, mixes a past that reaches six years before the heralded oldest city of St. Augustine with the raw beauty of the Gulf Islands National Seashore, a 150-mile strip of barrier islands, harbors and submerged lands. Outdoor adventures? How about canoeing and kayaking the Perdido River, sailing and jet-skiing the Gulf of Mexico and Pensacola Bay, or slipping on a scuba tank to explore the *USS Massachusetts*, a World War I-era battleship partly buried in 25 feet of sea water?

Venture 20 miles northeast and you can hitch a ride on a horse or canoe for a journey through long-leaf pine and white cedar forests, hardwood swamps and wiregrass that decorate the 186,475-acre Blackwater River State Forest, a site preserved as Old Florida was when the Native Americans settled it and the first wave of Spanish conquistadors came upon it. The forest and nearby Milton are called the "Canoe Capital of Florida." That's no idle boast, as you'll discover later in this chapter.

Every slice of Florida coast has a nickname, and this one is no exception. Chamber of commerce types call it the Emerald Coast, but they aren't ashamed of the other one – "The Redneck Riviera" – bestowed in part due to its proximity to Alabama and Georgia and in part to its eclectic beachfront lifestyles, which in the glitzier locations cater to the Southern party crowd.

Fort Walton Beach and Destin are the Riviera's westernmost provinces.

Just across Choctawhatchee Bay from each other, the two communities offer 24 miles of Appalachian Mountain quartz beaches (60% of which are preserves) and a blend of sun, sand and surf adventures. Destin, touted as The Billfishing Capital of the Gulf, is the home for more charter boats than any other port in Florida, and the area holds six saltwater fishing records. Destin and Fort Walton Beach are an offshore scuba diver's paradise, close to several wrecks, artificial reefs and the 100 Fathom Curve, which creates a living aquarium that, among other things, is one of the top shelling destinations on the planet. These two cities also feature plenty of activity for party-goers: The Hog's Breath Hobie Regatta is in June, the Destin Fishing Rodeo is in September-October (its 49th year and counting) and the Boggy Bayou Mullet Festival anchors October. Trust us, you haven't lived until you've tried mullet dip, which is nothing like sheep dip.

Back in South Walton, Seaside is not only a community but also a lifestyle that reaches to the postwar 1940s and 1950s, though it's a creation of the 1980s. It's an 80-acre village of tin-roofed cottages, porch swings and a layout that fosters evening strolls and chats across backyard fences. It's also one of Florida's most visual beaches. Its Victorian and post-modern residences, painted from a palate of rich pastels, boast names like Daydream Believer, Jack's Beanstalk, Villa Whimsy and Last Edition. Cary Grant would have loved this place.

Finally, Grayton Beach has several distinctions that set it apart. Its tree-lined streets were originally settled in the early 1900s, making it the oldest town between Pensacola and Apalachicola. The past remains in the beach's turn-of-the-century houses and wide front porches, many of them lined with jars of tea brewing in the sun. It's the sort of laid-back village where one of the favorite eateries, the Grayton Corner Café, posts a warning:

Seaside.

"Hours may vary due to quality of the surf."

It's no joke. The owners lower the shutters when the surf's up.

Speaking of surf, University of Maryland researcher Stephen Leatherman, known as "Dr. Beach," ranked Grayton Beach as the "Best Beach in America" in 1994 based on 50 yardsticks, ranging from sand quality and solitude to safety for children and the number of sunny days.

Neighboring Grayton Beach State Park and Campgrounds is a 356-acre testament to this area's natural beauty, while Eden State Gardens & Mansion at Point Washington pays tribute to Northwest Florida's antebellum past.

Diversity? It's as much a part of the Western Panhandle as anywhere else explored in this guide. Visitors find the kinds of adventure and creature comforts that exist in Florida's better-known seafront destinations (from fishing, diving and parasailing to pedal-down night life and pampering resorts), but they also find the other Florida, the one where canoeing, cycling and hiking can be enjoyed along virgin rivers, bayous, lagoons and thick forest trails.

Geography & History

Always remember the "F" word in Florida.

Flat.

That said, few, other than mountain climbers and bikers, snow skiers and rappelers of various disciplines, will be disappointed with their choice. The land rises no more than 291 feet above sea level at any point, yet its face changes at the drop of a hat in the Western Panhandle. As an added bonus, depending on your vantage point, many of the areas have sunrises and sunsets over the Gulf of Mexico or the Intercoastal Waterway.

It's also sprinkled liberally with Gulf frontage, sheltered inlets and coves, pristine rivers and vast forests. While the coastal region has been developed – in some cases overdeveloped – its barrier islands and many interior areas are preserved. Inland areas, in particular, remain much as they were when Spaniard Don Tristan de Luna set up a settlement in 1559 near what is now Pensacola.

The Spanish, of course, came late in the area's history and, as you'll see in the later chapters, weren't exactly ready, willing and able to deal with some of the more unexpected elements – no-see-ums (tiny sand gnats with piranha-size teeth), the tanning index and the Native American unwelcome mat among them.

While the topic is early Americans, four prehistoric tribes were in this area as early as 10,000 years ago. You can see artifacts from the ancient settlements at **Indian Temple Mound Museum**, ☎ 904-243-6521, 139 Miracle Strip, Fort Walton Beach. The exhibits include more than 6,000 pieces of pottery.

Don Tristan de Luna's colony didn't survive long, only two years, before it was abandoned, but the settlement was established six years before America's oldest continuous city.

Pensacola was not tamed again until another Spaniard, Don Andres de Ariola, landed with 350 soldiers in 1698. They built a permanent fort on the site of what is now the Pensacola Naval Air Station on Pensacola Bay and another one in 1719 near what became Fort Pickens on Santa Rosa Island. During one four-month period in 1719, the flag flying over the fort changed four times as the Spanish and the French battled for control. Later, the British and Spanish fought for the area, intermittently fending off pirates such as Billy Bowlegs, who some people say buried treasure on the coast, long before Florida became a state in 1845.

During the Civil War, Union forces held Fort Pickens. Today, it is part of the **Gulf Islands National Seashore** on Santa Rosa Island, ☎ 904-934-2600, 1801 Gulf Breeze Parkway, Gulf Breeze, FL 32561.

Much of the local history is retold at exhibits such as **Historic Pensacola Village**, ☎ 904-444-8905, 120 Church St. Its museums span 200 years of history, including artifacts and buildings from early Florida pioneers.

Near Point Washington, **Eden State Gardens & Mansion**, ☎ 904-231-4214, was the homestead of 19th-century lumberman William Henry Wesley. Following his death, the estate was vandalized, and the grounds were infested with weeds. But they were restored in the 1960s and deeded to the state park service. You'll learn more about the gardens and mansion in the touring section of this chapter.

One final, if elusive, historical note about the Western Panhandle. During Prohibition, leaders in the Destin and Fort Walton Beach area found themselves on the short end when it came to tourism. So they built casinos and speakeasys to lure vacationers away from more popular tourist haunts. Trouble is, in addition to the desirable elements, they attracted the likes of Al Capone and other bandits looking for "cool-off" spots away from the police. Nicknamed "Little Las Vegas," the idea soon died because of bad press and some of the clientele. Its remains, and maybe some of its clients' remains, became offshore reefs.

If you look hard enough, or ask some of the old-timers, you can find the storefronts that were engaged in the business. But don't expect to find any of the old one-armed bandits. This kind of gaming is illegal these days.

Getting Around

The largest airport in this region is **Pensacola Regional Airport**, ☎ 904-435-1746. The next largest is **Okaloosa County Air Terminal**, located in Destin, ☎ 904-651-7160. Together they are served by 13 national airlines and commuters. The **Tallahassee Regional Airport**, ☎ 904-891-7800, and **Panama City-Bay County Air Park**, ☎ 904-763-6751, are further east, if you're attacking from that side. Some of the air services connect through Atlanta, Nashville and New Orleans.

Ground travel is easy along the major feeder roads. Interstate 10 extends east from Mobile into southeast Escambia County and Pensacola, then wanders through the central portions of the three other counties discussed in this chapter: Santa Rosa, Okaloosa and Walton. US Highway 98 enters Escambia south of I-10 and travels along the Gulf Coast and Pensacola Bay. Highway 29 runs north and south through central Escambia from the Alabama line into Pensacola. And Highway 90 follows an east-west path through the counties between I-10 and the Blackwater River State Forest.

Unlike some of the more rural areas of Florida, even the secondary roads in this area are plentiful enough, and in good enough condition, to get you to any target in the least amount of time. Specific routes will be discussed in the touring section of this chapter.

While geographically this is North Florida, the winters are generally mild, thanks in part to the coast. That's what makes it a year-round destination. While there are a few days every year when temperatures dip into the low teens, the winter lows average 44°, with highs of 67°. Coast areas escape some of North Florida's summertime heat (the averages are 81° to 89°) and humidity due to Gulf breezes, but it's still wise to pack and pace yourself accordingly.

INFORMATION SOURCES

Emerald Coast Convention & Visitors Bureau, ☎ 800-322-3319, P.O. Box 609, Fort Walton Beach, FL 32549-0609.

Gulf Breeze & Navarre Beaches Tourist Information Center, ☎ 800-480-7263, 8543 Navarre Parkway, Navarre, FL 32566.

Pensacola Convention & Visitors Information Center, ☎ 800-874-1234, 1401 E. Gregory, St., Pensacola, FL 32501.

South Walton Tourist Development Council, ☎ 800-822-6877, P.O. Box 1248, Santa Rosa Beach, FL 32459.

Beaches of South Walton, ☎ 800-822-6877, P.O. Box 1248, Santa Rosa Beach, FL 32549.

Destin Chamber of Commerce, ☎ 904-837-6241, 1021 Hwy. 98, Destin, FL 32541.

Greater Fort Walton Beach Chamber of Commerce, ☎ 904-244-8191, P.O. Box 640, Fort Walton Beach, FL 32549.

Gulf Breeze Area Chamber of Commerce, ☎ 904-932-7888, P.O. Box 337, Gulf Breeze, FL 32562.

Pensacola Area Chamber of Commerce, ☎ 904-438-4081, P.O. Box 550, Pensacola, FL 32593.

Perdido Key Area Chamber of Commerce, ☎ 904-492-4660, 15500 Perdido Key Drive, Perdido Key, FL 32507.

Santa Rosa County Chamber of Commerce, ☎ 904-623-2339, 5247 Stewart St., Milton, FL 32570-4739.
Walton County Chamber of Commerce, ☎ 904-892-3191, P.O. Box 29, DeFuniak Springs, FL 32433.

Touring

Pensacola/Escambia County

Look! Up in the sky!! (Forget the UFOs.) The Pensacola Naval Air Station fills the skies with modern military war planes – the most spectacular of them are the home-based Blue Angels, the Navy's stunt-performing, aerial aces. They'll fill you in on aviation history at the **National Museum of Naval Aviation**, ☎ 800-327-5002, 1750 Radford Drive, Naval Air Station, Pensacola, FL 32508-6800.

The Blue Angels put on their homecoming air show each November, but you can catch their act year-round at the National Museum of Naval Aviation. It's located about 12 miles from downtown Pensacola. In addition to some thrilling in-flight videos of the team, there's a display, at the top of a seven-story atrium, of members cutting a diamond in their A-4 Skyhawks. The museum's 250,000 square feet of exhibit space feature early wood biplanes, blimps and space-age aircraft, such as the Skylab Command Module. Want to try your hand at flying? Strap yourself into a cockpit simulator for a test flight. There also are more than 100 vintage Navy, Marine Corps and Coast Guard aircraft parked outside. The guides (many of them retired aviators) provide informal tours punctuated by an amusing recollection of their own flying experiences.

For a scenic tour, travel another 10 minutes west on 292 and take a look at Perdido Key. Bridges link this tranquil barrier island to Florida and Alabama. Its high-rises and condominiums overlook the Gulf and Olde rivers that are part of the Intracoastal Waterway. Its shops and old-time honky-tonks keep the good times rolling. And its preserves keep nature for the next generation.

Seventy percent of the barrier island is the **Perdido Key Recreation Area**, ☎ 904-492-1595, which stretches along 1.4 miles of beachfront. The visitors center on Highway 292 has raised

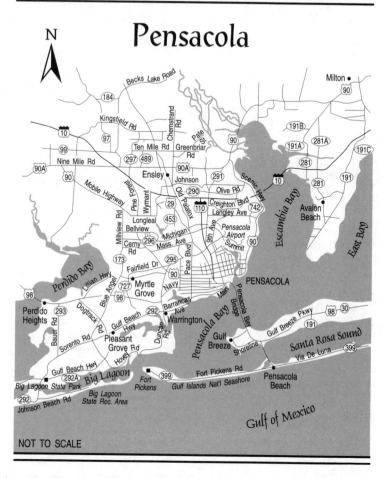

boardwalks and covered picnic areas ideal for viewing the surf, bird life, dunes, sea oats and scrubs that have been twisted and pruned by sometimes forceful winds. This is a good spot for swimming and shore fishing. Showers are available.

By the way, "Dr. Beach" ranked this No. 12 in the world in 1994.

(In case you wondered, well, even if you didn't, Perdido was called "lost island" by the Spanish.)

Nearby **Fort Pickens**, ☎ 800-874-1234, is a 21-million-brick fortress where Apache chief Geronimo was imprisoned for two years in the late 1880s. The fort includes cannon casemates and bulwarks where the shooters (if they ever had a fight, which they didn't) would have had a wider firing range.

Escambia County

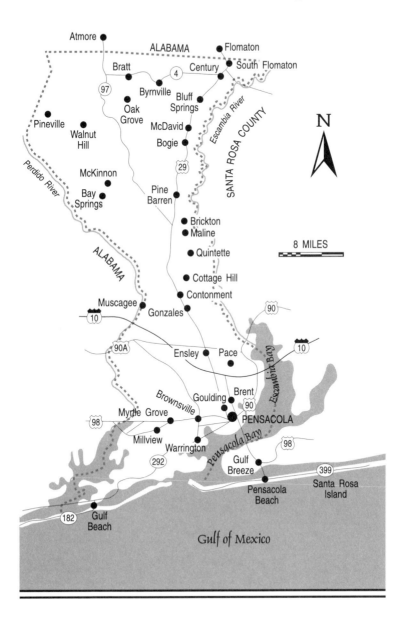

Santa Rosa County

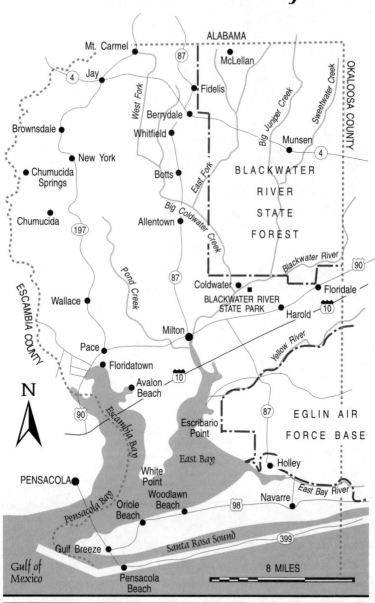

Public tours are available, and a visitors center is on site.

On the return voyage, follow 292 to 292A, turning right (east) and traveling 2.4 miles to **Big Lagoon State Recreation Area**, ☎ 904-492-1595, which features a view of wetlands and marshes that are the transition between coast and uplands. This is a great area to see a wide range of wildlife, including gray foxes, ospreys, great blue herons, raccoons and brown thrashers (which throw themselves onto the ground and flail away in anaphylactic shock – OK, OK, it's a joke!). The 698-acre park also has some short hiking trails, swimming and boating, campsites, showers and a 500-seat, all-weather amphitheater.

Back in town, don't miss a trip on Scenic Highway across Bayou Texar. The reward: a stunning view of Escambia Bay and The Bluffs. There are some walkways for easy viewing and photography.

Downtown, a great deal of the city's history dating to the early 1900s has been preserved in three settings, part of the **Colonial Architecture Trail**. All are based at ☎ 904-444-8905, 120 Church St., Pensacola, FL 32501:

Historic Pensacola Village is a collection of small museums tracing 200 years of history, including stories of French, Spanish and English occupations, told through artifacts and buildings of Florida's earliest pioneers. The **North Hill Preservation District** is an upper-class neighborhood that was platted between the 1870s and 1930s, while the **Seville Historic District** reaches from the 1780s to early 1800s, including Creole and Victorian homes. Markers point out sites.

Now, hop on your favorite mode of transportation. You're heading south.

GULF BREEZE

An artistic elephant?

Ellie the Elephant is billed as something of a Renaissance critter. She's one of the 700 animals at **The Zoo**, ☎ 904-932-2229, a delightful 30-acre natural-habitat zoological park and botanical gardens. The tenants include rare white Bengal tigers, lowland gorillas and pygmy hippos. You can take your kids, if you're packing any, to the petting area and giraffe feeding tower.

The star, though, is Ellie.

She plays her own brand of music and dabbles in watercolors. Actually, her paintings sell for significant amounts of money at charity fund-raisers. That's not necessarily an indication of her artistic talents but shows that people who give to charity have a bigger heart than an eye for art. To get there, take US 98 south from Pensacola, then follow the highway east 13 miles.

While Santa Rosa County isn't knee-deep in attractions or touring, you'll find it has plenty of challenges to tackle. But while you're sightseeing, consider:

- **Milton.** Actually, that's the current name, chosen a) to honor pioneer Dr. Milton Amos, b) to honor early Florida Gov. John Milton, or c) as a shortened version of the former name, Mill Town. While you're thinking about its former names, Milton in its earlier days also was called Hard Scrabble and Scratch Ankle – the latter, possibly due to the briar patches and thorn bushes that bit into the first settlers' lower extremities. The **Milton Opera House**, ☎ 904-623-4433, 6668 Caroline St. (Highway 90), was a cultural center when it was built in 1912. Today it's one of the town's several museums. Another, the **Arcadia Mill Site**, ☎ 904-626-4433, at 5709 Millpond Road, is in an 1820s-style building that once was part of the largest water-powered industrial center in territorial Florida. To reach Milton from Gulf Breeze, take US 98 back into Pensacola, head north on I-110 eight miles to I-10, turn east (right), then go 17 miles to Highway 191. Turn left and travel three miles into town.

- The **Blackwater River State Forest**, ☎ 904-957-4201, shares its 186,475 acres with neighboring Okaloosa County – it's the largest state forest in Florida. Over millions of years, erosion has shaped the forest surface into low rolling hills separated by meandering streams and broad flood plains that form a habitat for species such as red-cockaded woodpeckers and dozens of carnivorous plants. (Don't worry, they only eat insects.) The Blackwater River State Forest provides plenty of recreational activities, including hiking, fishing, canoeing, bicycling and horseback riding. To get to the forest from Milton, follow Highway 90 to Highway 191, traveling 17 miles to the main entrance.

Now, it's time to head east again.

Touring 35

Okaloosa County

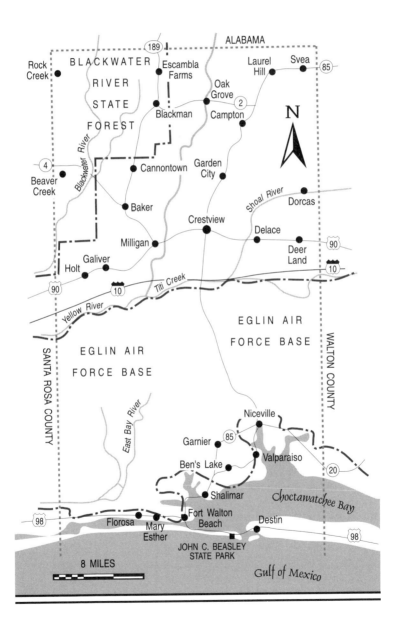

FORT WALTON & DESTIN

Why does a place get (and treasure) a name like The Redneck Riviera?

The "Redneck" part comes from the influences of its neighbors, Alabama and Georgia. Folks in those states, hungry for Gulf beaches, have made this one of their favorite getaways. The "Riviera" part comes from the style of architecture known as "Tourist Glitz." Fort Walton Beach and Destin – like the other province in the Riviera, Panama City, which is 45 miles east – are lined with neon calling cards, frenetic honky-tonks, miniature golf courses, amusement parks, fast-food joints, towering high-rises and hotels, and virtually anything else associated with a typical Florida beach destination. But much of it is confined to the thin strip of beachfront and, if you're inclined, it can be avoided.

That isn't to say the area is strictly glitz. On the contrary.

From Fort Walton Beach, take Highway 85 north about 13 miles, through Niceville and Valparaiso, to **Eglin Air Force Base**, ☎ 904-882-3933, for its double attraction. The first is the Eglin tour that includes a demonstration of the world's biggest environmental test chamber, McKinley Climatic Laboratory. It's capable of producing temperatures from 65° below zero to 165° above, as well as ice, rain, snow and 100 mph winds. After you comb your hair back in place, you'll also get a preview of the 33rd Tactical Fighter Wing, the "Top Guns" of Desert Storm. Limited primitive adventure opportunities are available on the Eglin Reservation, but a permit is needed. Call the base for information.

The **US Air Force Armament Museum**, ☎ 904-882-4189, is just off Eglin's main gate. Exhibits include an SR-71 Blackbird Spy Plane, B-52s, A-10s, F-15s, F-111s and vintage aircraft that reach across four wars. There's also a collection of guns, bombs, rockets, lasers, radar and "smart" bombs, in addition to a fighter cockpit simulator, war films and photography exhibits.

Back in Fort Walton, don't forget the **Indian Temple Mound Museum**, ☎ 904-243-6521, mentioned above. It's where Highway 85 meets US 98 (Miracle Strip Parkway). The **Focus Center**, ☎ 904-664-1261, is a children's favorite. This hands-on museum of science includes a reflecting Castle of Mirrors, adult-sized bubble makers, a hair-raising Vandergraph generator and an electrifying Illuma Storm, among other exhibits. It's located at 139 Brooks St., which crosses US 98 just east of Highway 85.

Speaking of US 98, the **Gulfarium**, ☎ 904-244-5169, is located right across the Brooks Bridge on the right. At 41, it's one of the oldest marine theme parks in America. In addition to the standard dolphin show, its residents include Peruvian penguins, California sea lions, Ridley sea turtles and dozens of fish species that can be observed in the panoramic living sea exhibit.

Destin may have the largest charter fleet on the Gulf Coast, something that will be explored further in the adventure areas of this chapter. Fishing reigns in Destin, and a good place to hear and see local fish tales is the **Destin Fishing Museum**, ☎ 904-654-1011, 20009 Emerald Coast Parkway (US 98). You'll get a look at world-record red snapper and cobia. There's also a hands-on tidal pool and some maritime memorabilia.

Henderson Beach State Recreation Area, ☎ 904-837-7550, has 6,000 feet of Gulf Coast shoreline and 208 acres sprinkled with sand pines, magnolias and a variety of wildflowers. Its boardwalks provide views of laughing gulls, pelicans and rare loggerhead sea turtles.

Ready to head east to a quieter time?

SOUTH WALTON

Five miles after US Highway 98 crosses into Walton County and passes the Sandestin Resort, the coast takes on a different face, much less commercial. In places, it appears to be a time tunnel into 1940s and 1950s Florida. Watch for Old Beach Highway 98 and follow it as it reconnects for a few miles with US 98, then turn back toward the coastline on Highway 30-A.

What's missing? The glitter and some of the present. Beginning with Frangista and stretching 26 miles to Seacrest, the 18 towns that comprise the Beaches of South Walton are in some places modern communities that lack the franchised glitter, while others seem like real-life videos from the movie **Summer of '42**.

People, in many places very few of them, come to walk the beaches, catch a little sun, regain their sanity and, maybe, recapture childhood memories.

Frangista, the westernmost of them, is an idyllic settlement carved out of the dreams of Greek immigrant John Nitsos. In 1948, his family told him he was going to the end of the world, but he came here to write his father's epitaph. The Nitsos home has been transformed into the Frangista Beach Inn and restored to its original charm. That means white-stuccoed walls, terra-cotta tile floors, pastel prints and an ambience generally reserved for yesterday's Florida.

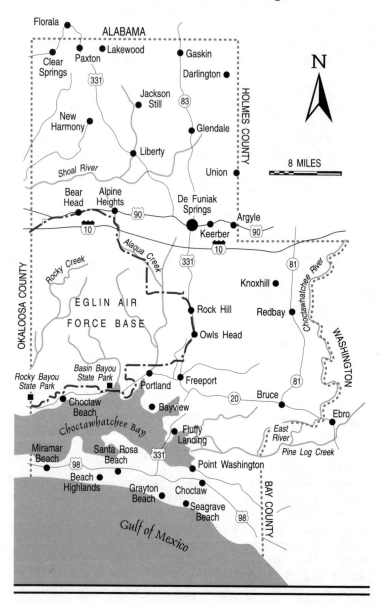

Old Beach Highway travels past beaches named Seascape, Surfside and Tops'l, past modern low-rises mingling with half-century-old cottages and past golden sea oats and ghost-white dunes on the edge of the Gulf. Where it rejoins US 98 for four miles, the landscape changes to pristine lakes, sawgrass and pine stands. Then 30-A reaches back to the shore and communities such as Dune-Allen, with its preponderance of dunes, Blue Mountain and Gulf Trace.

The **Grayton Beach State Recreation Area**, ☎ 904-231-4210, includes the 356-acre campground and Dr. Beach's top pick. It's accessible off 30-A and off Highway 283, which intersects 30-A on the western edge of the recreation area. This is a great place to swim, fish, walk the beach or see a diverse ecosystem, which includes dune migration, natural pruning and plenty of native wildlife.

The town of Grayton on Highway 283 has a delightful collection of shops, eateries and century-old architecture. There also is the funky world of **Patrone's Arts and Collectibles** – where you can mingle with roosters, turkeys and a beer-drinking potbellied pig while you shop for gifts, paintings, jewelry and furniture. If you ask any of the merchants, they'll be happy to point out the green clapboard "**Washaway Hotel**" built by Civil War Gen. William Miller and named because it was in the path of several hurricanes that hit the area.

Leaving the park and heading east on 30-A, take Highway 395 left to get to **Eden State Gardens & the Wesley Mansion**, ☎ 904-231-4214. The area, known as Point Washington, was built around the sawmill owned by the Wesley Lumber Company. Owner William Henry Wesley built this mansion in 1898. The Greek-Revival estate's French provincial furnishings and lush gardens were restored in the 1960s and it was given to the state park service. Tours, ranger- and self-guided, lead you through an estate filled with heirloom furnishings and gardens scented by thousands of azaleas.

Going south on 395, then less than a mile west on 30-A, you won't need a welcome mat to signal your arrival in **Seaside**. Developer Robert Davis has built

Seaside.

an idyllic community reminiscent of Nantucket or Martha's Vineyard, though on a much smaller scale. The 80-acre township's architecture is whimsical and ideal for a walking tour. In addition to the homes, many of which are available for rent, the town square features an open-air amphitheater that hosts frequent concerts; North Florida's most unusual grocery store, Modica Market; the tiniest and most photographed post office in North Florida (its architecture is Greek Revival); and the Mediterranean-style, outdoor shops, called Per-spi-cas-ity. While you're here, don't miss one of the nightly rooftop sunsets at Bud & Alley's Restaurant & Bar – which you'll come back to in the dining part of this chapter.

One final stop on the 30-A tour circuit: **Seagrove**. It's just east of Seaside, and its calling cards are oak, hickory, magnolia and holly trees that sit along the edge of 40-foot bluffs overlooking natural dunes.

Adventures

On Foot

Some of the best hiking paths are the sandlot trails along the 70 miles of public-access Gulf beach that trek through Escambia, Santa Rosa, Okaloosa and Walton counties. Fifty-two of the miles are within the **Gulf Islands National Seashore**, ☎ 904-934-2600 – including 16 breathtaking miles that begin south of Pensacola, where there isn't a whiff of commercial development. This is a trail lined with sea oats and sand dunes, pelicans and sand pipers, bluffs and sea breezes, to keep your biological radiator from boiling over. Again, there are no hills and the dunes are strictly off-limits, but if you need more resistance, walk in the Gulf to burn a little extra energy, but remember to take off your boots. The saltwater wrecks even the finest pair.

If you insist on leaving the beachfront, there are a few rewards awaiting.

The **Blackwater River State Forest**, ☎ 904-957-4201, offers three trails. The 21½-mile Jackson Red Ground Trail is part of the Florida National Scenic Trail and has a starting point close to the main forest entrance. The Sweetwater Trail, 4½ miles, is near the middle of the 186,475-acre forest, and the Wiregrass Trail, 5½ miles, is near its northeast corner. There are shorter trails at Hurricane and Bear lakes and the Krul and Bone creek recreation areas. The scenery includes long-leaf pines and scrub oaks, hardwoods and cedars, swamps and wiregrass that more than 200 species of wildlife call home. To get to the forest from Milton, follow Highway 90 to Highway 191, traveling 17 miles to the main entrance. You can get a detailed map at the forest's entrance.

There are three other ad lib hiking trails in the **Coldwater Recreation Area** of the forest adjoining the horse trails featured a little later in the chapter. Forest Road 64 is 4.4 miles one-way; Forest Road 66 is 3.4 miles one-way and Forest Road 13 is 4.4 miles. All are seldom-traveled dirt roads. To reach the recreation area's entrance, take Highway 191 north from Milton 13 miles to Forest Road 16, turn left and go three miles to the Coldwater sign (if you cross the Jernigan Bridge, you've gone too far).

The **Northwest Florida Water Management District**, ☎ 904-539-5999, offers trails at one property in the region. Its Choctawhatchee River and Holmes Creek tract has a pair of trails going through wetlands and dry hammocks that evolved from ancient dunes. You can reach an 11-mile trail system in the northern part of the tract by following US 90 east of DeFuniak Springs 23 miles to Caryville and Highway 179, turning left (north) and driving six miles to the entrance. A second set of trails, 6½ miles, is further south. From Caryville, take Highway 279 south five miles to Highway 280, turn right (west) and drive four miles to Highway 284, then travel four miles to the entrance. For a guide book with maps, call or write the district at Route 1, Box 3100, Havana, FL 32333-9700.

INFORMATION SOURCES

Florida Trail Association, ☎ 800-343-1882 (in Florida) or 352-378-8823, P.O. Box 13708, Gainesville, FL 32604.
Office of Greenways & Trails, ☎ 904-487-4784, Mail Station 795, 3900 Commonwealth Boulevard, Tallahassee, FL 32399-3000.

GOLF COURSES

- **The Club at Hidden Creek**, ☎ 904-939-4604, 3070 PGA Boulevard, Navarre, FL 32566, 18 holes, driving range, lessons, PGA rating R-70.8.

- **Creekside Golf Club**, ☎ 904-944-5498, 2355 West Michigan Ave., Pensacola, FL 32526, 18 holes, R-67.8
- **Emerald Bay Plantation**, ☎ 904-837-5197, 40001 Emerald Coast Highway, Destin, FL 32541, 18 holes, driving range, lessons, R-71.5.
- **Fort Walton Beach Municipal Golf Club**, ☎ 904-862-3314, P.O. Box 4009, Fort Walton Beach, FL 32549, 36 holes, driving range, lessons, R-68.0.
- **Foxwood Country Club**, ☎ 904-682-2012, Antioch Road, Crestview, FL 32536, 18 holes, driving range, lessons, R-68.0.
- **The Garden at Destin**, ☎ 904-837-7422, 40091 Emerald Coast Parkway, Destin, FL 32541, nine holes, driving range, lessons. No rating.
- **Green Meadows Golf Club**, ☎ 904-944-5483, 2500 Michigan Ave., Pensacola, FL 32506, nine holes. No rating.
- **Indian Bayou Golf & Country Club**, ☎ 904-837-6191, Airport Road, Destin, FL 32541, 27 holes, driving range, lessons, R-69.8.
- **Island Golf Center**, ☎ 904-244-1612, 1306 Miracle Strip Parkway, Fort Walton Beach, FL 32548, nine holes, lessons, R-70.8.
- **Marcus Pointe Golf Club**, ☎ 904-928-3930, 2500 Oak Pointe Drive, Pensacola, FL 32505, 18 holes. No rating.
- **The Moors**, ☎ 800-727-1010, 3220 Avalon Boulevard, Milton, FL 32583. 18 holes, R-72.9 at the championship level.
- **Osceola/City Municipal Golf Club**, ☎ 904-456-2761, 300 Tonawanda Drive, Pensacola, FL 32506, 18 holes, R-70.0.
- **Perdido Bay Resort**, ☎ 904-492-1223, One Doug Ford Drive, Pensacola, FL 32507, 18 holes, driving range, lessons, R-70.9.
- **Santa Rosa Beach & Golf Club**, ☎ 904-267-2229, Highway 30-A, Santa Rosa Beach, FL 32459, 18 holes, driving range, lessons, R-69.9.
- **Saufley Golf Club**, ☎ 904-452-1097, 2424 Saufley Road, Pensacola, FL 32508, nine holes.

- **Scenic Hills Country Club**, ☎ 904-476-0611, 8891 Burning Tree Road, Pensacola, FL 32514, 18 holes, driving range, lessons, R-70.0.
- **Seascape Golf & Racquet Club**, ☎ 904-837-9181, 100 Seascape Drive, Destin, FL 32541, 18 holes, driving range, lessons, R-69.7.
- **Shoal River Golf Club**, ☎ 904-689-1111, 1100 Shoal River Drive, Crestview, FL 32536, 18 holes, driving range. No rating.
- **Tanglewood Golf & Country Club**, ☎ 904-623-6176, Tanglewood Drive, Milton, FL 32570, 18 holes, driving range, lessons, R-70.9.
- **Tiger Point Gold & Country Club**, ☎ 904-932-1333, 1255 Country Club Road, Gulf Breeze, FL 32561, 36 holes, driving range, lessons, R-69.8/69.2.

On Horseback

Florida is a horse-lover's paradise, certainly second, albeit a distant second, to Kentucky in the number of thoroughbred farms, and within the top three or four for all breeds and riding disciplines. It's also a trail-rider's paradise – if you know the turf. State wildlife management areas (not to be confused with parks and preserves) offer a wealth of self-made trails for natives who know the politics, hunting seasons and indigenous wildlife such as rattlesnakes, vise-jawed alligators and feral hogs with a nasty disposition. And don't forget the black bears. Grizzlies they're not, but keep a safe distance anyway. For travelers, even natives who aren't schooled in the local mores, that means stay on the designated trail.

The **Blackwater River State Forest**, ☎ 904-957-4201, 11650 Munson Hwy., Milton, FL 32570, has it all. The **Spanish Trail**, accessible off Highway 191 right at the main entrance, consists of 19 trail miles through some of the most pristine areas of the forest, including a wonderful pit stop along Coldwater Creek and Jernigan Bridge, which has stables for overnighters or breaks and picnic areas. Spanish Trail crosses just two paved roads – 191 and 16 – and two hard-packed roads. Otherwise it's a forest journey through natural woodlands, including sweet gums, live and turkey oaks, sparkleberry, long-leaf pine and wiregrass. Wildlife? Sure, everything from otters and turkeys to bald eagles and ospreys. If you bring your own mount, don't forget a negative Coggins test. Florida is strict on this.

The forest's **Coldwater Recreation Area** is the best destination for riders. It has stables for 72 horses, 65 campsites, a kitchen/dining hall that's big enough for 110 hearty appetites, restrooms, showers, an amphitheater, a water play area for horses and riders and five marked trails leading through clear-water streams, shifting sandbars, hardwoods, junipers and long-leaf pines. Its color-coded trails (orange, red, yellow, white and blue) range from 3.5 miles to 5.3 miles one way. Maps and reservations can be obtained by writing the Blackwater Forest Center at 11650 Munson Highway, Milton, FL 32570. To reach the area's entrance, take Highway 191 north from Milton 13 miles to Forest Road 16, turn left and go three miles to the Coldwater Recreation Area sign.

On Wheels

Bikers, the self-propelled persuasion, always can ad lib a course, and this corner of Florida is no exception, whether the course is along city streets, country highways or dirt paths through the forests. While there are few designated trails, there are some routes that show off the West Panhandle's diverse countryside.

Foremost are those in the Blackwater River State Forest. The **Blackwater Heritage Trail**, ☎ 904-957-4201 or 488-3538, is scheduled to be completed by the spring of 1997. Its 8½-mile hard-surface route will reach from Milton to the Naval Air Station at Whiting Field, roughly parallel to Highway 87. Its path will take you through the same lush long-leaf pine, sweet gum and maple forests that populate the forest's riding trail.

The state forest has no designated trails, but it has a 30-mph vehicle speed limit (you can beat that on a bike, can't you?) and miles upon miles of paved and dirt trails ready for the adventurer. Highway 191, for example, runs a 16-mile path (32 miles roundtrip) through the forest's west side, crossing Juniper Creek at Juniper Bridge and again eight miles north. There are spurs available on this route that, at the 6½-mile mark, will point you south along Sandy Landing Road, nine miles over Sweetwater and Alligator creeks, or west-northwest just after the park entrance, 12 miles, over Coldwater Creek, to several unpaved road options. These include journeys on Simmons and McDaniel roads to rendezvous with Calloway swamp, a favorite canoe launching pad. If you choose the Sandy Landing Road course, 5½ miles after crossing Sweetwater

Creek, you might want to consider hanging a left on Bryant Bridge Road, which also crosses Alligator Creek. From that point it's 6.1 miles to a fish research center where you learn about the species you may land on a later fishing trip or, if you peddle less than a mile further, discover yet another canoe launching point at the Blackwater River. One more paved forest trail follows Highway 191, 6.2 miles from the main entrance to the park headquarters, then right (east) 5.7 miles to Old Martin Road and left (north) 2.8 miles to Hurricane Lake Road. From there, you can peddle on another 12 miles north, dipping into Okaloosa County and, at the eight-mile mark, a trail into Hurricane Lake, the forest's largest lake.

There also is a designated highway route (spell that, WARNING: cars and trucks traveling at asteroid speed) in Pensacola. If you're game (and, hopefully, not the road-kill variety), you can start the 5.6-mile leg from the Pensacola Visitors Center on Highway 98 north two blocks. Then go right on 17th Avenue three blocks to Cervantes Street (Highway 90), turn right and take Cervantes to Summit Boulevard (left) to the Pensacola Airport. A 16-mile leg from the Visitors Center heads south on Highway 98 over the Pensacola Bay Bridge, goes through Gulf Breeze and connects with Highway 399, turning right (west) to Fort Pickens.

INFORMATION SOURCES

Office of Greenways & Trails, ☎ 904-487-4784, 325 John Knox Road, Building 500, Tallahassee, FL 32303-4124.
Florida Department of Transportation, ☎ 904-487-9220, MS-82, 605 Suwanee St., Tallahassee, FL 32399-0450.

On Water

CANOEING

The state legislature designated Milton "The Canoe Capital of Florida."

But don't take it from the politicians.

Take it from the paddlers. They agree.

There are five excellent canoe trails in and around the Blackwater River State Forest in Santa Rosa and Okaloosa counties, plus a sixth that follows the Florida-Alabama state line west of Pensacola.

The latter, the **Perdido River Canoe Trail**, is a 24-mile run rated beginner. The current is two-three mph. The trail curves gently through pine and cypress stands, where you often can see deer and turkeys stopping for a sip. There are several small sloughs off the main run that can be explored, too.

For the full run, follow Highway 29 north from Pensacola about 18 miles to Highway 184 at Cantonment, drive west two miles to Highway 97, then north to Highway 99 at Bay Springs. Take Highway 97-A west three miles, through a 90° turn, then another 1½ miles to Pineville Road and the Walnut Hill Water Tower. Go west 2½ miles to the first dirt road on the left after the Brushy Creek Bridge to the Three Runs access point. (If you're feeling a bit light-headed from all the turns, pop a Dramamine and get in the canoe. You didn't drive this far to sit in the car.) For a short course (14 miles), at the intersection of Highways 99 and 196 at Barrineau Park, take the dirt road west a quarter-mile to the bridge. Both exit at the Muscogee Bridge on Highway 184 just west of Cantonment.

Now, on to Milton.

The **Coldwater Creek Trail** (18 miles) is a little more challenging but still rated for beginners. The current is three-plus mph. It flows through the Blackwater River and, since the river is spring-fed you'll find the shallow areas are cool, around 70°, which is particularly refreshing in Florida's hot summers. To reach the northern launch point, follow Highway 87 north from Milton 16 miles, go right (east) at Highway 4 five miles to the bridge over Big Coldwater Creek. The path goes through the Coldwater Creek Recreation Area, under the Berrydale Bridge, past Tomahawk Landing and under the Old Steel Bridge before ending at the Highway 191 bridge, around six miles northeast of Milton. If you're looking for a shorter course (nine miles), follow the directions from Milton on Highway 87 nine miles to Springhill Road, turning east to the Tomahawk Landing sign.

The **Blackwater River Trail** (31 miles) is rated beginner to intermediate with a two-three mph current. Cedar, maple and cypress trees form a dense canopy over the river in several locations and at some points there are high bluffs with pine and cedar stands. Don't be surprised if you see a bobcat, as well as deer and turkeys, in the area. From Milton, take Highway 191 north about 16 miles to Highway 4, head right (east) 2.6 miles to State Forest Road 31 (left), then go six miles to State Forest Road 24 (a dirt road with a Hurricane Lake sign), go right two miles to the Kennedy Bridge launch. For the shorter (20-mile) trail, from the intersection of

Highways 191 and 4, take Highway 4 east about nine miles to the Cotton Bridge entrance. The trail ends at Deaton Bridge.

The **Sweetwater-Juniper Creeks Canoe Trail** is a 13-mile course that has a beginners to intermediate skill rating. Current is three-plus mph on Sweetwater Creek and two-three mph on Juniper Creek. To reach the starting point, follow Highway 191 from Milton to Highway 4, turn right (east) at Highway 4 and go 1½ miles to the bridge. The upper portion of the trail is narrow, swift and winding. It ends at the Indian Ford Bridge.

The **Yellow River Trail**, at 56 miles, is the longest in the area. It's rated an intermediate course with a three-plus mph current on the upper portion and a two-three mph current on the lower end. The swift current on the north end occurs because the Yellow River drains the state's highest elevation, which descends quickly to sea level. The upper trail is bordered by hardwood forests and high sandy banks that remain as they were when Florida's early explorers came. Downstream, the river widens as it wanders through cypress-gum swamps and the fringes of the Eglin Air Force Base Reservation. From Milton, take Highway 191 south three miles to Interstate 10, traveling east on I-10 around 30 miles to Highway 85, then turn left (north) and follow the highway about 14 miles to Highway 2, turn left (west) once more and drive 4½ miles to the Highway 2 bridge at Oak Grove. A short course (20 miles) can be accessed by exiting I-10 to Highway 189 at Holt and traveling south 2½ miles to the river.

The **Shoal River Trail** (27 miles) is a beginner's run with a current of two-three mph. This is an area where there are few signs of civilization and an abundance of maple, oak, gum and cypress. There are creeks along the trail opening into lily-covered pools that can be excellent for fishing. From Milton, follow Highway 191 to connect with I-10, traveling east 42 miles to Highway 285, then north 3½ miles to the Highway 285 bridge. For the short run, exit I-10 at Highway 85 and drive north less than a mile to Crestview, turn east (left) on Highway 90 and go four miles to the Highway 90 bridge. This run is nine miles.

Maybe now you see why they call it "The Canoe Capital of Florida." And, if you're a lazier sort, many of the rental outlets listed below have tubes available for modified trips down some of these runs.

INFORMATION SOURCES

For designated trail maps, write to the **Office of Greenways and Trails**, ☎ 904-487-4784, 325 John Knox Road, Bldg. 500, Tallahassee, FL 32303-4124.
Florida Association of Canoe Liveries and Outfitters, ☎ 941-494-1215, P.O. Box 1764, Arcadia, FL 33821.
West Florida Canoe Club, ☎ 904-587-2211, P.O. Box 17203, Pensacola, FL 32522.
Adventures Unlimited, ☎ 800-239-6864 or 904-623-6197, Route 6, Box 238, Milton, FL 32570.
Action on Blackwater, ☎ 904-537-2997, P.O. Box 283, Baker, FL 32531.
Andrew Jackson Canoe Rentals, ☎ 904-623-4884, P.O. Box 666, Baghdad, FL 32530.
Blackwater Canoe Rentals, ☎ 800-967-6789 or 904-623-0235, 10274 Pond Road, Milton, FL 32583.
Bob's Canoe Rentals, ☎ 904-623-5457, 4569 Plowman Lane, Milton, FL 32585.

DIVING/SNORKELING

The underwater action is offshore in the Western Panhandle.

Dive a wreck or an artificial reef and watch a 20-pound grouper glide by. Take it or a tasty snapper home for dinner, if you've brought a speargun. The water temperature averages about 80°, though it can get much chillier during winter. Visibility generally is good, 50-60 feet, and on exceptional days as much as 100 feet. Shipwrecks, abundant marine life (barracudas, graceful manta rays and dolphins are common), natural and artificial reefs and bottom growth (coral and sponges) make scuba sites off Pensacola and Fort Walton Beach-Destin ideal for underwater photography. Shelling also is popular here.

Combined, these two areas offer 40 to 50 dive sites. As always, check with local shops and regulatory agencies for rules, current and tide conditions, and danger zones.

In the Pensacola area, the *USS Massachusetts*, a World War I-vintage battleship, is a favorite dive. Sunk by the Navy in 1927, portions of the 500-foot ship remain exposed in 25 feet of water, making it a nice shallow dive. It's only about one mile offshore from the Gulf Islands National Seashore pass where Pensacola Bay empties into the Gulf of Mexico. If you're looking for a grouper, snapper and flounder haven, try an artificial reef built with rubble from the old Pensacola bridge. Dumped in 75 feet of water, the reef and a barge scuttled seven miles off Santa Rosa Beach make an ideal spearfishing or marine life observation site. Three miles further out, the remains of the World War II-era Russian freighter *San Pablo* lie at 75 feet and serve as a habitat for grouper, barracuda and snapper. Nearby, the 65-foot tug *Sylvia* is on a sandy bottom at 82 feet. This is a good place for sand dollars, starfish and shells. Further east, about eight miles off Navarre Beach, **Brass Wreck** lies in 90 feet of water. The 250-foot, wood-hull schooner's true identity isn't known, but it earned its name from the brass pins that stick from its remains. The wreck has as much fish life as any spot in this portion of the Panhandle. **Timberholes**, two miles northwest of Brass Wreck, is a limestone reef at 110 feet with ledges that rise in several places 12 feet off the bottom. Spearfishing, shelling and lobstering are popular on this site.

In the Fort Walton Beach-Destin area, a good place to see sponges is at **Amberjack**, a rock reef lying three miles off Fort Walton Beach in 75 to 85 feet of water. There are a lot of ledges and tunnels in the reef. Another reef, **White Hill**, is 85 to 90 feet down and a good spot for spearfishing and lobstering.

INFORMATION SOURCES

Florida Association of Dive Operators, ☎ 305-451-3020, 51 Garden Cove Drive, Key Largo, FL 33037.
US Coast Guard, Mayport, ☎ 904-246-7315.
Florida Marine Patrol, ☎ 904-444-8978, 1101 E. Gregory St., Pensacola, FL 32501.
Ned DeLoach's Diving Guide to Underwater Florida, ☎ 904-737-6558, New World Publications, 1861 Cornell Road, Jacksonville, FL 32207.
Divers Den of Pensacola, ☎ 904-438-0650, 518 N. Ninth Ave., Pensacola, FL 32501.
Scuba Shack, ☎ 904-433-4319, 719 S. Palafox St., Pensacola, FL 32501.
Gulf Coast Dive Pros, ☎ 904-456-8845, 7203 Highway 98 West, Pensacola, FL 32506.
Gulf Breeze Pro Dive, ☎ 904-934-8845, 207-B Gulf Breeze Parkway, Gulf Breeze, FL 32561.
Aquanaut Scuba Center, ☎ 904-837-0359, 24 Highway 98 East, Destin, FL 32541.
ScubaTech of Northwest Florida, ☎ 904-837-1933, 5371 Highway 98 East, Destin, FL 32541.

SALTWATER & FRESHWATER FISHING

Fishing records? The Western Panhandle has more than its share.

On the saltwater side of things, 10 of Florida's 73 whoppers were caught out of Pensacola or Destin. Pensacola's trophies include cobia (114½ pounds), croaker (3 pounds, 12 ounces), tiger shark (1,065 pounds) and Lane snapper (6 pounds, 6 ounces). Destin holds the title for gag grouper (71 pounds, 3 ounces), Warsaw grouper (436 pounds, 12 ounces), speckle hind (42 pounds, 6 ounces), blue marlin (980½ pounds), thresher shark (544½ pounds) and red snapper (46 pounds, 9 ounces).

Additionally, in March or April, giant schools of Spanish mackerel, some as long as five miles, run along the Panhandle beaches. Cobia, great fighters, run in April and May; blackfin tuna and king mackerel are very common during May; and dolphin (often called mahi-mahi to avoid confusion with "Flipper") hit the offshore weed lines in June. July is the best time to go after those big blue marlins or sharks.

Western Panhandle freshwater fishermen have set their share of records, too, including a 122-pound alligator gar in the Escambia River, a 53-pound blue catfish in the same river and a 2.44-pound warmouth in the Yellow River.

The Escambia River also is noted for bluegill, bream and shellcracker in the spring, and sunshine and black bass fishing in the spring and fall. The lower sections of the Shoal and Yellow rivers noted above in the canoe section have their share of bass, bream, bluegill and shellcracker. The big alligator gar are pretty popular in the Choctawhatchee River in Walton County, as are bluegill in the spring and largemouth bass in spring and summer.

Make sure to get a fishing license. On the saltwater side, a non-resident license ranges from $5 for three days to $30 for a year. Non-resident freshwater licenses are $15 for seven days and $30 for one year. Florida also has size and bag limits on many species. Information on these can be obtained at area bait-and-tackle shops, marinas, or by contacting the **Florida Marine Patrol**, ☎ 904-444-8978, 1101 E. Gregory St., Pensacola FL 32501 or the Florida Game & Fresh Water Fish Commission, ☎ 904-265-3677, 3911 Highway 2321, Panama City, FL 32409-1658.

Fishermen who bring their own boats will find numerous ramps, including those at most area marinas, fish camps and state parks. Additionally, there are public ramps on the Yellow River in Santa Rosa County at **Brown's Fish Camp**, ☎ 904-623-6102, and

Couey's Fish Camp, ☎ 904-623-6164; on **Juniper Lake**, near DeFuniak Springs in Walton County at the campground, ☎ 904-892-3445; and at **Alaqua Creek**, in Walton County, ☎ 904-835-9890.

If you're looking for a charter, slip or boat rental, here are just a few of the many places in the area to hitch a ride, dock your yacht or lease a luxury liner for that fishing trip. **Got-Cha Charterboat**, ☎ 904-837-6637, Highway 98 East, Destin, FL 32540, has it all, from charter and head boats to guide service and rentals. Pier 1 Marina, ☎ 904-932-2224, 3 Gulf Breeze Parkway, Gulf Breeze, FL 32561, provides charter boats, guide service and rentals. **Dolphin Bait & Marine**, ☎ 904-438-3242, 600 S. Barracks St., Pensacola, FL 32501, features charters, guides and rentals. And **Oyster Bar Restaurant & Marina**, ☎ 904-492-4364, River Road, Perdido Key, FL 32507, has charters and rentals.

A sampling of the area's bait and tackle shops includes **Half Hitch Tackle Co.**, ☎ 904-837-3121, 621 E. Highway 98, Destin, FL 32541; **Gulf Breeze Bait & Tackle**, ☎ 904 932-6789, 825 Gulf Breeze Parkway, Gulf Breeze, FL 32561; and **Milton Sport Shop**, ☎ 904-623-8300, 714 Stewart St. SE, Milton, FL 32570.

Landlubbers don't have to worry. There are several fishing piers.

Pensacola Fishing Pier, ☎ 904-932-0444, Fort Pickens Road, Pensacola, stretches 800 feet into the Gulf and is lighted for night-time fishing. The **Navarre Beach Pier**, ☎ 904-939-5658, 8577 Gulf Boulevard, Navarre, is a lighted 880-foot pier. Want to go deeper? The **Okaloosa Island Pier**, ☎ 904-244-1023, Fort Walton Beach, reaches 1,260 feet into the Gulf, and it's lighted, too. One other site, **Bob Sikes Bridge**, links Gulf Breeze to Pensacola Beach and is an angler's favorite.

In The Air

All of the airports listed in the Getting Around section of this chapter offer aerial tours of their nearby areas. Additionally, there are a few lift-off sites along the coast that specialize in bird's-eye views. The ones on the beachfront include **Paradise Parasail & Watersports**, ☎ 904-664-7872, right across from the Tourist Information Center on Miracle Strip Parkway in Fort Walton, and **Boogies Water Sports**, ☎ 904-654-4497, in Destin at the Highway

98 bridge, where you not only can latch onto a parasail but also go for an ultralight flight.

Eco-Travel Excursions

Self-guided canoe and kayak tours are available on four rivers through **Adventures Unlimited**, ☎ 800-239-6864 or ☎ 904-623-6197, located north of Milton. Guides are available for an added price, but why waste the money? It's hard to get lost on any of these waterways. The Perdido River tour along the Alabama-Florida border is an overnighter that covers 24 miles. Overnight trips along the Sweetwater-Juniper and Coldwater creeks are 15 and 18 miles, respectively. Options on the Blackwater River tour include a two-day, 24-mile adventure as well as a three-day, 36-mile tour. The canoes are outfitted with a tent, sleeping bags, stove, lantern, cook kit and map. Primitive campsites, treehouses and cottages also are available at the main camp.

Where To Stay & Eat

There are literally tens of thousands of rooms available in this four-county area and hundreds of restaurants. You probably won't get locked out, or have to go to bed hungry, even during the peak seasons, winter and summer. But it's a good idea to plan ahead with reservations to ensure the room of your choice or a place to eat before your stomach starts grumbling.

Pensacola/Escambia County

The city and beach have the traditional chains. **Best Western**, ☎ 800-934-3301, 16 Via de Luna, Pensacola Beach, FL 32561, is on Santa Rosa Island, with a spectacular view of the Gulf of Mexico, sand dunes and sea oats. Right next door, **Clarion Suites Resort**, ☎ 800-874-5303, 20 Via de Luna, has an equal view with a clapboard-style architecture that doesn't scream "chain!"

If you're looking for something a little less conventional, you might try the **Eden Condominiums**, ☎ 800-523-8141, 16281 Perdido

Key Drive, Pensacola, FL 32507, which offers lush tropical foliage and solitude. Or if golf's your game the **Perdido Bay Golf Resort**, ☎ 800-874-5355, One Doug Ford Drive, Perdido Key, FL 32507, is right beside a challenging, 18-hole course.

Beef-eaters with big appetites usually find the way to **Mesquite Charlie's**, ☎ 904-434-0498, where the decor is definitely cowboy and the menu is piled high with ribs, chicken and steaks (including a belly-busting 32-ounce Porterhouse). **Skopelos on the Bay**, ☎ 904-432-6565, features an amusing mixture of seafood and Greek cuisine, while **McGuire's Irish Pub**, ☎ 904-433-6789, has an old-world atmosphere and a steak-and-seafood menu ranked among Florida's best. No visit to Pensacola is complete without a pit stop at Perdido Key's **Flora-Bama Lounge**, which literally sits along the state line. The seafood is tasty, but it's the shenanigans that delight customers. Owners Pat McClellan and Joe Gilchrist stage events such as the world championship mullet toss, a winter polar bear swimfest (OK, so it doesn't get as cold as Minnesota) and a songwriters' fest. They're also open to all sorts of crazy ideas, so bring one along.

Milton/Santa Rosa County

Santa Rosa's accommodations and restaurants are less commercial as well as less numerous than Pensacola's.

Bed-and-breakfast fans find two historic ones in Milton. **The Canal Street Inn**, ☎ 800-356-3537, 612A Canal Street, Milton, FL 32570, is a vernacular framed building that dates to 1890 and is located in the historic district. **The Creary-Ates House**, ☎ 904-623-8412, 507 Broad St., Milton, FL 32570, was built in 1879 for a local merchant. Owners Donald and Carol Barnhill restored the inn, which offers three rooms, in 1992. Their house combines yesterday's coziness and modern conveniences, including a Jacuzzi and cable television for those who cannot get away without having a tube fix. On the upscale side, the **Moors**, ☎ 800-727-1010, 3220 Avalon Boulevard, Milton, FL 32583, is another golfing resort. Its Scottish-style architecture is second only to a challenging, 18-hole course that hosts the Emerald Coast Classic, a stop on the Senior PGA Tour.

Dinner choices are reasonably sparse in this area. If you have a hunger for Cracker-style grub, **Reggie's Seafood & Bar-B-Que**, ☎ 904-623-3126, has a variety of all-you-can-eat specials, including mullet, gumbo, shrimp and ribs. If you want a good place to watch the sunset over the Intracoastal Waterway, try **Sam's Oyster Bar**, ☎ 904-939-1998, in Navarre, which features "topless oysters and live waitresses." Sam isn't lying on either count. His place is also topped with a miniature lighthouse for atmosphere. It's a grand place to shuck oysters and crack crabs without having to worry about the dress code or manners.

Fort Walton Beach/Destin

Hotels, condos, cottages, B&Bs and beach houses. They're all here.

The Henderson Park Inn, ☎ 800-336-4853, 2700 Highway 98 East, Destin, FL 32541, is perched on the dunes of Henderson Beach State Park. The Queen Anne structure has 39 suites and villas, shingle siding and a striking green roof topped by a cupola and widow's walk. **Sandcastle**, ☎ 904-837-4853, 461 Abalone Court, Fort Walton Beach, FL 32548, has beachfront units, including efficiencies. Several property management companies in the area provide a wide variety of accommodations. Among these agencies is **Abbott Resorts**, ☎ 800-336-4853, 35000 Emerald Coast Parkway, Destin, FL 32541, which manages Henderson Park Inn and many others.

The Back Porch, ☎ 904-837-2022, in Destin has an atmosphere much like Sam's Oyster Bar and a reputation as the creator of a local favorite – char-grilled amberjack. **Staff's**, ☎ 904-243-3482, in Fort Walton Beach, is the Emerald Coast's oldest restaurant, housed in a 1913 barrel-shaped warehouse that has pressed-tin ceilings and an abundance of antiques. The favorites here include a seafood skillet (yellowfin tuna, shrimp, scallops and crabmeat broiled in melted butter and topped with cheese) and fresh-baked wheat bread. **Joe's Crab Shack**, ☎ 904-650-1882, in Destin, is another eatery filled with local color. The sign out front boasts: "An Embarrassment to Any Neighborhood," but the food inside is anything but shameful. The treats include gumbo, grouper, softshell crabs, crab balls, catfish, crawfish and key lime pie.

Night life? Five neighboring bars – **Hog's Breath Saloon**, **Hoser's**, **Sam's Oyster House**, **Timbers** and **Thunderbirds** – comprise an area known as Shanty Town, where the party crowd doesn't begin to quiet down until 4 am in summer.

South Walton

There are three kinds of accommodations in these 18 communities.

The Frangista Beach Inn, ☎ 800-382-2612, 4150 Old US 98 East, Destin, FL 32541, provides a looking-glass into Florida of the 1950s. Restored in 1989 to its original charm, this hideaway sits on 700 feet of beach, and its rooms have the charm of a time not long ago when this part of Florida was mom-and-pop as well as predominantly undiscovered. In addition to the Old Florida-style rooms, John Nitsos's original cottage has been turned into a three-bedroom suite with balconies, a fireplace and hardwood floors.

Seaside, ☎ 800-635-0296, P.O. Box 4730, Seaside, FL 32459, is the creation of Robert Davis. It's a legacy of small-town America with an architectural look (Victorian, Greek Revival, Cracker, and neo-classic) that rivals Nantucket or Martha's Vineyard. Many of Seaside's houses are available for rent, as are the whimsical Honeymoon Cottages on the oceanfront (they come with a butler) and bed-and-breakfast lodgings like **Josephine's**, ☎ 800-848-1840.

The last type of accommodation, the modern, is at **Sandestin**, ☎ 800-277-0800, 5500 Highway 98 East, Destin, FL 32541. This is a 2,400-acre resort begun in 1953 by Winthrop Rockefeller. It has 550 rental units available, ranging from four-bedroom villas to suites and hotel-style rooms. The amenity package includes golf, tennis, a marina and a marketplace.

South Walton has some real treats at dinnertime.

Bud & Alley's Restaurant & Bar, ☎ 904-231-5900, named for a dog and cat that frequented the area, is the star attraction in Seaside. Owners Scott Witcoski and Dave Rauschkolb combine Mediterranean, Basque and Tuscan cuisine with influences from Louisiana and Cracker Florida. The menu changes regularly, but it might include delicacies such as wood-grilled cobia crostini, linguine with bay oysters and calico

Bud & Alley's upper deck.

scallops or apple-and-walnut stuffed quail. **Criolla's**, ☎ 904-267-1267, in Grayton Beach, tempts diners with dishes such as grouper gravlax and poached lobster, tortilla-fried softshell crab, and barbecued shrimp. **Frangista Seafood & Spirits**, ☎ 904-837-1223, located at the Frangista Beach Inn, has some of the most succulent cuisine in the region, including Old Florida-style catfish or wahoo, griddled rainbow trout with pecans and sautéed softshell crab in tomato-avocado salsa. And Sandestin's signature restaurant, the **Elephant Walk**, ☎ 904-267-4800, is a dining and visual pleasure. On the dining side, entrées include shrimp and lobster ragout, Sri Lanka tuna and grouper Elizabeth. On the visual side, the restaurant is named after the 1954 Elizabeth Taylor-Peter Finch movie and the art and artifacts are from India. They combine for sensory overload.

Campgrounds

If you're looking to sleep and eat a little closer to nature, the Western Panhandle offers plenty of places to pitch a tent, park a Winnebago, or camp in a primitive cabin.

All Star RV Campground, ☎ 904-492-0041, 13621 Perdido Key Drive, Pensacola, FL 32507, is a beachfront park that has a resident manager, cable television and telephone hook-ups. In addition to pull-through spaces for RVs, it has cabins, trailer rentals and tent spaces. **Cedar Pines Campground**, ☎ 904-623-8869, 6436 Robie Road, Milton, FL 32570, has pull-throughs, spaces for tents and trailer rentals. **Emerald Coast RV Resort**, ☎ 800-232-2478, 7525 W. Highway 30-A, Santa Rosa Beach, FL 32459, may be the most upscale of the area campgrounds. It's on 100 acres, with a nature trail to the beach. Its pull-throughs have concrete pads with patios, cable television, telephones, a heated pool, tennis courts and a clubhouse. Trailer rentals are available, but tents aren't allowed. **Navarre Beach Campground**, ☎ 904-939-2188, 9201 US 98, Navarre, FL 32566-2913, has pull-throughs, a large pool and playground, cable, boat ramp and pier, trailer rental, tent sites, on 8½ acres of beachfront.

Additionally, the following state parks and trails have limited campsites available: **Gulf Islands National Seashore**, ☎ 904-934-2600; **Blackwater River State Forest**, ☎ 904-957-4201; **Big Lagoon State Recreation Area**, ☎ 904-492-1595; and **Grayton Beach State Recreation Area**, ☎ 904-231-4210.

Central Panhandle

Ponce de Leon blew a sizable chunk of King Ferdinand's treasury on his search for the mythical fountain of youth. But the Spanish monarch kept sending checks until he got his hands on a college transcript. That's when he learned his wayward explorer failed Star Reading 101.

Instead of Bimini, his target, old Ponce landed in Florida in 1513, which he named "place of flowers." Of course, flowers weren't the only thing he found. There were arrow-packing natives, thirsty mosquitoes and alligators that were delighted to have a little Latin take-out.

Since he, Ferdinand, and Ferdinand's daughter, "Juana The Mad" (that's not a joke, look it up in the history books), are no longer among us, it's pretty safe to bet this quest went unfulfilled. If the fabled "fountain of youth" exists, it remains uncertified. This being so, several places stake a half-hearted claim to it. Among the contenders is the main spring (actually, the spot where two springs meet) at Ponce de Leon Springs State Recreation Area in Holmes County. Fantasy is seldom burdened by proof, so the possibility is as believable as claims made by St. Augustine, St. Petersburg and a few other places around "La Florida."

One thing is certain:

You'll have a youthful glow if you dive into the spring's 68° waters.

The same can be said for two short, but delightful, park trails that lead you over rolling hills, across a forest flood plain, through a swamp and along a spring flow that leads to the Choctawhatchee (don't you love Florida names) River and the Gulf of Mexico.

There are several other places for 21st-century explorers.

Sticking with the Central Panhandle's inland face for a few moments, two of Florida's more unusual geologic features are virtually side by side in Jackson and Washington counties.

Florida Caverns State Park in Marianna is a magical place of stalactites and stalagmites, rare gray bats and Barbour's map turtles, horseback trails and, if you are looking for a unique hiking experience, a half-mile subterranean loop where you don't have to worry about becoming overheated – no matter how many laps you take – even in the middle of summer.

A few miles southwest near Chipley, the **Falling Waters State Recreation Area** is equally unique to the Sunshine State. Niagara it isn't, but it's the closest thing in Florida to a legitimate waterfall. Its 67-foot cascade is created by water flowing in and out of a 100-foot-deep, 20-foot-wide cylindrical sinkhole.

You've had a glimpse inland. Let's take a peek at the coast.

The transition from Western to Central Panhandle is smooth.

There is mile upon mile of sugar-white beaches, shallow, grassy bays ripe with sweet scallops and Gulf waters that one guy will say are sapphire blue while another will swear are emerald green. One thing they won't argue: Mexico Beach is a time warp, the easternmost coastal town in the central time zone (the bars in St. Joe Beach, literally up the street, are open an hour later). It's a hamlet where the architecture and lifestyle are a yellowed page out of the 1940s and 1950s.

Cape San Blas.

Cape San Blas, an elbow of land between the Gulf and St. Josephs Bay, is an unspoiled oasis where rustic beach cottages and stilt condos doze among the dunes, and loggerhead turtles lay eggs on July nights. Ccommercialism is largely unknown. Remember Mr. Beach and his "gold star" rating for Grayton Beach in the last chapter? Cape San Blas was ranked fifth among the 650 beaches he rated worldwide.

This westernmost portion of the "Forgotten Coast," named because of its lack of crowds (with the exception of Panama City Beach, which you'll reach in a moment), has an abundance of other historic sites, including the town of Chipley; Port St. Joe's Constitutional Convention Museum, the site of Florida's first, albeit short-lived, capitol; and the ghost town of St. Joseph.

If you're looking for a reason to celebrate, the Central Panhandle is home to annual festivals honoring watermelons and the often-misunderstood opossum. Talk about down home, huh?

Moving northwest, Panama City Beach is the exception to the "Forgotten Coast" image.

This is the other half of the Redneck Riviera, a place to embrace if you're taking a break from adventures and nature, not that you can't find a little of either off its shores. There are some alluring scuba sites (the sunken World War II-era British tanker, the *Empire Mica*, is among them). You can hop on a riverboat for the ride to Shell Island, which has seven miles of untouched beaches, or take a slight detour and go on a snorkeling trip that lets you frolic with wild dolphins.

The beaches here, 27 miles of them, are made up of Appalachian quartz crystals washed down to the shore from the mountains. Over centuries, they have been bleached, ground and polished by nature. There's also the Museum of Man in the Sea, a gallery dedicated entirely to the history of diving and the sea world. Nearby St. Andrews State Recreation Area is the home of Dr. Leatherman's Number 1 beach for 1995.

What happened to Grayton, the top beach for 1994? It's still there and every bit as beautiful. But once a beach tops the chart, the good doctor removes it from contention for the next 10 years.

For the most part, though, Panama City Beach is more the exception to the natural flavor of this region. The waterfront strip is thick with more miniature golf emporiums, water and amusement parks, beach bars, dolphin shows and other standard tourist attractions per capita than virtually any other destination in North and Northwest Florida.

If you're still tempted, a final warning: This is a burgeoning spring-break spot, and many of the locals want it to reach the top spot. So even if you're after that break from nature and adventure, you might want to avoid the area during the spring when tens of thousands of wired college kids go on an annual tear.

You've been warned.

Geography & History

You've seen the highs (Falling Waters Recreation Area) and lows (Florida Caverns and a hint of the diving temptations). But the Central Panhandle follows the pattern of the rest of the state. It's basically flat land with a few speed bumps and shallow divots.

That has its perks, though, in the extensive coastline, varied canoe trails, swamps, savannas, deadwater lakes, cypress-lined rivers, hammocks and the panoramic, long-distance sunrises and sunsets.

You've learned a little about Ponce de Leon. He and his shipmates were the first white men to set foot in this region. Instead of the "fountain of youth," on a return trip he discovered an arrow lodged firmly between his ribs thanks to an unhappy native. He died back in Puerto Rico, where he was governor.

Similar to the Western Panhandle in the previous chapter and the Eastern Panhandle in the next, this area had Native American cultures dating back tens of thousands of years. And more recently, the Creek, Seminole, Muscogee and Apalachee nations settled the area. It's possible a wayward and historically lost Spaniard landed here in search of gold, a.k.a. copper, but records suggest there was little intrusion by Europeans after Ponce de Leon, except for a brief Spanish outpost in 1701 and a French bastion, "Le Fort de Dreve," which was located on the mainland opposite St. Joseph's Point in 1718.

Modern history came with Florida's American territorial status in 1821.

Washington County was established four years later. It was twice the size of the state of Delaware. At the same time, the towns of St. Joseph and Port St. Joe battled neighboring Apalachicola for the region's trade while the state's first constitutional convention met and on December 3, 1838, drafted what became the first of Florida's five constitutions.

Port St. Joe remained the capital until Tallahassee took control in 1845, the year Florida was admitted to the Union as a state. St. Joseph lost the battle with Apalachicola over commerce and soon virtually disappeared.

Getting Around

From a distance, commercial air travelers generally choose **Tallahassee Regional Airport**, ☎ 904-891-7800, if they're flying into the eastern part of the area, or **Pensacola Regional Airport**, ☎ 904-435-1746, if their landing pad is on the west side. Tallahassee is served by two jet-service major carriers and six commuters. Pensacola is roughly equivalent in both categories. **Panama City-Bay County Air Park**, ☎ 904-763-6751, is an option. It's served by three commuter services. All are open to private pilots.

Interstate 10 through the interior, US 98 along the coast and Highway 20 between them are the major east-west corridors through the Central Panhandle. I-10, in fact, reaches all the way from the westernmost tip of Florida to downtown Jacksonville near the Atlantic shore. The nearest thing to a north-south superhighway is US 231, which stretches out of Alabama, moving through Graceville and Marianna, before it empties into Panama City. Highway 79 spans from Esto in Holmes County through Bonifay on its way to Laguna Beach, 10 miles west of Panama City Beach. Finally, Highways 71/73 make the longest north-south run through the region, spanning the Central Panhandle's fat spare tire from Malone near the Alabama border, through Blountstown and Wewahitchka on the way to Port St. Joe on St. Josephs Bay. Even the secondary roads through this region are plentiful enough and in good enough condition to get you almost anywhere easily and quickly.

Weather?

Throughout the Panhandle, the winters are generally mild, more so in the coastal areas. Once you get around Marianna and Graceville, about as far from the coast as you can get here, subtract two degrees from the thermometer in the winter and add two during the summer. Elsewhere, expect winter averages of 54°, with anywhere from two to 10 days in the mid- to high teens. Panhandle summers generally are more tolerable than destinations in South Florida. On the coast, sea breezes keep summer's temperature and humidity manageable most days, though in that spare tire area you can forget the breezes. There are going to be some high-humidity, high-90s days in the hot spot; otherwise expect a few in the high 90s as well as several in the low to mid-90s in the coastal areas.

Be prepared for the heat index.

INFORMATION SOURCES

Panama City Beach Convention & Visitors Bureau, (US) ☎ 800-722-3224, (Canada) ☎ 800-553-1330, P.O. Box 9473, Panama City Beach, FL 32417.
Bay County Chamber of Commerce, ☎ 904-785-5206, P.O. Box 1850, Panama City, FL 32402.
Calhoun County Chamber of Commerce, ☎ 904-674-4519, 340-B East Central Ave., Blountstown, FL 32424.
Gulf County Chamber of Commerce, ☎ 904-227-1223, 501 5th St., Port St. Joe, FL 32456.
Holmes County Chamber of Commerce, ☎ 904-547-4682, P.O. Box 1977, Bonifay, FL 32475.
Marianna Chamber of Commerce, ☎ 904-482-8061, P.O. Box 130, Marianna, FL 32447.
Mexico Beach Chamber of Commerce, ☎ 904-648-8196, P.O. Box 13382, Mexico Beach, FL 32410.

Panama City Beaches Chamber of Commerce, ☎ 904-235-1159, P.O. Box 9348, Panama City Beach, FL 32407.
Washington County Chamber of Commerce, ☎ 904-638-4157, P.O. Box 457, Chipley, FL 32428.
Wewahitchka Chamber of Commerce, ☎ 904-639-2130, P.O. Box 628, Wewahitchka, FL 32465.

Touring

Panama City Beach/Bay County

You won't dally here long in the touring section, but there are a few stops worth noting before you leave town and start the circuit. Arguably, Panama City Beach's don't-miss feature is the **St. Andrews State Recreation Area**, ☎ 904-233-5140, 4415 Thomas Drive, Panama City, FL 32408. To reach it from Alternate US 98 (Front Beach Road) in Panama City Beach, drive east to Thomas Drive and turn right (south), continuing on Thomas three miles to the park. In addition to being the top-rated beach of 1995, the peninsula has 1,260 acres of Florida coast as it used to be. There's a nature trail through dunes and many types of plants. On the walk you'll probably see some wading birds and other small critters that populate the park. Occasionally, an alligator is spotted. The park has jetties that extend nearly a half-mile into the Gulf, two fishing piers and a boat ramp.

One of the more interesting developed attractions is the **Museum of Man in the Sea**, ☎ 904-235-4101, 17314 Back Beach Road, Panama City Beach, FL 32413. To get there from the park, retrace your path, following Thomas Drive to Front Beach Road (Alternate US 98), turn left and drive to Beckrich Road and turn right to Back Beach Road (US 98), take a left and go about four miles (past Highway 79) to the museum on the right. This is the only exhibit in the world dedicated solely to diving, man's attempts to become a two-legged fish and the wonders of the sea. Displays dating to the 1500s trace our fascination with the underwater world, moving from the first days of scuba and submerged exploration to the treasures of old shipwrecks, including the Spanish gold fleet sunk by a hurricane in 1715. Marine salvage, oceanography, construction and archaeology are among the

Bay County

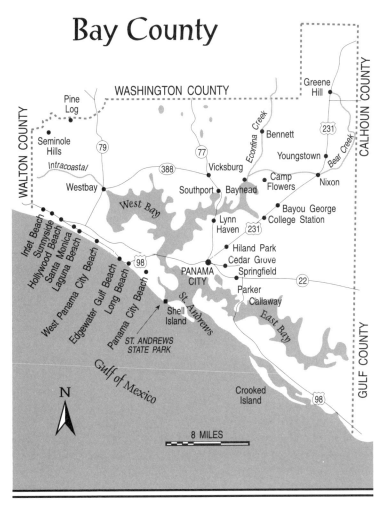

exhibits, and a 500-gallon saltwater aquarium lets you see the creatures that live in nearby St. Andrews Bay. A Toucha-Quarium lets you interact with shallow-water creatures and some hands-on experiments offer a lesson in how divers adapt to the underwater world.

The **Junior Museum of Bay County**, ☎ 904-769-6128, 1731 Jenks Avenue, Panama City, is a nice place to take the kids. Exhibits include a pioneer cabin, farming tools of the last century, puppet shows and a nature trail featuring three environments common to the area, a hardwood swamp, a hardwood hammock and a pine island. Children also get to play American Indian games and explore a life-size teepee in a hands-on room.

Several shops in the area will take you on snorkeling expeditions that let you see the undersea world while you play with wild dolphins. Among these are **The Super Shelling Safari Glass-Bottom Boat Tour**, ☎ 904-234-8944, at **Treasure Island Marina**, 3605 Thomas Drive; **Island Waverunner Tours**, ☎ 904-234-7245, at the same location; and **Sunra Charters-Aquastar**, ☎ 904-230-2800, which is at the Pass Port Marina on Thomas Drive.

You can see **Shell Island** from St. Andrews Park. Several tour companies operating from Panama City Beach provide transportation to the island, including **Capt. Anderson's**, ☎ 904-234-3435, 5550 N. Lagoon Drive, and *The Island Queen*, ☎ 904-234-3307, ext. 1816. The latter is a riverboat that sails into St. Andrews Bay and the Gulf from 100 Delwood Beach Road.

Elsewhere in town you can see one of the more traditional Florida marine parks (dolphin shows, aquariums, parrots, a shark tank, etc.) at **Gulf World**, ☎ 904-234-5271, 15412 Front Beach Road, and wildlife exhibits (350 big cats, reptiles and primates) at **Zoo World**, ☎ 904-230-1243, 9008 Front Beach Road.

One festival of note for adventurers: **The Gulf Coast Triathlon**, ☎ 904-234-6575, is working on its 15th year. Each May, 1,200 super-athletes tackle a 1.2-mile swim, 56-mile bicycle race and 13.1-mile run.

Are you man or woman enough?

If wind surfing or jet-skis and waverunners tempt you, there are dozens of places to rent the necessary tools and the wide-open Gulf of Mexico will test your skills. Rental sites include **Great Adventures Water Sports**, ☎ 904-234-0830, 8011 Thomas Drive; **Hathaway Marina Boat Rentals**, ☎ 904-234-9289, 6426 W. Highway 98; and **Fun Boat Rentals**, ☎ 904-233-7999, 5711 N. Lagoon Drive.

Amusement parks, miniature golf, go-cart tracks and bungee jumping – well, you can find these yourself. Trust us. If you drive along Front Beach Road (Alternate US 98), you can't miss the menagerie.

For a change of scenery, follow US 98 about 24 miles east to **Mexico Beach**, a charming community planned so that no place in town is further than a five-minute walk from the beach. Shelling, fishing and swimming are among the activities you can enjoy here. The beach is a relatively safe swimming hole due to the fact that St. Joseph Peninsula creates a barrier that all but eliminates the

Washington County

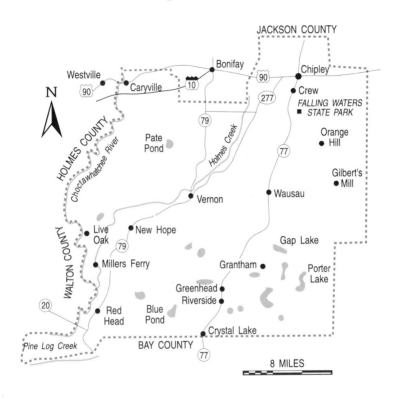

undertow. Mexico Beach has a pleasing mixture of modern as well as 50-year-old beach-bungalow architecture.

Washington County

Chipley, the county seat, was founded in 1882, though most of its historic buildings date to 1900 or later because two fires, the latter in 1901, destroyed a substantial portion of the original downtown. After that, the townspeople got the point and rebuilt with brick firewalls.

To reach Chipley, take US 98 east from Panama City Beach across the Hathaway Bridge and turn left (north) on Highway 77, traveling north 46 miles.

The town, once a stop on the L&N Railroad Line, has 280 sites listed on an historical survey. Forty-one of the more significant buildings form the core of a 1.4-square-mile walking tour, ☎ 904-638-6340. Among the properties are:

- **The Richardson Millinery Shop** (1904), 113 N. 6th St., which, during the town's heyday, had a roller-skating rink upstairs.
- **The Dunn Building** (1916), 103-109 S. Railroad Ave. E., which also is known as the Watts Building for the owner of the city's first telephone company. The vernacular-style building has a rich marble base.
- **First National Bank Building** (1905), 101 S. Railroad Ave. The building survived what the bank could not – the Great Depression. This three-story jewel has a mansard roof, 10 gable dormers, decorative cornice and a cutaway corner entrance.
- **The Old Cook House** (1905), 105 N. 5th St. Twice moved, this building at various times was the town library and the casket storage room for a former resident known only as Blackburn the Undertaker.

If you're planning a summer visit, you might plan it around the area's most notable festivals. Chipley hosts the annual **Panhandle Watermelon Festival** each June (the last weekend), where festivities include seed-spitting and melon-rolling contests in addition to (you saw this coming) a gala Miss Watermelon Pageant. The town of Wassau, which is 16 miles south of Chipley on Highway 77, has the heart-stopper – the **Wassau Possum** (in these parts there's no "O" in opossum) **Festival**, held the first Saturday in August. No self-respecting possum festival would be complete without crowning a king and queen and serving namesake vittles. Do you have the stomach for opossum pie?

Six miles south of Chipley on Highway 273, the **Falling Waters Recreation Area**, ☎ 904-638-6130, is one of the more unusual geological sites in Florida. While most sinkholes are funnel-shaped formations caused by the collapse of a cavern surface, this one has a smooth-walled chimney, which creates the falls and gives park guests an excellent view from a wood observation platform. The hilly terrain is honeycombed with other sinkholes. A private nursery, operated here during the 1920s, left the site rich in

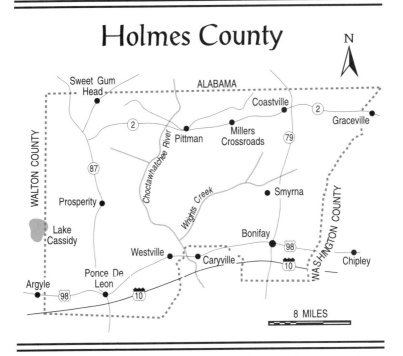

non-native trees such as mimosas, date palms and Japanese privets that mingle with native hardwoods, beech and dogwoods.

Holmes County

A quick stop now, a longer one later.

To get to **Ponce de Leon Springs State Recreation Area**, ☎ 904-836-4281, from Chipley, follow US 90 west 19 miles to Highway 181-A, turn left (south) and take it a mile to the 443-acre park. Its two flows produce 14 million gallons of chilly water per day. Twin nature trails, **Spring Run** and **Sandy Creek**, allow a nice view of wildlife and plant life along the 350-foot run to the Choctawhatchee River. Rangers conduct seasonal guided tours and, in no-swimming areas, you can try your luck for catfish, largemouth bass and panfish.

Vortex Spring, ☎ 904-836-4979, is north of the town of Ponce de Leon on Highway 81, about 3½ miles north of Highway 90. The private site is an outdoor playground that has swimming, canoeing, camping, fishing and diving available on 360 acres, complemented by rolling hills and tall pines. The main spring has a flow of 25 million gallons daily. This is a good site for conventional as well as cave diving. You'll explore it further under our diving adventures section.

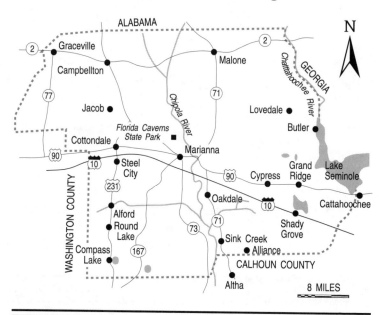

Jackson County

Do not miss a chance to visit **Florida Caverns State Park**, ☎ 904-482-9598. This is a treat, especially because of the unique geologic features. From the town of Ponce de Leon, take Highway 90 east 48 miles to Marianna and go left (north) on Highway 166 three miles to the entrance. The 1,284-acre park sits in the Appalachian foothills. The grounds include a beech-magnolia forest, a flood plain swamp, outcroppings of limestone and wildflowers. Birds that frequent this area range from barred owls and red-shoulder hawks to ruby-throated hummingbirds, American swallow tails and Mississippi kites in the spring.

Beavers, Barbour's map turtles and feisty alligator snapping turtles are among the other wildlife in the park. But the star attraction is the half-mile subterranean hiking loop through a marvelous cave system filled with stalactites and stalagmites, rimstone pools, columns and flowstones that took tens of thousands of years to develop. Hikers may come across a bat or two, but the caves most commonly inhabited by the endangered gray bat are closed to the public. Florida Caverns State Park has other amenities, including horse trails, covered under our adventures.

Back on Highway 90, go east again 22 miles to Highway 271, turn left (north) and travel about two miles to the **Three Rivers State Recreation Area**, ☎ 904-482-9006. This 682-acre park on Lake Seminole, which separates Florida and Georgia, offers hiking, boating and fishing activities. Its hammocks and pine woods are home to deer, fox squirrels, gray foxes and other species.

Gulf County

From Three Rivers State Recreation Area, return along Highway 271 to Highway 90, turn right (west), then left (south) on Highway 69 for the 21-mile voyage to Blountstown. Here, pick up Highway 71, continuing south 17 miles to Wewahitchka. In town, turn right on Lake Grove Road three miles to the **Dead Lakes State Recreation Area**, ☎ 904-639-2702. The name suitably describes the 83-acre reserve. The lake area was formed years ago when a flood of saltwater killed some of the lake's cypress trees, leaving stumps that have created a nice freshwater fishing habitat. The park's uplands include long-leaf pine, sweetbay, magnolia and cypress inhabited by deer, opossums, foxes, cotton rats, rabbits, beavers, alligators and several species of turtles. The town also prides itself on the Tupelo honey that's produced here.

From Wewahitchka, continue south 26 miles on Highway 71 to Port St. Joe, where history is kept alive at the **Constitution Convention State Museum**, ☎ 904-229-8029 (200 Allen Memorial Way, Port St. Joe, FL 32456). This 13½-acre site includes a marble monument erected in 1922 with the names of the convention's delegates. The museum hall has life-size delegates, four of which are audio-animated, providing a living history lesson on the site's brief tour as Florida's capitol.

From Port St. Joe, follow US 98 a short distance south to County Road 30, continue south five miles and turn right (west) for a tour of **St. Joseph Peninsula**. The first of two stops is **Cape San Blas**

Gulf County

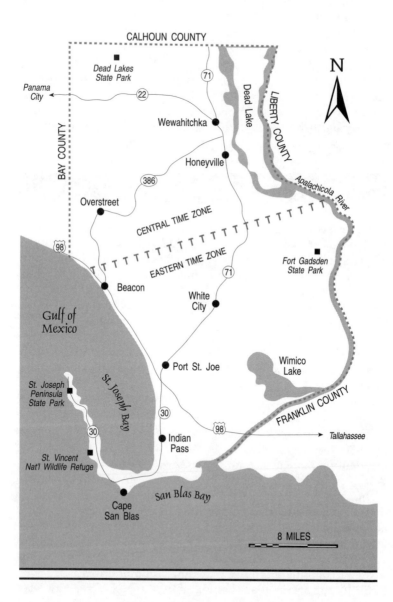

Calhoun County

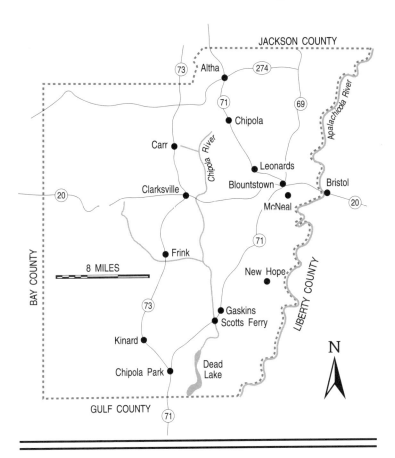

which, in addition to its Top Five Beach status, has an historic lighthouse and is a great place to swim, sun, scallop or go shelling along a vintage shore. While rental cottages and condos are available, motels, restaurants and other commercial fingerprints don't exist out here. It's a good place to see dolphins swimming 30 yards offshore, crabs darting in and out of their holes and pelicans diving for a snack. Eighteen miles further on County Road 30-E, at the furthest tip of the peninsula, is **St. Joseph State Park**, ☎ 904-227-1327. Bounded on three sides by water, this 2,516-acre park has a heavily forested interior (sandpine scrub and pine flatwoods), a seemingly endless stretch of beach and some striking dune formations. More than half of the park is a wilderness preserve. Developed areas include Gulf overlooks, a boardwalk and a hiking trail. Monarch butterflies are common during fall as they make their long migration from the North, and this is noted as one of the best places in Florida to see peregrine falcons. The shallow waters and beach are home to hermit, horseshoe and fiddler crabs.

Adventures

On Foot

You're about to discover this is not an area with a heavy concentration of designated trails, particularly those that will allow you to work up a lather. So the best bet, if that's your goal, is to use an improvised one. County Road 30 leaves the Gulf County mainland south of Port St. Joe, turning into CR 30-E for the 21-mile (one-way) journey to the tip of St. Joseph and the far reaches of the same-named state park. As noted earlier, this route is well-compensated with dune, woodland, beach and wildlife scenery and, if you're a true stormtrooper, you can do the full-length round-trip for a heavy-duty workout. The park has nine miles of beaches, and Cape San Blas has several miles more. If you're inclined, you can do more than half of the hike on the water. County Road 30 has moderate traffic. The 17-mile portion of CR 30-E from Cape San Blas has less. The last half of it is mainly used by the limited number of people who go to the park.

The other improvised hike is the 1.4-mile walking tour of Chipley's historic district, ☎ 904-638-6340. To reach it, take US 98 east from Panama City Beach across the Hathaway Bridge and turn left (north) on Highway 77, traveling north 46 miles.

Pine Log State Forest, ☎ 904-872-4175, is one of Florida's original forests, bought by the state in 1935-36. Pine Log's 6,911 acres include three lakes and an environmental center near the beginning of a three-mile nature trail that leads through slash, sand and long-leaf pines, as well as blackjack oaks, red maples, junipers and, for a short distance along the Pine Log Creek, cypress. It's also a peaceful spot for bird-watching (woodpeckers, mockingbirds and hawks). From Panama City, take US 98 west six miles to Highway 79, turn right (north) and drive 14 miles to the entrance on the right. For those who decide to lay over, the forest has 20 campsites, including 19 with electrical and water hook-ups. The Pine Log area also has a 31-mile portion of the Florida National Scenic Trail. Its western entry point is at the Choctawhatchee River on Highway 20 near Ebro, but a word of warning: Part of the trail is on private property and open only to Florida Trail Association members. For information, ☎ 800-343-1882.

Five area state parks offer designated hiking trails.

- ☐ **Falling Waters State Recreation Area**, ☎ 904-638-6130 (Washington), has two trails. One is about .8 miles roundtrip and passes by wiregrass, the site of an old well, the falls and outlying sinkholes. The other trail, .6 miles round-trip, goes from the parking area, past the amphitheater to the 24 campsites. The site is six miles south of Chipley on Highway 273.
- ☐ **Ponce de Leon Springs State Recreation Area**, ☎ 904-836-4281 (Holmes), has two short trails: Spring Run, 500 feet from the main spring halfway along the run to the Choctawhatchee River, and Sandy Creek, 750 feet along the opposite side. To get there from Chipley, follow US 90 west 19 miles to Highway 181-A, turn left (south) and take it a mile to the 443-acre park.
- ☐ **Florida Caverns State Park**, ☎ 904-482-9598 (Jackson), provides the very different perspective of hiking a half-mile course under the surface of the planet. The park has a half-mile of trails at ground level, too. The park is three miles north of Marianna on Highway 166.
- ☐ **Three Rivers State Recreation Area**, ☎ 904-482-9006 (Jackson), features a nearly mile-long, sometimes hilly trail along Lake Seminole. There also is a .4-mile Half Dry Creek Trail on the eastern side of the park. From Highway 90 in Marianna, go east 22 miles to Highway 271, turn left (north) and go two miles
- ☐ **St. Joseph Peninsula State Park**, ☎ 904-227-1327 (Gulf), offers three short trails that range from 1,400 feet to 2,000 feet, in case you don't have the energy for the 21-mile (one-way) marathon improvised earlier. The Gulf side trail is a link between two camping areas that

have 119 campsites. From Port St. Joe, follow US 98 a short distance south to County Road 30, continuing south five miles and turning right (west) on CR 30-E for an 18-mile spin to the park.

The **Northwest Florida Water Management District**, ☎ 904-539-5999, offers trails at three properties in the region. **The Choctawhatchee River-Holmes Creek tract** has two trails running through wetlands and upland hammocks that evolved from ancient dunes. You can reach an 11-mile trail system in the northern part of the tract by traveling US 90 west of Bonifay nine miles to Caryville and Highway 179, turning right (north) and going six miles to the entrance. A second trail set, totaling 6½ miles, is further south. From Caryville, take Highway 279 left (south) five miles to Highway 280, turn right (west) and drive four miles to Highway 284, then travel four miles to the entrance. **The Apalachicola River Management Area** has seven miles of trails through a forest flood plain inhabited by several species of birds, including swallow-tails and Mississippi kites. From Blountstown, hop on Highway 20 and drive five miles east to Bristol, turn right (south) on Highway 12 and go 16 miles to Highway 379, turn right and go 11 miles to the entrance. The **Econfina Creek tract** has one trail site that meanders through a diversity of flora (ash, magnolia, liverworts) and fauna (summer tanager and a large population of warblers). To reach the six-mile system from Blountstown, take Highway 20 west 28 miles to the entrance. For a guidebook with maps, call or write the district at Route 1, Box 3100, Havana, FL 32333-9600.

Additionally, **Tyndall Air Force Base**, ☎ 904-283-2641, about 10 miles east of Panama City on US 98, has two short nature trails and numerous other trails that are available for hiking. To get information about base access or maps, call or write the Natural Resources Office, Tyndall Air Force Base, FL 32403.

INFORMATION SOURCES

Florida Trail Association, ☎ 800-343-1882 (in Florida) or ☎ 352-378-8823, P.O. Box 13708, Gainesville, FL 32604.
Office of Greenways & Trails, ☎ 904-487-4784, Mail Station 795, 3900 Commonwealth Blvd., Tallahassee, FL 32399-3000.

GOLF COURSES

- **Bay Point Yacht & Country Club**, ☎ 904-235-6950, 100 Delwood Beach Road, Panama City Beach, FL 32411, 36 holes, driving range, lessons, PGA rating R-73.3.
- **Caverns Golf Club**, ☎ 904-482-4257, 2601 Caverns Road, Marianna, FL 32446, nine holes, driving range, lessons, R-67.4.
- **The Club at Sandy Creek**, ☎ 904-871-2673, 1732 Highway 2297, Panama City, FL 32404, nine holes, driving range, lessons, R-68.0.
- **Falling Waters Country Club**, ☎ 904-638-7398, Falling Waters Drive, Chipley, FL 32428, nine holes, driving range, R-69.0.
- **Great Oaks Golf Club**, ☎ 904-352-2060, US Highway 90, Marianna, FL 32446, nine holes, no rating.
- **Holiday Golf & Racquet Club**, ☎ 904-234-1800, 100 Fairway Boulevard, Panama City Beach, FL 32407, 18 holes, driving range, lessons, R-72.2.
- **Hombre Golf Club**, ☎ 904-234-3673, 120 Coyote Pass, Panama City Beach, FL 32407, 18 holes, driving range, lessons, R-70.3.
- **Magnolia Oaks Golf Club**, ☎ 904-482-8787, 5248 Clubhouse Drive, Marianna, FL 32446, 18 holes, driving range, lessons, no rating.
- **Majette Dunes Golf & Country Club**, ☎ 904-769-4740, 5304 Majette Tower Road, Panama City, FL 32404, 18 holes, driving range, lessons, R-70.3.
- **St. Josephs Bay Country Club**, ☎ 904-227-1751, County Road 30 South, Port St. Joe, FL 32456, 18 holes, driving range, lessons, R-70.7.
- **Signal Hill Golf Club**, ☎ 904-234-5051, 9615 Thomas Road, Panama City, FL 32407, 18 holes, R-63.55.

On Horseback

Trails for riders in the Central Panhandle are even more limited than the ones for hikers. One hedge: Florida has dozens of wildlife management areas in which locals sometimes ride, but many aren't included in this guide for a singular reason. Hunting. Without knowing the seasons or the aim of that person toting a shotgun, rifle or bow, why risk your safety and the safety of your animal?

Now the good news.

Florida Caverns State Park, ☎ 904-482-9598, has two trails in the northeast section of the park. The **South Flood Plain Trail** is 3.2 miles, while the **North Pine Island Trail** is 3.1 miles. Deer, turkey, barred owls, otters, bobcats, woodpeckers and other species of wildlife often are spotted along the trails. The native vegetation includes American beech, Southern magnolia, spruce pine, white oak and dogwood trees, as well as an assortment of wildflowers. The trails also pass some of the site's outlying sinks. Facilities include a stable, group camping area, individual campsites and showers. The park is three miles north of Marianna on Highway 166.

The **Northwest Florida Water Management District**, ☎ 904-539-5999, offers six miles of trails at its **Econfina Creek tract**. The scenics include ash, magnolias and a sometimes loud population of warblers. To reach it from Blountstown, take Highway 20 west 28 miles to the entrance. For a guidebook with maps, call or write the district at Route 1, Box 3100, Havana, FL 32333-9700.

As was the case for hikers, **Tyndall Air Force Base**, ☎ 904-283-2641, about 10 miles east of Panama City, has numerous interior trails open to riders. To get information about access to the base or maps, call or write the Natural Resource Office, Tyndall Air Force Base, FL 32403.

Don't forget to bring a negative Coggins for your mount(s).

On Wheels

The hiking trail improvised on County Road 30-E along the **St. Joseph Peninsula** makes a dandy, reasonably low-traffic bike trail as well. From Port St. Joe, peddle County Road 30 seven miles south, hooking a right at the "T," which is where the road becomes 30-E. From that point, pick your poison. The leg to Cape San Blas is 5½ miles. The pavement into the park and partway through is another 12.3 miles. These are one-way distances, of course, so don't forget the return voyage. If your radiator boils over along the way, there are plenty of places to pull over and cool off in the Gulf's waters, but don't forget where you are. This isn't downtown. The last store is four miles from the park entrance.

Another scenic improvised tour is further north in **Washington County**. To get there from Panama City and US 98, take US 231 north 44 miles, through Cairo, Fountain and Round Lake to Highway 276 at Alford. This is a secondary road that has relatively low traffic and passes North Florida woodlands and the Falling Waters State Recreation Area. Highway 276 has several jogs that allow you to peddle as much as 17 miles one-way to its intersection with Highway 277 near the Holmes River. Two alternate routes, each about 14 miles one-way, use Highway 276 to Highway 273. Turning right (north) leads you to Chipley. Turning left (south) takes you to Gilberts Mill in a forested area.

Off-road bikers, like hikers and horseback riders, might consider riding in **Tyndall Air Force Base**, ☎ 904-283-2641, where there are numerous interior trails. (Again, it's about 10 miles east of Panama City on US 98.) To obtain maps or information about base access, call or write the Natural Resource Office, Tyndall Air Force Base, FL 32403.

One final option: The six-day, 283-mile **Seven Hills to the Sea Bike Tour** is almost entirely in the Eastern Panhandle, but you can connect with it from this area. See page 117 for details on this marathon ride.

INFORMATION SOURCE

Florida Department of Transportation, ☎ 904-487-9220, Mail Station 82, 605 Suwanee St., Tallahassee, FL 32399-0450.

On Water

CANOEING

It's doubtful anyone can compete with Milton for canoeing. Yet the Central Panhandle has three designated canoe trails and two ad libbers that make it a venue worth considering. Paddles cocked? First, the designated runs.

The **Econfina Creek Canoe Trail** is a beautiful, swift-moving run that leads through high limestone walls, hammocks, bluffs and pine flatwoods. The 22-mile course stretches through Bay and Washington counties, beginning with a narrow section that has very tight curves and several fast-water chutes. The skill level is rated technical, the difficulty factor is rated strenuous and the current is three-plus mph on the upper portion of the trail. The lower part is spring-fed and slower, carrying a rating of beginner to moderate. A special note: There is a depth gauge under Scott's Bridge at the start of the trail. If it reads less than two feet, shallow water and log jams likely will make canoeing difficult. A reading of more than four feet means danger, the area is flooded. To reach the entry point from Panama City, follow US 231 north 27 miles to the town of Fountain, then another four miles to Scott's Road, turn left (west) and go four miles to the bridge. For a shorter, less taxing seven-mile run, take US 231 north 23 miles from Panama City, head left (west) at Highway 20 and drive 7.9 miles to the SR 20 bridge.

Easing back a little, the **Holmes Creek Canoe Trail** in Washington County is a more laid-back, 16-mile route through high, sandy banks, scenic hardwoods and low-lying swamps. The treats include a series of crystal-clear springs, some of which feed the creek. While low-hanging branches and submerged tree trunks offer a wee challenge, the curves are lazy and the current is slow (zero-one mph). The skill and difficulty levels are rated beginner and easy, respectively. The starting point is at the Vernon Wayside Park. To get there from Chipley, go west on US 90 nine miles to Bonifay, then south 11 miles on Highway 79, across the bridge. Take the first dirt road east a quarter-mile to the park. For the shorter course, seven miles, continue south of Vernon four miles on Highway 79 to Hightower Springs Road, then go right (north) one-half mile to the landing.

The **Chipola River Canoe Trail**, at 52 miles, is the marathoner's choice. It begins at Florida Caverns State Park, so among the attractions are the outlying caves and limestone formations. This trail flows through swamp and hardwood forests of beech, magnolia, oak and dogwood. Critters? As with the others in this chapter, you're likely to run into a variety of turtles, a few woodpeckers and, if your timing is right (or wrong), a beaver or an alligator or two. Look for limestone bluffs and caves along the way. The difficulty factor is easy to moderate and the skill level is beginner to intermediate with the current usually two-three mph. Now the manufacturer's warning: The first three miles of the run, starting at the state park, are sometimes dangerous and always require technical paddling skills (low water and lower branches). There are some rapids including "Look and Tremble Falls." (Falls? Well, that may be an overstatement.) If you're up for it, take Highway 167 north of Marianna three miles to the caverns entrance. Otherwise, launch at the State Road 167 bridge entrance a mile north of Marianna. (It's still a 49-mile endurance test. No one will call you a wimp.) For the short course (23 miles), take Highway 73 south about 26 miles to Clarksville, turn left (east) and go one mile to a wayside park.

One other note for those of you who carry snorkeling gear when paddling: The Chipola River yields plenty of artifacts to sharp-eyed adventurers, including arrow tips and large, prehistoric shark's teeth.

Now, let's ad lib a little.

St. Joseph Peninsula State Park, on County Road 30-E southwest of Port St. Joe, ☎ 904-227-1327, has 17 miles of paddling in St. Joseph Bay and up to 22 miles in the Gulf of Mexico. Depending on weather and skill level, a sea kayak is usually a better choice than a canoe.

The Three Rivers State Recreation Area, ☎ 904-482-9006, near Sneads, is another good place to create your own trail. It's on Lake Seminole and is fed by the Chattahoochee and Flint rivers, which divide Florida, Alabama and Georgia.

The hilly terrain is surrounded by hardwood hammocks and pines. The lake area is controlled by the Jim Woodruff Lock & Dam. It's inhabited by deer, fox squirrels and alligators, as well as an abundance of freshwater fish (so don't forget to bring a rod along).

To reach the recreation area from Marianna, take US 90 east 23 miles to Highway 271, turn left and go two miles to the entrance.

INFORMATION SOURCES

For designated trail maps, write to the **Office of Greenways and Trails**, ☎ 904-487-4784, 325 John Knox Road, Bldg. 500, Tallahassee, FL 32303-4124.

Florida Association of Canoe Liveries and Outfitters, ☎ 941-494-1215, P.O. Box 1764, Arcadia, FL 33821.

Bear Paw Canoe Trails, ☎ 904-482-4948, P.O. Box 621, Marianna, FL 32446.

Cypress Springs Canoe Trails, ☎ 904-535-2960, P.O. Box 726, Vernon, FL 32462.

Econfina Creek Canoe Livery, ☎ 904-722-9032, Route B, Box 1570, Youngstown, FL 32466.

Arrowhead Campgrounds, ☎ 904-482-5583, 4820 Highway 90 E., Marianna, FL 32446.

DIVING/SNORKELING

Once you get down, you won't want to come up, particularly offshore.

Yes, chamber of commerce types and industry members shouldn't always be trusted when they claim to have the best anything. But Panama City and Port St. Joe may have some of the best saltwater diving in Florida. Between them, the two launch pads have more than 60 dive sites – wrecks and natural as well as artificial reefs ranging from depths of 40 to 120 feet. Spearfishing spots? They have them. Photo opportunities? Them, too. Small and not-so-small marine life? You bet. From colorful tropicals and microscopic crustaceans to bottle-nose dolphins and giant manta rays, there's an abundant supply nourished by reefs, wrecks and the Gulf Stream's warm waters. And all of these sites are located in a compressed area. You don't have to drive miles between them. Park your van at one of the area's many dive shops and leave the driving to them.

The Wrecks

If you count the ones intentionally scuttled as reefs (there are at least 20 ships, planes and tugs), the Central Panhandle's Gulf Coast earns its reputation as the "Wreck Capital of the South."

It's hard to pick favorites, but the *Chippewa* and the *Empire Mica* are two of the most spectacular. The *Chippewa*, about 12 miles off Panama City Beach, is a 205-foot tug sunk intact and standing upright in 96 feet of water. Her deck is 70 feet down, and she has a large open cabin 50 feet down. The *Empire Mica*, a British tanker sunk in 1942 by a German U-boat, rests on the bottom at 110 feet, about 20 miles south of Cape San Blas. Her calling card: an 18-foot spare prop. While some of her remains have decomposed, there's enough left to reveal the two torpedo holes that doomed her. If you make this dive, you'll be in the company of amberjack, snapper, barracuda and grouper.

A 441-foot **Liberty Ship** 15 miles southwest of Panama City Beach is a good place to see giant manta rays and sea turtles during the summer months. Her hull is 57 feet across and rises 20 feet above a bottom at 72 feet.

The Reefs

An abundance of manmade reefs complement the natural ones in this corner of the Gulf, making it a hot spot for spearfishing, underwater photography or simply observing marine life in frequently thick schools. When it comes to spearfishing, few places are hotter than a Quonset hut that rests in 87 feet of water, eight miles off Panama City Beach. The 40-by-30-foot cylinder is an attractant for amberjack and barracuda in summer and grouper and snapper in winter. Visibility is usually 25 feet but sometimes it's substantially better. Fish aren't the only trophies – 1937 beer bottles are the booty at the *Tarpon*, a 160-foot freighter lost with 18 crew members. She lies, partly intact, at 92 feet, and some of her vintage cargo remains with her.

The Springs

While inland sites can't rival the Gulf in volume, there are two sites well worth the trip. **Vortex Spring** is a big (360-acre) commercially run site. The main spring produces 25 million gallons per day, and the four-mile run, known as Blue Creek, is a relaxing course for snorkelers or canoeists. The dive site has student training platforms at 20 feet and the spring basin, 50 feet down, has a ledge-like, well-lit cavern where divers cavort with freshwater eels (they're harmless), redhorse suckers and catfish. Experienced divers tackle a garage-size tunnel that runs around 100 yards to a depth of 100 feet. (☎ 904-836-4979.) From Chipley, follow US 90 west 31 miles to Ponce de Leon and Highway 81, exiting right (north) 4.2 miles to the site. A wet suit? You decide. The spring is a chilly 68°.

Another commercial cavern site, **Cypress Springs**, is near Vernon. At a depth of 25 feet, there is a small (6-by-10 feet) opening with a strong flow. Once inside, the cavern opens into a room that's about 40 feet wide and 15 feet high. Those who feel comfortable and experienced enough to do so swim through a shaft that angles to a depth of 70 feet. You can still see the surface and natural daylight at this point. The spring produces about 90 million gallons of water per day. (☎ 904-535-2960.) To get there from Chipley, follow US 90 west nine miles to Bonifay, head left (south) 7.6 miles to Cypress Springs Road (it's dirt) and continue to the spring entrance.

Additionally, snorkeling is permitted at the **Ponce de Leon Springs State Recreation Area**, which features a 350-foot run into Sandy Creek, a tributary of the Choctawhatchee River,

☎ 904-836-4281. From Chipley, take US 90 west 19 miles to Highway 181-A, turn left (south) and go a mile to the 443-acre park.

INFORMATION SOURCES

Florida Association of Dive Operators, ☎ 305-451-3020, 51 Garden Cove Drive, Key Largo, FL 33037.
US Coast Guard, Mayport, ☎ 904-246-7315.
Florida Marine Patrol, Panama City, ☎ 904-234-0211.
Ned DeLoach's Diving Guide to Underwater Florida, ☎ 904-737-6558, New World Publications, 1861 Cornell Road, Jacksonville, FL 32207.
Capt. Black's Dive Center, ☎ 904-229-6330, 301 Monument Ave., Port St. Joe, FL 32456.
Diver's Den, ☎ 904-871-4777, 4720 East Business 98, Panama City, FL 32404.
Emerald Coast Diver's Den, ☎ 800-945-3483 or 904-871-2876. Two sites: 6222 East Highway 98, Panama City, FL 32404; 5121 Thomas Drive, Panama City Beach, FL 32408.
Hydrospace Dive Center, ☎ 800-874-3483, 904-234-3063. Two sites: 6422 W. Highway 98, Panama City Beach, FL 32407; 3605-A Thomas Drive, Panama City Beach, FL 32407.
Panama City Dive Center, ☎ 800-832-3483, 904-235-3390, 4823 Thomas Drive, Panama City Beach, FL 32408.
Cypress Springs, ☎ 904-535-2960, P.O. Box 726, Vernon, FL 32462.
Vortex Springs, ☎ 904-836-4979, Route 2, Box 650, Ponce de Leon, FL 32455.

SALTWATER & FRESHWATER FISHING

The same good news for saltwater fishermen in the Western Panhandle is waiting for those who land in the Central Region. Hang onto your rod.

Panama City Beach is one of Florida's oldest recreational fishing spots, dating to the 1920s. Bottom fishing for red snapper and grouper on the offshore reefs are among the favorites. Unlike areas further south along the peninsula, the depth here falls as much as 200 feet just 20 miles off the beach. Closer to shore, the spring brings giant schools of Spanish mackerel, occasionally up to five miles long, one wave after another. Another springtime favorite is cobia, 40- to 100-pounders that cruise the white-sand bottom just off the beach. May is the best time for king mackerel, blackfin tuna and bonita; June marks the arrival of dolphin in the offshore weedlines; and July means blue marlin, for which the area has several major tournaments. Flats fishermen find redfish (spring and fall) and sea trout (all but summer). For those who don't bother with rod and reel, crabbing and scalloping are generally good at St. Joseph Peninsula State Park.

Freshwater enthusiasts shouldn't feel snubbed.

The Three Rivers State Recreation Area, ☏ 904-482-9006, is a hot spot on Lake Seminole. This area has a reputation for an abundance of largemouth and smallmouth bass, catfish, bluegill, speckled perch and bream. Directions are in the canoeing portion of this chapter. **The Lake Victor Fish Management Area**, ☏ 904-265-3677, is a 130-acre artificial fishing hole created by an earth dam that runs across Limestone Branch. Depths average eight feet and fish attractors are in place to help your luck. Species include largemouth bass, bluegill, shellcracker, warmouth, black crappie and channel catfish. From Chipley, take Highway 77 north 13 miles to Graceville, then go left (west) 21 miles on Highway 2. About a mile after you cross Highway 179-A, look for a dirt road and the entrance to Lake Victor on the left. **The Merritt's Mill Pond Fish Management Area**, ☏ 904 265-3677, is near Marianna. The reservoir is fed primarily by springs, making it crystal clear, with a cypress backdrop. Shellcracker (a.k.a., redear sunfish), largemouth bass and bluegill are very common. The springs' minerals and nutrients produce some whoppers, including a world record shellcracker. More on that in a minute. To get to the pond's public ramp, take US 90 three miles east of Marianna, then turn left (north) on Highway 71 for 1.1 miles, then right on Highway 164 for 1½ miles. At Hunter Fish Camp Road go right (south) for one-half mile to the ramp.

Dead Lakes State Recreation Area, ☏ 904-639-2702, is another freshwater gold mine. The dark water and cypress snags and stumps make it a great place to hook bluegill, shellcracker and largemouth bass. From Marianna, go 17 miles east on Highway 90 to Highway 69, turn right (south) for a 21-mile voyage to Blountstown. Pick up Highway 71, continue south 17 miles to Wewahitchka. In town, turn right on Lake Grove Road and drive three miles to the recreation area.

OK, the records. That shellcracker – 4.86 pounds – was caught 10 years ago on the pond. Lake Seminole boasts one of its own, a 16.31-pound sunshine bass, and the Washington County side of the Choctawhatchee River produced a chain pickerel that tipped the scale at 5.55 pounds.

Back in the salt, there are three current records: Tripletail, 32 pounds, in Apalachicola Bay; black sea bass, 5 pounds, 1 ounce, Panama City; and a bull shark that weighed in at 517 pounds off Panama City Beach.

Freshwater anglers looking to park it at a camp can choose among several that offer a range of services from ramps, bait and gas to lodging, licenses and guides. On the Chipola River, they include **Douglas Landing**, ☎ 904-639-5481, and **Bryant's Landing**, ☎ 904-639-2853, both on County Road 381 off Highway 71 near Wewahitchka. Dead Lake camps such as **Cypress Lodge**, ☎ 904-639-5414, and **Lake Side Lodge**, both off Highway 71, also are just outside Wewahitchka. The **Arrowhead Campground**, ☎ 904-482-5583, is at Merritt's Mill Pond on Highway 90 east of Marianna. **Seminole Lodge**, ☎ 904-593-6886, is located (not coincidentally) on Lake Seminole off Highway 90 near Sneads. **Hide-A-While Camp**, ☎ 904-535-4834, is along the Choctawhatchee River on Highway 20 close to Ebro.

The Panama City Beach area is thick with charter operators.

If you don't mind crowds, **Capt. Anderson's Marina**, ☎ 904-234-3435, is the place to go. It has a six-pack of 85-footers, each capable of taking 60 people on Gulf trips, while **Don Tyler at Treasure Island Marina**, ☎ 904-234-8246, can take up to 40 fishermen. **Gotta Believe/Gotcha Charters**, ☎ 904-234-9409, offers a fleet of seven vessels that have room for six to 14 anglers. If you're looking for less competition and more room, try Don Williams' "**Hyperactive**," ☎ 904-233-5634, and Dave Jacobs' **Reel 'Em In Charters**, ☎ 904-271-0184. Each carries parties of four out of Hathaway Marina. Most marinas also offer rentals for sea dogs who insist on finding the best spots themselves.

If you're looking to get away from the crowds on land as well as at sea, go to **Guilford Charter Service**, ☎ 904-648-8211, in Mexico Beach, or hook up with the folks at **Bay Charters**, ☎ 904-229-1086, in Port St. Joe.

Dan Russell Pier in Panama City Beach, ☎ 904-234-5080, is the Gulf Coast's longest (1,642 feet) and it's lighted for night owls. **M.B. Miller Pier**, ☎ 904-784-4066, in Panama City, is 586 feet and also is lighted. The **Mexico Beach Fishing Pier** – sorry, no telephone – sticks 386 feet into the Gulf. It's lighted, too.

One final note:

Make sure to get a fishing license. On the saltwater side, a non-resident license ranges from $5 for three days to $30 for a year. Non-resident freshwater licenses are $15 for seven days and $30 for one year. Florida also has size and bag limits on many species. Information on these can be obtained at area bait-and-tackle shops, marinas, or by contacting the **Florida Marine Patrol**, ☎ 904-233-5150, Ctr. Bldg. 432, Panama City, FL 32407, for saltwater fishing or the **Florida Game & Fresh Water**

Fish Commission, ☎ 904-265-3677, 3911 Highway 2321, Panama City, FL 32409-1658, for freshwater.

In The Air

Talk about contrast:

Turquoise waters, ghost-white beaches and forest green woodlands.

What better way to see them than the way the pelicans and gulls do, from high above. You can hook onto a parasail at **The Boardwalk Beach Resort**, ☎ 800-224-4853 or 904-234-3484, 9450 Thomas Drive, **Coastal Parasailing**, ☎ 904-233-0914, or **Great Adventures**, ☎ 904-234-0830, all on Panama City Beach. **Coastal Helicopters**, ☎ 904-234-8642, puts a different spin on aerial sightseeing with tours that lift off right from the beachfront.

Eco-Travel Excursions

Anna and Rickie McAlpin at **Bear Paw Canoe Trails**, ☎ 904-482-4948, in Marianna, offer three-, eight- and 15-mile adventures along the Chipola River. The tour gives you a chance to explore crystal-clear springs and dry caves such as The Ovens (don't forget to bring a flashlight). From Marianna, take Highway 71 south 4½ miles to Magnolia Road/Highway 280, turn right, go one mile, cross a bridge and turn right again at the sign on a dirt road just past the bridge.

Where To Stay & Eat

Much like the Western Panhandle, the Central Panhandle has undergone a building boom in its tourism sector primarily in Panama City Beach, which has become a magnet for spring breakers, young families, avid fishermen and those looking for the social life – but not quite the crowds – of places like Daytona Beach, Miami, Tampa-St. Petersburg and Fort Lauderdale.

Also much like the Western Panhandle, this region has tens of thousands of motel, hotel and condominium units and hundreds of restaurants that offer just about any cuisine you crave. Reservations? They're a smart move, especially in the peak spring-summer seasons to ensure your first choice in lodging and meal times, but Panama City during spring break is the only spot where you risk being shut out.

Panama City/Bay County

One of the more delightful, self-sustaining parking spots is **The Boardwalk Beach Resort**, ☎ 800-224-4853 or 904-234-3484. This isn't one but four properties (Comfort Inn & Suites, Gulfwalk, Beachwalk and Howard Johnson Resort Hotel), with 626 guest rooms (suites to motel units and efficiencies), more than one-third of a mile of beachfront and an eclectic amenity package – including a beach bar and grill, the Copper Cowboy Saloon, a gourmet pizzeria, a convenience store, cafés, markets and its own jet-ski and parasailing venues. It's a great hangout if you're into '50s music, too. Slip into your poodle skirt or letterman's sweater and saddle oxfords and head over to The Hangout. The properties are connected by an 1,800-foot boardwalk along the coast.

Most of the well-known chains are represented along a one-mile piece of the miracle strip (Front Beach Road). Included are **Holiday Inn SunSpree Resort**, ☎ 904-234-1111; **Days Inn Beach**, ☎ 904-233-3333; **Best Western Casa Loma**, ☎ 904-234-1100; **Best Western Del Coronado**, ☎ 904-234-1600; and **Ramada Inn Beach & Convention Center**, ☎ 904-234-1700. Combined, these five have 875 rooms and they share a toll-free number: ☎ 800-633-0266.

St. Andrews Bay Resort Management, ☎ 800-621-2462, is one of several agencies in the area specializing in condominium, townhouse and private beach house rentals. They range from modern luxury accommodations to the Art Deco look that is common on Miami's South Beach. **Gulfaire Vacation Rentals**, ☎ 800-643-6392, offers condominium rentals at several locations, while **Marriott's Bay Point Resort**, ☎ 800-874-7105, displays another face of Panama City Beach. It's surrounded by 1,100 acres that are part of a national wildlife refuge.

When your stomach starts rumbling, you won't lack choices, but seafood is a natural specialty. Menus include char-grilled grouper topped with crabmeat and Hollandaise sauce, mesquite-grilled snapper, blackened tuna, Grecian-style pompano, Cajun crawfish and Apalachicola Bay oysters. **Billy's Oyster Bar**, ☎ 904-235-2349; **Key West Bar & Grill**, ☎ 904-230-9009; **Kokomo's Oyster Bar**,

☎ 904-230-8411; **Scampy's,** ☎ 904-235-4209; and **Shuckums Oyster Pub,** ☎ 904-235-3214, are just a few of the scores of restaurants in the beach area.

Washington County

Chipley has a scattering of modestly priced chain members, including the **Budget Inn,** ☎ 904-638-1850; **Days Inn,** ☎ 904-638-7335; and a **Super 8 Motel,** ☎ 904-638-8530, as well as the **Chipley Motel,** ☎ 904-638-1322. At mealtime, you might consider some of the area's home-style or barbecue restaurants. Among these are **Bailey's Barbecue,** ☎ 904-638-1914, Chipley; **Granny's Country Kitchen,** ☎ 904-638-1339, Chipley; **The Pit Restaurant,** ☎ 904-535-9180, Vernon; **Shirley's,** ☎ 904-535-6449, Vernon; and **Uncle Billy's,** ☎ 904-638-3571, Chipley.

Holmes County

Bonifay offers three modest- to moderate-priced motels: **Best Western Tivoli Inn,** ☎ 904-547-4251; **Budget Inn,** ☎ 904-547-4167; and **Econo-Lodge,** ☎ 904-526-3710. In addition to fast-food eateries, the town continues the family-style and barbecue theme common in small-town North and Northwest Florida. The options include **Blitch's Family Restaurant,** ☎ 904-547-4835; **Diane's Restaurant,** ☎ 904-547-4473; and **Paige's Barbecue,** ☎ 904-547-3000.

Jackson County

Marianna is a little more populated with motels and restaurants. Chains include **Best Western,** ☎ 800-528-1234 or 904-526-5666; **Comfort Inn,** ☎ 800-228-5150 or 904-526-5600; **Days Inn,** ☎ 800-329-7466 or 904-526-4311; and **Econo-Lodge,** ☎ 800-446-6900 or 904-526-3710. Those looking to avoid the chains can choose among **Durden's Family Inn,** ☎ 904-592-9113; **Lee's Motel & Apartments,** ☎ 904-482-5793; and **Seminole Lodge and Marina,** ☎ 904-593-6886.

There's a broader range of cuisine here than in Holmes and Washington counties. Some of the options: **Red Canyon Grill,** ☎ 904-482-4256; **Rob's Bar-B-Q and Steak House,** ☎ 904-482-4256;

Tony's Restaurant, ☎ 904-482-2232; **Parramore Landing & Restaurant** (in Grand Ridge), ☎ 904-592-2091; and **Peacock's Country Kitchen** (Grand Ridge), ☎ 904-592-2211.

Calhoun County

The **Lodge** and **The Lodge Restaurant**, ☎ 904-674-2626, in Blountstown, are among the few places to park and refuel in Calhoun County, which is pretty void of tourism trappings. The inn has a homey atmosphere and the restaurant has a daily country lunch buffet, as well as seafood buffets Friday and Saturday nights. **The Garden House Grill**, ☎ 904-643-3366, in Bristol, is a local favorite. Steaks and seafood as well as lighter things (salads and sandwiches) are featured.

Gulf County

If your budget allows a few dollars more for accommodations, **Cape San Blas** is a picturesque place to rent a beach house, set amid the dunes, sea oats and white-sand beach. Many of them are stilt homes with decks and glorious views. The region's semi-privacy spells romance, more so for mid-week guests. Several agencies specialize in these rentals, including **Rosasco Realty**, ☎ 800-648-6531; **Tom Todd Realty**, ☎ 800-876-2611; and **Elizabeth W. Thompson**, ☎ 904-648-5449. You'll find traditional beachfront motel-style accommodations at **El Governor Motel**, ☎ 904-648-5757, in Mexico Beach; the **Gulf Sands Motel**, ☎ 904-647-5711, in Port St. Joe; and the **Surfside Inn**, ☎ 904-648-5771, in Mexico Beach. **Old Saltworks Cabins**, ☎ 904-229-6097, in Port St. Joe, and **Whispering Pines** of Cape San Blas, ☎ 904-227-7252, feature rustic cabins and cottages, respectively.

Top of the Gulf Restaurant, ☎ 904-648-5275, located at El Governor Motel, and **Butlers by the Bay Restaurant**, ☎ 904-227-1386, near Mexico Beach, are good spots to dig into fresh local seafood, char-broiled steaks and prime rib. Some of the other local favorites include **Betty Lee's Wewa Restaurant**, ☎ 904-639-2318, in Wewahitchka; **Jim McNeil's Indian Pass Raw Bar**, ☎ 904-227-1670, at Port St. Joe; and **Cap'n Jack's**, ☎ 904-227-2046, also at Port St. Joe.

Campgrounds

Campers have plenty of choices in the Central Panhandle.

Arrowhead Campgrounds, ☎ 904-482-5583, 4820 Highway 90-E, Marianna, FL 32446, offers 250 sites, showers, cable television, a recreation hall, a pool, a store and docks. **Cape San Blas Camping Resort**, ☎ 904-229-6800, P.O. Box 645, Port St. Joe, FL 32456-0645, has tent and RV sites as well as cottages along the Gulf. **Northwest Florida Campground & Park**, ☎ 904-638-0362, Route 5, Box 830, Chipley, FL 32428-9501, is a 19-acre site near Interstate 10. The park provides a large recreation room, covered pavilion and a busy activities schedule. **Ocean Park RV Resort**, ☎ 904-235-0306, 23026 W. Highway 98, Panama City Beach, FL 32413-1107, is across from the Gulf Beach and adjacent to Lake Powell. It has a pool, game room, laundry, pull-through sites and full hook-ups. **The Rustic Sands Resort Campground**, ☎ 904-648-5229, 800 N. 15th St., Mexico Beach, FL 32456, is quiet and family-oriented. It has a recreation room, cable television, marina and a boat ramp.

Finally, these state sites feature limited camping:

- **Falling Waters State Recreation Area**, ☎ 904-638-6130, Chipley.
- **Florida Caverns State Park**, ☎ 904-482-9598, Marianna.
- **Pine Log State Forest**, ☎ 904-872-4175, Panama City.
- **St. Joseph Peninsula State Park**, ☎ 904-227-1327, Port St. Joe.
- **Three Rivers State Recreation Area**, ☎ 904-482-9006, Sneads.

Eastern Panhandle

The town that Coke built?

Well, yes, but it was inadvertent.

Shortly after the turn of the century, Quincy residents who needed a loan had one place to turn, Quincy State Bank. Its president, Mark W. "Pat" Munroe, made no bones about it: Applications would get his special blessing if some of the money was used to buy stock in the new Coca-Cola company.

Munroe's motives are unclear. The results are not.

Reluctantly or otherwise, townspeople at one point owned more than 65% of Coke's stock. Munroe's "strong-arm" financial planning turned 24 of them into millionaires long before World War II and made Quincy, for a while, the richest town per capita in the nation. That was a blessing when the area's main industry, shade tobacco (the leaves used to make the outer wrapper of a cigar), bailed out in the 1960s in favor of cheaper labor and quarters. Coke's influence remains in Quincy's architecture and independence. Tobacco's departure didn't have nearly the impact it had on nearby Havana, which had to scrape to survive. In the past decade, however, this hamlet named for the Cuban capital has been reborn as one of the largest antique centers in the Southeast and the home of a blossoming artists' colony. Many of its shops have settled in restored, red-brick tobacco warehouses and auto dealerships left over from its heyday. These, with its narrow, tree-lined streets, have led to a colorful and continuing renaissance.

Today, the sister cities are two of the prettiest small towns in Florida and among the easternmost points where you'll still find dominant architecture out of the 19th and early 20th centuries, including the **Davidson House** (1859), **Allison House** (1843) and **Empire Theater** (1910).

But Gadsden is just one of six counties you're going to see in this chapter, which includes the northern reaches of areas simultaneously known as Big Bend and The Nature Coast. This region of the panhandle has a range of "looks," from the vibrant, densely settled state capital of Tallahassee in Leon County to ultra-rural Liberty County, where the population has only quadrupled to 6,538 people since 1880. That's partly because the huge Apalachicola National Forest saves a large share of Liberty, Wakulla and Leon counties for outdoor adventurers, as do other state and federal parks and preserves. One of these, the **Torreya State Park**, has 1,000 acres of deep ravines, 150-foot bluffs and a species of the rare evergreens for which the park is named. These stately trees only grow along the Apalachicola River's bluffs. Speaking of rivers, this region nearly rivals Milton in the number of trails available to paddlers of varying talents. Stay tuned for more about canoeing in the adventures section.

You'll also have some fun on a needle-thin strip of four barrier islands: **St. George, Cape St. George, Dog Island** and **St. Vincent Island** off Apalachicola in Franklin County. The latter three are only accessible by boat. All of them feature pristine, powder-white beaches (you can rent your own), marshes, great fishing and shelling, a limitless horizon and wildlife ranging from the native to the novel – sambar deer and rare red wolves are among them. By the way, at mealtime, think "oyster." You haven't feasted on one until you've tasted the Apalachicola Bay's variety. The bay also leads the way to several good offshore dive sites, including the photogenic **Miss Gem** and, for deeper water fans, the **Exxon Tower** rising partway from a floor at 105 feet.

The treasures awaiting in adjacent Wakulla County include the **St. Marks Lighthouse** (built in 1829), which is a national historic site; **Edward Ball Wakulla Springs State Park**, home of a rustic lodge and a first-magnitude spring (at 250 feet it's one of the deepest freshwater springs on the planet and the spot where underwater scenes for some of Johnny Weissmuller's Tarzan moves were shot); and the **Gulf Specimen Marine Laboratory**, a hands-on center where you'll get to meet native and exotic marine life.

Tallahassee is the largest city in the region but, even here, you won't find fake sharks or humans dressing in mouse costumes. Instead you'll find some of Florida's richest history lessons, particularly on the government side. Chamber of commerce types like to call it a place of pow-wows, plantations, politics and pride, the first due to early Native American presence and, to a lesser degree, Florida State University's national champion "Seminoles," the last three due to the city's antebellum roots and Southern personality. This is where you can view the stately old Capitol, an 1845 American Renaissance structure with red-and-white striped awnings; Herman, a nine-foot mastodon skeleton (this guy's 12,000 years old) at the Museum of Florida History; the princely Governor's Mansion; and the Southeast's answer to the Vietnam Veterans Memorial, 40-foot, twin-granite towers that face the old Capitol.

The city has 122 properties on the National Register of Historic Places, and several other historic sites are within a short drive, including the site of San Marcos de Apalache and the Civil War-era Natural Bridge Battlefield.

One more point for bikers before you move into more specific information about the area: The six-day, 283-mile Seven Hills to the Sea Bicycle Tour moves through this area. Here's hoping you catch your second wind.

For the wimps among us, there are several shorter trails.

Either way, wimp or warrior, the countryside wanders through rolling hills dotted with 150-year-old live oaks, pines, snowy dogwoods, fragrant magnolias, blue-water springs, swamps, sinkholes and, yes, even skinny-dipping ponds. On the way, you'll encounter several plantation houses as old as those live oaks.

Geography & History

Except for the Tallahassee metropolitan area, much of the countryside in the Eastern Panhandle is a patchwork of barrier islands, fishing villages, farms, timberland and uninhabited, occasionally unexplored, forests and refuges under public ownership. As mentioned earlier, this area is a treasure chest of bluffs, dramatic ravines and winding rivers, beginning with the powerful Apalachicola River, which forms the western boundary of the region and serves as a dividing line between eastern and central time zones. To the east, forests and preserves reveal sloughs, hammocks, savannas and grassy marshes. Resident creatures include deer, otters, wild hogs, turkeys, rabbits, quail and, though less abundant, black bears, bobcats and coyotes. This region has several places where history was made, including the first camps established by Spanish explorers and early American military forts. On a railroad bed that dates to 1837, the state has built the 16-mile Tallahassee-St. Marks Trail, which is a great spot for cycling, hiking, and horseback riding.

More history?

The Native Americans were here first. They shared this land tens of thousands of years ago, when the Panhandle and North Florida were the end of the continent and South Florida was an island well off its shore.

More recent tribes (1250 AD through the mid-1800s) include the Creek, Seminole, Muscogee and Apalachee cultures. It was the promise of Apalachee gold (in reality it probably was copper) that lured the Spanish to the area around what is now Tallahassee. Panfilo de Narvaez was the first in 1528. His visit and his life were cut short by the Apalachee, who didn't lack fighting skills. Hernando de Soto came 11 years later with 600 troops, holding off the Indians and setting up camp for a year. Historians believe this camp celebrated the first Christmas Mass in the United States on a hill overlooking Tallahassee. Missions and a fort were built at what is now the San Marcos de Apalache State Historic Site at St. Marks. Except for two brief periods, the Spanish controlled the region until 1821, when Florida was ceded to the United States. Today, **San Marcos de Apalache,** ☎ 904-925-6216, displays the remnants of a Spanish bastion wall, magazines and earthworks from its occupation by Confederate troops, as well as a cemetery.

St. Marks has another noteworthy historic site, **Natural Bridge**, ☎ 904-925-6216, where a rag-tag army of old men, young boys and wounded Confederate troops, who were home to recuperate, held off Union forces in the closing days of the Civil War. That made Tallahassee the only Southern capitol east of the Mississippi never to be captured by the Union. In addition to battle markers, breastworks and a monument, the park has an annual re-enactment each March.

The descendants of our first three presidents – Washington, Adams and Jefferson – as well as Prince Achille Murat, the nephew of Napolean Bonaparte, were among Tallahassee's early settlers. In the social event of the 1826 season, Murat married Washington's great-grandniece, Kate. He wooed her by drinking from her slipper. (Yes, today, he would be considered a bit odd.) Their mansion is now located at the **Tallahassee Museum of History and Natural Science,** ☎ 904-576-1636. Her slipper? Well, honestly, no one knows.

You'll learn more about the Eastern Panhandle's more recent history, from statehood and plantation life to archaeological digs and the first years of the 20th century, as you start touring the region. But first a few air and ground rules.

Getting Around

The area is compressed enough that most folks coming by air would use the **Tallahassee Regional Airport**, ☎ 904-891-7800, which is served by two major carriers and a half-dozen commuter airlines, some of them connecting through Atlanta and New Orleans. The **Panama City-Bay County Air Park**, ☎ 904-763-6751, is an option if you're beginning your adventure further west. Either of these airports is suitable for private pilots, as is the **Quincy-Gadsden Municipal Airport**, which has a 3,700-foot lighted runway and fuel facilities.

Ground travel is reasonably easy and quick, though obstacles, such as the Apalachicola National Forest, make some destinations a bit less direct. Interstate 10 cuts through the north part of the area, through Gadsden, Leon and Jefferson counties. One of its most distant and lonely connections is the commute from the hamlet of Gretna south on Highway 65, about 80 miles, to Eastpoint, located on Apalachicola Bay, midway between Carrabelle and Apalachicola. US Highway 27 runs south of I-10 in the eastern part of the region before crossing I-10 west of Tallahassee and reaching north. Arguably, the most scenic route is US 98, which parallels the coast in Wakulla and Franklin counties. In addition to giving you glimpses of the shoreline, the highway passes through many fishing villages and 1940s-style settlements. Highway 263, which is also called Capital Circle Southwest, is an ideal north-south loop that avoids downtown Tallahassee and points you to destinations north and south of Leon County.

Like other parts of the Panhandle, the winters are generally mild, more so in the coastal areas. Expect a few days each year in the mid-teens, but a winter average of 54° (even this far north it isn't unusual to have an 80° Christmas Day) is what's expected. Fry days? Yes, Florida's summers often are brutal, but, like the Western Panhandle, this area's northern reaches extend 35 to 60 miles from the Gulf, which means sea breezes keep heat and humidity down. You can expect some stifling, mid-90s days, but not nearly as many as in South and Central Florida. Just in case, though, take the necessary precautions when packing, planning and pacing activities.

INFORMATION SOURCES

Apalachicola Bay Chamber of Commerce, ☎ 904-653-9419, 84 Market St., Apalachicola, FL 32320-1776.
Carrabelle Area Chamber of Commerce, ☎ 904-697-2585, P.O. Drawer DD, Carrabelle, FL 32322.
Gadsden County Chamber of Commerce, ☎ 904-627-9231, P.O. Box 389, Quincy, FL 32353.
Liberty County Chamber of Commerce, ☎ 904-643-2359, P.O. Box 523, Bristol, FL 32321.
Monticello-Jefferson County Chamber of Commerce, ☎ 904-997-5552, 420 W. Washington St., Monticello, FL 32344.
Tallahassee Area Chamber of Commerce, ☎ 904-224-8116, P.O. Box 1639, Tallahassee, FL 32302.
Tallahassee Area Convention and Visitors Bureau, ☎ 800-628-2866 or ☎ 904-413-9200, 200 W. College Ave., Tallahassee, FL 32301.
Wakulla County Chamber of Commerce, ☎ 904-926-1848, P.O. Box 598, Crawfordville, FL 32326-0598.

Touring

Gadsden County

Navigator, map, compass and cell phone in hand? Then lock 'n' load.

You're going to start from Tallahassee Regional Airport, book it to Havana and Quincy, then make a methodical march through the Eastern Panhandle, as if you're part of Gen. William Tecumseh Sherman's Army, except you're not going to burn Atlanta or (hopefully) take any casualties.

Baggage and rental (or otherwise) car in hand, turn left onto Highway 263, which doubles as Capital Circle Southwest, then drive 12 miles to US Highway 27, going left about eight miles into Havana.

Breathe deeply.
No mills.
No smog.
No exhaust fumes.
Not even a whiff of tobacco any more.

It's like much of the rest of North and Northeast Florida in those respects.

You've already learned about the shade tobacco industry and the vacuum its departure created. You've also heard about a renaissance. So now, let's fill in the blanks.

The best way to see Havana is by taking a self-guided walking tour of the historic district. It's pretty easy to find, since Highway 27 also is Main Street, with ample parking on the south side just past Ninth Avenue or (right) off Sixth. The reward is a growing stable of antique shops and galleries.

Lee Hotchkiss and Keith Henderson were pioneers of the rebirth.

"When my husband and I came here (from Tallahassee), just about the whole downtown was empty storefronts. It was a perfect area for an antique shop. We bought the block, sold some to friends and spent the summer sandblasting."

That was 1985, when the husband-and-wife team opened their shop in an 80-year-old building, one of five businesses to open simultaneously.

Today, there are 39 specializing in old collectibles, including the couple's **H&H Antiques**, ☎ 904-539-6886, on Main at West Seventh, **Berry Patch**, ☎ 904-539-0877, on Sixth Avenue off Main; and the **Antique Center**, ☎ 904-539-7711, a small mall located between Sixth and Seventh Avenues on Main. Those who love to browse through yesterday's goodies literally spend days in Havana.

Galleries and shops add two dozen more places to poke.

Lee Mainella's Florida Art Center & Gallery, ☎ 904-539-1770, is located on First Street just east of Seventh Avenue (use the parking lot on Main and Eighth Avenue). The restored auto body shop and tractor store showcases a number of Florida artists in a variety of media, including Mainella's incredible watercolors. **The Nice Picture Gallery**, ☎ 904-539-5952, on First between Seventh and Eighth, specializes in paintings, photography, sculpture and pottery from several artists. **The Historical Bookshelf**, ☎ 904-539-5040, on Seventh just north of Main, features an incredible selection of rare books, including many by Southern authors. If you happen to be here in mid-October, don't miss the annual Havana Bead Festival. Beads may sound a little unusual to celebrate, but this is a juried show featuring contemporary and antique beads and jewelry from more than 100 exhibitors.

Moving west, take Highway 12 in a zigzag pattern seven miles to Quincy.

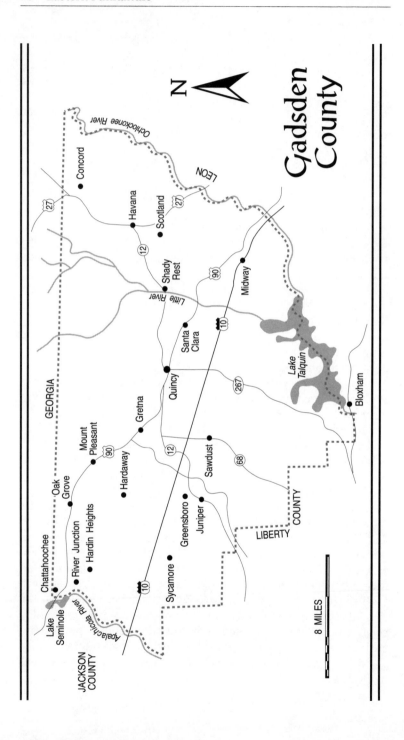

You'll know you've arrived when the neighborhoods change to a delightful collection of Queen Anne, Victorian, Georgian and antebellum architecture. The best way to see the town, whose 36-block downtown area has been designated a Nationally Registered Historic District, is to take a walking tour (maps and site biographies can be picked up at the Chamber of Commerce in Quincy, ☎ 904-627-9231). The reward is a peaceful morning or afternoon among splendors such as:

- ❑ **Banker "Mr. Pat" Munroe's Victorian mansion**, built big enough in 1893 to accommodate his 18 children (whew!), complete with wide porches, stained-glass windows, ornate fireplace mantles and a rose garden. Located at 204 E. Jefferson St., it's now the home of the Quincy Garden Club.
- ❑ **The Eastern Cemetery**, dating to the 1820s, where headstones include one for Archibald Sumpter, an Indian trader and one of Quincy's first settlers.
- ❑ **The John Lee McFarlin House** (1895). Built for a planter instrumental in the early development of shade tobacco, his mansion is as experimental as his work, a melange of irregularity and intersecting planes that are tied together by an extravagant verandah and leaded double doors.

Liberty County

This is an area of raw natural beauty and few manmade attractions – or distractions, depending on your viewpoint – due in large part to the Apalachicola National Forest, other natural havens and the locals' insistence on keeping their independence and ultra-rural lifestyles. Many of the county's natural adventures will be explored later in this chapter, but two neighboring sites deserve special mention from a touring perspective: Apalachicola Bluffs and Ravines Preserve and Torreya State Park.

From Quincy, take Highway 90 West two miles to Highway 267, travel south 13 miles to Highway 20, then west 24 miles to Bristol, the county seat and the only incorporated town in the county. From there, take Highway 12 about six miles north, turning left onto Highway 270. Both highways skirt the southern end of the spectacular **Apalachicola Bluffs and Ravines Preserve**, ☎ 904-643-2756, a 6,267-acre tract owned by The Nature

Torreya State Park

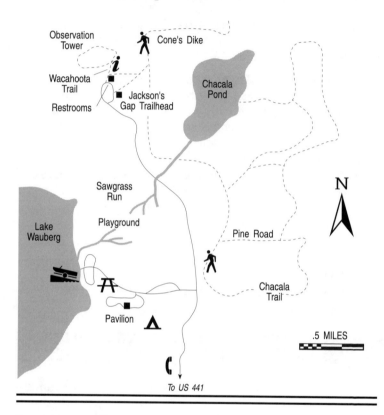

Conservancy. This preserve is a refuge and restoration habitat for ancient flora, long-leaf pines and wiregrass. A unique ecological burn project is being used in hopes that the smoke will settle into the ravines and stop the growth of a fungus that may be consuming the endangered Torreya tree.

Torreya State Park, ☎ 904-643-2674, is a visual wonderland. As mentioned earlier, its 1,000 acres are home to deep ravines formed by centuries of erosion. In addition to its namesake trees, the park's grounds have an abundance of yews and US champion winged elms. Some of the 150-foot bluffs form the backyard for the **Gregory House**, an antebellum mansion that was the core of an extensive cotton plantation built in 1849. Originally located a short distance away, the home was given to the state in 1935, dismantled, floated

Liberty County

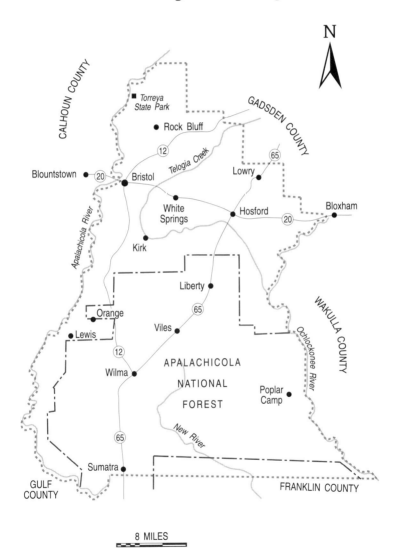

across the Apalachicola River and reassembled on this site. The mansion has furnishings from the mid-1850s, when Jason Gregory and his family lived in it. Elsewhere on the park's grounds, there are Confederate gun pits that once held six cannons meant to stop Union gunboats from passing on the river. There also are hiking trails, a wide range of wildlife (beavers, bobcats, grey foxes and the unusual Barbour's map turtle) and a stone bridge that crosses Rock Creek.

Franklin County

It's part of the Forgotten Coast, so-named because it's overshadowed, at least in a publicity sense, by the higher profiled Panhandle beaches to the west. While inland areas are rural and sometimes primitive, Franklin County's Gulf Coast stretch has several great tour stops without the congestion of the bigger tourist draws. The latter is underscored by the fact that Franklin County doesn't have a stoplight – the only blinker light is at the intersection of Main Street and Avenue E (US 98).

From Bristol, travel Highway 12 south about 25 miles, through Sumatra, to **Fort Gadsden State Historic Site,** ☎ 904-670-8988. Its roots date to 1814, when the British established a post to recruit American Indians and blacks during the War of 1812. While the site is well-marked, the fort is nowhere to be found. A hot shot from one of Gen. Andrew Jackson's cannons hit the powder magazine, sending the British fortress into the ever after. Fort Gadsden, built on the west side of the site along the Apalachicola River, was a Confederate stronghold until 1863 when malaria drove the soldiers to healthier terrain. The 78-acre site came under state control in 1961. The park has a miniature replica of the Confederate fort and six exhibits of its life and times in an interpretive center.

From Fort Gadsden, continue on Highway 65 about six miles to US 98 at Green Point. You'll begin touring at Apalachicola, an Indian name meaning Land of Friendly People, which is located eight miles west on US 98. Then you'll go east along the mainland before moving to the barrier islands just offshore.

The center of downtown **Apalachicola** is a National Historic District, ☎ 904-653-9419, that covers 2½ square miles and features more than 200 interesting homes, commercial buildings and additional historic sites. Among them are the **Ruge Brothers Seafood Canning Factory,** dating to 1895 and once the largest cannery in the world; the **Orman House,** a Greek Revival home

Touring 103

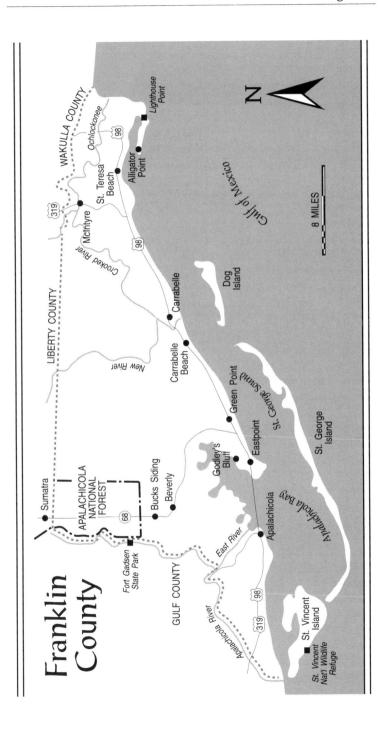

assembled with pegs in 1838 by a planter and merchant (during the Civil War, the owner placed a nail keg on its roof to warn the townspeople when Union troops were in town); **Trinity Episcopal Church**, another Greek Revival structure that was constructed in sections in New York in 1837-38, then assembled in Apalachicola; **Chestnut Street Cemetery**, which dates to 1832 and includes the graves of Confederate soldiers; and the **George S. Hawkins House**, the cottage home of the first chief justice of Florida's Supreme Court. The **John Gorrie State Museum**, ☎ 904-653-9347, located in the center of the district on Gorrie Square, is another popular stop. This was the home of a young physician who became mayor, postmaster and a city council member. But his most important work was medicine. Gorrie's treatment of patients during an 1851 yellow-fever outbreak led him to invent an ice machine to cool their rooms, laying the groundwork for modern refrigeration and air conditioning. The original machine is at the Smithsonian; but a replica is in the museum. Self-guided tour maps of the historic district are available at the **Apalachicola Chamber of Commerce**, ☎ 904-653-9419, also located in the district at 84 Market St., Apalachicola, FL 32320. (If you're in town the first Saturday of May, Trinity Episcopal Church members conduct a guided tour.)

Battery Park, located on Bay Avenue at the eastern point of the district, hosts Apalachicola's biggest annual bash – the **Florida Seafood Festival**, ☎ 904-653-8051. This day-long blowout is held the first Saturday of November. It lures some 15,000 people to savor world-famous Apalachicola Bay oysters, browse through arts and crafts booths and sing along to hours of live entertainment. The festival includes crowning King Retsyo (yes, that's oyster spelled backwards) and Miss Florida Seafood, an oyster-eating contest (the winner is the man or woman who guzzles the most raws in 15 minutes and manages to keep them down) and an oyster-shucking contest in which quality and quantity are important. Shuckers are penalized heavily for unthinkable atrocities, such as puncturing the meat and leaving shell fragments behind.

Since seafood and the marine estuary are such vital parts of this region, there's one other stop before heading east: the research and education center at the **Apalachicola National Estuarine Research Reserve**, ☎ 904-653-8063. The center, located at 261 7th St. in the historic district, has several exhibits of plant and animal life found in the 193,758-acre ecosystem that's comprised of rivers, barrier islands, sounds, flood plains and Apalachicola Bay.

Now, forward march.

From Apalachicola, follow US 98 east across Gorrie Bridge to the town of **Eastpoint**, the heart of the county's commercial seafood industry. Take a late afternoon hike along the historic waterfront and you'll see oyster boats returning with the day's haul or shrimp boats being readied for the long night's run. For the record, local oystermen supply 1.8 million pounds of these tasty critters per year (10% of the nation's harvest). It's enough to cover a football field three feet deep. Shrimpers net more than 1 million pounds of white, brown and pink shrimp annually (20% of Florida's crop). Eastpoint also offers the only road link – Highway 300 – between the mainland and St. George Island. (The other barrier islands are accessible only by boat.) More on the islands in a few minutes.

Continuing east on US 98, **Carrabelle**, at the mouth of the same-named river, is another port city that, in addition to a commercial fishing operation, has a tiny fleet of charter boats for recreational fishermen and women. It's home to the Big Bend Saltwater Classic, a three-day tournament held Father's Day weekend (the grand prize is a fishing trip to Puerto Rico) and the simultaneous Carrabelle Waterfront Festival, a big block party featuring arts and crafts, a gumbo cooking contest, music, a bass fishing tournament, hot-air balloon rides and much more. One final stop in Carrabelle: the satellite police station. It's in a telephone booth (honest) in the heart of the town's business district, which is nearly as tiny as the "world's smallest police station."

OK, it's time to head to the islands.

St. Vincent Island is not a typical barrier island. The entire island, 12,358 acres, is a national wildlife refuge, ☎ 904-653-8808. The isle is dissected by dune ridges that are geological records of ancient beaches and fluctuating sea levels during the last 5,000 years. The areas between the dunes range from lakes and sloughs to upland pine forests and wetlands. St. Vincent is a refuge for several endangered or threatened species such as bald eagles and indigo snakes. It's also a temporary home for a variety of migrating species (loggerhead turtles, wood storks and peregrine falcons, among others). The island also has a small herd of sambar deer, a Southeast Asian elk native that reaches 600 pounds (in comparison, Florida's native white-tail deer only grow to 130 pounds) and a very small colony of red wolves. The latter, introduced here in 1990, are part of an in-the-wild breeding program meant to save the endangered species. Pups, after weaning, are reintroduced to habitats such as the Great Smoky Mountains National Park. Fourteen miles of beaches on the south and east sides are open for day-time use. St. Vincent is accessible from Apalachicola. The refuge office and interpretive center are in the harbor master's building on Market Street.

Little St. George Island was part of St. George Island until 1957, when the US Army Corps of Engineers cut a pass to make it quicker for fishing boats to reach the Gulf. The three-square-mile, state-owned island's most notable feature is a lighthouse, built in 1852 on an elbow known as Cape St. George. This area is an excellent shelling location, also accessible by boat from Apalachicola.

St. George Island has 30 miles of white-powder beaches, great fishing, some dandy accommodations and restaurants, and the 1,962-acre **St. George Island State Park**, ☎ 904-927-2111, a nine-mile stretch of beaches and sand dunes surrounded by the Gulf of Mexico and Apalachicola Bay. The turf, ranging from sandy coves and salt marshes to long-leaf pine and oak forests, is the home of diamondback terrapins, black skimmers and ghost crabs. While the lecture is about crabs, hermits are the featured attraction at one of the island's festivals, the **Oyster Cove/Cajun Café Restaurant annual crab races** held in late August. Colorfully painted, named and numbered, the crabs are the field for six races (the reticent ones are encouraged with a squirt gun to race a circular course). But the main-draw festival is the **St. George Island Chili Cookoff**, held the first Saturday in March. Billed as the largest regional chili cookoff in the country, it attracts 50 cooks and 5,000 spectators. St. George is the most developed of Franklin County's four barrier islands, with 500 full-time residents, an inn and several restaurants. But much of it remains natural, including the **Dr. Julian G. Bruce St. George Island State Park**, ☎ 904-670-2111, where a series of trail boardwalks and observation platforms allow a close-up view of nature.

Dog Island, accessible from Carrabelle, is the smallest of the four (100 residents and an eight-room motel). Most of the island is a nature preserve. It has a single sand road that wanders from the ferry dock through salt marshes, pine forests, a beach, dunes and a horizon that seems to stretch forever. In the fall and early spring, the island is a pit stop for migrating birds.

Wakulla County

From Carrabelle, follow US 98 about 26 miles to **Panacea** and the **Gulf Specimen Marine Laboratory**, ☎ 904-984-5297, at 222 Clark Drive (it's one block east of US 98 off Otter Lake Road). This partly hands-on center has a 25,000-gallon aquarium and dozens of exhibits. You get to meet hermit crabs that aren't the racing

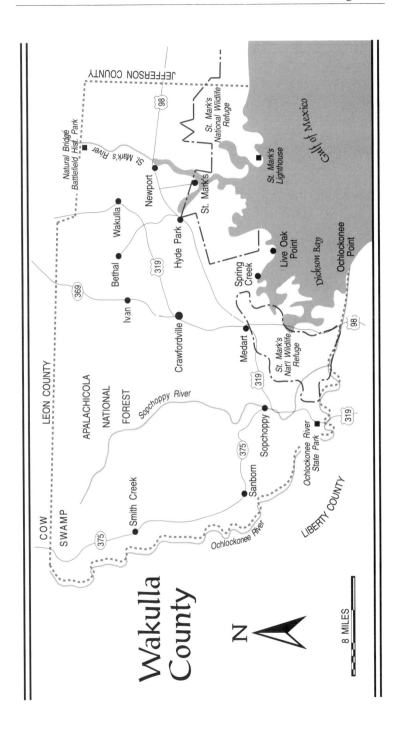

variety, see what a shrimp looks like before it lands on your plate and watch black-and bronze-headed sea horses dodge in and out of seaweed. The lab features hundreds of invertebrates, fish and algae from the Gulf of Mexico.

Three miles north on US 98, turn right (northeast) on Highway 319, then right (south) on Highway 363 for the two-mile trip to St. Marks. Town attractions are both historic and natural. The **St. Marks Lighthouse**, a national historic site, ☎ 904-926-1848, is four miles south on County Road 59. The lighthouse was built in 1829 using limestone blocks from the ruins of a nearby fort. The 80-foot tower had continuous lightkeepers until 1957. Today, the light is automated. The **San Marcos de Apalache State Historic Site**, ☎ 904-925-6216, on Canal Street in St. Marks, has a history dating to 1528 when Panfilo de Narvaez landed here with 300 men. The site has remnants of its various occupations: a Spanish bastion wall, a moat, Confederate magazines and earthworks, and a military cemetery. There also is a small museum and visitor center that has exhibits and artifacts covering the fort's history. The lighthouse, like much of coastal Wakulla County, is part of the **St. Marks National Wildlife Refuge**, ☎ 904-925-6121, which features some adventures covered later in this chapter.

Tarzan flicks weren't the only ones shot at **Edward Ball Wakulla Springs State Park**, ☎ 904-224-5950. *Creature from the Black Lagoon*, *Airport '77*, among others, contain scenes from this first-magnitude spring, where the water quality is clear enough to see fish and a few fossilized mastodon bones that lie 100 feet below the surface. You don't even have to get wet: Glass-bottom boats give landlubbers a wonderful view of what's below, as do the other boat tours of the treasures that lie above it. The park also has a rustic lodge and some other amenities that will be detailed in the "Where To Stay & Eat" part of the chapter. To get to the park, travel Highway 365 north 10 miles to Highway 267, turn right (east) and proceed two miles to the park entrance.

One more stop before packing it in for Tallahassee: **Natural Bridge State Historic Site**, ☎ 904-925-6216, is where one of Florida's two biggest Civil War battles occurred (the other is at Olustee, which will be covered below on page 139). From the springs, continue on Highway 267 east four miles to Highway 363, heading left (north) eight miles to Woodville and a paved road (right) that leads to the site.

Tallahassee

Leon County

Turn the ignition and aim the sedan right (north) from Natural Bridge on Highway 363 for five miles until it merges with Highway 61 (Monroe Street) and the short run to the heart of downtown Tallahassee. When you hit its intersection with Apalachee Parkway, you're at Florida government central.

Eyes left and you'll see the contrasting architecture of the twin capitols. If politics is your thing, you can see the House and Senate at their rhetorical finest during the February-April legislative session in the **New Capitol**, ☎ 904-413-9200. Otherwise, the best bet is to hop aboard the elevator and punch in coordinates for the 22nd floor, where an observatory gives a panoramic view of a city nestled by dogwoods and azaleas, springs and lakes, rolling hills and plantations. The **Old Capitol**, ☎ 904-487-1902, is a charming place where you can learn about the area's architectural and political past. This pearl of Capitol Hill, built in 1845 and restored in 1902,

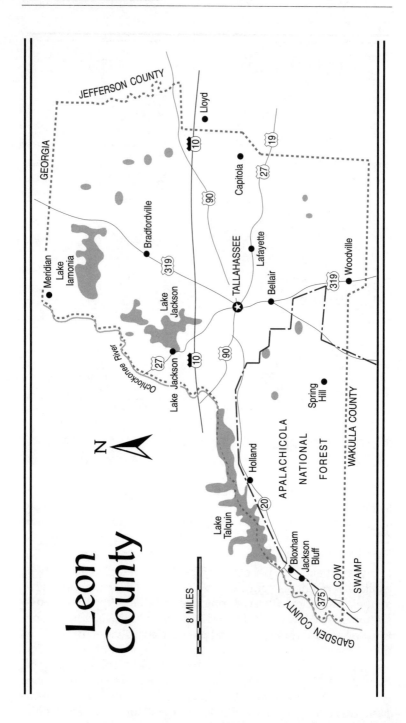

is adorned with stained-glass windows, candy-striped awnings, antique furnishings and memorabilia that convey a strong sense of old-style Southern politics.

For a moving experience, just walk across Monroe Street to where a pair of flags flank the Southeast's version of the Vietnam Veterans Memorial.

Remember Herman, our mastodon buddy? He's among the treasures at the **Museum of Florida History**, ☎ 904-488-1484, 500 S. Bronough St. The others include Spanish heirlooms, Civil War relics and a full-size riverboat. Over at the **Tallahassee Museum of History and Natural Science**, ☎ 904-576-1636, located at 3945 Museum Drive, you'll find more than Princess Murat's plantation. Exhibits on this 55-acre site include an 1880s farmhouse, a hands-on discovery center, and natural habitats occupied by Florida panthers, red wolves and alligators.

The Georgian-style **Governor's Mansion**, ☎ 904-488-4661, 700 N. Adams St., features tours during the legislative session and December holiday season. Built in 1956, the portico is patterned after Andrew Jackson's columned home, The Hermitage. Inside, there is a delightful collection of 18th-and 19th-century furnishings and collectibles. Just up the street, **Adams Street Commons**, ☎ 904-224-3252, is a one-block-long district anchored by historic buildings, enticing shops and tempting restaurants.

Tallahassee's oldest surviving residence, known as **The Columns**, is a white-columned brick home built in the 1830s and rumored to have a nickel in every brick. Today, The Columns, ☎ 904-224-8116, 100 N. Duval St., is home to the Tallahassee Chamber of Commerce. This is a good place to stop. The chamber has walking and driving tour maps leading the way to the area's scenic roads and trails, plantations and other attractions.

On the way out of town, don't miss the **Alfred B. Maclay State Gardens**, ☎ 904-487-4556. Located at 3540 Thomasville Road (Highway 61, which is the extension of Monroe Street), it's the former winter home of wealthy New York financier Alfred Maclay and his wife, Louise. Their estate is set on a rolling hill above Tallahassee. The Maclays began a floral masterpiece that now has 150 varieties of camellias, 50 kinds of azaleas and 150 species of exotic flowers.

Jefferson County

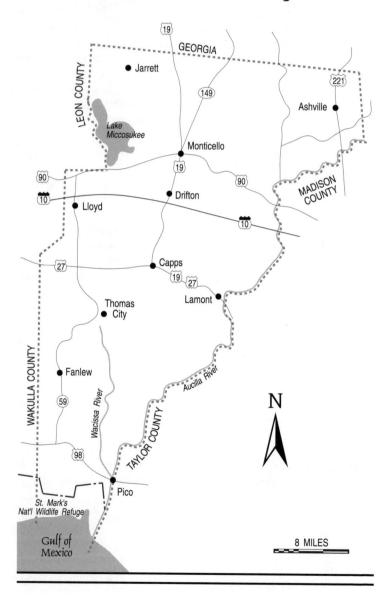

Jefferson County

One final, and brief, stop before you launch into specific adventures.

Historic Monticello is 32 miles east of Tallahassee.

From Maclay Gardens follow Highway 61 south one mile to Interstate 10, go east to the Highway 90 exit, then left (or north) for the 19-mile drive to the Jefferson County seat. **Monticello's historic district**, ☎ 904-997-5552, includes 27 blocks of turn-of-the-century architecture. Many of the properties, including the Perkins Opera House and the buildings along Courthouse Square, are on the National Register of Historic Places.

Adventures

On Foot

It's hardly a forced march, but one place to start is the walking tour of the historic district in Quincy, a three-mile, flatland tour, start to finish. You can grab a map that identifies specific properties at the Chamber of Commerce's office, ☎ 904-627-9231. At certain times, docents take groups on guided tours.

There are several great trails located in the area, including four in the **Apalachicola National Forest**, ☎ 904-643-2282, near Bristol on Highway 20 or, ☎ 904-926-3561, near Crawfordville on US 319. The **Wright Lake Trail** stretches 4½ miles through a pine forest that adjoins a cypress-lined lake. To get there, take Highway 65 along the west side of the forest two miles south of Sumatra, turn right at Forest Road 101 and go three miles to the Wright Lake trail sign. **Leon Sinks Geological Trail** is three trails totaling 5.4 miles, all of which showcase the area's wet and dry sinkholes and hardwood hammocks. From Tallahassee, pass the US 319-Highway 263 intersection, continue on US 319 six miles south and turn right at the sign. The Eastern Panhandle has 66 miles of the **Florida National Scenic Trail** going along the Ochlockonee River south of Bristol. Hikers can reach the eastern entrance, which is north of the forest, by driving Highway 65 to Highway 67 at Telogia, turning south and continuing 16.9 miles, then going left at Forest Road 13. The entrance is three miles away at Porter Lake. There also is a 12-mile loop trail at Camel Lake. It can be reached by driving south on Highway 12 from Bristol. After 12 miles turn left on Forest Road 105, then proceed two miles to the lake. The aesthetics? Otters, bald eagles, black bears and alligators are just a few of the 400 species of birds, reptiles and mammals that live here.

    Torreya State Park, ☎ 904-643-2674, in Bristol, has a seven-mile loop that goes through the park's dramatic ravines and other natural features. To get to it from Bristol, follow Highway 12 north eight miles to Highway 271, turn left (north) and continue four miles to the entrance. The **St. Marks National Wildlife Refuge**, ☎ 904-925-6121, has five-and nine-mile trails along US 98 in the Panacea area and seven- and 13-mile trails near St. Marks off Highway 59. Both travel through the marshes, swamps, flatwoods and uplands that surround Apalachee Bay. To get detailed maps of the refuge's trails and various access points, call or write the refuge at P.O. Box 68, St. Marks, FL 32355. The refuge also has a 43-mile section of the **Florida Trail** that can be reached at two spots: 1.1 miles west of Medart on Highway 319 or .75 mile west of the Aucilla River bridge on US 98.

    If you decide to take the short trip from Apalachicola across St. Vincent Sound to the wildlife refuge, ☎ 904-653-8808, there's plenty of self-guided hiking room on the island's 14 miles of beach and 80 miles of sand roads. The refuge office and visitor center in the harbor master building on Market Street will give you a map that should keep you from getting lost or storing calories.

    The **Northwest Florida Water Management District**, ☎ 904-539-5999, offers seven miles of trails at its Apalachicola River tract. They wander through a forest flood plain inhabited by several species of birds, including Mississippi kites and swallow-tails. From Quincy, follow Highway 267 south 12 miles to Highway 20, turn right (west) and go 20 miles to Bristol, then turn left (south) on Highway 12 and travel 16 miles to Highway 379. Turn right and go 11 miles to the entrance. For a guidebook with maps, call or write the district at Route 1, Box 3100, Havana, FL 32333-9700.

    Tallahassee's most notable hiking route is the **Tallahassee-to-St. Marks Historic State Trail**, ☎ 904-922-6007, a 16-mile journey along a railroad route that once connected the two cities. A paved parking lot is located on Highway 363, also known as Woodville Road, two miles south of Tallahassee at the north end of the state trail. **Alfred B. Maclay State Gardens**, ☎ 904-487-4556, has five miles of trails surrounding Lake Overstreet, which has vegetation such as water lilies, pickerelweed, purple cabomba, dogwoods and magnolias. Don't be surprised when a deer, grey fox or bobcat darts across your path. The property is located at 3540 Thomasville Road (Highway 61, the extension of Monroe Street).

The **Fort Braden Trail** in the **Lake Talquin State Forest**, ☎ 904-488-1871, has an east loop (6.2 miles) and a west loop (2.9 miles) marked in blue paint. The forest is south of Quincy. To get there, take Highway 267 south 12 miles, across Lake Talquin, and turn left (east) to the entrance. Maps are available at the **Florida Division of Forestry**, 1214 Tower Drive, Tallahassee, FL 32301.

Also, Tallahassee's **Elinor Klapp-Phipps Park**, ☎ 904-891-3975, has about 11 miles of hiking trails west of Lake Jackson. The trails wind through land that's inhabited by wood storks, bobcats, turkey, deer, ospreys and other species. The park is located along Millers Landing Road. To get there, follow Meridian Road (Highway 155) seven miles north of Tallahassee to Millers Landing Road, then turn right.

INFORMATION SOURCES

Florida Trail Association, ☎ 800-343-1882 (in Florida) or ☎ 352-378-8823, P.O. Box 13708, Gainesville, FL 32604.
Office of Greenways & Trails, ☎ 904-487-4784, Mail Station 795, 3900 Commonwealth Blvd., Tallahassee, FL 32399-3000.

GOLF COURSES

- **Gadsden Country Club**, ☎ 904-627-8386, Solomon Dairy Road, Quincy, FL 32353, 18 holes, driving range, PGA rating R-69.8.
- **Hilaman Park Golf Club**, ☎ 904-891-3935, 912 Myer Park Drive, Tallahassee, FL 32301, 18 holes, driving range, lessons, R-68.5.
- **Seminole Golf Club**, ☎ 904-644-2582, 2550 Pottsdamer St., Tallahassee, FL 32304, 18 holes, driving range, lessons, R-71.0.
- **Seminole Valley Golf Club**, ☎ 904-663-2223, Main Street, Florida State Hospital Grounds, Chattahoochee, FL 32324, nine holes, driving range, R-69.5.

❏ **Summerbrooke Golf & Country Club,** ☎ 904-668-2582, Summerbrooke Drive, Tallahassee, FL 32312, 18 holes, driving range, lessons, no rating.

On Horseback

Get along little doggee.

The **Vinzant Trail** stretches through 29 scenic miles on the northeast side of the **Apalachicola National Forest,** ☎ 904-926-3561. From Tallahassee, go west on Highway 20 nine miles to Forest Road 325 (there's a sign), turn south and go 1½ miles to the trail's starting gate. The 16-mile **Tallahassee-St. Marks Historic Railroad State Trail,** ☎ 904-922-6007, is another nice ride. A paved parking lot is on Highway 363, also called Woodville Road, two miles south of Tallahassee at the north end of the trail. The five-mile trail at **Alfred B. Maclay State Gardens,** ☎ 904-487-4556, is open to riders. The property is located at 3540 Thomasville Road (Highway 61, the extension of Monroe Street in Tallahassee). The **Fort Braden Trail** area of the **Lake Talquin State Forest,** ☎ 904-488-1871, offers two trails, the west loop (4.4 miles) and the east loop (4.3 miles), marked with pink paint. To get there from Quincy, take Highway 267 south 12 miles, cross Lake Talquin and turn left (east) to the entrance. Maps are available from the **Florida Division of Forestry,** 1214 Tower Drive, Tallahassee, FL 32301. Also the **Elinor Klapp-Phipps Park,** ☎ 904-891-3975, in Tallahassee has about 11 miles of horse trails off the west shore of Lake Jackson. The trails wind through land inhabited by wood storks, bobcats, turkey, deer, ospreys and other Florida species. The park is located along Millers Landing Road. To get there, follow Meridian Road (Highway 155) seven miles north of Tallahassee to Millers Landing Road, then turn right. Warning: Riders need a city permit because this is a limited access area for horses.

Remember to bring a negative Coggins for your horses.

On Wheels

Let's start with the shorter trails and build to the monster.

The five-mile trail at the **Alfred B. Maclay State Gardens,** ☎ 904-487-4556, welcomes cyclists, as well as hikers and horseback riders. Again, the site is located at 3540 Thomasville Road (Highway 61), which is an extension of Monroe Street in Tallahassee. The **Munson Hills Off-Road Bicycle Trail**, ☎ 904-926-3561, in the Apalachicola National Forest, has two trails – the **Munson Hills Loop** (a shade more than 7½ miles through rustic forest lands, oak, cherry, sassafras and wild blueberries) and the **Tall Pine Shortcut** (4.25 miles around the area's pristine lakes). From Tallahassee, take Highway 363 south 1.25 miles beyond Capital Circle (Highway 319/263) to the entrance of the trail. The 16-mile **Tallahassee-St. Marks Historic Railroad Trail**, ☎ 904-922-6007, is open to peddlers. A paved parking lot is located on Highway 363, also known as Woodville Road, two miles south of Tallahassee at the northern end of the state trail.

Now, behold the beast.

The **Seven Hills to the Sea Bicycle Tour**, ☎ 904-487-4784, is a six-day, 283-mile loop through the region. Those of us with tired muscles can break it into any of six legs. For the diehards, start at **Wakulla Springs State Park**, ☎ 904-222-7279, and eat a lot of pasta. Here's a quick and dirty breakdown of each leg and what's waiting for you.

- ❏ Wakulla Springs to Ochlockonee State Park, 28 miles. Under the touring part of the chapter you read about beautiful Wakulla Springs. This leg also takes you past a submarine cavern at Spring Creek, the rural hamlet of Sopchoppy and skirts the St. Marks National Wildlife Refuge.
- ❏ Ochlockonee State Park to St. George Island State Park, 47 miles. This ride has spectacular views of open water, offshore barrier islands and the area's quaint fishing villages, such as Carrabelle and Eastpoint.
- ❏ St. George Island to St. Joseph Peninsula Park, 45 miles. This segment of the ride includes more coastal vistas, a tour of historic downtown Apalachicola and a brief venture into some of the picturesque areas covered in the section with Cape San Blas and the pencil-thin St. Joseph Peninsula.
- ❏ St. Joseph Peninsula Park to Dead Lakes Recreation Area, 53 miles. A return along the peninsula is half-coastal, half-flood plain forest, where thousands of sun-bleached tree skeletons rising from nearby lakes are a reminder of what hurricane surges do to inland forests.

- Dead Lakes Recreation Area to Torreya State Park, 47 miles. Tip: Get an early start because the early part of the ride is along well-traveled State Road 71. It's also a good idea to call the Liberty County Sheriff's Office, ☎ 904-643-2235, in advance to help arrange transport of bikes and gear across the narrow – spell that, VERY narrow – Apalachicola River Bridge. The eye candy further along this route includes rural farmlands, red clay hills, bluffs and swift descents.
- Torreya State Park to Wakulla Springs, 64 miles. This spectacular tour takes you along ravines, rolling hills, and the fabulous spring awaiting you at the end of the line.

INFORMATION SOURCES

The Office of Greenways & Trails, ☎ 904-487-4784, Mail Station 795, 3900 Commonwealth Blvd., Tallahassee, FL 32399-3000.
Florida Department of Transportation, ☎ 904-487-9220, Mail Station 82, 605 Suwannee St., Tallahassee, FL 32399-0450.

On Water

CANOEING

Grab a paddle and get ready to rocket. There are seven runs in the area.

The **Upper Ochlockonee River Trail** is a 26-mile run rated for beginners. The current is two-three mph. The trail, shallow and often silty, is lined with willows, as well as wild hogs, raccoons and wading birds. For the full run, take Highway 12 east from Havana seven miles to the bridge at the Gadsden-Leon county lines. For a short course (12 miles), take Highway 63 south from Havana seven miles to Highway 263, turn right to Tower Road and right again to the landing.

The **Lower Ochlockonee River Trail** is a 63-mile run rated for beginners. The current is two-three mph. This is a dam-controlled route through the Apalachicola National Forest and the Ochlockonee River State Park. For the full run, connect with

Highway 20 west from Tallahassee 22 miles to the river's bridge. The short course, at Wood Lake (26 miles), can be reached by taking Highway 20 west of Tallahassee 21 miles to Highway 375, then south to Forest Road 340 and south again for 2½ miles. If you follow Forest Road 338 south another two miles to the sign and turn, bingo, you're there.

The **Sopchoppy** (it has a nice tongue lash to it, doesn't it?) **River Trail** is a 15-mile course rated beginner to intermediate with a two-three mph current, a bit more difficult on the upper portion. The upper part is a narrow bending course through cypress knees and high, heavily wooded banks, but the river widens in the lower portion. From Sopchoppy, take Highway 375 to Forest Road 346 and the launch point. The short course (five miles) is at the bridge on Highway 375.

The **Wakulla River Trail**, four miles, is a beginner's trail with an extremely slow current. The spring-fed river is lined with cypress trees and a lot of wildlife. From the town of Wakulla, head due south of Tallahassee on Highway 363, turn left (west) on Highway 365 and go two miles to the bridge access point.

The **Wacissa River Trail** is 14 miles for beginners, with a two-three mph current. The spring-fed stream is lined with dense woodlands and numerous tributaries. To get there, take Highway 319 (Capital Circle) from Tallahassee to Highway 259, turn right and go about 14 miles to Wacissa, then south on Highway 59. When the highway goes west (left), stay straight until you reach the park. Short course to prepare yourself? Aw, you won't need it.

The **Aucilla River Trail** is 19 miles, rated intermediate to technical due to its three-plus mph current that leads over shoals and the remains of two old rock dams, making it a challenge at low tide. The trail is framed by high limestone banks, and portions flow through a cypress-gum swamp. From Tallahassee, head east 23 miles on US 27 to the bridge and entry point just beyond Lamont.

There is one other option for triathletes and kamikaze types: the **Historic Big Bend Saltwater Paddling Trail**, a 91½-mile journey in the Gulf of Mexico that is accessible from St. Marks and stretches south to the town of Suwannee. Sea kayaks are recommended over canoes. While the weather is generally mild, the waves can reach two to four feet. If you feel you're up to this one, call or write the Office of Greenways & Trails, ☎ 904-488-3701, 325 John Knox Road, Bldg. 500, Tallahassee, FL 32303, for a brochure with the necessary warnings and a list of additional entry-exit points for shorter ventures.

ADDITIONAL INFORMATION SOURCES

For designated trail maps, write to the **Office of Greenways and Trails**, ☎ 904-487-4784, 325 John Knox Road, Bldg. 500, Tallahassee, FL 32303-4124.
Florida Association of Canoe Liveries and Outfitters, ☎ 941-494-1215, P.O. Box 1764, Arcadia, FL 33821.
TNT Hideaway, ☎ 904-925-6412, Route 2, Box 4200, Crawfordville, FL 32327.
Canoe Shop, ☎ 904-576-5335, 1115-B West Orange Ave., Tallahassee, FL 32310.
Gulf Coast Excursions, ☎ 904-984-5895, Route 1, Box 3201, Panacea, FL 32346.
Apalachee Canoe Club, P.O. Box 4027, Tallahassee, FL 32315.

DIVING/SNORKELING

Wakulla Springs?
Sorry, divers.
Despite its beauty and allure, it's only open to swimmers and snorkelers. If you can do without tanks on this one, **Wakulla Springs**, ☎ 904-224-5950, can be reached from Tallahassee by following Highway 319 south 11 miles to Highway 267, turning left (east) and proceeding two miles to the park entrance.

Emerald Sink is a nifty dive with an easy-access wooden dock. It begins with a beautifully clear, 60-foot-across access point, drops to several explorable walls and a maximum depth of 120 feet. A 15-foot cave opening narrows before reaching a depth of 200 feet. But a warning: This leg is for well-prepared cave-divers only. To get there from Tallahassee, follow Highway 319 south 8.2 miles, turn right at the first hard-surface road past the Wakulla County line (look for the New Light Church sign), then drive .3 mile to the first sand road on the left. The sink is 100 yards in on the right.

Clearcut Sink is cypress-lined with a wooden staging platform some 30 feet below the surface. The cavern entrance starts at 45 feet and quickly drops to 90 feet, where it joins a stream that runs deeper. (This is an advanced cave dive with narrow limits, silt and a heavy flow.) Follow the directions to Emerald Sink. From the church sign, turn left on C.J. Spear Road, make an immediate right, go about one-half mile and take the second sand road to the left.

Wacissa River Springs is a series of 12 possible dives connected to the **Wacissa River Canoe Trail**. All are located within 1½ miles of the launch point, and all are reasonably shallow dives (8 to 48 feet) with limestone vents and, in some cases, good photography. To get there, take Highway 319 (Capital Circle) from Tallahassee to Highway 259, turn right and go about 14 miles to Wacissa, then south on Highway 59. When the highway goes west (left) stay straight until you reach the park.

Offshore diving, in which most rely on area outfitters, also is available.

Franklin County's artificial reef is a scattering of metal spans and concrete from an old bridge over Apalachicola Bay. It's in 80 feet of Gulf water and about 11 miles off St. George Island. This dive features swim-throughs and its share of barracuda and blue angelfish. The **Exxon Template** is a 65-foot tower in 105 feet of water, 28 miles off the island. It attracts schools of a variety of fish and usually has visibility of 40 feet. *Miss Gem*, a 50-foot shrimp boat resting at 71 feet, has been draped with old shrimp nets, which can yield nice underwater photos. This dive is 16 miles off the west end of Dog Island. At the **Carrabelle Two-Mile Reef**, a dive of 35 feet, you'll encounter sea bass, snapper and grouper. **Turtle Towers Ledge Reef**, eight miles off Dog Island, is named for the sea turtles often seen in the area. A limestone ledge, 50 feet down, stretches for several hundred yards. Another good place for turtles – as well as nurse sharks – is **Caves Ledge**, a natural reef with undercuts and caves reaching to a depth of 75 feet. This site is 42 miles off the end of St. Vincent Island.

INFORMATION SOURCES

Florida Association of Dive Operators, ☎ 305-451-3020, 51 Garden Cove Drive, Key Largo, FL 33037.
US Coast Guard Mayport, ☎ 904-246-7315.
Florida Marine Patrol, ☎ 904-697-3741, South Marine St., Carrabelle, FL 32322.
Ned DeLoach's Diving Guide to Underwater Florida, ☎ 904-737-6558, New World Publications, 1861 Cornell Road, Jacksonville, FL 32207.
Blue Water Scuba, ☎ 904-681-2628, 1604 S. Monroe, Tallahassee, FL 32301.
Scuba Discovery, ☎ 904-656-7665, 2320-B Apalachee Parkway, Tallahassee, FL 32301.
Discount Divers Supply, ☎ 904-877-5980, 4377 Crawfordville Road, Unit E, Tallahassee, FL 32310.
Florida Sports, ☎ 904-488-8347, 107 W. Gaines St., #466, Tallahassee, FL 32399-2000.
Stamas Pro Dive, ☎ 904-229-6330, 301 Monument Ave., Port St. Joe, FL 32456.

SALTWATER & FRESHWATER FISHING

One word describes the freshwater challenge in the Eastern Panhandle: Paradise. Seven Florida records have been set here:

- Redeye bass, 7.83 pounds, Apalachicola River, Gadsden County.
- Striped bass, 42.25 pounds, Apalachicola River, Gadsden County.
- White bass, 4.69 pounds, Apalachicola River, Gadsden County.
- Black crappie, 3.93 pounds, Lake Talquin, Gadsden County.
- Flier, 1.24 pounds, Lake Iamonia, Leon County.
- Carp, 40.56 pounds, Apalachicola River, Gadsden County.
- Flathead catfish, 35.50 pounds, Apalachicola River, Liberty County.

These lakes and the river also are noted for a range of other freshwater species, including bream, bluegill, pickerel, shellcracker and more. Base your expedition at any of the area's many fish camps. **Bay City Lodge,** ☎ 904-653-9294, State Road 384 in Apalachicola, is a full-service camp (ramp, bait, gas, lodging, licenses and guides), as are many of those listed on these pages. It's located along the Apalachicola River. **Gainey's Talquin Lodge,** ☎ 904-627-3822, and **Ingram's Marina,** ☎ 904-627-2241, are on Lake Talquin (both are along Highway 65-C off State Road 267, about eight miles south of Quincy). Ingram's ramp is public. **Lake Jackson Fish Camp,** ☎ 904-562-5590, is on Lake Drive off Old Bainbridge Road north of Tallahassee, while **Reeve's Lake Iamonia Landing,** ☎ 904-893-0361, is on Lake Iamonia Road off Highway 12 and US 319, north of the capital. Both of these provide most services and public ramps. **Ed & Bernice's,** ☎ 904-379-8122, located on the Ochlockonee River, is on Bernice Lane off Highway 20, just on the Liberty County side of the bridge. **Shell Island Camp,** ☎ 904-925-6398, is located on the Wakulla River in St. Marks. It, too, has a public ramp and most services.

Saltwater anglers generally find the same trophies that exist elsewhere in the Panhandle: Spanish mackerel in spring, summer and fall, though more so in March and April; cobia in April and May; sea trout are plentiful in every season except summer (the same for wahoo); while snapper and redfish are abundant in all but the winter months. But keep in mind that this isn't the saltwater hot spot that some other regions of Florida are. **Pelican Dockage**, ☎ 904-984-0190, runs a charter boat out of Panacea, and brothers **Chris and Tommy Robinson**, ☎ 904-653-9669, are saltwater and freshwater guides in Apalachicola. The town also has two fishing piers: a 500-foot pier at **Battery Park Marina**, ☎ 904-653-8715, and a 100-footer at **Lafayette Park**, ☎ 904-653-8715.

Don't forget to pick up a fishing license. Non-resident saltwater licenses range from $5 for three days to $30 per year. Non-resident freshwater licenses cost $15 for seven days and $30 for a year. Also, there are size and bag limits on many species. Information on these is available from bait-and-tackle shops, marinas, local guides, the **Florida Marine Patrol**, ☎ 904-697-3741, South Marine St., Carrabelle, FL 32322, or **Florida Game & Fresh Water Fish Commission**, ☎ 904-265-3677, 3911 Highway 2321, Panama City, FL 32409-1658.

Eco-Travel Excursions

The barrier islands off Franklin County provide some of the most scenic eco-tours in Florida. Jeanni McMillan, the operator of **Jeanni's Journeys** on St. George Island, ☎ 904-927-3259, leads sightseers on motorboat tours of the four islands. The teacher and environmental planner-turned-outdoors woman offers guided canoe and kayak adventures, scalloping and shelling excursions, night hikes that include netting feisty blue crabs by flashlight and sunset cruises. If you want to learn to sail or cast net, Jeanni will teach you that, too.

Tom Gray, operator of **Captain Tom's Adventures** in Apalachicola, ☎ 904-653-8463, provides many of the same adventures and lessons in addition to a Baybottom University Fun School. This is a day-long chance to experience an area fisherman's life. The excursion includes dragging a shrimp trawl, tonging oysters, pulling crab pots and throwing a cast net. Gray's fascination for nature has been shaped by careers that include shrimper, commercial fisherman and biology teacher.

If you're after a more leisurely pace, the 40-foot *Apalachicola Belle*, ☎ 904-653-8803, cruises the Apalachicola River, while the 63-foot schooner *Governor Stone*, ☎ 904-653-8708, takes passengers on a two-hour sail of the bay area. By the way, the two-masted schooner was christened in 1877, so you get a history lesson in addition to one about nature.

Further north, **Lake Talquin Tours**, ☎ 904-877-3198, offers fishing ventures as well as pontoon boat sightseeing excursions on the pristine lake.

Where To Stay & Eat

Gadsden County

Quincy and Havana have several warm and cozy (not to mention historic) bed-and-breakfasts. **The Allison House**, ☎ 904-875-2511, in Quincy, is a Georgian-style inn that dates to 1843, when it was built by Florida's sixth governor. Owned by Stuart and Eileen Johnson, the inn has five guest rooms with private baths, a colorful history and a decor to match the inn. Breakfasts include some delicious homemade muffins, fresh fruits and yogurt. **The McFarlin House**, ☎ 904-875-2526, in Quincy, is a three-story Queen Anne-style structure built in 1895. The inn has nine luxurious rooms, a delightful wrap-around porch, clawfoot tubs and stained-glass windows. Innkeeper Susan Mick spoils guests with Southern hospitality. If you're looking for intimacy, **Gaver's Bed & Breakfast**, ☎ 904-539-5611, in Havana, has two charming guest rooms with contemporary and antique appointments. Its 12-foot ceilings provide an open, airy atmosphere, and owners Bruce and Shirley Gaver provide a full or continental breakfast.

Did someone sound the dinner bell?

Nicholson's Farmhouse, ☎ 904-539-5931, was built in 1828 by Dr. Malcolm Nicholson and was the homestead of four generations of the family before it was converted into a restaurant operated by Nicholson's great-great-grandson Paul and his partner, Willard Rudd. Outside, the historic farmhouse's charm remains. Inside, the Havana restaurant's specialties of the house are aged steaks. Dutch and Sophia Swart's **Place Down Under**, ☎ 904-875-4660, in Quincy, treats guests to duck nipernaise (boneless duck with ginger plum sauce) and pork medallions paprika (roasted and sautéed with mushrooms, sherry and cream), among other extraordinary entrées.

Franklin County

Landside, there are several inns and bed-and-breakfasts along the coast, such as **Coombs House Inn**, ☎ 904-653-9199, in Apalachicola, **Brigitte's Romantic Retreat,** ☎ 904-653-3270, also in Apalachicola, and **Ell's Court On The Gulf**, ☎ 800-697-2050, in Carrabelle. But many visitors choose to spend at least part of their stay in the delightful cottages, houses and condominiums on St. George Island. Many of these are set high on dunes with wood walks leading through sea oats to the ghost-white beaches. Agencies that handle them include **Collins Vacation Rentals**, ☎ 800-423-7418, **Accommodations St. George**, ☎ 800-332-5196, and **Gulf Coast Realty**, ☎ 800-367-1680. If you're really after solitude, ask one of the rental agencies about setting you up with your own beach.

At chow time, think seafood. This is, after all, one of Florida's finest when it comes to meals – fried, broiled or raw – from the sea. Some of the best eateries in the region are **Boss Oyster**, ☎ 904-653-9364, Apalachicola; **Caroline's Riverfront Restaurant**, ☎ 904-653-8139, Apalachicola; **The Happy Pelican**, ☎ 904-927-9826, St. George Island; and **Oyster Cove**, ☎ 904-927-2600, St. George Island.

Wakulla County

Ed Ball Wakulla Springs State Park, ☎ 904-224-5950, is a perfect place for a back-to-nature stay. The park has a rustic lodge built in 1937 and outfitted with Tennessee marble floors, intricate ceilings, Moorish arches, antique furnishings and a wonderful stone fireplace. It has 27 guest rooms, six conference rooms, an old-fashioned, 60-foot marble soda fountain and an elegant restaurant. At the tip of St. Marks, **Shell Point Resort**, ☎ 904-926-7163, is on Highway 367, right on the bay. It features a 26-unit motel, restaurant and marina. Other notable places for dinner include **Grady's Galactic Gumbo Pot**, ☎ 904-984-2080,

Panacea; **Mom's Seafood & Steaks**, ☎ 904-962-2655, Sopchoppy; and **Oyster Bay Inn Restaurant**, ☎ 904-926-1669, Crawfordville.

Leon County

The Tallahassee area has more accommodations and restaurants by far than any other destination in the region. Remember the "R" word – reservations – particularly (and sufficiently in advance) if your trip is during the February-April political season, or on fall weekends when Florida State University's Seminoles are at home on the gridiron.

Modestly priced accommodations in the downtown area include **Days Inn**, ☎ 904-224-2181, and **Ramada Inn Capitol View**, ☎ 904-877-3171. A more moderate-priced group includes **Cabot Lodge North**, ☎ 904-386-8880, and **Courtyard**, ☎ 904-222-8822. Those with deeper pockets might choose the **College Inn** (each room is a complete apartment), ☎ 904-561-0002, or the **Governor's Inn**, ☎ 904-681-6855.

When hunger strikes, **Andrews Second Act**, ☎ 904-222-3444, is a perennial Golden Spoon award winner where the creative, continental treats include Tournedoes St. Laurent (filet mignon and asparagus spears topped with garlic, scallions and parsley-butter sauce) and oak-roasted salmon in a honey and balsamic mustard glaze. **The Silver Slipper**, ☎ 904-386-9366, also is a Golden Spoon winner, where the Old South atmosphere and steak-to-seafood entrées have delighted an assortment of political heavyweights, from John F. Kennedy to George Bush.

Campgrounds

Do-it-yourselfers have several choices in the Eastern Panhandle.

A Camper's World, ☎ 904-997-3300, Route 1, Box 164B, Lamont, FL 32336-9717, is located less than 30 minutes from the capitol and features shaded pull-through sites and hot showers. **Alligator Point Campground**, ☎ 904-349-2525, Route 1, Box 3392, Panacea, FL 32346-9714, has a white-sand beach on the Gulf of Mexico, camping cabins, pull-throughs, lakefront sites and a tackle shop. **Holiday Park & Campground**, ☎ 904-984-5757, 14 Coastal Highway, Panacea, FL 32346, is on Ochlockonee Bay. It has shaded waterfront sites, cable television, a 200-foot fishing pier, pool, hot showers and recreation center. **Tallahassee East KOA**, ☎ 904-997-3897, Route 3, Box 25, Monticello, FL 32344, has 30 acres of shaded grounds, long pull-throughs, a pool and game room. **Tallahassee RV Park**, ☎ 904-878-7641, is 10 minutes from the state capitol and features long pull-throughs and lighted, paved roads.

Additionally, the **Apalachicola National Forest** has many tent and camper sites in Liberty, Franklin, Wakulla and Leon counties. A brochure called *National Forests in Florida* has full details of all of the locations. The brochure is available by contacting the Supervisor's Office, National Forests of Florida, ☎ 904-942-9300, Woodcrest Office Park, 325 John Knox Road, Suite F-100, Tallahassee, FL 32303.

The following state parks also cater to campers: **Torreya State Park**, ☎ 904-643-2674, Bristol; **St. George Island State Park**, ☎ 904-927-2111, Eastpoint; and **Ochlockonee River State Park**, ☎ 904-962-2771, Sopchoppy. A brochure called *Florida State Parks* can be obtained from the Department of Environmental Protection, ☎ 904-488-9872, Mail Station 535, 3900 Commonwealth Blvd., Tallahassee, FL 32399-3000.

Suwannee Region

True story:
(They're all true actually. After all, this is non-fiction.)
Stephen Foster's most famous composition, not to mention Florida's state song, almost got blind-sided with the lyrics: *Way Down Upon the Pee Dee River*.

That was Foster's first choice because 1) it fit, 2) he'd seen the Pee Dee, 3) he'd never been within 100 miles of the Suwannee and 4) it beat the heck out of his brother Morrison's suggestion – the Yazoo River.

The closest the Pee Dee comes to Florida is South Carolina. The closest it came to being lyrics in "Old Folks At Home" was the first draft. Foster changed rivers in 1851, and the rest is history that's kept alive at the **Stephen Foster State Folk Culture Center**, ☎ 904-397-4331, near White Springs. The memorial to one of the nation's most prolific songwriters (284 titles including Camptown Races, Oh! Susanna and My Old Kentucky Home) includes a museum, a carillon tower and a folk park where craftsmen and women keep yesterday's trades alive.

It also gives a hint of how vital water is to this area. North Florida's calling cards are the rivers and streams that wind through the region, and the Suwannee is as much the blood of the Real Florida as any other body of water in the state. This storied, gloried river wanders 245 miles from Georgia's Okefenoke Swamp to the Gulf of Mexico. More than a century ago, *New York Telegram and Evening Mail* editorial writer James Craig described it this way:

"The real Suwannee River does not rise in any part of Georgia. It rises in the highest mountains of the human soul and is fed by the deepest springs of the human heart. It does not flow through the northern part of Florida but through the pleasant sunny lands of memory. It does not empty into a material sea but into the glorious ocean of unfulfilled dreams."

No one ever said that about the Pee Dee. Trust us.

Too bad Foster missed what captured Craig's heart and imagination.

He missed stands of water-swollen cypress, alligator hatchlings emerging from the nest, transparent springs, falling creeks, mist-tickled mornings, solitude, and a Cracker culture that

Marjorie Kinnan Rawlings immortalized in *Lord Bill of the Suwannee River*.

During your adventures in the Suwannee River region, you're going to get to know many of the other calling cards. Despite a lack of coastline, the region has a number of enticing scuba sites, including Ginnie Springs, which makes a strong claim to the title of Cave Diving Capital of Florida. Ginnie Springs actually is nine springs that feed the Santa Fe River, and the addition of caverns and caves make this a natural wonder for divers, snorkelers, swimmers, paddlers, tubers and campers. Beautiful Blue Springs just off the Withlacoochee River is another favorite site among the "get down" crowd, while Ichetucknee Springs State Park is a scenic, laid-back venue for those with a lazy streak. The 3.2-mile spring run is ideal for a leisurely tube, float or snorkel trip. With this many treasures, there might be a claim or two for this being the Spring Diving Capital of Florida, too.

Canoe trails? There are five dandy ones winding through the five counties covered in this chapter. Peddling paths? This is home turf for the event-oriented Suwannee Bicycle Association. And the five state parks and forests in the region offer plenty of additional adventures at their respective locations.

When you start touring you'll learn the South lives in Madison. The town's roots reach to December 26, 1827, and its passion is found in two of its more notable attractions. The antebellum-style Wardlaw-Smith-Goza Conference Center, also called "Whitehall," was built in 1860. When war broke out, it served as a hospital for Confederate troops injured during Florida's biggest Civil War encounter, the Battle of Olustee, near what today is Lake City. The beautifully restored mansion and gardens are a wonderful example of Old South architecture. That heritage is well represented, too, at the Confederate Soldier's Memorial at Four Freedoms Park. The park has a second monument, this one honoring Madison native son Capt. Colin Kelly, who posthumously received the Distinguished Service Cross and Distinguished Flying Cross for a dive-bomber attack that sank a Japanese battleship.

You'll learn a little more about these and other areas during the touring part of this chapter. But first, take a peek at the natural and manmade history inherent in Florida's northern Suwannee River basin.

Geography & History

There are some subtle differences (no sea breezes or coastline) between this corner of North Florida and the Panhandle, but a great deal of the landscape remains the same. In other words, there are plenty of rivers, springs, woodlands and rolling hills. Perhaps the most notable difference is also a blessing for some: No big cities. Small towns and villages exist, for the most part, as they did a half-century ago and more. While there is spotty development and some occasional intrusions, such as chain motels and fast-food outlets, nature pretty much has its way. That means farms, timberlands and huge tracts of forest and refuge lands. The earth includes hammocks, sloughs, savannas and grassy marshes. People are far outnumbered by deer, otters, wild hogs, turkeys and, well, just about any upland and marine creature you can imagine. Even manatees are occasionally found way down upon the Suwannee River.

The area's history doesn't stretch quite as far back as coastal Florida, in large part because the Spanish, French and English explorers couldn't get their fat, heavy ships up the shallow rivers. Even notable foot travelers, such as Hernando de Soto, pretty much left this part of North Florida to the American Indians who called it home. Of the more modern nations, Seminoles and Muskogees were among the early inhabitants. Local lore suggests Osceola, the great Seminole chief, was raised in what is now Hamilton County. It goes on to suggest a white man killed his son on the shore near White Springs, fueling a hatred that led to his bravery in the Seminole Indian wars. Of course, Osceola legends are as common as the ones about Ponce de Leon's "fountain of youth." So maybe you ought to be from Missouri on some of these.

Madison was settled in the early 1800s by cotton farmers. There are two leftovers from the industry's heyday: a small patch of sea-island cotton growing near an AMTRAK station on Range Street and, near it, a 500-horsepower steam engine that once hauled 65 cotton gins at the world's largest processing plant. In the last days of 1827, Madison and Hamilton counties were created from lands that previously were Jefferson County.

The Suwannee River region's most notable historical event may have been the Battle of Olustee. On February 20, 1864 the Union and Confederate armies met about 15 miles east of what is now Lake City. The battle raged for four hours. By its conclusion, the Union had suffered a stinging defeat – of the more than 5,000 troops, 2,000 were killed, wounded or captured. **The Olustee Battlefield Historic Site,** ☎ 904-752-3866, is the stage for an impressive re-enactment each February. The annual event draws about 2,500 re-enactors and is second only to Gettysburg in magnitude. There's a small interpretive center and a monument located at the site on US 90.

More history? Stay tuned. There's plenty more once you begin touring.

Right now, though, let's lay the groundwork for your arrival.

Getting Around

There are no major airports in the five-county area, but there are three – two regionals and one international – within 75 miles of most destinations.

The largest, **Jacksonville International Airport**, ☎ 904-741-4902, is 75 miles east of the Lake City area. It's served by eight major airlines and four regionals. **Tallahassee Regional Airport,** ☎ 904-891-7800, is 70 miles west of the region and it's served by two major carriers and a half-dozen commuters, some connecting through Atlanta and New Orleans. The closest of the three, **Gainesville Regional Airport,** ☎ 352-373-0249, is about 27 miles from the southern tip of the Suwannee River region. Gainesville is served by two major carriers and four commuters.

The main east-west highway is Interstate 10, which spans all of North and Northwest Florida. Interstate 75 cuts a slightly diagonal north-south path through the region, from Valdosta and the Georgia-Florida line south to Gainesville and beyond. Other major roads include US 90 (east-west), US 441 (north-south), and US 129 (north-south). Despite the rural character, there is an abundance of secondary roads that provide direct routes to virtually all of the destinations that you'll be visiting in the Suwannee River area.

By northern standards, expect reasonably mild winters (less so if you hail from South Florida). Being inland and devoid of sea breezes, the five counties are literally melting pots some days during the peak of summer (mid-July to the first two weeks of September). Temperatures generally are similar to those found in the "spare tire" parts of the Central Panhandle. Expect winter averages of about 52°, six to 10 days in the mid- to high teens and maybe even a day or so where the thermometer drops to a single digit. The summer average is about 84°, but expect at least a dozen high-humidity, high-90s days, and at least a couple where the thermostat boils over the century mark.

So, if you're coming at either peak, pack, dress and pace accordingly.

INFORMATION SOURCES

Lake City/Columbia County Tourist Development Council, ☎ 904-758-1312, P.O. Box 1847, Lake City, FL 32056-1847.
Original Florida, ☎ 904-758-1555, P.O. Box 1300, Lake City, FL 32056-1300. (Represents Hamilton, Lafayette, Madison and Suwannee counties.)
Suwannee County Tourist Development Council, ☎ 904-362-3071, P.O. Drawer C, Live Oak, FL 32060.
Branford Area Chamber of Commerce, ☎ 352-935-3722, P.O. Box 674, Branford, FL 32008.
Hamilton County Chamber of Commerce, ☎ 904-792-1300, P.O. Box P, Jasper, FL 32052.
High Springs Chamber of Commerce, ☎ 352-454-3120, P.O. Box 863, High Springs, FL 32655.
Lafayette County Chamber of Commerce, ☎ 904-294-2705, P.O. Box 416, Mayo, FL 32066.
Lake City/Columbia County Chamber of Commerce, ☎ 904-752-3690, 106 S. Marion St., Lake City, FL 32025.
Madison County Chamber of Commerce, ☎ 904-973-2788, 105 N. Range St., Madison, FL 32340.

Touring

Madison County

Covered bridges? Sorry, this is the other Madison County. It's located two miles north of Interstate 10. Both the Highway 14 and Highway 53 exits take aim on the center of town. The best stop: a walking tour of Madison's historic district. Maps are available at the **Chamber of Commerce,** ☎ 904-973-2788, located at 105 N. Range St., which is in the heart of the district.

City Park at the corner of Range and Base streets has a large, Southern-style gazebo and the Confederate Soldier's Memorial, a

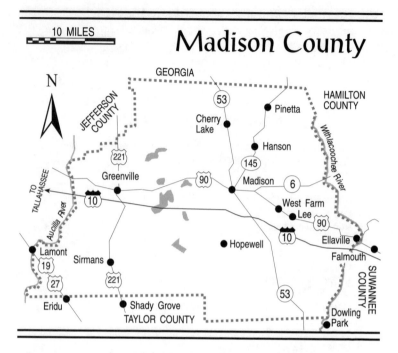

solitary statue of a rifle-carrying infantryman. The park's other monument, the Four Freedoms Memorial, is named for Franklin Delano Roosevelt's stirring 1941 speech and is dedicated to World War II hero, Colin Kelly. **St. Mary's Episcopal Church** is one block north on Marion Street. The narrow frame structure was built in 1851 and is a beautiful example of Carpenter Gothic Architecture, which was popular in North Florida at the time. The church has the original pews and two large stained glass windows, one of Jesus and the other of its namesake, the Virgin Mary. On the outskirts of town you can get another glimpse of the Civil War's influence. A cemetery simply known as **Confederate Soldiers Graves** has the remains of 31 soldiers who were killed at The Battle of Olustee. The neat rows of markers are inscribed only with the letters C.S.A. The soldiers who rest here were never identified. Nearby, **Oak Ridge Cemetery** is the final resting place of a state governor, many early settlers and Colin Kelly.

One last stop before leaving Madison.

The **Wardlaw-Smith-Goza Conference Center**, named for various owners but better known locally as Whitehall, is just off US Highway 90 at the west side of town. It's now part of the North Florida Junior College campus, ☎ 904-973-2288, and tours are available by appointment. Its last owner, William M. Goza, paid for a major restoration. The two-story, heart-pine mansion has the original windows and shutters, 20 fluted columns, a free-standing stairway, mahogany furnishings and a heart-pine floor assembled with wood pegs. The grounds include gardens bursting with azaleas, camelias and wisteria. And near the north entrance, there is a huge live oak that took root long before Whitehall was built in 1860.

Hamilton County

From Madison, follow US 90 three miles east until Highway 6 forks to the left. Follow Highway 6 about 21 miles, through an Interstate 75 interchange, then turn right (east) at US 129 for the six-mile spin into Jasper. This will be a quick, albeit a little bizarre, stop before you're off to one of Florida's oldest resorts. But you don't want to admit you were in picturesque little Jasper without a stop at its No. 1 tourist attraction – **The Old Jail**, ☎ 904-792-1300.

What a trip.

The bizarre part? This is a museum devoted as much to the hangman as the heritage of Jasper, which, in a not-so-odd way, intermingle. (Editor's warning: If you have a weak stomach or are opposed to the death penalty you might want to skip the next paragraph. Otherwise, welcome to Building 1, Room B-167 and

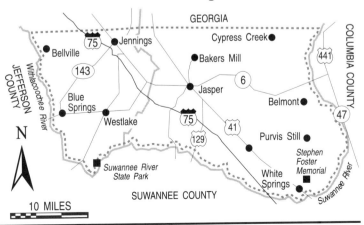

Capital Punishment 101.)

In the days before Florida converted to the electric chair (1924), the legal means of execution was a hangman's knot on the steps of the respective county jails. Enter the Hamilton County Jail in Jasper, built in 1893. Just how many poor stiffs stepped onto the gallows at the rear of Northeast First Street? No one kept count, though the last was a fellow in 1916 who killed a deputy sheriff. Some say this was the site of the last legal hanging in Florida (note the prior disclaimers on Osceola and Ponce de Leon). Anyway, if you have a taste for somewhat unusual attractions, the Old Jail deserves a reservation on your dance card. First, it's the oldest building in Jasper. It's where the county's sheriffs (and their families) lived side-by-side with assorted desperadoes. Today, the two-story jail is home to the Hamilton County Historical Society and its (somewhat) offbeat collection of early 20th-century memorabilia. Spend an hour walking through areas where inmates were housed and hung. Feast your eyes on a photograph (here goes your lunch, but you were warned) of the chap who in 1916 went to the gallows for killing a deputy, get a close look at the hangman's noose, 13 knots swinging in the tower above the jail's entrance, and don't miss a trip to the bowels of the jail, known to the inmates as "The Dungeon." A little less unsettling, but at least as rewarding, are the exhibits of the early farm life, Indian artifacts and Cracker homesteads of Jasper's early years.

You were promised a resort more tame than the jail. Some say that Osceola came here for the cleansing waters. FDR? Well, maybe he made a pit stop, too. But **White Springs** on the banks of the Suwannee River is noted for a series of documented facts. In its prime, around the turn of the century, this spot had 16 resort hotels, a fashionable shopping district, a skating rink and a blue-water, mineral spring, which stays a pleasing 72° year-round. During the early part of this century, many came here hoping to cure various afflictions. **The Telford Hotel**, built in 1903 during the resort's boom days, is no longer a hotel, but it's still hanging around. A walking tour of the historic area visits the Telford; the **Adams Country Store**, erected in 1865 and one of the few original buildings to survive fires that ravaged the town shortly after the turn of the century; and the palatial **Hamilton Hotel**, a four-story, Victorian masterpiece that, in its prime, was one of the only places to stay if you were among the upper crust who visited White Springs. Twenty additional historic sites are on the walking tour. For more information, holler at the **Hamilton County Chamber of Commerce**, ☎ 904-792-1300, P.O. Box P, Jasper, FL 32052.

OK, pack the baggage compartment, climb into your Winnebago or Yugo and set your compass north-northwest for a two-mile drive up US 41 to Stephen Foster land and the (kiss it goodbye) Pee Dee River.

There are camping sites, outdoor grills and even a chart-it-yourself hiking trail, but **Stephen Foster State Folk Culture Center,** ☎ 904-397-4331, differs from a lot of state parks in that it's oriented to two themes – its namesake composer as well as folk arts and trades that linger from yesterday's Florida. In addition to supplying a wealth of Foster history and trivia, the site includes an antebellum-style museum with eight dioramas commemorating his songs and several antiques, including a piano on which he composed "Nelly Bly." Above the treetops, the park's 97-bell carillon tower literally fills the countryside with his music, and its folk center is the place where weavers, wood carvers, blacksmiths, quilters and painters work. The center also hosts several festivals during the year, including the **"Jeanie With The Light Brown Hair" audition and ball** (in October), the **Rural Folklife Days** (November), a **Storytelling Festival** (April) and the big blowout, the **Florida Folk Festival** (May), a three-day extravaganza that features folk songs and dances, legends and crafts.

Ready to move again?

Columbia County

Lake City is about as developed and eclectic as the region gets. But don't expect the stereotypical Florida tourist trappings. The closest thing to congestion occurs within a half-mile radius of where Interstates 10 and 75 cross, a few miles northwest of here, and most of that is a service area for travelers and truckers.

The city has one stop of particular note to adventurers and sports fans: **The Florida Sports Hall of Fame,** ☎ 800-352-3263 or 904-758-1310. This modern memorial to sports heroes is located a quarter-mile west of Interstate 75, just off Highway 90 (look for a tourist welcome station and you won't miss it – it's in the same building). The sometimes interactive museum honors nearly 100 athletes (football, baseball and basketball stars to jockeys, Triple Crown winners and powerboat racers). Athletes enshrined in Aprils past include Babe Zaharias, Garo "Oh No-The Ball's In My Hands" Yepremian, Frank Shorter, Larry Csonka, "Fireball" Roberts, Chris Evert, Angelo Dundee, Tracy Caulkins, Red Barber and 1956 Triple Crown winner Needles.

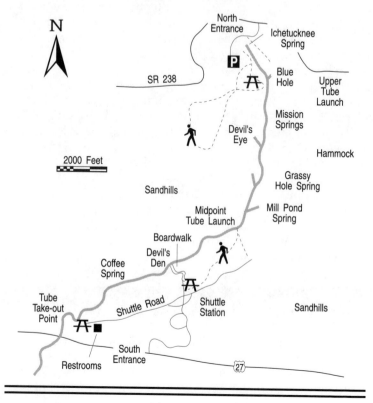

Ichetucknee Springs State Park

A respite for antique hunters, which can be an adventure the way some of you shop, **Webb's Antique Market South**, ☎ 904-758-5564, is a seven-day-a-week operation (open until 6 pm) at the US 41/441 exit on I-75. It's a mall with more than 300 dealers (furniture, primitives, glass, pottery, silver, etc.). One exit north at US 90, go east into Lake City to stops at **The Pink Magnolia**, ☎ 904-752-4336 (Depression glass), on US 90; **Britannia Antiques**, ☎ 904-755-0230 (British and European furniture, stained glass), at 131 W. Madison St.; and **Gateway Gallery**, ☎ 904-752-2485 (folk art, crackle painting, lamps, polished metal), 901 N. Marion.

Those of you who are geographically correct know you've been cheated a little by including the **Olustee Battlefield State Historic**

Columbia County

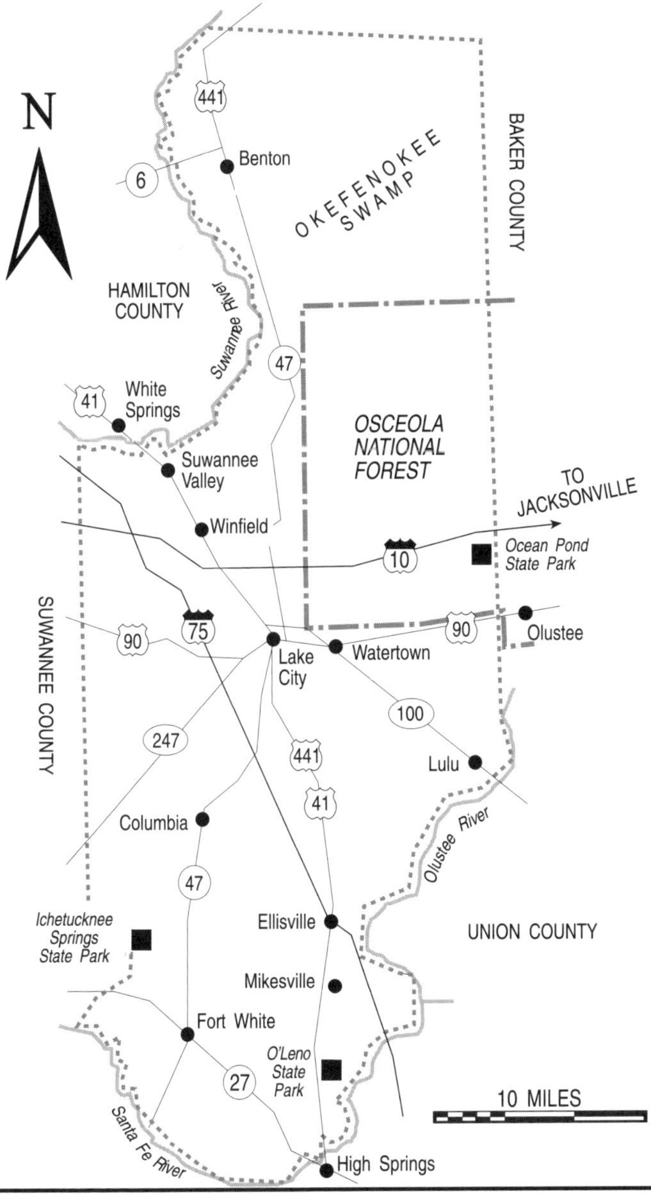

Site, ☎ 904-752-3866, as a part of this chapter. You're right – it's really in Baker County, which is part of the next chapter, but it's included here because of its proximity to Lake City (15 miles east on US 90). Another great stop, and one that will be explored further in our adventures, is **Ichetucknee Springs State Park**, ☎ 904-497-2511. As noted earlier, this is a nifty tubing, snorkeling or floating venue (see a brief note under the hiking adventures, too). To get to the park, travel from Lake City on US 41 south three miles to Highway 47, turn right and follow it south 11 miles to Highway 238 (right) and then book it two miles to the park's entrance.

Risking motion sickness, let's get on the road again.

Suwannee County

From Lake City, find your place in the caravan for the 23-mile ride on US 90 to beautiful Live Oak and the **Suwannee County Historical Museum**, ☎ 904-362-1776. While you won't find gallows and hangman's knots in this one, the treats in this converted railroad depot include a moonshine still (sorry, there isn't a tasting room), a pioneer-life household exhibit, pony cart (1850) owned by Florida's first governor, an antique dental chair (they didn't use anesthetic in those days, so you might find fingernails imbedded in the arm rests) and a telephone switchboard. The museum also has exhibits that let you view some of the large animals that roamed this area hundreds of thousands of years ago and get an idea what it was like to travel the ancient Suwannee River in a dugout. The museum is located at 208 N. Ohio Avenue.

Now, it's showtime.

The Spirit of the Suwannee Music Park, ☎ 904-364-1683, three miles north of Live Oak on Highway 129, is a campground (250 RV sites) located on one of the more scenic runs of the river. It's also Florida's version of Bluegrass Central. Its special events include the **Spring Bluegrass Festival** (April), **Suwannee River Gospel Jubilee** (June), **Hot Cajun Nites** (August) and **New Rising Star Bluegrass Festival** (November). The privately run camp also is the home of the **Spirit of the Suwannee Balloon Classic**, a three-day festival and competition that fills the sky with 30 hot-air balloons. But the headliner is the annual **Suwannee River Jam** in October. The celebrities include Alabama, the Oak Ridge Boys, Eddie Rabbitt, Trisha Yearwood, Pam Tillis and Sammy Kershaw, among others.

Suwannee County

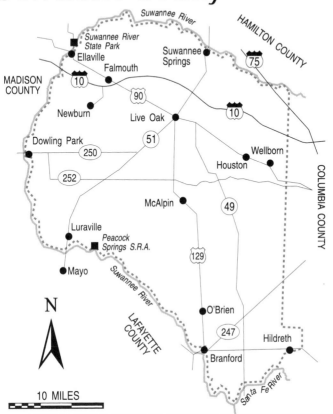

There are a slew of other parks, recreation areas and springs, but let's save some of the surprises for our adventures area. Speaking of adventures, it's time to water your horses, lace your boots, fill your scuba tanks, unpack your rod, grab your paddle and otherwise prepare for liftoff.

Adventures

On Foot

Work those buns (and thighs and calves and cardiovascular systems).

There are trails and trails and more trails in the Suwannee River region.

Leading the pack is the **Florida National Scenic Trail's leg in the Osceola National Forest**, ☎ 800-343-1882 (Florida only), 904-752-2577 and 352-378-8823. This 23-mile trail segment has access points in two areas. For the full route (that means 46 miles round-trip, unless you have a road crew), follow US 90 15 miles east of Lake City, just beyond the Olustee Battlefield Site, and park on the south (right) side of the highway, opposite the trail entrance on the left. For the short course, about 13 miles one-way, take Hwy 250 just east of Lake City off US 90 and catch the trail's other entrance, 13 miles in at Highway 250-A. The aesthetics include mist-shrouded cypress swamps (if you start early), sawgrass marshes interrupted by hardwood hammocks, vast pine forests and crystal-clear springs. You will find 20 boardwalks, from which you can watch nature, including local wildlife – turkey, deer, grey fox, American swallow-tail kite, red-cockaded and pileated woodpecker, warblers and Bachman's sparrows.

On deck is the **Big Gum Swamp Wilderness Area**, ☎ 904-752-2577, which has a pair of primitive trails worthy of note inside the Osceola National Forest. A 6.2-mile trail begins at an entrance off Highway 262 (from US 441 in Lake City head north to Highway 262, turning right or east nine miles to the trail entrance). The other, a three-mile loop, begins off Highway 250 (from Lake City take Highway 250 across I-10 about seven miles to a parking area on the right). The scenics on this trail include cypress-gum swamps, pine flatwoods, shallow sloughs and, if you're sharp-eyed, the remnants of a turpentine still.

There are several additional hiking paths in the Suwannee River region, including:

- **Twin Rivers State Forest**, ☎ 904-208-1462, an eight-mile trail along the river that provides glimpses of sinkholes, wildflower carpets and stands of American elm, sweet gum, hickory, river birch and bald cypress. To get to the forest from Madison, head east on US 90 about 16 miles to the outskirts of Ellaville. Note: If you pass a state agricultural inspection station you've gone about one mile too far east.

- **The Holton Creek Trail**, 16 miles, is located 12 miles northwest of Live Oak on Highway 249 (turn south on the second dirt road past the river, then turn left on the next dirt road and follow the signs). This area includes a first magnitude spring, dozens of sinkholes and outcroppings, two state champion cypress trees, plus oak, hickory, magnolia and beech.

- **The Mattair Spring Trail**, 11 miles, is located on Highway 129, 3½ miles northwest of I-10, then turn right (east) on 40th Street and follow it 1½ miles and turn left (east) at 75th Drive, which becomes unpaved after .3 miles. Look for the entrance road and a sign on the right, .6 miles after the pavement ends. There's ample parking, and the scenic trail includes very high limestone banks and an occasional patch of white-sand beach.

- **Camp Branch** is a six-mile trail located nine miles from White Springs on County Road 25-A (River Road). After passing over I-75, look for the entrance to the tract on the left a half-mile after it makes a 90° turn to the right. The trail has bluffs, ravines, flood plain areas and sinks where the branch run disappears underground.

- **Carter Camp** is a six-mile trail in the **Stephen Foster State Folk Culture Center**, ☎ 904-397-1920, in White Springs. From Lake City, take US 41 north about 14 miles to Highway 135 in White Springs and follow the signs.

- **Ichetucknee Springs State Park**, ☎ 904-497-2511, offers two short trails. The two-mile **Pine Ridge Trail**, which is located off the river's run, forms an oval around sinkholes, hardwood hammocks, sandhill and long-leaf pines, wiregrass and various sprouts of lichens. The .7-mile **Trestle Point Trail** parallels the river for part of its path, then ventures to abandoned phosphate pits, an old railroad trestle and the tram road. Wildlife in the park ranges from gopher tortoises and frogs to river otters and flying squirrels. To get to the park from Lake City, take US 41 south three miles to Highway 47, turn right and follow it south 11 miles to Highway 238 (right), then go two miles to the park's entrance.

- **Suwannee River State Park**, ☎ 904-362-2746, has five hiking trails (**Lime Sink, Suwannee, Balanced Rock, Sandhills** and **Earthworks**) that can be tackled as one trail (2.93 miles). Combined, the trails wander along the river, the old ferry landing, Lime Sink's beaver colony – if you can't spot the beavers, search for the teeth marks they leave on standing trees – and the Columbus Cemetery. (Sorry, this isn't the graveyard where Christopher is buried. It's the final resting place for those who settled an old riverboat town.) From Madison, follow US 90 east 14 miles to Ellaville and Highway 132, then turn left (north) for the short drive to the park.

Additionally, the **Suwannee River Water Management District**, ☎ 904-362-1001 or (in Florida) 800-226-1066, provides several good trails throughout this region, including the following ones along the river.

- **Little Shoals Tract**, a 2½-mile marked trail, which has small rapids in an area where early explorers and American Indians crossed the river. From White Springs, take US 41 south two miles across the river. The entrance road is just past the river on the left, before that agricultural inspection station.

- **Big Shoals Tract**, a 2½- and three-mile trail along high bluffs, large rapids, limestone outcroppings, tupelo and wild azaleas. Follow Highway 135 north out of White Springs to Godwin Bridge Road, turn right (east) and follow it to the tract's entrance.
- **Gar Pond Tract**, a six-mile marked trail through river sloughs, wet prairies and a sinkhole. From White Springs, travel US 41 south two miles across the river. The entrance road is just past the river on the right.

The **Holton Creek Tract** listed above also is a district trail.

INFORMATION SOURCES

Florida Trail Association, ☎ 800-343-1882 (in Florida) or 352-378-8823, P.O. Box 13708, Gainesville, FL 32604.
Office of Greenways & Trails, ☎ 904-487-4784, Mail Station 795, 3900 Commonwealth Boulevard, Tallahassee, FL 32399-3000.

GOLF COURSES

- **Tartaruga Creek Golf & Village**, ☎ 800-738-7739, Route 2, Box 121-K, Greenville, FL 32231, 18 holes, driving range, lessons, PGA rating R-72.8.
- **Lake City Country Club**, ☎ 904-752-2266, Route 13, Lake City, FL 32055, 18 holes, driving range, lessons, R-69.7.
- **Quail Heights Country Club**, ☎ 904-752-3339, Route 17, Box 707, Lake City, FL 32055, 18 holes, driving range, lessons, R-68.6.
- **Suwannee River Valley Country Club**, ☎ 904-792-1990, Route 1, Box 127, Jasper, FL 32052, nine holes, driving range, lessons, R-71.5.
- **Suwannee Country Club**, ☎ 904-362-1147, US 90, Live Oak, FL 32060, nine holes, driving range, lessons, R-68.9.

On Horseback

The cavalry (the **Suwannee River Water Management District**, ☎ 904-362-1001 or, in Florida, 800-226-1066) comes to the rescue with several good trails in this area.

- ❏ The **Holton Creek Trail**, 16 miles, is located 12 miles northwest of Live Oak on Highway 249 (turn south on the second dirt road past the river, then turn left on the next dirt road and follow the signs to the opening of the trail). The area has a first magnitude spring, dozens of sinkholes and two state champion cypress trees (yes, they have state records for odd things in Florida), plus oak, hickory, magnolia and beech. This also is a bicycling area, so be ready for the occasional horse flinch, if your steed happens to be prone to sudden surprises of the rolling variety.

- ❏ The **Mattair Spring Trail**, 11 miles, is located on Highway 129, 3½ miles northwest of I-10, turn right (east) on 40th Street and follow it 1½ miles, then turn left (east) at 75th Drive, which becomes unpaved after .3 miles. Look for an entrance road and a sign on the right, .6 miles after the pavement ends. There is plenty of parking. This scenic trail section includes high limestone banks and an occasional pleasant interruption by a white-sand beach. Again, this is a bike trail, so be ready for sudden and fast movements.

- ❏ **Camp Branch** is a six-mile trail located nine miles from White Springs on County Road 25-A (River Road). After passing over I-75, look for the entrance to the tract on the left a half-mile after it makes a 90° turn to the right. The trail has bluffs, ravines, flood plain areas and sinks where the Camp Branch run disappears underground.

- ❏ **Little Shoals Tract**, a 2½-mile marked trail, which has small rapids in an area where early explorers and American Indians crossed the river. From White Springs take US 41 south two miles across the river. The entrance road is just past the river on the left, before – yes, you've been paying attention – that agricultural inspection station again.

- ❏ **Big Shoals Tract**, 2½- and three-mile trails along high bluffs, swift rapids, limestone outcroppings, tupelo and wild azaleas. Follow Highway 135 north out of White

Springs to Godwin Bridge Road, turn right (east) and follow it to the entrance.

- **Gar Pond Tract**, six-mile marked trail through river sloughs, wet prairies and a sinkhole. From White Springs, travel US 41 south two miles across the river. The entrance road is just past the river on the right.

The district permits horseback riding on unmarked trails at several other locations. For information or maps, call or write the district at 9225 County Road 49, Live Oak, FL 32060.

Other riding trails in the area include **Carter Camp**, a six-mile trail in the **Stephen Foster State Folk Culture Center**, ☎ 904-397-1920. From Lake City, take US 41 north 14 miles to Highway 135 in White Springs and follow the signs. At **Twin Rivers State Forest**, ☎ 904-208-1462, there's an eight-mile trail with glimpses of the riverfront, sinkholes, wildflower carpets and patches of American elm, sweet gum, hickory, river birch and bald cypress. From Madison, head east on US 90 16 miles to the outskirts of Ellaville.

One more note for riders: The **Osceola National Forest** offers nearly 40 miles of primitive trails, mainly in its West Tower district north of Lake City. For information, maps and the steer-clear-of-the-place hunting dates, call or write the District Office, ☎ 904-752-2577, P.O. Box 90, Olustee, FL 32072.

On Wheels

If you paid attention earlier in this battle plan, you know this is home court to the event-oriented **Suwannee Bicycle Association**, in White Springs, ☎ 904-397-2347, in Tallahassee ☎ 904-878-2042, or in Jacksonville ☎ 904-387-9858. The SBA offers custom tours to special groups, small group tours every month and several long events. How long? Try the **Suwannee Sweetheart Cycling Weekend**, held in February (30-, 53-, 63-and 100-mile options); or the **Suwannee Bicycle Festival**, held in May (several choices including a 41-mile White Springs historic district tour; the 100-mile Suwannee Circuit Century around Live Oak; a 27-mile Ice Cream Ride to the Spirit of the Suwannee Campground; and the Suwannee Springs Peddle & Paddle, a 23-mile ride that includes two hours of canoeing at half-time). The **Florida Flat-Tire Festival** in November has 15 routes to many of the region's water management district preserves. Distances range from 2½ to 25 miles. The **Secret Santa Cycling Weekend** in December offers 40- and 60-mile rides the first day and 25-, 60- and 100-mile options the second. If you're not ready for the holiday break after that one, well, you're a certified hardcore.

Several trails that are available year-round are worth special note, too.

The marathoner's choice is the six-day, 327-mile **Florida Springs Bicycle Tour**, ☎ 904-487-4784. While this tour traditionally begins at Payne's Prairie State Preserve in Alachua County (see page 176), it's easy to improvise by launching from the Olustee Battlefield, 15 miles east of Lake City on US 90. The six legs lead from Olustee to Stephen Foster State Folk Culture Center (30 miles), Stephen Foster to O'Leno State Park (47 miles), O'Leno to Manatee Springs State Park (58 miles), Manatee to Payne's Prairie (63 miles), Payne's Prairie to Gold Head Branch State Park (63 miles) and Gold Head Branch to Olustee (67 miles). Directions for each leg are pretty doggone involved. You can obtain a copy by writing to the Office of Greenways & Trails at the address listed in the Information Sources at the end of the cycling portion of this chapter.

Our friends at the **Suwannee River Water Management District**, ☎ 904-362-1001 or (in Florida) 800-226-1066, provide several other bicycle trails thanks to the district's aggressive land-buying habits, which are intended to preserve land in its natural state. Many of the trails are already familiar if you've read the hiking and bicycling adventures earlier:

- ❑ The **Holton Creek Trail**, 16 miles, is 12 miles northwest of Live Oak on Highway 249 (turn south on the second dirt road past the river, turn left on the next dirt road, then follow the signs). This area has a first magnitude spring, dozens of sinkholes and those two state champion cypress trees, plus oak, hickory, magnolia and beech.

- ❑ The **Mattair Spring Trail**, 11 miles, is on Highway 129, 3½ miles northwest of I-10. Turn right (east) on 40th Street and follow it 1½ miles, then turn left (east) at 75th Drive, which becomes unpaved after .3 miles. Look for an entrance road and a sign on the right, .6 miles after the pavement ends. There's ample parking and the trail's course includes very high limestone banks and an occasional stretch of white-sand beach.

- ❑ **Little Shoals Tract**, a 2½-mile marked trail, which has small rapids in an area where early explorers and American Indians crossed the river. From White

Springs, take US 41 south two miles across the river. The entrance road is just past the river on the left, before that familiar agricultural inspection station.

- **Big Shoals Tract**, a three-mile trail along high bluffs, large rapids, limestone outcroppings, tupelo and azaleas. Take Highway 135 north out of White Springs to Godwin Bridge Road, turn right (east) and follow it to the entrance.
- **Gar Pond Tract**, a six-mile marked trail through river sloughs, wet prairies and a sinkhole. From White Springs, travel US 41 south two miles across the river. The entrance road is just past the river on the right.
- **White Springs Tract**, four- and five-mile marked trails along the river and into the town. From the caution light in White Springs (the intersection of US 41 and Highway 136), head south on US 41 and turn south on Adams Memorial Drive. Go past the cemetery to the entrance.
- **Saunders Tract**, a six-mile marked trail partly along Camp Branch Creek. From Live Oak, take Highway 129 north to Highway 132. Go east to 25-A and follow it 3.3 miles to an open gate at the entrance.

The district permits cycling at several other tracts. For information or maps, call or write the district at 9225 County Road 49, Live Oak, FL 32060.

INFORMATION SOURCES

Office of Greenways & Trails, ☎ 904-487-4784, 325 John Knox Road, Building 500, Tallahassee, FL 32303-4124.
Florida Department of Transportation, ☎ 904-487-9220, Mail Station 82, 605 Suwanee St., Tallahassee, FL 32399-0450.
Suwannee Bicycle Association, ☎ 904-397-2347, 904-878-2042, or 904-387-9858, P.O. Box 247, White Springs, FL 32096.

On Water

CANOEING

Paddlers find five designated state trails in the Suwannee River region.

The **Aucilla River Trail**, introduced on page 119, is a 19-mile course rated intermediate to technical due to three-plus mph currents that stretch over shoals and the remains of two old rock dams that make it especially challenging at low tide. The trail is framed by high limestone banks and portions of it flow through a cypress-gum swamp. From Madison, go west on US 90 about 21 miles to Highway 257 and turn left (south), traveling nine miles to US 19/27. Turn left and go one mile to the bridge, which is the starting point.

The **Santa Fe River Canoe Trail**, 26 miles, is rated beginning and easy in the skill and difficulty departments, with an average current of two-three mph. It's a nice trail for beginners, passing through hardwood hammocks and swamps, by some clear-water springs and across an occasional small shoal. For the full run, follow US 27 east from Branford 26 miles to High Springs, turn left on US 41/441 and travel two miles to the public ramp. The short course, 13 miles, starts at the Highway 47 bridge. From Branford, use US 27 east 16 miles to Fort White and turn right (south) on Highway 47, proceeding four miles to the bridge.

The **Upper Suwannee River Trail**, at 69 miles, is the longest in the area. It's rated beginner and easy, except for some rapids, and its current averages about two-three mph. The most challenging of the rapids is Big Shoals. You can hear its roar well before you get there and even experienced canoeists carry their craft along the banks in this area. There are white-sand beaches, springs and swamps at a number of spots along this trail. Limestone outcroppings contain ancient fossils and the woods, waters and skies along the way are home to otters, beavers, red-tailed hawks, ospreys and several species of songbirds and wading birds. Are you man or woman enough for a full run? If so, take Highway 135 north of White Springs seven miles to Highway 6, turn right (east) and go less than a mile to the bridge. A shorter option, about 44½ miles, begins at the US 41 bridge one mile south of White Springs. The shortest route, 22.6 miles, launches at the US 129 bridge. From

Live Oak, follow US 129 north six miles and just before the bridge turn right to the Suwannee Springs entrance.

The **Lower Suwannee River Canoe Trail**, at 51.4 miles, is rated beginner and easy with a two-three mph current. This stretch of the river is wide and gentle. The scenery includes craggy limestone bluffs and more ancient fossils. The wildlife is similar to what you see on the upper trail and there are numerous wide sandbars where you can camp, if you happen to have a somewhat primitive, bold personality. The starting point is the Suwannee River State Park on US 90, nine miles west of Live Oak. The short course for this one, 22 miles, launches at the Highway 51 bridge, two miles north of Mayo.

The **Withlacoochee River North Canoe Trail**, 32 miles, is rated beginner in skill level and moderate in difficulty. The current averages two-three mph. The river curves gently through swamps, hardwood forests and pastures. The limestone outcroppings have some swirling water.

Cypress trees on the Withlacoochee River.

The river changes with rainfall, turning high and swift during rainy seasons, so it's a good idea to check local weather conditions before setting off. The trail begins at the Florida-Georgia border on Highway 145, 16 miles north of Madison. The short course, 12 miles, begins at the Suwannee River State Park on US 90, nine miles west of Live Oak.

In addition to the five designated state trails, canoeing is available at the **Ichetucknee Springs State Park**, ☎ 904-497-4690, by reservation. Moonlight and sunrise canoe trips, led by rangers, are available down the 3.2-mile run, starting at Blue Hole. To get to the park from Lake City, take US 41 south three miles to Highway 47, turn right and follow it south 11 miles to Highway 238 (right), then go two miles to the park's entrance.

The **Suwannee Canoe Outpost**, which is at **Spirit of the Suwannee Campground**, ☎ 800-428-4147 or 904-364-4991, features one-to 19-mile self-guided excursions down the scenic Suwannee. The campground is three miles north of Live Oak on Highway 129.

INFORMATION SOURCES

For designated trail maps, write to the **Office of Greenways and Trails**, ☎ 904-487-4784, 325 John Knox Road, Bldg. 500, Tallahassee, FL 32303-4124.
Florida Association of Canoe Liveries & Outfitters, ☎ 941-494-1215, P.O. Box 1764, Arcadia, FL 33821.
Santa Fe Canoe Outpost, ☎ 904-454-2050, P.O. Box 592, High Springs, FL 32643.
Steamboat Outfitters, ☎ 352-935-0512, P.O. Box 28, Branford, FL 32008.
River Run Campground, ☎ 352-935-1086, Route 2, Box 811, Branford, FL 32008.
Suwannee Canoe Outpost, ☎ 800-428-4147, Route 1, Box 98-A, Live Oak, FL 32060.
Suwannee Outdoor, ☎ 904-397-2347, P.O. Drawer 247, White Springs, FL 32096.
American Canoe Adventures, ☎ 904-397-1309, Route 1, Box 8335, White Springs, FL 32096.

DIVING/SNORKELING

If you insist on saltwater dives, you'll draw a blank in the Suwannee River area, but it would be a sin to skip this destination and miss the wonderful diving and snorkeling sites that certify this as the Cave Diving Capital of Florida – and make it a strong contender for the Spring Diving Capital, too.

Ginnie Springs, ☎ 800-874-8571 or 904-454-2202, is located off the Santa Fe River near the point where Columbia and Gilchrist counties meet. From Fort White, follow Highway 47 south six miles and watch for the sign on your left. The privately operated site has a full-service diving center, lodging and some of the most beautiful springs in Florida. The nine springs offer options for open water, cavern and cave divers. The open water area is a large basin that's surrounded by eel grass, with a white-sand bottom and an excellent photo opportunity. That's just as true once you swim into the cavern and look back at the silhouettes of the other divers and snorkelers lingering in the basin. The cavern entrance is four to six feet wide, and it leads to two chambers. The first is about 30 feet wide with a nine-foot ceiling, followed by a room, about 60 feet wide and 70 feet long, which angles from a depth of 35 feet to 60 feet. **Devil's Eye Spring** is on the same 200-acre site. Its limestone shaft drops to a sand bottom at 20 feet. A cave entrance, three feet high and 18 feet wide, leads to the dark 30-by-20-foot room called the "Devil's Dungeon." Certified cave divers can squeeze through a dangerous two-by-four-foot tunnel that leads to a small room and a depth of 65 feet. This isn't an adventure for a diver without proper training and state of mind. Another spring at the site, "Little Devil," doesn't require cave-diving certification. It has a 45-foot drop and a beautiful view from the bottom.

Blue Springs, ☎ 904-971-2880, is another privately run site that has a dive center, accommodations and open-water, cavern and cave diving options. The spring has a large basin, 75 feet across, and a 20-foot-by-30-foot cavern at 30 feet down. This is a comfortable option for recreational divers. Cave divers find an interesting maze, more than 3,500 feet in length, leading off the cavern. Blue Springs is located in Lee. From Madison, follow US 90 east 2½ miles, turn left at Highway 6 and go six miles. Look for the Blue Springs sign just before the Withlacoochee River Bridge. (Blessedly, you don't have to be on the lookout for an agricultural station.)

Ichetucknee Springs State Park, ☎ 904-497-2511, has nine springs along the 3.2-mile run, which is an excellent snorkeling trip. While diving isn't allowed in the head spring, a tank really isn't necessary since most of the springs are in shallow water, making it easy for anyone to reach the bottom in their search for relics or fossils.

Peacock Springs State Park, ☎ 904-497-2511, does welcome divers. Its three springs, six sinks and caves (about 28,000 feet of passages have been explored and surveyed by certified cave divers) provide a full range of venues. Note: Underwater lights are not allowed unless a diver has proper certification. The site's springs feed the Suwannee, but most options are caverns or caves. The main spring has a cavern entrance at 18 feet that provides a comfortable berth into an open room with, in one corner, a ceiling 15 feet off the bottom and, in another, a depth of 45 feet. From there, cave divers can venture through a narrow slit, reaching depths of 65 feet, and a winding tunnel that after 400 feet leads to the shaft at Pot Hole Sink. From Branford, go north six miles on US 129, turn left onto Highway 349 and go 12 miles, turning left on another paved road (look for two dumpsters), then travel 1½ miles, turning left again at the stop sign. Then drive 3.3 miles to the entrance sign on the left.

The Branford area has several sites radiating from it. **Troy Springs**, a big circular hole with a depth of 75 feet, also has a short run to the Suwannee River and the ribs of a Civil War-era steamer. **Royal Springs** is a site that has a depth of 50 feet and a 200-foot run to the Suwannee. **Orange Grove Sink**, another 50-footer, has a scenic cavern with unique limestone formations. **Yana Springs** has a cavern with two domed ceilings, a spacious room and a 40-foot reading on your depth gauge. Branford is 24 miles south of Live Oak. To get there, follow US 129 south to where it meets US 27.

INFORMATION SOURCES

Florida Association of Dive Operators, ☎ 305-451-3020, 51 Garden Cove Drive, Key Largo, FL 33037.
US Coast Guard, Mayport, ☎ 904-246-7315.
Florida Marine Patrol, ☎ 904-359-6580, 2510 Second Ave. N., Jacksonville Beach, FL 32250.
Ned DeLoach's Diving Guide to Underwater Florida, ☎ 904-737-6558, New World Publications, 1861 Cornell Road, Jacksonville, FL 32207.
Ginnie Springs Dive Center, ☎ 800-874-8571 or 904-454-2202, 7200 N.E. Ginnie Springs Road, High Springs, FL 32643.
Blue Springs Resort, ☎ 904-971-2880, Route 1, Box 1950, Lee, FL 32059-9732.
Branford Dive Center, ☎ 352-935-1141, P.O. Box 822, Branford, FL 32008.
Steamboat Dive Inn, ☎ 352-935-2283, US 27 & 129, Branford, FL 32008.

SALTWATER & FRESHWATER FISHING

This is a good area for do-it-yourselfers, though you can get information about guides and all the gear you need at places like **Jim's Live Bait & Tackle**, ☎ 904-364-1089, in Live Oak; **Bass Assassin Lures**, ☎ 904-294-1049, in Mayo; or **Jim's Sports Shop**, ☎ 904-362-1305, also in Live Oak.

Your prey: largemouth, smallmouth and black bass, crappie, bluegill and catfish. And don't forget to try your luck with the scrappy Suwannee River bass – it only thrives in the region for which it's named. (Tip of the day: These beauties can best be landed along the river banks, but they're also found in limited supply in the Santa Fe and Withlacoochee rivers.)

Many anglers don't bother with boats, particularly on the area rivers. They just park themselves on the banks and use a rod and reel or a cane pole. It cuts the overhead, and the fishing is just as good on the shore in most spots, including the Suwannee, Withlacoochee and Santa Fe rivers. The Withlacoochee at **Blue Springs** (11 miles east of Madison on Highway 6) is noted for largemouth bass from February into May and redbreast sunfish from March through September.

Another productive fishing hole is **Cherry Lake** (10 miles north of Madison on Highway 53, then 1½ miles east on Highway 253). This is a good bass fishing spot, particularly for smaller ones, though a few 10-pounders are hauled up each year. The peak is February and March. Bluegill and redear sunfish are abundant on or near the bottom May through July. The best period for sunshine bass is the heart of winter, November through February.

The **Suwannee River State Park**, ☎ 904-362-2746, and the **Stephen Foster State Folk Culture Center**, ☎ 904-397-4331, also welcome anglers. The state park is on US 90, about 15 miles west of Live Oak. The folk culture center is two miles northwest of White Springs on US 41. The species available include most of the ones listed in earlier freshwater holes.

Every one of the **Suwannee River Water Management District**'s 33 tracts in the region is open to anglers, including those listed earlier in the hiking, biking and canoeing adventures. For a 72-page booklet on the tracts, call the district at ☎ 800-226-1066 or 904-362-1001 or write to 9225 County Road 49, Like Oak, FL 32060. Save a stamp or another call – ask the district to send its handy guide to boat ramps and canoe launching points in the region. There are 51 on the upper and lower Suwanee River, 12 more on the Santa Fe River and five on the upper Withlacoochee River.

The **Twin Rivers State Forest** has six tracts open to fishermen. A brochure that includes a map of the sites can be obtained by calling ☎ 904-208-1462 or write to Live Oak Work Center, 7620 133rd Road, Live Oak, FL 32060. The **Osceola National Forest** has four good fishing spots, including one at the **Olustee Beach State Recreation Area** that features a fishing pier. You can get a forest brochure by calling or writing the District Office, ☎ 904-752-2577, P.O. Box 70, Olustee, FL 32072.

Don't forget to pick up a fishing license. Non-resident freshwater licenses cost $15 for a week and $30 for a year. There are size and bag limits on several species. Information on these is available from bait-and-tackle shops, guides, or the **Florida Marine Patrol**, ☎ 904-359-6580, 2510 Second Ave. N., Jacksonville Beach, FL 32250, or the **Florida Game & Fresh Water Fish Commission**, ☎ 904-758-0525, Route 7, Box 440, Lake City, FL 32055-8713.

Where To Stay & Eat

The lack of crowds and rural character of the region mean fewer choices, but there are some cozy and interesting accommodations as well as down-home places to eat.

Madison & Hamilton Counties

The **Manor House Bed & Breakfast**, ☎ 904-973-6508, located in the town of Madison, is an elegant 19th-century brick motel surrounded by majestic live oaks and magnolias. The inn features five luxury suites, breakfast served in your room and three dining areas, including Miss Virginia's Café. Make sure to save some time to browse through Blind Pig Antiques, which is located in the hotel.

Deerwood Inn, ☎ 904-973-2504, also in Madison, features motel rooms and spaces for RVs and campers on a 20-acre wooded site bordered on three sides by the Suwannee River.

Madison also has a **Days Inn**, ☎ 904-973-3330, and a **Super 8 Motel**, ☎ 904-973-6267, on Highway 53 just off Interstate 10.

In addition to the dining rooms at The Manor House, a local favorite is the **Three B's Restaurant**, ☎ 904-963-1115, in White Springs, owned by three brothers – Luke, Dana and Robie Faucher. Unlike many of the restaurants in this region, you won't find collard greens, cornbread or barbecue here. You will find chicken, steaks, seafood and Italian specialties. If your taste buds are set on barbecue, try **Smoke House Bar-B-Q**, ☎ 904-948-2270, in Greenville or **Ken's Bar-B-Que**, ☎ 904-973-2545, in Madison. Homestyle Southern cooking is the specialty at **Latrelle's Family Restaurant**, ☎ 904-973-3115, also in Madison.

Suwannee County

The **McLeran House Bed & Breakfast**, ☎ 904-963-4603, in Wellborn, dates to 1909, when it was built for a wealthy banker. The inn's five acres have a cedar gazebo, fountain, garden swing and goldfish pond. Inside, there are two rooms, one downstairs with a private entrance and private bath, and one upstairs with a shared bath. The decor includes heart-pine floors, six fireplaces with curly-pine mantles and a grand stairwell. The inn also has a large, wrap-around porch for watching the world pass by slowly.

There also are several motels in the area, including **Suwannee River Best Western**, ☎ 904-362-6000, and **Parker's Motel & Restaurant**, ☎ 904-362-2790, both in Live Oak; **Colonial House Inn**, ☎ 904-963-2104, and **Scottish Inn**, ☎ 904-963-2501, both in White Springs; and **Steamboat Dive Inn**, ☎ 904-935-3483, and **Sandy Point Motel, Restaurant & Campground**, ☎ 352-935-0615, both in Branford.

The Dixie Grill & Steer Room, ☎ 904-364-2810, in Live Oak, specializes in aged beef and great homemade pies. **Jay's Restaurant**, ☎ 904-362-3534, also in Live Oak, features homestyle Southern cooking and all-you-can-eat Suwannee River catfish specials.

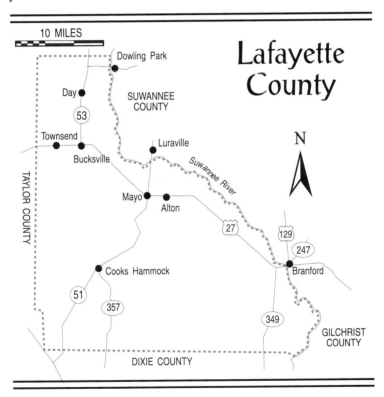

Columbia & Lafayette Counties

Le Chateau de Lafayette Bed & Breakfast, ☎ 904-294-2332, started life in Mayo as the Lafayette County Courthouse, in 1883. It was turned into a spacious home in 1907, then an apartment house, before its restoration in 1995 as an inn. The rooms have high ceilings and cozy beds. There's a wrap-around veranda where you can unwind. And in the morning, breakfast includes plenty of fresh baked goods.

The Smoakhouse Ranch, ☎ 352-935-2662, near Branford, is set amid ranch and timberlands. Two cottage suites have private baths, one with a sleeping loft, plus modern kitchens, sitting areas and decks. The grounds include old tobacco barns, trails through the woods, hammocks, swings and porches, plus gardens where you can snitch blackberries. There's also a bridge across a pond, where you can drop a line or watch the antics of the frogs and water skates.

Nearby, Lake City has 34 motels from which to choose, including **Holiday Inn**, ☎ 904-752-3901; **Ramada Inn**, ☎ 904-752-7550; **Hampton Inn**, ☎ 904-752-3419; **Thunderbird Motor Lodge**, ☎ 904-752-2741; and **Quail Heights Lodge**, ☎ 904-752-3339.

A favorite place at dinnertime is the **Wayside Restaurant**, ☎ 904-752-1581, which has a menu rich in Western steaks and Suwannee catfish.

Campgrounds

The close-to-nature crowd has some unique options in this region.

For instance, the **Spirit of the Suwannee Campground**, ☎ 904-364-1683, in Live Oak, always has musical offerings. Even if you land here when there isn't a big event scheduled, you'll run into a smaller one, such as a sandlot jam. The campground is a magnet for pickers, fiddlers and crooners, and there's a bluegrass mini-extravaganza every Saturday night. The park has 250 RV sites, walking trails, boat ramps, canoe rentals, fishing on the river and Rees Lake, the Old Tyme Farm Museum, an indoor concert hall, an amphitheater, a swimming pool and cable television hook-ups. If you want to time your arrival to one of the special events, call or write for a schedule: 3076 95th Drive, Live Oak, FL 32060.

Another unique place to park a camper or pitch a tent is **Jim Hollis' River Rendezvouz**, ☎ 800-533-5276 or 904-294-2510. River Rendezvouz has its own dive shop and air station, plus a Jacuzzi, steam room, sauna, canoe rentals, lounge (305 kinds of beer, preferably to be ingested well between dives), restaurant and fishing. The campground is located in Mayo.

Jennings Outdoor Resort Campground, ☎ 904-938-3321, not coincidentally located in Jennings, has pull-through campsites with full hook-ups, hot showers, a recreation hall, food store, cable television, a swimming pool and lake fishing.

Ginnie Springs Resort, ☎ 800-874-8571 or 904-454-2202, in High Springs, also has a dive shop. It has primitive sites, 55 campsites with electric and water hook-ups, RV pull-through sites, heated bath houses, covered pavilions, hiking trails and canoe, tube, scuba and snorkeling rentals.

Madison Blue Spring and Campground, ☎ 904-971-2880, in Lee, has RV and wilderness campsites, a dive shop, bath houses, hot showers and pavilions.

In Lake City, **Inn & Out RV Camp Park**, ☎ 904-752-1648, and **Wagon Wheel RV Resort**, ☎ 904-752-2279, also are full-service campgrounds.

Additionally, campsites are available at the following:

- **American Canoe Adventures**, ☎ 904-397-1309, in White Springs, 20-acre primitive campsite, restrooms and showers.
- **Suwannee River State Park**, ☎ 904-362-2746, in Live Oak, 31 campsites.
- **Stephen Foster State Folk Culture Center**, ☎ 904-397-4331, sites for RVs and tents.
- **Twin Rivers State Forest**, ☎ 904-208-1462, near Live Oak, primitive camping at its Chitty Bend, Nekoosa, Ellaville and Anderson Springs tracts.
- **Ocean Pond Campground** in the **Osceola National Forest**, ☎ 904-752-2577, near Olustee, 50 sites for camper trailers and tents, showers, water and restrooms. The forest also provides primitive campsites at its West Tower, East Tower and Hog Pen Landing tracts.

Northern Heartland

Strange encounters of the abnormal, paranormal and nearly normal kind:
(You be the judge: Which is which?)
Old Sparky. That's the politically incorrect nickname for Florida's electric chair at the Florida State Prison. You can't see the real McCoy – unless you're a working journalist, an official execution witness, or have a reserved seat. But you can get the drift at **Carla's Sandwich Shoppe & Prison Museum**. It seems like an odd combination, until Carla Hawthorne explains the facts of life in Starke. First, she's an ex-prison guard who had to find some means to make a living when she left the system. Second, there are five state prisons within a nine-mile radius of her front doorstep. Third, folks in this part of Florida have a law-and-order state of mind. So, maybe it isn't such a stretch. Besides, if jail and gallows mementos are good enough for downtown Jasper, heck, maybe it's a natural that prison and death-row memorabilia found a home within a chip shot of the Bradford County seat. Carla's is the kind of stop where honky-tonk music mingles with Elvis-and-Marilyn shrines. They mingle, in turn, with the creativity of some of Florida's more ingenious inmates and our very own criminal justice system. But enough on Carla for now.

A haunted bed-and-breakfast? Meet Sonny Howard. Sonny's hideaway is the **Herlong Mansion**, which is located in picturesque Micanopy, an antiques epicenter that's caught the eye of several Hollywood types (among them, Michael J. Fox and his film *Doc Hollywood*). The mansion looks anything but eerie with its tall columns, roomy porches and Greek Revival architecture wrapped around the original Cracker home. It's a stately building, with a turn-of-the-century ambience and a collection of somewhat unusual walking sticks. Let's not spoil the surprise, but if you stop, ask Sonny to show you the pair that used to be attached to bulls. Among guests, they're lively conversation pieces, though not nearly as much as Inez, the reputed friendly ghost. Beyond her titillating overnighters, whether in reality or simply legend, there's another perk to having (or at least believing you have) a ghost on the premises:

"You don't need to buy an alarm system," Sonny says.
"The undesirables won't come near this place."

You'll come back to the Herlong later.

The Skin Shop. It may be North Florida's weirdest gift shop. For the man or woman who has everything, what about: a python cummerbund, a gator-claw back scratcher for those hard to reach places, a toad skeleton bigger than Larry Bird's foot, or a coiled rattlesnake that, on a double-take, has a small gator head? Dwayne McGee does some normal stuff, such as selling skins for Lucchese and Tony Lama boots. But, when his sense of humor shines through, this guy has splashes of down-home genius.

Ready for something a little less bizarre but a lot more adventurous? How about crawling into the skeletal cab of a dragster for an up to 200-mph zip down the quarter-mile? **Frank Hawley's Drag Racing School** near Gainesville provides the experience on the same strip where the annual Gatornationals are held. That is one of the more expensive adventures in this five-county region. But there are plenty of others considerably cheaper, and many of them free.

For peddlers, marathon madness returns in the form of that six-day, 347-mile **Florida Springs Bicycle Tour** visited earlier, this time beginning at the designated starting point. And the **Gainesville-Hawthorne Trail** is a great one for wheels, hiking boots and the horseshoe crowd. Paddlers find fewer designated trails – OK, confession time, there's one – but there are several trails that can be improvised on the area's lakes and rivers. **Payne's Prairie** is a vast preserve that's a hiker's and nature-lover's paradise, while divers and snorkelers can dive into a wealth of wonderful caverns, caves and springs, including our return to the **Branford** area and **Ginnie Springs**, mentioned on page 183. Oh, and just a tickler here, let's not leave out hot-air ballooning. There are a pair of adventures that let you ride in gondolas in the flight paths of eagles.

When you start touring, you're going to visit several quaint towns including Micanopy, which, in addition to its ghostly haunts, has become a thriving antiques center; Alachua, where you're going to visit an incredible retirement home for the horses many folks don't want; and Santa Fe, where college kids are groomed as our next generation of zookeepers. While Santa Fe Community College doesn't let madcap adventurers try their luck feeding a hungry rattlesnake or caracal, the college is an adventure day-off treat that may plant the seed of a new career for you or, if you're as old as us, your kids.

Gainesville? Well, that's the big city in the area, the cultural star; many of its sidelines are based at, or connected to, the University of Florida. Gainesville has a wealth of natural treasures inside the

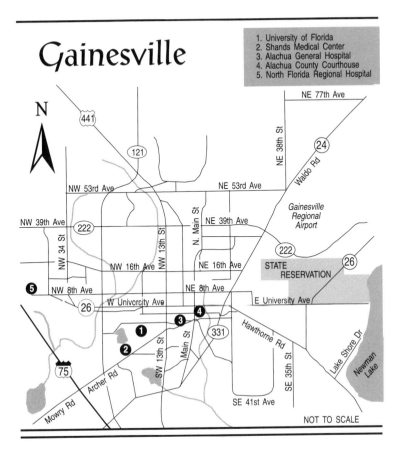

Florida Museum of Natural History – which is located on campus – and the Fred Bear Archery Museum, which isn't. There also are plenty of great vittles and natural adventures at the other destinations in Alachua County.

One final note before you learn a little about the region's geography and history, synchronize our compasses, see the sights and sounds and at last dig into our adventures: Marjorie Kinnan Rawlings. She won the Pulitzer Prize for *The Yearling*, set in south Alachua County, and further immortalized the area with *Cross Creek*. Her home and favorite backwoods places are just a hop, skip and a speed trap or two (watch out chiefly for Waldo) down US 441. The entire town is like taking a step back in time, but wait until you get a gander at what the state park service has done to her homestead.

But enough teasing. Let's roll.

Geography & History

Yep, still flat. Forever flat. And no coast.

But still wooded, wet and often wild.

Even the major city, Gainesville, has abundant parks and greenbelt areas. The rest of the region has geographic features similar to those of many other areas in Northwest and North Florida. That means rivers, springs, refuges, timberlands, rolling hills, farms, prairies, savannas, hammocks and sloughs. The Northern Heartland's small towns have changed little in the past 50 to 100 years. Wildlife? This is a naturalist's dream. The same species of mammals, reptiles, fish and birds you've encountered in other chapters thrive here, too, as do some that are, well, a little unusual, such as the wild horses in the **Payne's Prairie State Preserve**. Their roots trace back to the early Spanish explorers.

Now, let's take a short walk on the pre-American history trail.

Ancient Indians date at least as far back as 10,000 years in the Payne's Prairie area, nine miles south of what today is Gainesville. They were followed by the Timucuans, a peaceful, mound-building culture (about 500 to 1500 B.C.), but they disappeared around the time Hernando de Soto and his stormtroopers marched through the area in 1539. Many historians believe the Timucuans were wiped out by the white man's diseases – but not the Seminoles and the Creeks. They established themselves here well into the Spanish (as early as 1720), English and early American occupations. Truth is, they drove the Spanish and English from the area. Naturalist and explorer William Bartram spent time in the area during the 1770s and established a rapport with the native tribes, which Andrew Jackson didn't. His tactics didn't exactly follow the Marquess of Queensberry rules, particularly with Osceola and other Seminole chiefs, but they ended the Seminole Indian Wars around the time Florida attained statehood in 1845.

Plantations developed over the next 20 years. Gainesville was born. High Springs and Newberry sprouted up around phosphate mining operations. Archer evolved as a railroad and then a citrus crop town. Union County had its beginnings in cattle, lumber and sea-island cotton. But the backwoods character wasn't truly "discovered" until Marjorie Kinnan Rawlings came to Cross Creek in the 1920s and began sharing her experiences, and the area's treasures, with her readers.

More on Marge later. First, you have to get here.

Getting Around

Gainesville Regional Airport, ☎ 352-373-0249, is served by two commercial carriers and four commuter airlines. Jacksonville's International Airport, ☎ 904-741-4902, is 45 miles east of Macclenny and 95 miles northeast (driving distance) of Gainesville. Jacksonville is served by eight major airlines and four regionals.

Roads: There's a better system here than in all but the first chapter, on the Western Panhandle. Interstate 10 continues as an east-west feeder through the region, from east of Lake City to Macclenny, then continuing on into Jacksonville, featured in the next chapter. Interstate 75, on its slightly diagonal course, runs a north-to-south course through Alachua (west of Gainesville) and Union counties, while US 441 and 301, also north-south, run through the west and east frontiers, respectively, of the area, and US 90 follows a path roughly parallel to the one plotted by I-10. And those are just the federal highways. This area has plenty of secondary roads, with the exception of Baker County, which has part of the Osceola National Forest, and the west-to-east corridors in Union County.

Now, it's time for the Willard Scott weather report. Expect pretty mild winters by northern standards and summers that are less than mild. Located inland and lacking sea breezes, Baker and Union counties literally can be melting pots in the peak of summer (early July through mid-September). The summer average is 84°, but expect at least a dozen high-humidity, high-90s days, as well as a few where the temperature shoots over the century mark. Subtract two degrees on average when you're in the southern regions, around Gainesville and Newberry. Expect winter averages of 52-56°, with a few days as low as the mid- to high teens. At the northern extremities, you can count on a day or so where the thermometer drops to a single digit.

INFORMATION SOURCES

Alachua County Visitors and Convention Bureau, ☎ 352-374-5231, 30 E. University Ave., Gainesville, FL 32601.
Original Florida, ☎ 904-758-1555 (Alachua, Gilchrist and Union counties), P.O. Box 1300, Lake City, FL 32056-1300.

Baker County Chamber of Commerce, ☎ 904-259-6433, 20 E. Macclenny Ave., Macclenny, FL 332063.
Branford Area Chamber of Commerce, ☎ 352-935-3722, P.O. Box 674, Branford, FL 32008.
City of Alachua Chamber of Commerce, ☎ 352-462-3333, P.O. Box 387, Alachua, FL 32616.
Gainesville Area Chamber of Commerce, ☎ 352-334-7100, P.O. Box 1187, Gainesville, FL 32602-1187.
Gilchrist County Chamber of Commerce, ☎ 352-463-6327, P.O. Box 186, Trenton, FL 32693.
Hawthorne Area Chamber of Commerce, ☎ 904-481-4436, P.O. Box 125, Hawthorne, FL 32640.
High Springs Chamber of Commerce, ☎ 352-454-3120, P.O. Box 863, High Springs, FL 32655.
Newberry Area Chamber of Commerce, ☎ 352-472-6611, P.O. Box 495, Newberry, FL 32669.
Starke-Bradford County Chamber of Commerce, ☎ 904-964-5278, 202 S. Walnut St., Starke, FL 32091.
Union County Chamber of Commerce, ☎ 904-496-3624, P.O. Box 797, Lake Butler, FL 32054.

Touring

Gilchrist County

You won't spend much time touring because Gilchrist is small and largely undeveloped (less than 10,000 people). Much of what there is to do is going to be covered in the adventures, including returns to Branford and Ginnie Springs and introductions to Otter Springs, Hart Springs, some state preserves and the area's favorite fishing holes.

If you're following our tour circuit from earlier chapters, you can enter the region from Live Oak by taking US 129 south 58 miles, through burgs such as McAlpin, O'Brien, Branford and Bell, an old railroad town that is the smallest of Gilchrist's three incorporated cities. At Highway 26, turn right (west) and drive eight miles to US 19 at Fanning Springs on the Suwannee River. The **Fanning Springs State Recreation Area** is a small wayside park with a few hiking trails, picnic areas and a steel section of the old Suwannee River bridge (circa 1923) replaced a decade ago. If you begin the

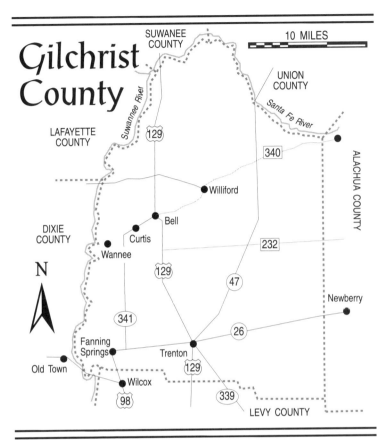

tour by flying or driving into Gainesville, you can get to Fanning Springs by following Highway 26 west 38 miles, through Trenton, the county seat. The highway goes through farm and timberlands.

Alachua County

If you fly into Gainesville, no problem, you're there.

If your landing zone is Jacksonville, the fastest, easiest and most scenic route is to follow I-10 west 25 miles, then go south on US 301 through towns such as Lawtey and Waldo before (43 miles later) reaching the outskirts of Gainesville. (Warning: Waldo is noted for getting a large chunk of its budget from speeders, so pay attention.) If you're marching through Florida chapter-by-chapter, skip Gilchrist County, at least for now, and set your sights on Gainesville

Northern Heartland

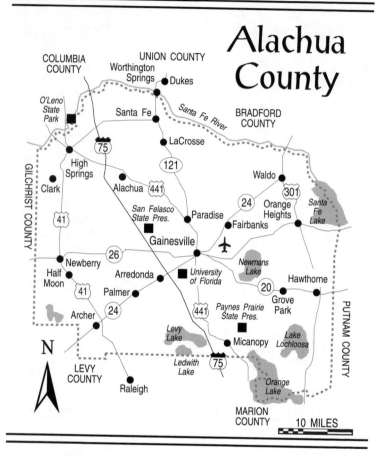

from Lafayette County. Drive the sedan east on US 27 to US 441, then turn left (still east), moving through the university city and continuing (now south) on US 441 for a south-to-north march.

First stop: **Marjorie Kinnan Rawlings State Historic Site**, ☎ 352-466-3672. This is a wonderful tribute to the Cracker lifestyle and to the Pulitzer Prize-winner. Cross Creek sits between Orange and Lochloosa lakes. This is where Rawlings and her first husband, Charles, learned self-sufficiency and the ways of the woods. Rawlings fell in love with rural Florida, as evident in her writings. She died in 1953 at age 57. Her farmhouse has been restored to the way she left it, including her writing spot on the front porch. Park rangers slip into character, giving portrayals of life here during the 1930s and 1940s, reading from the author's works, and providing snippets of trivia about her life. Guided tours also are provided.

The house is closed Mondays, Tuesdays and Wednesdays and throughout August and September for preservation work. To get to the park, turn left (east) off US 441 on Highway 346, go six miles and bear right on Highway 325 for a six-mile trip to the site.

To get to the next stop, the historic town of **Micanopy**, retrace your route on Highways 325 and 346 to US 441, turning left (south) for the one-mile jaunt to Alternate Highway 25. There's a sign directing you to the town, which begins less than one mile in (turn right on Cholokka Boulevard).

You probably remember Sonny Howard and Inez at the **Herlong Mansion**, ☎ 352-466-3322 (see page 88). The stately building, whose core dates to 1845, is at the far end of Cholokka. The main drag, for that matter the only drag, is lined with wonderful old architecture and a healthy collection of antique shops. They include **Sun Glo Farm**, ☎ 352-466-3037 (New England furniture, porcelain, glass), **House of Hirsch Too**, ☎ 352-466-3774 (an old Victorian house filled with collectibles), **Whippoorwill**, ☎ 352-466-4903 (brass, copper, china, rugs) and **Shady Oaks Study Gallery**, ☎ 352-466 0725 (stained glass, jewelry, local art works).

Now it's time to visit **Gainesville**. Take Seminary Street in the center of Micanopy west to Highway 234, turn left for a quick run to Interstate 75, then north for a 12-mile trip to Highway 24 (Archer Road), exiting left under the interstate. Watch on the left for the sign to the **Fred Bear Museum**, ☎ 352-376-2411, less than half a mile from I-75. The museum's late namesake was a world-renowned archer, naturalist and collector of historic treasures. His museum, primarily, though not entirely, dedicated to archery, has a unique assortment of exhibits, from trophies such as bull elephants and Kodiak bears to the evolution of the bow and arrow to thumb rings and arrow points from as early as 2700 B.C. There's also an area where you can watch modern craftsmen and women making 21st-century Bear Archery equipment.

Kanapaha Botanical Gardens, ☎ 352-372-4981, is one-half mile west off Highway 24. Turn right onto S.W. 63rd Boulevard. This is a plant-and flower-lover's paradise. The entrance road is the site of an old American Indian game trail and part of the route naturalist William Bartram took when he explored the area during the time of the American Revolution. Today, the grounds are filled with color and life. One stop is the herb garden (ever see a toothache tree?); another is a classic bamboo garden; a third is the hummingbird garden where the namesakes and butterflies perform aerial acrobatics. The palm hammock has two rare, double-crowned cabbage palms (you're right – that's the Florida state tree); a rock garden features desert plants and textures; while the sunken garden has gingers, ferns and rare Torreya trees flourishing around a sinkhole.

The heart of Gainesville has an incredible selection of historical, cultural, and natural exhibits operated by the city, the private sector and the University of Florida. Historic Gainesville combines a 23-block walking tour and a three-mile windshield tour of the city's past. The start and finish line for the walking tour is the **Thomas Center**, ☎ 352-334-2197, 306 N.E. 6th Ave. The beautifully restored, Mediterranean-style hotel has art galleries, 1920s period rooms, exhibits of the city's history, and it's surrounded by gardens. Other tour stops include the 1897 **H.L. Phifer House**, a Queen Anne cottage built for an early banker and his new bride; the 1897-98 **Bodiford House**, a Victorian with a wrap-around porch; and **Epworth Hall** (1884), a two-story, brick Renaissance Revival structure that began life as a school and later was acquired by First United Methodist Church. For tour maps of the area or information, write to **Historic Gainesville**, P.O. Box 466, Gainesville, FL 32602, or call the **Alachua County Visitors and Convention Bureau**, ☎ 352-374-5231 or **Gainesville Chamber of Commerce**, ☎ 352-334-7100.

The **Samuel P. Harn Museum of Art** at the University of Florida, ☎ 352-392-9826, has continually changing exhibits, including paintings and sculptures from various cultures (African, American and pre-Columbian), cinema, musical and dance performances, workshops and lectures. UF's **Center for the Performing Arts**, ☎ 904-392-2787, features performances that range from Broadway, opera and dance to pop, jazz and classical. UF's **Florida Museum of Natural History**, ☎ 352-392-1721, features a full-size limestone cave, a Mayan palace, skeletons and fossils of some of Florida's earliest residents and an Object Gallery where you can get a close look at hundreds of natural science exhibits.

One last taste of culture before you hit the road again. The **Hippodrome State Theater**, ☎ 352-375-4477, at 25 S.E. 2nd Place, is the former home of the city's post office (1911). It has been restored with a three-quarter round stage, where musicals, drama and improvisational teen theater are performed.

From the Hippodrome, drive west on University Avenue (which starts as Highway 24; make sure you stay straight when Highway 24 splits a diagonal to the left; you're now on Highway 26 or Newberry Road). After seven miles, you'll reach I-75. Turn right (north) one exit to Highway 222 and go right again (east) to the **Santa Fe Community College Teaching Zoo**, ☎ 352-395-5604. Lions and tigers and bears? Oh, no. This is a place where hopeful zookeepers learn from 70 small, less ferocious species. Long-time zoo director Jack Brown explains things this way: "Our students are beginners. Beginners make mistakes. If you make one with a lion or tiger you may not get a second chance." That's why the zoo's menagerie includes caracals, lemurs, otters, Sika deer, alligators, poison dart frogs, gila monsters, bald eagles – in all, 275 mammals, reptiles and birds. Best of all, it's relatively undiscovered (spell that, no crowds) and it's free.

The **Retirement Home for Horses**, ☎ 904-462-1002, has a menagerie of a different sort – unwanted, abused and neglected horses taken in by an English couple, Peter and Mary Gregory, who have a soft spot for our equine friends. At present the farm has more than 70 star boarders. Wendy has wires sticking out of her belly, a reminder of a former life as a research animal; Peanut, the youngest at six years old, is deformed by a hunched back; and Bandit is scarred from a bit that cut deeply into his mouth. The Gregorys, realizing their lifetime dream to provide shelter for such animals, make them two promises. First, they will never be ridden or worked again. Second, they will live out their lives here with TLC – much more than they had at their former homes. Their Mill Creek Farm is open only on Saturdays from 11 am to 3 pm. (If you decide to go, stop at a grocery store along the way and pick up a five-pound bag of carrots. The residents will show their appreciation.) For more information, write the Gregorys at Mill Creek Farm/Retirement Home for Horses, P.O. Box 2100, Alachua, FL 32615-2100.

On deck: **High Springs**. From Alachua, take US 441, beneath I-75, seven miles to this historic railroad town. Platted in 1885, many of High Springs' original wood buildings didn't survive the great windstorm of 1896 or a series of fires that swept the town in the next few years. But it was quickly rebuilt. Its historic district includes **St. Bartholemew's Episcopal Church** (1896), a Gothic structure that has heart-pine and board-and-batten construction; the **Will Godwin House**, an 1890s residence with unique triple gables in the front; the **Priest Theater**, originally built as a car dealership in 1926 but converted into (and still operating as) a theater; the **Roach-Rawls House** (1897), with its classic Southern two-story porches; and the 1896 **High Springs Opera House**, which is now home to the Great Outdoors Trading Co. If you need a shopping break, there are plenty of places to browse, including **Wisteria Corner Antique Mall**, ☎ 904-454-3555; **Greentree Pottery**, ☎ 904-454-1991; **High Springs Antique Mall**, ☎ 904-454-4770; **Country Emporium**, ☎ 904-454-4433; and the **Joy of the Spirit**

Gallery and Tea Room, ☎ 904-454-4930. For information or a map, call or write the **Chamber of Commerce,** ☎ 904-454-3120, P.O. Box 863, High Springs, FL 32643.

OK, it's been a long time since you got a little weird, so aim the nose of your groundship at **The Skin Shop,** ☎ 352-468-1548, in Waldo (speed traps – try to remember them). From High Springs, take US 441 east around 23 miles to Highway 20, bearing to the left (east) three miles to Highway 20, then left again on Highway 24 for the 12-mile journey to Waldo. Dwight McGee owns the shop. This was our nearly normal tickler at the opening of the chapter. Be forewarned though: If you're an animal rights activist, this probably isn't a place to visit. (But one thing to note – most of the once-living things inside either were road-kills or varmints that posed a legitimate threat to human or pet life forms.) Remember the python cummerbund, the toad skeleton bigger than Larry Bird's foot and the raw materials custom-made for Lucchese boots? They're just the appetizers. McGee sells legendary jackalopes mounted on wood plaques, cobra-head belt buckles, 24-foot python skins and the ultimate motorcycle helmet – an armadillo shell, fringed with a generous splash of nondescript fur, accented with a pair of buffalo horns, and topped with an alligator-head crown.

Now it's time to zoom into the sunset, easy rider. Set your compass north-northeast.

Bradford County

Carla's Sandwich Shoppe & Prison Museum, ☎ 904-964-4050 (about six miles west of Starke on Highway 100 – follow the Florida State Prison's signs), is worth a trip if for no other reason than the "hoot" factor. There's a honky-tonk atmosphere and the prison- and death-row memorabilia, but there's also one of Carla's famous hugs. ("Hugs are better than drugs; they chase the blues away.") Things can get a little blunt at times – like her "Burn, Bundy, Burn" T-shirts made to commemorate the 1989 execution of infamous serial killer Ted Bundy. But on the more sedate level, Carla's museum has an ingenious collection of zip guns, crude swords and other unique items taken from prison inmates. If you're a law-and-order type, this is a must.

Of course, despite the proximity of five prisons, it isn't just a penitentiary town. There are plenty of adventure areas that you'll explore later in this chapter, plus some historic structures

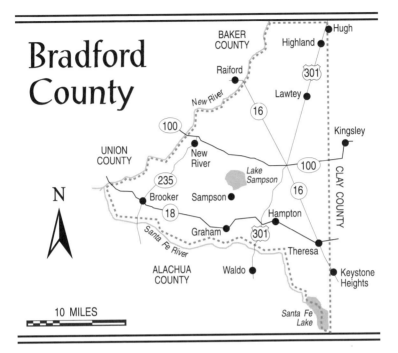

downtown on US 301 (the old courthouse, dating to 1902, and several other buildings that are more than a century old) and good old **Camp Blanding**, ☎ 904-964-3357: This is not only an active Florida National Guard base, but the site of a museum that's a living monument to a World War II training camp (if you weren't around to experience the military at the time, you'll get a strong sense here). The museum and grounds include a memorial to Medal of Honor and Purple Heart recipients, and prisoners of war.

Union County

From Starke, let's take the scenic Highway 100 through the fancy wrought-iron overhead arch that announces you're on your way to Florida State Prison. (Yes, you're busting a gut to go into the prison, but you'll have to take a bye on this run. Maybe in the next book, *Cell Blocks of 21st-Century America*, you'll get inside.) Continue on Hwy 100 west from US 301 in Starke 17 miles, past Carla's again, to its intersection with Hwy 121 and **Lake Butler**, the largest town in the county. If you're up for another tour, there is a nice historic district. Tour stops include the **Odom House** (1890), a

Union County

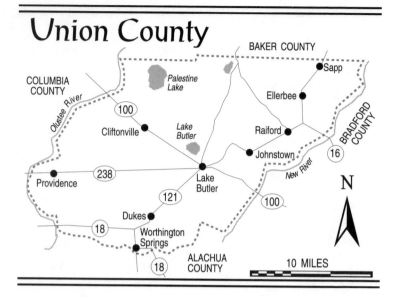

Queen Anne treat with wide porches, an irregular roof, gingerbread trim and 14-foot ceilings; the **Old Jail** (1910), with two cells, iron-grate doors and the distinct look of a giant bread oven; and the **York House** (1872), a Victorian Revival home with big brick chimneys and large porches. You can get a detailed tour map and biography of each site by contacting the **Union County Chamber of Commerce**, ☎ 904-496-3624, P.O. Box 797, Lake Butler, FL 32054.

Baker County

The region's most notable historical event was the Battle of Olustee. On February 20, 1864, Union and Confederate armies met near Olustee, 15 miles east of what is now Lake City. The battle raged for four hours. When it was over, the Union had suffered a stinging defeat. Two thousand of its 5,000 troops were killed, wounded or captured. **Olustee Battlefield Historic Site**, ☎ 904-752-3866, stages an impressive re-enactment each February. The event draws about 2,500 re-enactors, four times as many spectators, and it's considered second only to Gettysburg in magnitude. There's a small interpretive center and a monument. It's located on US 90. From Lake Butler, follow Hwy 238 north seven miles, bearing left on Hwy 229 and going 10 miles to US 90. Turn left. The park is a four-mile drive (on the right) from that point.

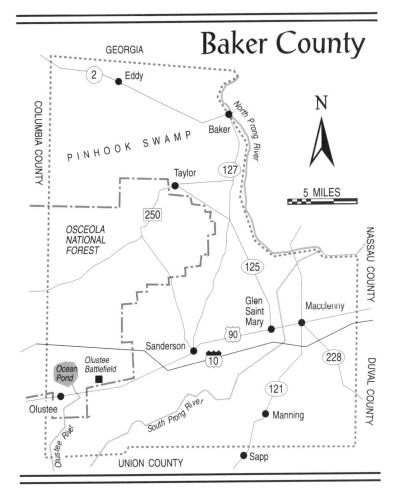

Adventures

On Foot

Let's put some mileage on those walking boots, beginning with the 17-mile **Gainesville-Hawthorne State Trail**, ☎ 352-466-3397 or 352-336-2135. This one is a former railroad line, about equal parts limerock, gravel and pavement. It passes through the marshes, hammocks and flatwoods of Payne's Prairie, Prairie Creek and the Lochloosa Wildlife Management Area, before ending at Hawthorne, near US 301. From University Avenue (Highway 24) in Gainesville, follow S.E. 15th Street south 2½ miles to the city's Boulware Springs Park and the trail entrance.

Payne's Prairie State Preserve, ☎ 352-466-3397, near Micanopy, has a mix of lakes, marshes, prairies and uplands where hikers encounter North Florida's native and not-so-native species. If you're lucky, you may see the preserve's wild horses, American bison or, from mid-October to late November, sandhill cranes that make an extended rest stop here. Payne's Prairie has five designated trails ranging from .3 miles to 8.24 miles, round-trip. Additionally, three ranger-led hikes are available by reservation: a three-mile wildlife walk (Saturdays, November to April), a 3½-mile prairie rim ramble (Sundays, November to April) and a 6½-mile overnight backpack trip (first full weekend each month, November to April). The reservations telephone number is ☎ 352-466-4100. The main entrance to Payne's Prairie is nine miles south of Gainesville on the left (east) side of US 441. But some of the trails are better accessible from the north rim area, the directions to which are the same as to Boulware Springs Park and the Gainesville-Hawthorne Trail in the previous paragraph. If you want maps or more information in advance, call or write the preserve at Route 2, Box 41, Micanopy, FL 32667-9702.

These other state parks in Alachua County have modest hiking trails:

- **O'Leno State Park**, ☎ 352-454-1853, Route 2, Box 1010, High Springs, FL 32643, offers a half-mile trail along the Santa Fe River, a half-miler through pine and hardwood forests to an old limestone quarry and a 3½-mile trail that passes through hammocks, sandhills and wet sinks on its way to the remnants of an old road and dam that served a now-forgotten lumber town. The park entrance is five miles north of High Springs on the east side of US 441.

- **Devil's Millhopper State Geological Site**, ☎ 352-336-2008, 4732 N.W. 53rd Ave., Gainesville, FL 32606, has a one-third-mile trail around the main attraction – a 120-foot-deep sinkhole. Explorations have produced fossils, teeth, bones and shells of animals that lived here thousands of years ago. Follow N.W. 13th Street (US 441) six

miles north of University Avenue (Highway 24) and go left (west) on N.W. 53rd Avenue four miles to the site.
- **San Felasco Hammock State Preserve,** ☎ 352-336-2008, 4732 N.W. 53rd Ave., Gainesville, FL 32606, has a one-mile trail around springs, sinkholes and a large prairie basin. From Devil's Millhopper, take N.W. 53rd Avenue to Highway 232 and turn right, going about four miles to the preserve.

The St. Johns River Water Management District, with the help of other city and state government agencies, has blazed trails in two Alachua County areas:

- **Gum Root Swamp,** ☎ 904-329-4404 or 352-334-2197, has about five miles of trails through an undisturbed hardwood swamp that's thick with cypress knees and wildlife such as bald eagles, wood storks, wading birds, leopard frogs, deer, otters and more. The swamp is located on the east side of Gainesville. You can reach it on Highway 26.
- **Lochloosa Wildlife Conservation Area,** ☎ 352-732-1225 or 904-329-4404, has four-, seven- and 10-mile trails in separate areas of the 10,333-acre tract. The area meanders through the Lochloosa Lake system, the River Styx (this, of course, is the other River Styx – it doesn't get anywhere near Hades), and Cross Creek near the home of Marjorie Kinnan Rawlings. From Micanopy, turn left (east) off US 441 on Highway 346, go six miles and then bear right on Highway 325. All three trail sites are off Highway 325.

Maps and more information can be obtained by calling the water district, or writing to P.O. Box 1429, Palatka, FL 32178-1429.

Additionally, the following Alachua County parks provide trails:

- **Bivens Arm Nature Park,** ☎ 352-334-2056, 3650 S. Main St., Gainesville, 1½-mile trail.
- **Morningside Nature Center,** ☎ 352-334-2170, 3540 E. University Ave. (Highway 26), Gainesville, seven-mile trail and a boardwalk under a cypress dome. This is the site of a turn-of-the-century farm.
- **Westside Park,** 1001 N.W. 34th St., Gainesville, 1½-mile trail.

Moving north into Baker County, arguably the best system in the region is the **Florida National Scenic Trail**'s leg through the **Osceola National Forest**, ☎ 800-343-1882 (Florida only), ☎ 904-752-2577 and 352-378-8823. This 23-mile stretch has access points in two areas. For the full route (that means 46 miles, round-trip, unless you have a road crew), take Highway 121 north from Gainesville 28 miles to Lake Butler, go left on Highway 100, then quickly right on Highway 231 for the 15-mile trip to Olustee and US 90. Turn right (east) and travel just past the battlefield, parking on the right (south) side of the highway, opposite the trail entrance on the left. The aesthetics include mist-shrouded cypress swamps (if you start early), sawgrass marshes interrupted by hardwood hammocks, large pine forests and transparent springs. Twenty boardwalks along the trail provide breaks to watch wildlife, including turkey, deer, grey fox, American swallow-tail kite, red-cockaded and pileated woodpeckers and Bachman's sparrows.

On deck is the **Big Gum Swamp Wilderness Area**, ☎ 904-752-2577, which has a pair of primitive trails worthy of note inside the Osceola National Forest. A 6.2-mile trail begins at an entrance off Highway 262. From US 441 in Lake City, which is 15 miles west of Olustee in Columbia County, go north to Highway 262, turn right or east and go nine miles to the trail entrance. A three-mile loop begins off Highway 250 (from Lake City, take Highway 250 across I-10 about seven miles to the parking area on the right). The scenery includes cypress-gum swamps, pine flatwoods, sloughs and, if you're sharp-eyed, the remnants of a turpentine still.

The **Suwannee River Water Management District**, ☎ 800-226-1066 (Florida only) or 904-362-1001, offers hiking trails at its Lindsey, Beardsley and Koogler tracts, all on the Suwannee River in Gilchrist County. Take Highway 26 about six miles east of Trenton, turn right (north) at Highway 232 (N.W. 70th Avenue) and go 12 miles to the entrances on S.W. 25th Street. For maps or information, call or write the district at 9225 County Road 49, Live Oak, FL 32060.

INFORMATION SOURCES

Florida Trail Association, ☎ 800-343-1882 (in Florida) or 352-378-8823, P.O. Box 13708, Gainesville, FL 32604.
Office of Greenways & Trails, ☎ 904-487-4784, Mail Station 795, 3900 Commonwealth Blvd., Tallahassee, FL 32399-3000.

GOLF COURSES

- **Heritage Links Country Club at Turkey Creek**, ☎ 904-462-4655, 3500 Turkey Creek Blvd., Alachua, FL 32615, 18 holes, driving range, lessons, no PGA rating.
- **Ironwood**, ☎ 352-378-5240, 2100 N.E. 39th Ave., Gainesville, FL 32607, 18 holes, driving range, no rating.
- **Meadowbrook Golf Club**, ☎ 352-332-0577, 10401 N.W. 37th Place, Gainesville, FL 32606, 18 holes, driving range, lessons, R-66.5.
- **Pineview Golf & Country Club**, ☎ 904-259-3447, Highway 23 North, Macclenny, FL 32063, 18 holes, driving range, no rating.
- **University of Florida Golf Club**, ☎ 352-375-4866, 2800 S.W. 2nd Ave., Gainesville, FL 32607, 18 holes, driving range, lessons, R-69.2.
- **West End Golf Club**, ☎ 352-332-2721, Highway 26/Newberry Road, Gainesville, FL 32607, 18 holes, driving range, lessons, no rating.

On Horseback

While riding trails are not as numerous as in the Suwannee Region, there are some scenic places to explore by horse.

The 17-mile Gainesville-Hawthorne State Trail, ☎ 352-466-3397 or 352-336-2135, is an old railroad line that has been surfaced with limerock, gravel and pavement in different areas. It passes through the marshes, hammocks and flatwoods of Payne's Prairie, Prairie Creek and the Lochloosa Wildlife Management Area before ending at the village of Hawthorne, near US 301.

From University Avenue (Highway 24) in Gainesville, follow S.E. 15th Street south 2½ miles to where it ends at the city's Boulware Springs Park and the trail entrance.

Payne's Prairie State Preserve, ☎ 352-466-3397, near Micanopy, has trails through lakes, marshes, prairies and uplands where horses and riders might run into North Florida's native species (deer, turkey, eagles). There's also a chance of seeing the preserve's wild horses, which have roots dating to the days of the Spanish explorers, a small herd of American bison or, from mid-October to late November, sandhill cranes.

The prairie has one designated horse trail, the 6½-mile **Chacala Trail** that runs through shady hammocks and pine flatwoods. This trail is accessible from the main entrance, nine miles south of Gainesville on the left (east) side of US 441.

If you want maps or more information in advance, call or write the preserve at Route 2, Box 41, Micanopy, FL 32667-9702.

Lochloosa Wildlife Conservation Area, ☎ 352-732-1225 or 904-329-4404, has four-, seven- and 10-mile trails within the 10,333-acre tract. They curve through the Lochloosa Lake system, the River Styx and Cross Creek, close to the Marjorie Kinnan Rawlings State Historic Site.

From Micanopy, go left (east) off US 441 on Highway 346 for six miles, and then bear right on Highway 325. All three trail sites are off Highway 325. There are also several graded roads in the area that are available for improvised trails. The site is managed by the **St. Johns River Water Management District**, P.O. Box 1429, Palatka, FL 32178-1429.

The **Suwannee River Water Management District**, ☎ 800-226-1066 (Florida only) or 904-362-1001, offers riding trails at its **Santa Fe Swamp Tract** (Bradford County) and **Lindsey Tract** (Gilchrist County). The **Santa Fe Trail** is on Highway 21 about 10 miles south of Starke.

To get to the Lindsey Tract, which is on the Suwannee River, follow Highway 26 about six miles east of Trenton, turn right (north) at Highway 232 (N.W. 70th Avenue) and go 12 miles to the entrance at S.W. 25th Street. For maps and information, call or write the district at 9225 County Road 49, Live Oak, FL 32060.

San Felasco Hammock State Preserve, ☎ 352-336-2008, 4732 N.W. 53rd Ave., Gainesville, FL 32606, has a trail around springs, sinkholes and a prairie basin. Follow N.W. 13th Street (US 441) six miles north of University Avenue (Highway 24) and turn left (west) on N.W. 53rd Avenue to Highway 232, going right about four miles to the preserve.

O'Leno State Park, ☎ 352-454-1853, Route 2, Box 1010, High Springs, FL 32643, has a 3½-mile trail through hammocks, sandhills and sinks on its way to the remnants of an old road and dam that served a now-forgotten lumber town. The entrance is five miles north of High Springs on US 441. The park has stalls available.

One more note for riders: The **Osceola National Forest** offers nearly 40 miles of primitive trails, mainly in its West Tower district north of Lake City. For information, maps and the hunting seasons (do you really want to go riding when the forest is thick with hunters?), call or write the **District Office**, ☎ 904-752-2577, P.O. Box 90, Olustee, FL 32072.

On Wheels

Six days and 327 miles. Can you handle it?

The **Florida Springs Bicycle Tour** leads through rural back roads, palmetto jungles, oak canopies, cypress swamps and blue-water springs. It passes horse farms and the majestic Suwannee River as it goes through much of north-central Florida. For those who are not out to set endurance records, each of the six days can be tackled as individual legs ranging from 30 to 67 miles. The launching pad is Payne's Prairie, nine miles south of Gainesville on US 441. The six legs are Payne's Prairie to Gold Head Branch State Park in Keystone Heights (63 miles), Gold Head Branch to Olustee Battlefield State Historic Site east of Lake City (67 miles), Olustee to Stephen Foster State Folk Culture Center near White Springs (30 miles), Stephen Foster to O'Leno State Park near High Springs (47 miles), O'Leno to Manatee Springs State Park in Chiefland (58 miles) and Manatee to Payne's Prairie (63 miles). For a comprehensive set of directions for each leg, write to the Office of Greenways & Trails at the address listed in the Information Sources at the end of the cycling portion of this chapter.

In addition to hikers and riders, the 17-mile Gainesville-Hawthorne State Trail, ☎ 352-466-3397 or 352-336-2135, welcomes cyclists. This old railroad line has been resurfaced with limerock, gravel and pavement in different areas. The trail cuts through marshes, hammocks and flatwoods located in Payne's Prairie, Prairie Creek and the Lochloosa Wildlife Management Area, before ending at Hawthorne near US 301. From University Avenue (Highway 24) in Gainesville, follow S.E. 15th Street south 2½ miles to where it ends at the Boulware Springs Park and the trail entrance.

Payne's Prairie State Preserve, ☎ 352-466-3397, has two designated bike trails: the 6½-mile **Chacala Trail** that moves through shady hammocks and pine flatwoods and the 8.24-mile **Cone's Dike Trail** that goes into a marsh. Both trails are accessible from the main entrance on US 441. Additionally, the prairie has a 10-mile, ranger-led mountain bike tour the third Saturday of each month. Make sure to call (☎ 352-466-4100) or write (Route 2, Box

41, Micanopy, 32667-9702) in advance for reservations. They're required, as are helmets.

Lochloosa Wildlife Conservation Area, ☎ 352-732-1225 or 904-329-4404, has a 10-mile off-road trail. It cuts through Lake Lochloosa to Burnt Island. From Micanopy, turn left (east) off US 441 on Highway 346 for six miles, then right on Highway 325. The tract is managed by the **St. Johns River Water Management District,** P.O. Box 1429, Palatka, FL 32178-1429.

The **Suwannee River Water Management District,** ☎ 800-226-1066 (Florida only) or 904-362-1001, offers biking trails at its **Santa Fe Swamp Tract** (Bradford County), **Beardsley Tract** and **Lindsey Tract** (both in Gilchrist County). Santa Fe is located on Highway 21 about 10 miles south of Starke. To get to the Lindsey and Beardsley Tracts, on the Suwannee River, follow Highway 26 six miles east of Trenton, go right (north) at Highway 232 (N.W. 70th Avenue) and go 12 miles to the entrances at S.W. 25th and S.W. 10th streets, respectively. For maps and information, call or write the district at 9225 County Road 49, Live Oak, FL 32060.

While it's not a designated trail, another good ride is to follow the three scenic roads (Alternate 25-A and Highways 325 and 346) that go through Micanopy, Cross Creek and Island Grove. You can access the area either from US 441 (the Micanopy side) or US 301 (the Island Grove side).

Finally, the city of Gainesville has 60 miles of roads with on-street bicycle lanes or paved shoulders and another 17 miles with wide curb lanes. A brochure is available for $2 from the **Traffic Engineering Department,** ☎ 904-334-2130, 3rd Floor, Thomas Center, 302 N.E. 6th Ave., Gainesville, FL 32601.

INFORMATION SOURCES

Office of Greenways & Trails, ☎ 904-487-4784, 325 John Knox Road, Building 500, Tallahassee, FL 32303-4124.
Florida Department of Transportation, ☎ 904-487-9220, Mail Station 82, 605 Suwanee St., Tallahassee, FL 32399-0450.

On Wheels II

Ready for a different kind of spin?

Frank Hawley's Drag School, ☎ 909-392-5925, delivers it. While Hawley is based in California, he comes to the Gainesville

Raceway, home of the Gatornationals, several times a year to teach dragster, funny car and motorcycle racing. They aren't for the weak at heart (you might hit 200 mph in the quarter-mile) or for hot dogs – Hawley doesn't let students near the cockpit or saddle until they're thinking and preaching safety as strongly as he does. One-, two- and three-day classes are available, including some for beginners. For more information, call or write to the school at P.O. Box 484, La Verne, CA 91750-0484.

On Water

CANOEING

There's but one designated trail in the region, the **Santa Fe River Canoe Trail**, but it's a nice, 26-mile course along a gorgeous river lined with hardwood hammocks, springs and swamps. The trail starts where the Santa Fe returns to the surface after a three-mile journey underground. The trail's skill level is rated for beginners and the difficulty rating is easy with a two-three mph current. There are some small shoals during low water times, but most of them are passable. The Ichetucknee River is a tributary of the Santa Fe near the end of the run. You can paddle upstream to **Ichetucknee Springs State Park**, ☎ 352-497-2511. For the full run, take US 441 two miles north of High Springs to the bridge and turn left to a public boat ramp. For a shorter, 13-mile course, take Highway 340 about eight miles west of High Springs, turning right (north) on Highway 47 and go six miles to the bridge.

Other paddling options include **Otter Springs RV Resort**, ☎ 352-463-2696, which offers three- to 35-mile adventures on the Suwannee River. To get there, take Highway 36 west 37 miles from Gainesville to the town of Wilcox and follow the signs to the resort. **Ginnie Springs**, ☎ 800-874-8571 or 352-454-2202, offers runs along the Santa Fe River (from High Springs head west on Highway 340 to the entrance sign), as does **Poe Springs**, ☎ 352-454-1992, which also is on Highway 340 west of High Springs.

Suwannee River canoe launch points also are available at the **Suwannee River Water Management District's Beardsley, Koogler** and **Lindsay tracts**, ☎ 800-226-1066 (in Florida) or 904-362-1001. From Trenton, take Highway 26 six miles east and turn right (north) at Highway 232 (N.W. 70th Avenue). Entrances to the three tracts are at S.W. 25th and S.W. 10th streets.

The **Lochloosa Wildlife and Prairie Creek** conservation areas, ☎ 352-732-1225 or 904-329-4404, feature canoeing on Lake Lochloosa and Prairie Creek, respectively. To get to the Lochloosa area from Micanopy, turn left (east) off US 441 on Highway 346 for six miles, then turn right on Highway 325. Prairie Creek is located five miles southeast of Gainesville on Highway 20. Both of these sites are managed by the St. Johns River Water Management District.

INFORMATION SOURCES

For designated trail maps, write to the **Office of Greenways and Trails**, ☎ 904-487-4784, 325 John Knox Road, Bldg. 500, Tallahassee, FL 32303-4124.
Florida Association of Canoe Liveries & Outfitters, ☎ 941-494-1215, P.O. Box 1764, Arcadia, FL 33821.
Ginnie Springs, ☎ 800-874-8571 or 352-454-2202, 7300 N.E. Ginnie Springs Road, High Springs, FL 32643.
Santa Fe Canoe Outpost, ☎ 352-454-2050, P.O. Box 592, High Springs, FL 32643.
Steamboat Canoe Outfitters, ☎ 352-935-0512, P.O. Box 28, Branford, FL 32008.
Otter Springs RV Resort, ☎ 352-463-2692, Route 1, Box 1400, Trenton, FL 32693.
River Run Campground, ☎ 352-935-1086, Route 2, Box 811, Branford, FL 32008.
Cross Creek Fish Camp, ☎ 352-466-3424, Route 3, Box 126-A, Hawthorne, FL 32640.
Twin Lakes Fish Camp, ☎ 352-466-3194, Route 3, Box 209, Hawthorne, FL 32640.

DIVING/SNORKELING

Two things are going to be familiar if you read the last chapter. One, there is no coast, so the area has no saltwater dives. Second, since some of the best freshwater diving and snorkeling spots straddle the Northern Heartland and Suwannee regions, many of the adventures are repeated. As mentioned earlier, this destination is certifiable as the Cave Diving Capital of Florida – and it's a strong contender for the Spring Diving Capital, too.

Ginnie Springs, ☎ 800-874-8571 or 904-454-2202, is located off the Santa Fe River near the point where Columbia and Gilchrist counties meet. From High Springs, go west on Highway 340 to the entrance sign on the right. This privately run site has a full-service diving center, lodging and some of the most beautiful springs in Florida. Nine springs feature options for open water, cavern and cave divers. The open water area is a large basin that's surrounded by eel grass with a white-sand bottom and an excellent photo opportunity. That's just as true once you swim into the cavern and look back at the silhouettes of the other divers and snorkelers lingering in the basin. The cavern entrance is four to six feet wide, and it leads to two chambers. The first is about 30 feet wide with a nine-foot ceiling, followed by a room, about 60 feet wide and 70 feet long, which angles from a depth of 35 feet to 60 feet. **Devil's Eye Spring** is on the same 200-acre site. Its limestone shaft drops to a sand bottom at 20 feet. A cave entrance, three feet high and 18 feet wide, leads to the dark, 30-by-20-foot room called the "Devil's Dungeon." Certified cave divers can squeeze through a dangerous two-by-four-foot tunnel that leads to a small room and a depth of 65 feet. This isn't a dive for those who aren't certified cave divers! Another spring at the site, "**Little Devil**," doesn't require cave certification and has a 45-foot drop and a beautiful view from the bottom.

Ichetucknee Springs State Park, ☎ 904-497-2511, has nine springs along the 3.2-mile run, which is an excellent snorkeling trip. While diving isn't allowed in the head spring, a tank really isn't necessary since most of the springs are in shallow water, making it easy for anyone to reach the bottom in their search for relics or fossils. From High Springs, follow US 27 northwest 12 miles to Fort White, turn right (north) on Highway 47 for a two-mile drive to Highway 238 and turn left (west) to the park entrance, about two miles in.

Branford is in Suwannee County but some of its best offerings reach into Gilchrist County. They include **Troy Springs**, a large, circular hole with a depth of 75 feet and, on the short run toward the Suwannee River, the ribs of a Civil War-era steamship; **Royal Springs**, a dive that has a depth of 50 feet and a 200-foot run to the Suwannee; **Orange Grove Sink**, another 50-footer that includes a nice cavern with unique limestone formations; and **Yana Springs**, a cavern that has a pair of domed ceilings, a large room and a 40-foot reading on your depth gauge. The best way to launch a Branford diving expedition is to head into town, located on Highway 27, 26 miles northeast of High Springs, and connect with one of the dive shops listed below.

INFORMATION SOURCES

Florida Association of Dive Operators, ☎ 305-451-3020, 51 Garden Cove Drive, Key Largo, FL 33037.
US Coast Guard, Mayport, ☎ 904-246-7315.
Florida Marine Patrol, ☎ 904-359-6580, 2510 Second Ave. N., Jacksonville Beach, FL 32250.
Ned DeLoach's Diving Guide to Underwater Florida, ☎ 904-737-6558, New World Publications, 1861 Cornell Road, Jacksonville, FL 32207.
Ginnie Springs Dive Center, ☎ 800-874-8571 or 904-454-2202, 7200 N.E. Ginnie Springs Road, High Springs, FL 32643.
Branford Dive Center, ☎ 352-935-1141, P.O. Box 822, Branford, FL 32008.
Steamboat Dive Inn, ☎ 352-935-2283, US 27 & 129, Branford, FL 32008.

SALTWATER & FRESHWATER FISHING

Trophies awaiting anglers in the region include some old favorites found in other lakes and rivers across North and Northwest Florida – bluegill, crappie, catfish and the many varieties of bass.

Orange and **Lochloosa lakes,** 10 miles south of Gainesville near the towns of Cross Creek and Island Grove, are good spots for trophy bass (10 pounds and over) in January, February and March. Black crappie, bluegill and redear sunfish are abundant here, too.
Newnans Lake, which is 1½ miles east of Gainesville, is a good spot for largemouth bass in February and March. It's accessible on three area highways – 20, 26 and 234.

Lake Samson and **Lake Rowell** in Bradford County are helped by hydrilla (yes, it's a navigation problem, but your prey loves it). The best time for bluegill is May through July, when they're spawning. Black crappie bite best in these lakes the last two weeks of February. From Starke, follow Highway 100 west six miles to Sampson Trestle Road and the lakes.

Santa Fe, Altho and **Hampton lakes** benefit from fish attractors, vegetation transplanting and sunshine bass restocking. Largemouth, redear, crappie, bream and bluegill also are plentiful in these lakes. Santa Fe is located on Highway 21, two miles north of Melrose (15 miles east of Gainesville). Altho is on US 301 at Waldo; Hampton is five miles north of Waldo (take US 301 to Highway 18, turn left and you're there).

Payne's Prairie State Preserve, ☎ 352-466-3397, located nine miles south of Gainesville on US 441, has fishing available and a ramp at Lake Wauberg. The **St. Johns River Water Management District**, ☎ 904-329-4404, courts anglers with its **Lochloosa Wildlife** and **Gum Root Swamp** conservation areas (maps as well as additional information can be obtained by calling or writing to P.O. Box 1429, Palatka, FL 32178-1429). Last but not least, the **Suwannee River Water Management District**'s **Beardsley, Koogler, Lindsay** and **Santa Fe tracts** have some good fishing spots, too. For maps and information, ☎ 800-226-1066 (in Florida) or 904-362-1001, or write to 9225 County Road 49, Live Oak, FL 32060.

By the way, don't forget the Suwannee River. Gilchrist County's stretch of the river has two records – Suwannee bass (3.89 pounds) and redbreast sunfish (2.08 pounds).

Fish camps and boat rental spots?

Griffin's Lodge (☎ 904-475-1444; Route 2, Box 512, Melrose, FL 32666) is on Santa Fe Lake, offering boats and motors, guides, a ramp, bait, lodging and an area for campers. **Twin Lakes Fish Camp** (☎ 352-466-3194; Route 3, Box 209, Hawthorne, FL 32640) has boats, guides, bait and access to lakes Lochloosa and Orange at Cross Creek. **Cross Creek Lodge** (☎ 352-466-3228; Route 3, Box 124, Hawthorne, FL 32640) provides ramps, bait, guides and boats.

Don't forget to pick up a fishing license. Non-resident freshwater licenses cost $15 for a week and $30 for a year. There are size and bag limits on several species. Information on these is available from bait-and-tackle shops, guides, or the **Florida Marine Patrol**, ☎ 904-359-6580, 2510 Second Ave. N., Jacksonville Beach, FL 32250, or the **Florida Game & Fresh Water Fish Commission**, ☎ 904-758-0525, Route 7, Box 440, Lake City, FL 32055-8713.

WATER SKIING

Just in case you want to get another kind of thrill – and perhaps a natural aquatic enema if you don't wear a ski suit and are lazy enough to drag your keister – consider hauling yours over to the **Cleveland Ski School & Training Center**, ☎ 352-481-2152, on Lake Jeffords in Hawthorne. If you know the sport and want to pick your own lake (but forgot to pack skis), stop by **Alachua Marine**, ☎ 352-373-7862, 4031 N.W. 6th St. in Gainesville, for rentals.

In The Air

Another teaser early in the chapter, another punchline here: Hot-air ballooning.

Bill Folkert's place (**Wet Willie's Balloon Team**), ☎ 352-481-3626, is based in Hawthorne, but most of his lift-offs are from Ocala (see page 263), with some in the Gainesville area. The 60- to 90-minute flights in the Ocala area give adventurers a bird's-eye view of the area's beautiful horse farms and forests. It's not unusual to see deer from tree-top level. On clear days, he'll shoot to 3,000 feet, where you can see the Atlantic Ocean and the Gulf of Mexico.

Wendy and Bill Pearson's **Personal Flight Ballooning**, ☎ 352-378-6223, will give you an overhead view of the Gainesville area, and a champagne punch-line at the end of your flight.

Where To Stay & Eat

Gilchrist & Alachua Counties

Three things about the Herlong Mansion, ☎ 352-466-3322, in Micanopy:

Sonny Howard doesn't tell his Inez story until after the first breakfast, just in case first-night guests are a bit skittish about ghosts. His breakfasts include several egg recipes, homemade bread and muffins, fresh fruits and juices, and more. And he has an incredible 200-cane collection that includes walking sticks from around the world.

Shady Oak Bed & Breakfast, ☎ 352-466-3476, is another taste of yesterday kept alive in Micanopy. This warm 19th-century three-story mansion comes with five suites (one with a widow's walk, another with a claw-foot tub and yet another with a mirrored headboard for romantics), wide porches and two large common areas for those who want to get acquainted with their neighbors.

Moving to Gainesville and keeping the B&B theme for a moment, consider **Sweetwater Branch Inn** (circa 1885), ☎ 800-451-7111 or 352-373-6760, located at 625 E. University Ave.

Sweetwater combines Southern hospitality with Victorian elegance that features six large rooms (each with private bath and claw-foot tub) and a completely tranquil atmosphere. **Magnolia Plantation**, of the same vintage, ☎ 352-375-6653, 309 E. Seventh St., is named for the lusty trees that surround this inn. It features six rooms (sleigh beds, claw-foot tubs, four-posters and more), 10 fireplaces, a mahogany staircase and breakfasts in a dining room or on the front or back verandas.

Gainesville's more modern accommodations include the **Radisson**, ☎ 800-333-3333; **Cabot Lodge**, ☎ 800-843-8735; **Comfort Inn**, ☎ 800-228-5150; **Days Inn**, ☎ 800-325-2525; **Econo Lodge**, ☎ 800-424-4474; **Hampton Inn**, ☎ 800-426-7866; **La Quinta**, ☎ 800-531-5900; and, if you're looking for more modestly priced lodgings, **Budget Lodge**, ☎ 352-331-1601, or **Super 8**, ☎ 352-378-3888.

Moving north to High Springs, there are two offerings: **Grady House Bed & Breakfast Inn**, ☎ 904-454-2206, is a five-room house (dating to 1917) with porches, swings and plenty of wildlife to encounter. **The Great Outdoors Inn**, ☎ 904-454-2900, is a six-room pit stop that offers porches, rocking chairs and 40 acres where you can pick wild blackberries.

If you want to stay the night in Gilchrist County, there's the **Cadillac Motel**, ☎ 352-463-2188, located near the Suwannee River in downtown Fanning Springs; the **Suwannee Gables**, ☎ 352-542-7752, in Old Town; the **Suwannee River Cove**, ☎ 352-935-1666, in Branford; and the **Crystal Oaks Motel**, ☎ 352-463-7214, back in Fanning Springs.

By now, with all this reading, you've worked up an appetite. Good. You'll need one in Gainesville.

Want to go Latin? **Emiliano's Café and Bakery**, ☎ 352-375-7381, provokes your appetite with spicy mango salmon, paella, roast pork loin glazed with honey and cilantro and some of the best Latin pastries you ever put your lips around. At **Amelia's**, ☎ 352-373-1919, the cuisine turns to Italian favorites – such as baked ziti with mozzarella and ricotta, veal scaloppine and flounder in a plum tomato sauce with capers and olives. Elegance in the form of great steaks and seafood is what brings diners to the **Sovereign Restaurant**, ☎ 352-378-6307, while **Harry's Seafood Bar & Grille** has an open-air atmosphere and a menu that speaks for itself.

High Springs? Don't miss a meal at **The Great Outdoors Trading Co. and Café**, ☎ 904-454-2900. Brunch is the featured attraction (belly-busting omelets and Everglades French toast – grilled in egg batter with plenty of cinnamon sugar and maple syrup and jam). Accessories include pancakes, country biscuits and, you better try these in Florida, down-home grits.

In Gilchrist County, it's a little less formal, but you can get your belly full at the **Lighthouse Restaurant**, ☎ 352-463-2644, in Fanning Springs; **Atkins Grill**, ☎ 352-463-6859, in Bell; or **Trenton Café**, ☎ 352-463-1609, in, you guessed it, Trenton.

Bradford County

Starke is a little more basic when it comes to lodging, mainly moderately priced chains and mom-and-pop accommodations where frills are replaced with neighborliness. Choices range from the **Best Western Motor Inn**, ☎ 904-964-6722, **Days Inn**, ☎ 904-964-7600, and **Budget Inn**, ☎ 904-964-7143, to the **Bradford Motel**, ☎ 904-964-5332, **Jo-Lu Motel**, ☎ 904-964-8810, and **Sleepy Hollow Motel**, ☎ 904-964-5006.

At meal time you'll run into the some of the national chains, a few regional ones, such as **Sonny's Real Pit Barbecue**, and a sprinkling of one-of-a-kinders – such as **Carla's Sandwich Shoppe & Prison Museum**, ☎ 904-964-4050.

Campgrounds

But, honey, I want to sleep under the stars.

No problem.

Ginnie Springs Resort, ☎ 800-874-8571 or 904-454-2202, in High Springs, features primitive campsites, 55 sites with electric and water hook-ups, RV pull-throughs, a heated bath house, covered pavilions, hiking trails and canoe, tube, scuba and snorkeling rentals at its on-site dive shop. At **Hart Springs**, ☎ 904-463-6486, Gilchrist County operates a recreation park (fishing, boating, swimming) that includes water and electric hook-ups, primitive sites, a dump station, grills, hot showers and dressing rooms.

Moving east, Alachua County has several options.

Cross Creek Fish Camp, ☎ 352-466-3424, has 16 RV sites with hook-ups, six cottages and three tent sites. **Cross Creek Lodge**, ☎ 352-466-3228, offers 12 RV sites and seven motel rooms. **Finway Fish Camp**, ☎ 352-481-2114, located in Hawthorne, provides 35 RV sites, 10 campsites and seven cabins. **Twin Lakes Fish Camp**, ☎ 352-466-3194, in Hawthorne, has 15 full hook-ups, three cottages,

20 campsites and showers. And **High Springs Campground**, ☎ 904-454-1688, offers large shady pull-throughs with full hook-ups.

In Starke, where the name doesn't do justice to the scenery, you can park it at **KOA Kampground**, ☎ 904-964-8484, which features full hook-ups, tenting sites, a pool, showers, a playground, restrooms, laundry facilities and a grocery.

State parks?

Payne's Prairie State Preserve, ☎ 352-466-3397, in Micanopy, offers 35 RV spots with electric hook-ups, 15 tent sites, showers, grills and a playground. You also can camp-in at **O'Leno Springs State Park**, ☎ 904-454-1853, in High Springs, where for groups there are 18 cabins, a dining hall and kitchen.

Additionally, the **Suwannee River Water Management District**, ☎ 800-226-1066 in Florida or 904-362-1001, has primitive canoe trail camping available at its **Beardsley, Koogler** and **Lindsey tracts** on the Suwannee River if you first get a special-use permit. Call the district for details or write to 9225 County Road 49, Live Oak, FL 32060.

OK, after a good night's rest, a hearty breakfast and a last check for maps and undies left lying about, it's time to jump-start the starship, beat the compass into submission and head to the Northeast.

Northeast Florida

Of course, being attentive students of the adventure game, you remember King Ferdinand and his lovely daughter, "Juana the Mad," from page 61. When you last met Ponce de Leon, their slightly wayward explorer, he was desperately blowing the king's fortune and searching for the "fountain of youth" in the Central Panhandle. Well, Ponce slept around a lot, including here, on that ill-fated quest.

Discounting plastic surgery, which probably was discovered in California and only has short-term success, the secret of eternal life has never been found, unless you're into that Bela Lugosi thing. That doesn't stop at least three Florida locations from staking a claim to the fountain, including **St. Augustine**, which has a more legitimate right to say it's America's oldest, continuously occupied city. It was established by the Spanish in 1565, about a half-century after a quiver of blunt-tipped arrows and other unpleasant natural elements (giant mosquitoes, fire-breathing cockroaches and ill-tempered rattlesnakes) convinced Ponce to high-tail it back to the governor's mansion in Puerto Rico. Alas, a short while after his exit he bought the farm, adding a significant obstacle to Spanish royalty's dreams of sticking around.

Still, Ponce de Leon and his followers left us something. There is no place in Florida where the heritage runs deeper and richer. Sure, St. Augustine has its tourist side (sometimes gaudy attractions, fast-fooderies and neon distractions), but many of its structures are made of an ancient coquina and coral shell mixture that has stood up to the centuries – not to mention an uncommon amount of cannon shot. St. Augustine seems to have the oldest *everything* in Florida: the oldest jail, the oldest school, the oldest house, the oldest store and even the oldest alligator farm. But not the oldest bar. Uh-uh. At least not the oldest, continuously operated bar. That honor goes to the town of **Fernandina Beach**, in the northeastern corner of the state. It's the home of the **Palace Saloon**, a century-old gentleman's tavern that was a favorite haunt for seafarers and, when the Rockefellers unwound on nearby **Cumberland Island**, for many of America's wealthiest businessmen. Its swinging front doors form a time tunnel. Through them, the 40-foot oak-and-black-mahogany bar is as friendly as it was when it arrived after the World's Fair of 1904. The carved buxom maidens that support its weathered mirror are as flirtatious as they were when yesterday's barkeeps used them in a unique scheme to get tips from unwitting seamen. If they could toss a coin so as to make it stay on the maidens' attributes they won the night's haul. But the most noteworthy, if somewhat reclusive, fixture may be Uncle Charlie, a bartender at the Palace for 54 years, who in death (if you're a believer) is the tavern's resident spirit.

Fort Clinch, now a state park, is another postcard from the past. Work on this 4½-million-brick fortress began in 1847, but it was never completed. During the Civil War, it was held by both Confederate and Union troops who, despite its strategic location on the Atlantic Ocean and St. Marys River, never fired a single cannonball – not even in practice. Today, Florida Park Service rangers such as George Berninger bring back the heyday. Eight hours a day, five days a week, he's a grunt in Uncle Sam's First New York Engineers, even if it means wearing authentic wool trousers, linen shirt and wool jacket in the 97° summer sun. His interpretation of this era is as much entertainment as education. When visitors stop by the quartermaster's supply room, Berninger tells them they can choose among four flavors of hardtack:

"Plain, mold, weevils and mold with weevils."

You want aesthetics?

The coast south of Fernandina Beach reaches deeper into **Amelia Island**, a barrier finger where modern resorts snuggle against marshes, hammocks and swamps. Here, some believe cutthroats such as Blackbeard and Captain Kidd buried unimaginable treasures. **American Beach**, a key stop on the Black History Trail, is a transition zone between yesterday and today. If you're lucky, you might run into MaVynee Betsch, a free-spirited environmentalist who will: a) give you a lesson in black culture, b) make a pitch on behalf of the endangered whales and butterflies, and c) let you know her given name was MarVynee, but she dropped the "R" because she wasn't real happy about President Reagan's environmental policies or (as she puts it) the lack thereof. If you decide to track down MaVynee be prepared for the visuals. She carries 14-inch fingernails in a plastic bag, and her salt-and-pepper hair, somewhere near 14 feet of it, is shaped like the Niger River and adorned with dozens of funky buttons making statements such as "No Nukes" and "Save the Whales."

Big Talbot Island State Park is an honor system stop that has a dramatic beach carved by erosion and adorned with large driftwood formations. **Mayport** is the home of some of America's mightiest warships, while **Jacksonville Beach** is one of the region's two tourist meccas but also a great adventuring base.

Moving inland, the **St. Johns River** is one of the state's most beautiful and natural waterways. It's also unique in that it runs south to north, going from east-central Florida to the Northeast. There are several idyllic hamlets along the way, but otters, ospreys, sabal palms and cypress stands are far more common than any signs of man's handiwork. With a few exceptions, development is restricted to spotty homes and rustic getaways such as **Gateway Fish Camp**, a time warp that's set in the woodlands, just north of where the river meets Lake George. By the way, if you make it to Gateway, don't miss a voyage on the **Fort Gates Ferry**, the eighth or ninth version of a crossing service that began more than a century ago. Today's rendition is a tiny tug-like boat called the *Too Wendy* that has a metal-barge sidecar (big enough for four cars or 18 Harleys) and a canine first mate that answers to the name "T.S. Skipper."

Big Talbot Island.

Adventures? Heck, yes. You can fish, kayak, sail, jet-ski, windsurf and go up in a hot-air balloon. Hiking trails? Eat a lot of carbs, because there are plenty of trails, and if you don't like the designated ones, there's mile after mile of beachfront on which to improvise. There are two designated canoe trails and some ad libbers. You can horseback ride on designated trails or even go for a ride on the beach at Seahorse Stables. Bicyclists can catch the easternmost leg of that six-day, 327-mile Florida Springs Bicycle Tour, as well as some shorter routes. Last, but not least, there is saltwater diving. Off Jacksonville Beach, the dive crowd can savor natural and artificial reefs, sunken freighters and tugs, or the Lost Phantom, an F4-A that slipped off a carrier deck (oops, there went a Navy career) and into a 102-foot grave.

The five-county region has four state parks, two state forests and several water management district tracts that provide plenty of additional (spell it, cheap) adventures. But before you barnstorm into this mix, take a few minutes to learn a little more about the area's turf and heritage.

Geography & History

The inland areas of Nassau, Duval, Clay, St. Johns and Putnam counties put on faces that are similar to the other regions of North and Northwest Florida. The interior is dotted with moderate hills, timberlands, farms, sloughs, hardwood hammocks, springs and a prairie or two. The St. Johns River, because of a lack of development in all but its northernmost parts, lends a vision of Old Florida, where backwoods camps, fishing boats and riverfront retreats are about the only intrusions on nature. Wildlife? For the most part, you're going to encounter pretty much the same mammals that have crossed your path in the other regions (river otters, raccoons, opossums, white-tail deer and more), as well as the customary assortment of wading birds and sunbathing reptiles, especially on the St. Johns.

The Atlantic Coast areas are more developed, particularly at Fernandina Beach, Jacksonville Beach, St. Augustine and, to a lesser degree, some parts of Amelia Island. The barrier islands, the Intracoastal Waterway and the beaches are distinct portions of the coastal geography, as are tall sand dunes and sea oats.

Historically, Northeast Florida was inhabited at least as early as 500 B.C. by the Timucuan Indians but, like most of the rest of Florida's north, was probably the home of Native Americans 10,000 years ago or longer. The age of colonization started in 1513 with Ponce de Leon's visit. Fernandina Beach on Amelia Island has had eight flags flying above it since Frenchman Jean Ribault landed here in 1562. The French, Spanish and British often traded occupations because of the area's significance as a port. In 1821 it became a US possession with the rest of Florida. Along the way, this section of coastline has been a haven for pirates, a bustling cargo port and a commercial fishing center, the latter giving birth to a shrimping industry that continues to thrive today.

Jacksonville's history traces to a short-lived French Huguenot colony called "La Caroline" in 1564 and, until 1821, it was occupied by the French, Spanish and British, like Amelia Island and St. Augustine to the south.

The Spanish colonized St. Augustine 42 years before Jamestown and 55 years before the Pilgrims landed at Plymouth Rock. Actually, the Spanish tried to gain a foothold in Florida five times after Ponce de Leon's visit, but each of them failed. The sixth time was the charm, maybe because the Spanish had a little more incentive this time: The 1564 French fort on the St. Johns River was considered to be a threat to King Philip II's treasure ships, so he sent Don Pedro Menendez de Aviles, who set up the colony on August 28, 1565, the Feast Day of St. Augustine. The Spanish had a pretty easy time kicking out the peace-loving Timucuans. The French were sent packing, as well. But St. Augustine was a prize not easily kept over the next 200 years. Englishman Sir Francis Drake attacked and burned the town in 1586, and pirate captain John Davis plundered it during 1668. But the Spanish built two forts to discourage such exuberance: Castillo de San Marcos (in 1695) and Fort Matanzas (in 1742). Eventually, though, Spain was intercepted, and the keys to the city landed in a British cornerback's hands in 1763. Spanish rule returned in 1783 for 37 years before Florida was sold to the United States as a territory.

Although Florida sided with the Confederacy during the Civil War, the city of St. Augustine was occupied by Union forces through most of the war. Its birth as a tourist spot came in the 1880s, when capitalist and railroad pioneer Henry Flagler developed the city and Anastasia Island as a resort for the leisure set.

Now, before you arrive, a few snippets of historical trivia you won't find in the history (or other guide) books:

- An Italian sculptor carved the two kings of beasts on the historic Bridge of Lions. (Today, it's the bridge that leads to Anastasia Island State Recreation Area, 24 miles of beaches and luxury resorts.) But he forgot to carve the tongue on one of his subjects and the ear on the other. He was the object of such ridicule from the townsfolk that he stabbed himself to death with a blunt sculpting knife.
- Datil chilies, which have a reputation as the fieriest in the country, have been grown here since 1777, when the Minorcans brought them from their small island off the coast of Spain. How hot are they? Hot enough that just one pepper usually is enough to blaze a lasting memory on the toughest tongue and palate.
- Yankee Beach, a name bestowed by the locals, is the first small strip of white-sand beyond the Bridge of Lions on Anastasia Island. From Flagler's days to the present, it's often been cluttered with Northerners who aren't aware that, beyond it, there are 24 miles of less crowded beaches lined with sabal palms, sea oats and sand dunes.

Getting Around

Jacksonville International Airport, ☎ 904-741-4902, is served by eight major airlines and four regionals.

Ground travel is easy, more so in the coastal areas, thanks to interstates, US highways and a good secondary road system. Interstate 10 is an east-west feeder through the center of the region, from Baldwin to Jacksonville and Atlantic Beach. Interstate 95 runs north-south from the Florida-Georgia border in Nassau County, through Jacksonville (I-295 forms a loop around the city congestion) and points south. A1A is the primary beach route throughout the region, moving from Fernandina Beach on the north end, through Atlantic and Jacksonville beaches, then Ponte Vedra, St. Augustine and Crescent Beach. US 1 runs north-south a bit further inland, occasionally intertwining with I-95, while US 17 parallels the St. Johns River, running north-south through the heart of the region.

Weather: There's a slight deviation from the last few chapters since you're back in coastal Florida. The summer average is consistent through much of this region – about 82 to 84°, maybe a shade warmer on the western fringes or among the concrete and highrises of downtown Jacksonville. Expect 10 to 12 high-humidity, high-90s days, but rarely one reaching to three digits. The winters average 52 to 56°, with perhaps two to four days in the high teens to low twenties. Chilly, but it isn't Grand Rapids.

INFORMATION SOURCES

Amelia Island Tourist Development Council, ☎ 800-226-3542 or 904-277-0717, 102 Centre St., Fernandina Beach, FL 32035.
Clay County Tourist Development Council, ☎ 904-284-6300, P.O. Box 1366, Green Cove Springs, FL 32043.
Jacksonville and The Beaches Convention & Visitors Bureau, ☎ 800-733-2668 or 904-798-9148, 3 Independent Drive, Jacksonville, FL 32202.
St. Johns County Visitors & Convention Bureau, ☎ 904-829-1711, 88 Riberia St., Suite 250, St. Augustine, FL 32084.
Clay County Chamber of Commerce, ☎ 904-264-2651, 1734 Kingsley Ave., Orange Park, FL 32073.
Jacksonville Chamber of Commerce, ☎ 904-366-6600, 3 Independent Drive, Jacksonville, FL 32202.

Greater Nassau County Chamber of Commerce, ☎ 904-879-1441, P.O. Box 98, Callahan, FL 32011.
Putnam County Chamber of Commerce, ☎ 904-328-1503, P.O. Box 550, Palatka, FL 32178-0550.

Touring

Nassau County

First stop: **Fort Clinch State Park**, ☎ 904-261-4212. If you're coming from Jacksonville International Airport, jump aboard I-95 and go north 16 miles to the A1A exit, turning right (east) for 18 miles to Fernandina Beach. The Fort Clinch entrance (look for the signs) is just west of where A1A ends at Atlantic Avenue.

If you're following a chapter-by-chapter itinerary, take I-10 at Macclenny 22 miles east to I-295, going left (north-northwest) 18 miles to I-95, then go left (north) again on I-95 to the A1A exit and use the directions from that point that are listed in the previous paragraph (A1A to Atlantic Avenue).

There is a small museum and store near the parking area, and a nature trail leads through a coastal hammock and huge dunes to the fort site. The interpretive programs and personal amenities are what sets this fort apart from many others. Ranger George Berninger's repertoire and the fort's period furnishings give a stark, though accurate, picture of a soldier's life in the 1860s.

"Let me give you some advice, ma'am," he warns a woman who has a cast on her arm. "Do not take yourself to the surgeon. His motto is: 'Lemme cut that off so it won't hurt anymore.' "

Speaking of the surgeon, if you can "convince him you're sick, you can get four ounces of whiskey a day. You don't need to be sick – you just need to be convincing."

And speaking of whiskey, "We worry when the preacher comes with the 'do-gooder' women. You know what I mean. Temperance women. We promise to drink no more," then with a wink, he confides in a whisper, "no less, either."

In addition to the daily interpretations, the fort has candlelight tours every Friday and Saturday evening. The first weekend every month (all day Saturday, half a day Sunday) 40 volunteers stage a larger demonstration of daily routines in the surgeon's office,

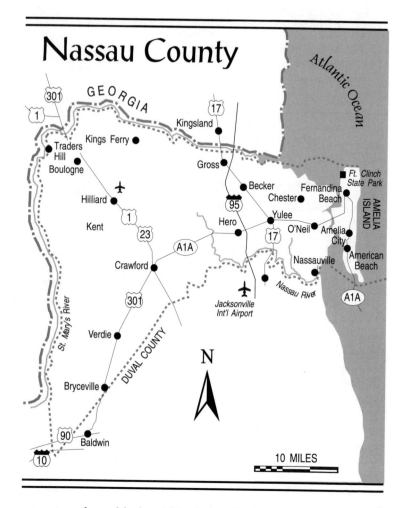

carpentry shop, blacksmith's forge, kitchen and several other mid-18th-century work stations that have been recreated.

Leaving the fort, turn right on Atlantic Avenue for a short drive to historic Fernandina and Centre Street (the extension of Atlantic Avenue). One sure-fire stop is the **Amelia Island Museum of History,** ☎ 904-261-7378, at 233 S. 3rd St., just off Centre. The museum, located in the former county jail, offers guided oral history tours led by docents, who retrace the island's development through eight flags. One room shows life aboard the Spanish treasure ships; another reveals archaeological finds from the region; and others focus on Fernandina's heyday, in the latter 19th and early 20th centuries. Docents also lead walking and driving tours of the historic in-spots, by appointment for groups of four or more. Another option is hitching a ride aboard the giddy-ups at **Historic Tours,** ☎ 904-277-1555, which let you roll through downtown, Old Town and Fort Clinch by horse-drawn carriage. Or, get a map at the tourist council office, ☎ 800-226-3542 or 904-277-0717, 102 Centre St., and set off by yourself. The tour circuit includes the chance to quench your thirst (and maybe bump into Charlie) at the **Palace Saloon,** ☎ 904-261-6320, 117 Centre, which began life in 1878 as a haberdashery; the **Florida House Inn,** ☎ 904-261-3300, 22 S. 3rd St., whose guest ledger (since opening in 1857) has the signatures of Ulysses S. Grant, Cuban patriot José Marti and the Rockefellers – who weren't quite sober enough to make it back to the mansion on Cumberland Island; and the **Fairbanks House,** ☎ 800-261-4838, 227 S. 7th St., a splendid Victorian home built in 1885 by renowned architect Robert S. Schuyler and now a bed-and-breakfast. The tour route also includes the **Classical Revival First Presbyterian Church** (1860) and the Mediterranean-style **Villa Las Palmas** at the corner of Alachua and North 4th Street, which was built in 1910 by lumber baron N.B. Borden for his bride. One other retreat stop before you leave Fernandina – Burbank Trawl Makers behind Standard Marine, ☎ 904-261-3671, at 101 N. 2nd St., is a place where you can see the third generation of Burbanks make shrimp nets by hand, like their grandfather did a century ago.

Heading south on A1A (Fletcher Avenue), watch for the sign directing you to turn left to **American Beach**. This village was established in 1930 by Abraham Lewis, founder of the Afro-American Insurance Co. There are no phone numbers or advance reservations here. The beach is well beyond its resort prime. Today, there are about 40 full-time residents. Down at the water the **Ocean Rendezvous** still stands. In its day, jazz greats such as Charlie Parker, Cab Calloway and Ray Charles cut their musical teeth at the club. American Beach is one of nine stops on the **Black Heritage Trail,** ☎ 800-733-2668, which includes Kingsley Plantation, Edward Waters College and Mt. Zion A.M.E. Church. For a map, call or write to the **Jacksonville & The Beaches Convention & Visitors Bureau,** 3 Independent Drive, Jacksonville, FL 32202. A final note before leaving American Beach – if you run into MaVynee Betsch, she'll be happy to answer the question:

Why do the best seashells open to the left?

(The answer has something to do with her politics.)

On the south end of the island, beyond the environmentally aware resort of Amelia Island Plantation, you'll encounter the wild side. Dunes, palms, scrub thickets and moss-bearded oaks are the order of the day here. You may see a sign, just before the bridge, to Seahorse Stables. You'll come back when you go horseback riding later in the chapter.

For now, though, wagons ho!

Jacksonville

DUVAL & CLAY COUNTIES

A three-pack of state properties as you drive down A1A as it merges with Highway 105: Big Talbot Island, Little Talbot Island

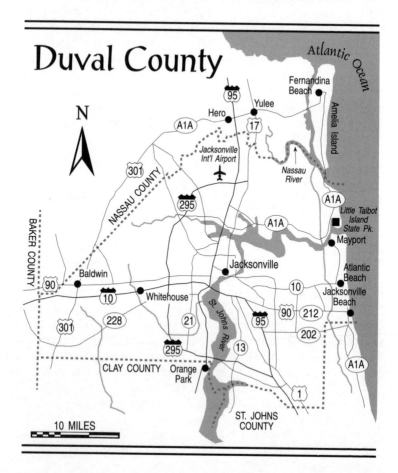

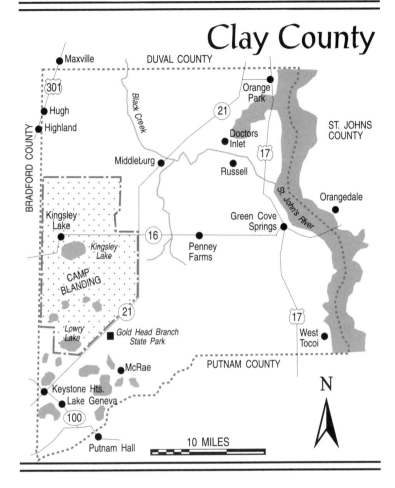

and Fort George Island. **Big Talbot Island State Park**, ☎ 904-251-2320, is the one with some spectacular bluffs carved by erosion, 11½ miles of undeveloped trails, the ruins of two plantations, huge driftwood formations on the beach and five marked trails that wind through dunes, salt marshes, tidal creeks and wet prairie. **Little Talbot Island State Park**, ☎ 904-251-2320, is another part of the 2,500-acre, undeveloped barrier island. It's a bird-lover's paradise (nearly 200 species are known to inhabit it), and there are five miles of white-sand beaches, plus a 4.1-mile hiking trail. **Fort George Island State Cultural Site**, ☎ 904-251-2323, has oyster-shell mound mementos of the Timucuan Indian settlement that date back thousands of years. The

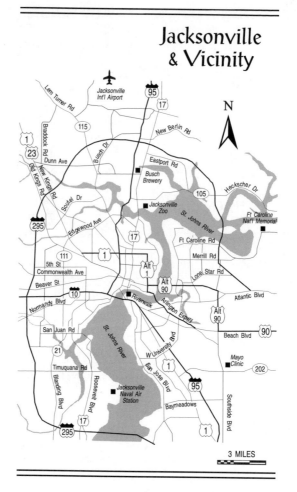

Jacksonville & Vicinity

island also has a 4.4-mile trail up **Mount Cornelia** (don't get a rush – it's only 65 feet above sea level) and **Kingsley Plantation**, ☎ 904-251-3537. Kingsley, along the Avenue of Palms, offers a taste of 19th-century Florida plantation life. It was built by Zephaniah Kingsley, whose slaves produced sugarcane and sea-island cotton. The site includes the original plantation house, as well as the ruins of 23 tabby slave quarters. As mentioned earlier, the plantation is a stop on the Black Heritage Trail.

There's one eco-friendly stop to hit before you move a little south. Back at Big Talbot Island, **BEAKS** (Bird Emergency Aid and Kare Sanctuary), ☎ 904-251-2473, is a public-access center that raises and cares for thousands of injured or deformed wild birds including bald eagles, ospreys, pelicans and owls. It's open to the public, but call in advance for reservations.

If you take A1A south across the St. Johns River, where it separates from Highway 105, there are a pair of military installations (one past – one present) to cure any cravings in that realm. **Fort Caroline National Memorial**, ☎ 904-641-7155, is a shrine to the short-lived French Huguenot settlement in 1564. The park has a replica of the fort, a museum of French and Native American artifacts and a trail. **Mayport Naval Station**, ☎ 904-270-5226, offers a peek at a 21st-century, high-tech fort. It's home to 13,000 sailors and the aircraft carrier *USS John F. Kennedy*, as well as cruisers, destroyers and frigates. Public tours can be arranged, but don't expect them to take you out for a test drive.

Need a shot of culture? There are a lot of quick fixes, and the **Jacksonville & The Beaches Convention & Visitors Bureau**, ☎ 800-733-2668 or 904-798-9148, at 3 Independent Drive, Jacksonville, FL 32202, and **Jacksonville Chamber of Commerce**, ☎ 904-366-6600, (same address), will be happy to send a city map with easy directions to any of the following and more:

- **Cummer Museum of Art and Gardens**, ☎ 904-356-6857, at 820 Riverside Drive, celebrates Florida's history through the art work of Winslow Homer, Louis Tiffany and Thomas Moran, among others. Its 12 galleries feature an impressive collection of Western paintings from 2000 B.C. to the day before yesterday. The museum also has lush gardens on the St. Johns River.
- **Jacksonville Maritime Museum**, ☎ 904-355-9011, on the riverwalk, has ship models, paintings, old photographs and artifacts related to the maritime industry, from 1842 through the near present.
- **Museum of Science and History**, ☎ 904-396-7062, offers several exhibits, including the Civil War-era ship *Maple Leaf*, "Atlantis Tails," which examines five marine mammals that inhabit (or migrate through) Northeast Florida, and several other displays – such as cutting edge magnetic technology, a peek at the invisible forces around us and "Kidspace," an interactive area where children learn about science through hands-on toys. If those aren't enough, there's a planetarium and a 1,200-gallon aquarium at the site.

Before you load the cannons and aim south-southeast, consider one more stop that's not exactly an adventure (unless you go ballistic and jump in with the resident wildlife) – **Jacksonville Zoological Gardens**, ☎ 904-757-4463. Its Birds of the Rift Valley is a free-flight aviary, a 1,200-foot boardwalk snakes through an East Africa exhibit and the interactive shows include "Let's Talk to the Animals," "Raptor Rap" and "Elephant Encounters." In all, there are 500 animals, including the rare and surely non-indigenous (to Florida) white rhinoceros. Maybe it's a blessing it isn't one of our natives – imagine the impact it could have on your hiking adventure.

Ignitions cranked? Southward bound.

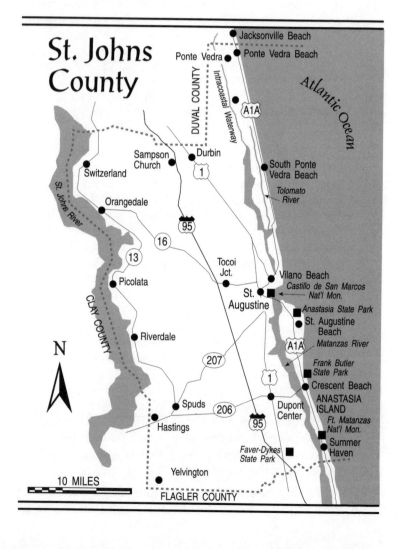

St. Augustine

ST. JOHNS & PUTNAM COUNTIES

From Jacksonville, do a stutter step, run a slant pattern right (southwest), and buttonhook at Palatka. In mapmaker's lingo, that means skip the interstates and take US 17 south 47 miles to the Putnam County seat, where the hotspots include **Ravine State Gardens,** ☎ 904-329-3721, an 85-acre park that boasts a two-mile drive/cycle/walk trail around the scenic namesake ravines; the **Welaka Fish Hatchery and Aquarium,** ☎ 904-467-2374, which features the freshwater gamefish you could land if you decide to sportfish in this neck of the woods; and the **David Browning Museum,** ☎ 904-329-5538, where you can see a model train exhibit and photos, documents and memorabilia from Florida's railroading past.

From Palatka, follow US 17 southeast across the St. Johns River to the point where it meets Highway 309 (about 13 miles), and turn right (south) for the eight-mile run to **Gateway Fish Camp,** the **Fort Gates Ferry** and one of the more scenic places to view the river. There's not much reason to hop aboard the ferry unless it's for the pure experience. This isn't a sightseeing ferry, and your route doesn't lend itself to any great adventures close to the other side. Rather, the driving path would take you down eight teeth-rattling miles on a washboard national forest road and another 18 on a paved forest road before you came near anything but hunting lands. But this is a place to kick it back at the fish camp, drop a line for a bass, and maybe sip a cool one. Besides, ride or not, you'll meet T.S. Skipper and the ferry master, Richard Cothron, because they own the place. If you decide simply to park it, you can help them watch the far side for customers, who call the ferry by pulling onto the ramp and flashing their headlights.

From the fish camp, follow Highway 309 back to US 17, turn left and go three miles to Highway 207, turn right (north) and travel 26 miles to US 1 (left), which skirts the west side of St. Augustine.

How can you tour the city? Let us count the ways:

- ❏ By horse-drawn carriage (**Colee's Sightseeing Carriages,** ☎ 904-829-2828, and **Gamsey Carriage Co.,** ☎ 904-829-2391).

- By open-air trolleys or sightseeing trains (**St. Augustine Historical Tours**, ☎ 904-829-3800, and **St. Augustine Sightseeing Trains**, ☎ 904-829-6545).
- By boat (*Matanzas Queen*, ☎ 904-471-0116, and **Scenic Cruise**, ☎ 904-824-1806).
- On your own.

The special effects are pretty overwhelming for history freaks: 144 blocks of houses and buildings on the National Register of Historic Places – which equals precisely 12 miles, shoulder to shoulder. The center of the district is on St. George Street, which lies a few blocks east of US 1, and many of the pit stops are on St. George and two other north-south streets, the Avenida Menendez (Marine Street) and San Marcos, a couple of west-east thoroughfares (King and Castillo) or over the Bridge of Lions,

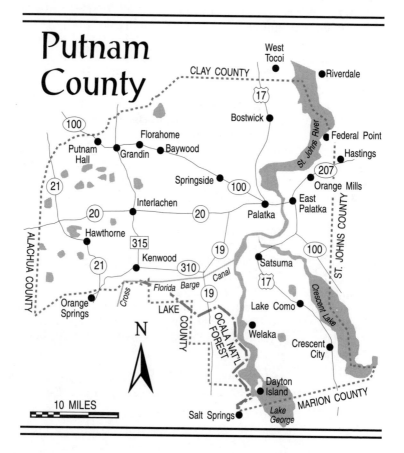

which leads the way to Anastasia Island. If your pleasure is self-guided touring, ask for a detailed map from the **St. Johns County Visitors & Convention Bureau**, ☎ 904-829-1711, 88 Riberia St., Ste. 250, St. Augustine, FL 32084.

First, let's tackle the official "oldest" stuff, which starts with the marvelous brick streets, tabby cottages and coquina-and-coral buildings (topped with red-clay roofs) that are throughout the historic district. **Castillo de San Marcos**, ☎ 904-829-6506, was erected between 1672 and 1695 and is the nation's oldest and last surviving masonry fort. It guarded Matanzas Bay from English invasion and is a designated national monument. Interpreters tell its tales, while re-enactors fire cannons from ramparts that are surrounded by moats and outer works. The **Gonzalez-Alvarez House** (built in 1727), ☎ 904-824-2872, recreates life from the 1700s to Henry Flagler's times; the **Oldest Wooden Schoolhouse** (1763), ☎ 904-824-0192, is a cypress-and-red-cedar structure where lessons continue to be taught; the **Oldest Store Museum** (1840), ☎ 904-829-9729, is literally stuffed with 100,000 antiques from lace corsets and Edison phonographs to high-wheeled bikes and a steam tractor; and the **Old Jail** (1891), ☎ 904-829-3800, has scores of exhibits recalling its 63 years as the local pokey.

This is a place rich with Spanish military, religious and social influences. The **Spanish Quarter** (1740), ☎ 904-825-6830, is a living-history village that features spinning, blacksmithing, woodworking and other trades; the **City Gate** (1808) is the ruins of a defensive wall that served as the entrance to the city; the **Mission of Nombre de Dios** (1565), ☎ 904-824-2809, whose 208-foot cross is visible from more than 25 miles at sea, marks the place where the first Catholic Mass was said in the New World; and **Fort Matanzas** (1742), ☎ 904-471-0116, is a tower built off Anastasia Island to protect the inlet from pirates and British warships. If you choose to visit Matanzas, it's accessible only by boat. Those who don't bring a boat can find a number of tours on the waterfront.

St. Augustine has an abundance of museums, too.

The **Lighthouse Tower & Museum on Anastasia Island** (1887), ☎ 904-829-0745, has nautical mementos, a video of the lightkeepers' tasks and – if you're up to it – a 219-step climb to its lantern room, with a spectacular view of the Atlantic Ocean and the historic district. The **Lightner Museum** (1888), ☎ 904-824-2874, was Flagler's elaborate resort spa; now it houses substantial collections, including cut glass, cloisonné vases, Jumeau wood-jointed dolls and a music room. **Government House Museum** (1598), ☎ 904-825-5033, has early European exhibits such as a 16th-century ship's hold and gold and silver pieces salvaged from treasure-ship wrecks. As the name suggests, the **Museum of Weapons & Early American History,** ☎ 904-829-3727, features a varied collection of firearms including a feathered Indian rifle used in the Battle of Little Big Horn. And finally, for those with a quirky streak, the **Tragedy in the US Museum,** ☎ 904-829-1711, let's you see the Buick in which actress Jayne Mansfield was decapitated (ugh) or the bullet-riddled, almost-a-getaway-car of Bonnie and Clyde.

St. Augustine's plays and festivals range from the stately to the strange.

The headliner is Florida's official state play, **Cross and Sword,** ☎ 904-471-1965, a symphonic drama depicting the settlement of St. Augustine by Spanish colonists. It's held every night except Monday, June through September, in the amphitheater on Anastasia Island. **Menendez Day,** ☎ 904-825-1010, honoring the guy who founded the city, is held in February; **Drake's Raid,** ☎ 904-829-9792, in June, recreates Sir Francis' attack; and **Spanish Watch Night,** ☎ 904-824-9550, retraces by torchlight the procession of the 1740s Spanish garrison with a stop (ignoring history a little) at the 1797 Cathedral Basilica and a conclusion at the Castillo de San Marcos. Ready for a three-pack of less serious festivals? First up is the **Cabbage & Potato Festival,** ☎ 904-692-1420, which, each April, turns the nearby town of Hastings into a mecca for cloggers, gospel singers and spuds-and-cabbage connoisseurs. Also each April, there's a birthday bash for Queen Isabella (she turned Ferdinand into a widower when she saw Ponce's expense voucher), ☎ 800-653-2489; it's celebrated by a large number of locals and tourists. Last, but far from least, the **Great Chowder Debate,** ☎ 800-653-2489, puts reputations on the line with a battle of the chowders (conch, clam, crab, lobster and scallop).

The **Fountain of Youth,** ☎ 800-356-8222, is a national archaeological park that has artifacts of the first mission and colony, the burial grounds of Christian Indians and a spring, but there's no evidence of anyone walking away immortal. **Zoradyda Castle,** ☎ 904-824-3097, a replica of Spain's "Alhambra," exhibits the impressive treasures and lifestyles of the Moorish monarchs.

The **Alligator Farm,** ☎ 904-824-3337, is as Old Florida tourist-trendy as the roadside orange juice stands. This puppy opened in 1893 and features "land of crocodiles," which has all 22 species from around the world. One of the original stars was Gomek, 17 feet and 1,700 pounds of raw reptilian eating machine. Unfortunately, this native New Guinea crocodile passed on of old age in 1997. There are 2,000 or so alligators at the farm as well, though you don't need to come here to find one. Hike (not too close) any marsh or paddle any backwoods river and you're bound to encounter one. The state is literally crawling with them. But these are not crocs. The only native species, the American crocodile, is in very short supply in South Florida.

You've ventured onto **Anastasia Island** a couple of times already. To reach it take King Street east from US 1, one mile (the distance is shorter by catching King off Riberia, St. George or Avenida Menendez) to the **Bridge of Lions**. Try to remember two things. First, the Carrara marble lions are sculpted after those of the Loggia dei Lanzi in Florence – please, ignore the sculptor's screwups with the lions, so he can rest in peace. Second, go beyond Yankee Beach. Your reward, in addition to some of the already mentioned tour stops, is **The Anastasia Island State Recreation Area**, a delightful 1,700-acre bird sanctuary that has five miles of beaches (of a total shoreline of 24 miles), lagoons, sabal palms and sea oats growing wild out of 20-foot dunes.

One more quick touring option: **Ponte Vedra Beach**, about six miles north of St. Augustine on A1A, is a barrier island with some of the highest dunes (up to 40 feet) in Florida. The island also is home to the **Guana River State Park**, which has five miles of coastline, ancient Spanish wells and a 2,000-year-old Indian shell mound. This is another area you'll get back to once you start adventuring.

Speaking of which... it's about time.

Adventures

On Foot

Think of it as spring training. You can warm up with the 30-block walking tour of **Old Fernandina**, which combines the town's historic scenery with a bit of exercise. The tour begins on Centre Street, just east of the docks, at the depot of Florida's first cross-state railroad. A detailed itinerary, including descriptions of historic sites, is available at the **Amelia Island Tourist Development Council**, ☎ 800-226-3542 or 904-277-0717, 102 Centre St., Fernandina Beach, FL 32035.

Amelia Island Plantation, ☎ 800-874-6878 or 904-261-6161, a 1,250-acre, environmentally sensitive resort on A1A near the island's southern tip, has more than 10 miles of hiking and jogging trails through uplands, dunes and marshes.

East of Jacksonville, straddling the Nassau-Duval County line, **Cary State Forest**, ☎ 904-693-5055, has 18 miles of marked forest trails. The best time to see some of the forest's wildlife (deer and raccoons to wild hogs and, occasionally, a black bear) is near sunrise or sunset. The main entrance is on US 301 about 12 miles south of Callahan and six miles north of Baldwin. Maps are available by calling or writing the forest office, 8719 W. Beaver St., Jacksonville, FL 32220.

Trails also are available at three state properties on A1A in northeastern Duval County, about 13 miles south of Fernandina Beach and 14 miles north of Jacksonville Beach. **Big Talbot Island State Park**, ☎ 904-251-2320, has bluffs carved by erosion, a trail along 11½ miles of primitive beach and five other marked trails through dunes, salt marshes, tidal creeks, and prairies. **Little Talbot Island State Park**, ☎ 904-251-2320, a bird metropolis, has some five miles of beaches and a 4.1-mile hiking trail. **Fort George Island State Cultural Site**, ☎ 904-251-2323, offers a 4.4-mile trail through shell mounds to the summit (again, it's all of 65 feet above sea level) of Mount Cornelia. For maps or more information on the Talbot Island parks, call or write to

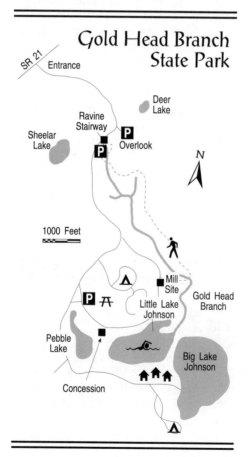

12157 Heckshire Drive, Jacksonville, FL 32233. If you want to know more about the Fort George Island park, call or write to 11676 Palmetto Ave., Fort George Island, FL 32232.

Jennings State Forest, ☎ 904-693-5055, is a spot where you can improvise along several miles of unimproved roads. Scenics include dome swamps, black water streams, ravines and the scores of mammal, reptile and bird species that are common to North Florida. To reach the forest, follow US 301 south from Jacksonville 13 miles to Highway 218, turn left (east) and travel about six miles to the entrance on the left. For maps and additional information, call or write to the **Division of Forestry**, 8719 W. Beaver St., Jacksonville, 32220.

Gold Head Branch State Park, ☎ 904-473-4701, has four marked trails that total about 1½ miles one-way. They pass sandhills, a steep ravine, springs, lush vegetation and an old mill. The park (6239 Highway 21, Keystone Heights, FL 32356) is in Clay County. To get there from Jacksonville, follow Highway 21 south 42 miles to the park entrance. The park also has a 3.2-mile section of the Florida National Scenic Trail.

Welaka State Forest, ☎ 904-467-2388 (P.O. Box 174, Welaka FL 32193-0174), has several trails that weave through a mosaic of wetlands, hammocks, flatwoods, sandhills and bayheads. Trails can be tackled individually (.6 miles to 4½ miles) or combined for 12 miles of hiking. The forest is about 65 miles south of Jacksonville. Take US 17 through Green Cove Springs and Palatka, then turn right onto Highway 309 at Satsuma for the six-mile drive to the forest.

Guana River State Park, ☎ 904-825-5071 (2690 South Ponte Vedra Blvd., Ponte Vedra Beach, FL 32082), has nine miles of old service roads between the Intracoastal Waterway and the Atlantic. The park is about 13 miles north of St. Augustine on A1A.

The **St. Johns River Water Management District**, ☎ 904-329-4404, has trails available at four sites in the region:

- The **Bayard Point Conservation Area**, on the St. Johns River just east of Green Cove Springs, has 18 miles of trails along the river and inland. To get there, take US 17 south of Green Cove Springs to Highway 16, turn right (east) and go 2½ miles to the entrance.
- **Caravelle Ranch Conservation Area**, also on the St. Johns near Palatka, has 17 miles of trails along the Cross

Florida Greenway. From Palatka, go south on Highway 19 about 20 miles to the entrance.
- The **Dunns Creek Conservation Area** provides 4½ miles of trails through Long Swamp. From Palatka, follow US 17 south five miles to Highway 100 and go left about four miles to the entrance.
- **St. Marys River State Forest** has about 15 miles of trails in northeastern Nassau County, along the St. Marys River and the Florida-Georgia border. From Fernandina Beach, take A1A west 23 miles to US 1 and 23 at Callahan, turn right (north) 19 miles to Boulogne and go right 1.2 miles on Lake Hampton Road to the entrance.

One warning before you move on: Any time you venture into a state forest (not a state park) or conservation area, there's a chance of encountering hunters. Call or write in advance for hunting seasons as well as a detailed booklet on the district's properties (P.O. Box 1429, Palatka, FL 32178-1429).

INFORMATION SOURCES

Florida Trail Association, ☎ 800-343-1882 (in Florida) or 352-378-8823, P.O. Box 13708, Gainesville, FL 32604.
Office of Greenways & Trails, ☎ 904-487-4784, Mail Station 795, 3900 Commonwealth Boulevard, Tallahassee, FL 32399-3000.

GOLF COURSES

- **Baymeadows Golf Club**, ☎ 904-731-5701, 7981 Baymeadows Circle W., Jacksonville, FL 32256, 18 holes, driving range, lessons, PGA rating R-70.2.
- **Blue Cypress Golf & Country Club**, ☎ 904-744-2122, 4012 N. University Blvd., Jacksonville, FL 32211, 18 holes, no rating.
- **Champions at Julington Creek**, ☎ 904-287-4653, 1111 Durbin Creek Blvd., Jacksonville, FL 32259, 18 holes, driving range, lessons, no rating.
- **Cimarrone Country Club**, ☎ 904-287-2000, 2690 Cimarrone Blvd., Jacksonville, FL 32259, 18 holes, driving range, R-68.7.

Adventures 215

- **Deerfield Lakes Golf Club**, ☎ 904-879-1210, Route 4, Callahan, FL 32011, 18 holes, driving range, lessons, R-68.2.
- **Dunes Golf Club**, ☎ 904-641-8444, 11751 McCormick Road, Jacksonville, FL 32225, 18 holes, lessons, R-69.2.
- **Fernandina Beach Golf Club**, ☎ 904-277-7370, 2800 Bill Melton Road, Fernandina Beach, FL 32034, 27 holes, driving range, lessons, no rating.
- **Golf Club of Jacksonville**, ☎ 904-779-0800, 10440 Tournament Lane, Jacksonville, FL 32222, 18 holes, driving range, lessons, R-68.
- **Hyde Park Golf Club**, ☎ 904-786-5410, 6439 Hyde Grove Ave., Jacksonville, FL 32210, 18 holes, driving range, lessons, R-68.8.
- **Jacksonville Beach Golf Club**, ☎ 904-249-8600, 605 S. Penman Road, Jacksonville Beach, FL 32250, 18 holes, driving range, lessons, R-70.5.
- **Keystone Heights Golf & Country Club**, ☎ 904-473-4540, Highway 21 S., Keystone Heights, FL 32656, 18 holes, driving range, no rating.
- **Mill Cove Golf Club**, ☎ 904-646-4653, 1700 Monument Road, Jacksonville, FL 32225, 18 holes, driving range, lessons, R-67.9.
- **Palatka Golf Club**, ☎ 904-329-0181, 1715 Moseley Ave., Palatka, FL 32177, 18 holes, driving range, lessons, R-66.
- **Palm Valley Golf Club**, ☎ 904-285-8978, 1075 Palm Valley Road, Ponte Vedra Beach, FL 32082, nine holes, no rating.
- **Ponce de Leon Golf & Conference Center**, ☎ 904-829-5314, 4000 US 1 N., St. Augustine, FL 32095, 18 holes, driving range, lessons, R-68.6 (and no promise of eternal life, but a hope for par).
- **Ravines Golf Club**, ☎ 904-282-7888, 2932 Ravines Road, Middleburg, FL 32068, 18 holes, driving range, lessons, R-70.
- **Reynolds Golf Club**, ☎ 904-284-3502, 659 Highway 16, Green Cove Springs, FL 32043, nine holes, driving range, lessons, R-70.
- **St. Johns County Golf Club**, ☎ 904-825-4900, 4900 Cypress Links Blvd., Elkton, FL 32033, 18 holes, driving range, lessons, R-71.2.

❏ **West Meadows Golf Club,** ☎ 904-781-4834, 11400 West Meadows Road, Jacksonville, FL 32221, 18 holes, driving range, lessons, R-68.1.

❏ **Windsor Parke Golf Club,** ☎ 904-223-4653, 4747 Hodges Blvd., Jacksonville, FL 32224, 18 holes, no rating.

On Horseback

The same warning for hikers applies to the horse crowd – some of the best trails for riding in the region are in state forests and conservation areas, where hunters may be encountered. Call or write in advance for hunt season dates and detailed maps of the trails.

Welaka State Forest, ☎ 904-467-2388 (P.O. Box 174, Welaka FL 32193-0174), has the 6½-mile **Sandhill Horse Trail** that loops through sandhill stands of long-leaf pines and wiregrass. The trail is removed from hunting areas. Welaka also has a 72-horse stable, training arenas and a show area. The site is about 65 miles south of Jacksonville (follow US 17 through Green Cove Springs and Palatka, then turn right on Highway 309 at Satsuma for six miles).

The 18 miles of hiking trails in the **Cary State Forest,** ☎ 904-693-5055 (8719 W. Beaver St., Jacksonville, 32220) also are open to horseback riders. The main entrance is on US 301, 12 miles south of Callahan on the Nassau-Duval County line.

You can ride at five St. Johns Water Management District sites, ☎ 904-329-4404, (P.O. Box 1429, Palatka, FL 32178-1429).

The **Bayard Point Conservation Area,** located on the St. Johns River just east of Green Cove Springs, has seven miles of horse trails near the river. Take US 17 south of Green Cove Springs to Highway 16, turn right (east) and go 2½ miles to the entrance.

Caravelle Ranch Conservation Area, also on the St. Johns near Palatka, has 17 miles of trails along the Cross Florida Greenway. From Palatka, go south on Highway 19 about 20 miles to the entrance.

The **Dunns Creek Conservation Area** provides 4½ miles of trails through Long Swamp. From Palatka, follow US 17 south five miles to Highway 100 and go left about four miles to the entrance.

St. Marys River State Forest has about 15 miles of trails in northeastern Nassau County, along the St. Marys River and the Florida-Georgia border. From Fernandina Beach, take A1A west 23 miles to US 1 and 23 at Callahan, turn right (north) 19 miles to

Boulogne and go right 1.2 miles on Lake Hampton Road to the entrance.

Jennings State Forest, ☎ 904-693-5055 (8719 W. Beaver St., Jacksonville, 32220), has a three-mile equestrian trail along Yellow Water Creek, passing some of the site's ravines and Nolan Ridge Cemetery. Take US 301 south from Jacksonville 13 miles to Highway 218, turn left (east) and go six miles to the forest on the left.

Amelia Island State Recreation Area, ☎ 904-251-2320 (c/o The Talbot Islands GEOPark, 11435 Fort George Road E., Fort George, FL 32226) has some scenic trails, the best of which is operated by a concession, **Seahorse Stables,** ☎ 904-261-4878, which conducts guided beach rides.

Remember: Florida requires a negative Coggins if you bring horses.

On Wheels

Here's one more place to tackle all or part of the **Florida Springs Bicycle Tour,** designed as up to a six-day, 327-mile assault of some of the state's most scenic roads.

The tour leads through rural back roads, palmetto jungles, oak canopies, cypress swamps and blue-water springs. It passes horse farms and the majestic Suwannee River as it goes through much of north-central Florida. For those who aren't after endurance records, each of the six days can be tackled as individual legs ranging from 30 to 67 miles. To get a detailed set of directions for each of the legs, call or write to the Office of Greenways & Trails at the address listed in the Information Sources at the end of the cycling portion of this chapter.

In this region, the tour begins at **Gold Head Branch State Park,** ☎ 904-473-4701. From Jacksonville, follow Highway 21 south 42 miles to the park entrance. The attack plan: Gold Head to Olustee Battlefield State Historic Site (67 miles), Olustee to Stephen Foster State Folk Culture Center (30 miles), Stephen Foster to the O'Leno State Park (47 miles), O'Leno to Manatee Springs State Park (58 miles), Manatee Springs to Paynes Prairie State Preserve (63 miles) and finally Paynes Prairie back to Gold Head (63 miles).

Guana River State Park, ☎ 904-825-5071 (2690 South Ponte Vedra Blvd., Ponte Vedra Beach, FL 32082), has nine miles of old service roads between the Intracoastal Waterway and the Atlantic. The park is located about 13 miles north of St. Augustine on A1A.

You can cycle at three St. Johns Water Management District sites, ☎ 904-329-4404 (P.O. Box 1429, Palatka, FL 32178-1429); all of them have off-road trails. As was the case in our hiking and riding adventures, it's smart to contact the district in advance about hunting seasons so you're out of the line of fire.

The **Bayard Point Conservation Area**, on the St. Johns River just east of Green Cove Springs, has nine miles of trails on the river side of the tract. Follow US 17 south of Green Cove Springs to Highway 16, turn right (east) and go 2½ miles to the entrance.

The **Dunns Creek Conservation Area** has a three-mile trail along a tram road through Long Swamp. From Palatka, take US 17 south about five miles to Highway 100 and go left about four miles to the entrance.

St. Marys River State Forest has two-mile and five-mile bicycle trails. To get to the forest from Fernandina Beach, follow A1A west 23 miles to US 1 and 23 at Callahan, turn right (north) 19 miles to Boulogne, then go right 1.2 miles on Lake Hampton Road to the entrance.

As is the case for hikers, **Jennings State Forest**, ☎ 904-693-5055, is a spot where you can improvise along several miles of unimproved roads. The scenery includes swamps, black water streams, ravines and a lot of mammal, reptile and bird species common throughout North and Northwest Florida. Follow US 301 south from Jacksonville 13 miles to Highway 218, turn left (east), then travel six miles to the forest on the left. For maps and additional information, call or write to the Division of Forestry, 8719 W. Beaver St., Jacksonville, FL 32220.

If you're in the market for guided touring, **Outdoor Adventures** in Jacksonville offers two-to five-day adventures ranging from a 67-mile outing to a 150-miler. There also are shorter trips. Peddling options include routes through Fernandina Beach, Fort Clinch and St. Augustine. To get further information, call ☎ 904-393-9030, or write to 1625 Emerson St., Jacksonville, FL 32207.

INFORMATION SOURCES

Office of Greenways & Trails, ☎ 904-487-4784, 325 John Knox Road, Building 500, Tallahassee, FL 32303-4124.

Florida Department of Transportation, ☎ 904-487-9220, Mail Station 82, 605 Suwanee St., Tallahassee, FL 32399-0450.

On Water

CANOEING

Cock your paddles. You're going to begin with two designated state trails, then visit several other places where you can ad lib a route.

The **St. Marys River Canoe Trail** is a 51-mile run rated beginner and easy in the skill and difficulty categories, respectively. The current is two-three mph. The run follows the gentle curves of the river through hardwood forests that are inhabited by ospreys, herons and egrets. You also might see a deer or bear. For the whole run, you're going to have to drive a little beyond the region's western limits. From downtown Jacksonville, take US 90 west 23 miles to Macclenny, then turn right (north) on Highway 121 and continue 5½ miles to the bridge. For a 30-mile trip, take A1A 23 miles west of Fernandina Beach to US 1, turning right (north) and driving 12 miles to Hilliard and Highway 115, traveling west six miles to Highway 121, then right (north) 2½ miles to the first graded road on the left (north) of Dunn Creek and following the road to the landing.

The **Pellicer Creek Canoe Trail** is an easy four-mile course with virtually no current (zero-one mph). It winds through a tidal marsh where canoeists usually see wading birds, waterfowl, alligators, otters and raccoons. Bald eagles also nest in the area. The current is slow enough so that you can paddle upstream for a round-trip. From St. Augustine, travel US 1 south 17 miles to the bridge at Pellicer Creek.

Gold Head Branch State Park, ☎ 904-473-4701 (6239 Highway 21, Keystone Heights, FL 32356), has a delightful path of more than one mile down the branch to Little Lake Johnson. There are a couple of spurs to explore within 1,500 feet of the beginning of the run, several springs and the ravines. There's a concession where you can rent canoes in the summer. From Jacksonville, take Highway 21 south 42 miles to the park entrance.

Fort Clinch State Park, ☎ 904-261-4212, and **Little Talbot Island State Park**, ☎ 904-251-2320, have some nice canoeing opportunities in their tidal creeks. Fort Clinch is just west of where A1A runs into Atlantic Avenue in Fernandina Beach. Little Talbot Island is on A1A about six miles north of Mayport.

There are two canoeing sites in the St. Johns Water Management District, ☎ 904-329-4404, (P.O. Box 1429, Palatka, FL 32178-1429):

- **Bayard Point Conservation Area** (St. Johns River). Follow US 17 south from Green Cove Springs to Highway 16, turn right (east) and go 2½ miles to the entrance.
- **Stokes Landing Conservation Area** (Tolomato River). Take US 1 north from St. Augustine six miles to Venetian Boulevard (right), go right again on Old Dixie Road and left on Lakeshore Drive to the entrance.

Jennings State Forest features canoeing on Black Creek and several adjoining branches. Take US 301 south from Jacksonville 13 miles to Highway 218, turn left (east), then travel six miles to the forest. For maps and more information, call ☎ 904-693-5055, or write to 8719 W. Beaver St., Jacksonville, FL 32220.

Outdoor Adventures, ☎ 904-393-9030, in Jacksonville, has several guided adventures, ranging from half- to multi-day trips on waterways including the St. Marys and Suwannee rivers. While a few tours are by canoe, many are in kayaks because the trips lend themselves to more stable craft.

INFORMATION SOURCES & ADDITIONAL OUTFITTERS

For designated trail maps, write to the **Office of Greenways and Trails**, ☎ 904-487-4784, 325 John Knox Road, Bldg. 500, Tallahassee, FL 32303-4124.

Florida Association of Canoe Liveries & Outfitters, ☎ 941-494-1215, P.O. Box 1764, Arcadia, FL 33821.

Seminole Canoe & Kayak Club, ☎ 904-287-2820, 4619 Ortega Farms Circle, Jacksonville, FL 32210.

Surf Station, ☎ 904-471-9463, 1020 Anastasia Blvd., St. Augustine, FL 32084.

Pier 17 Marina, ☎ 904-387-4669, 4619 Roosevelt Blvd., Jacksonville, FL 32210.

DIVING/SNORKELING

Inhale deeply and smell the salt air. You're finally back to offshore diving.

Tanks, regs, charts, cameras and spearguns in hand, it's time to explore.

Nine-Mile Reef, 11 miles off the Mayport jetties, is scattered with wrecks, including several barges and an old 52-foot steamer, all of which are good spots to find moderate-size grouper, flounder and sheepshead. The depth is about 75 feet, but visibility is only about 30 feet. Paul's Main Reef, also about 11 miles off the jetties, has two photogenic tugs next to each other. It's another good place to look for grouper up to 15 pounds. The depth is 75 feet, and the visibility is a little better than at Nine-Mile. **Amberjack Reef**, 21 miles from the jetties, is a natural reef that has an abundance of coral and sponges on a 10-foot ledge. Amberjack, as the reef's name implies, are common on this dive, which reaches 85 feet and has 40-foot visibility. Tiny crustaceans and tropicals live in the reef's crevices.

Another good photo opportunity is the *Hudgins*, a 150-foot freighter sitting at 105 feet. She draws schools of spadefish, amberjack and snapper. Visibility in the area, 27 miles from shore, can be as good as 50 feet. **Blackmar's Reef**, also about 27 miles offshore, has five wrecks (barges, tugs and a ferry) and a number of small reefs that attract amberjack, grouper, snapper and, occasionally, jewfish to the area. Fat lobster seem to love this site. There's also a fighter and a World War II-era Corsair to raise the bet that this is one of the most diverse dives in the area. The depth ranges from 95 to 110 feet and visibility is as good as 100 feet.

Last, but not least, the **Lost Phantom**, another 100-foot visibility dive, is an F4-A that sits at 102 feet. Its canopy is blown off and cable is tangled around its landing hook. Amberjack and jewfish love to hang out around the tail section.

INFORMATION SOURCES

Florida Association of Dive Operators, 305-451-3020, 51 Garden Cove Drive, Key Largo, FL 33037.
US Coast Guard, Mayport, ☎ 904-246-7315.
Florida Marine Patrol, ☎ 904-359-6580, 2510 Second Ave. N., Jacksonville Beach, FL 32250.
Ned DeLoach's Diving Guide to Underwater Florida, ☎ 904-737-6558, New World Publications, 1861 Cornell Road, Jacksonville, FL 32207.
Aqua Explorers Dive Center, ☎ 904-261-5989, 2856 Sadler Road, Fernandina Beach, FL 32034.
Divers Supply, ☎ 904-646-3828, 9701 Beach Blvd., Jacksonville, FL 32216.
Atlantic Pro Dive, ☎ 904-246-2401, 2294 Mayport Road, Jacksonville, FL 32233.
Mandarin Dive Center, ☎ 904-262-1606, 9735-11 St. Augustine Road, Jacksonville, FL 32257.

Sea Hunt Enterprises, ☎ 904-824-0831, 1114-C S. Ponce de Leon Blvd., St. Augustine, FL 32086.
Palatka Scuba International, ☎ 904-325-4575, 506 Madison St., Palatka, FL 32177-3431.

SALTWATER & FRESHWATER FISHING

If you're after king mackerel, **St. Augustine** is the place to launch. During the summer months, heavyweights in the 50- to 60-pound class run offshore, though strays occasionally come in close enough to be nailed off piers. Dolphins, blue marlins, swordfish and wahoos are other summer favorites well offshore. Closer in, small grouper, snapper, sea bass, flounder and cobia are common. Redfish, trout and flounder are waiting year-round in the Intracoastal Waterway. Tarpon and redfish run along the beaches of **Amelia Island** during the summer. One of the best spots for them is the **St. Marys River**'s southern jetties. Sharks (tigers, hammerheads, bull and more) are other summertime trophies.

Northeast Florida has three state saltwater records: flounder, 20 pounds, 9 ounces; black drum, 93 pounds; and jewfish (watch out for the hernia, please), 680 pounds. All were caught off Nassau County.

On the freshwater side, the **St. Johns River** is a factory for several kinds of bass, although it's better known than one river further south. The river is so wide and well traveled near Jacksonville that the good fishing is pretty much limited to the shore. **Jacksonville** has eight urban ponds managed and stocked by the Florida Game & Freshwater Fish Commission and the freshwater area of the St. Marys River is noted for largemouth and striped bass, especially in winter and summer. **Lake Geneva** and **Brooklyn Lake**, located just southeast of Keystone Heights on Highway 100, have been respectable holes for largemouth during winter and spring.

Amelia Island fishing.

The **Nassau River**, which is accessible at the US 17 bridge, four miles south of Yulee, yields striped bass December through May. The St. Marys, which you can reach at Boulogne (US 1/23) and Macclenny (US 90), produces bass, bluegill and redear sunfish February through September.

The region's two state freshwater records are a seven-pound Florida gar that was taken in Putnam County's portion of the Oklawaha River and a 5.72-pound brown bullhead in Duval County's Cedar Creek.

Saltwater anglers can find charter boats, boat rentals and guide services at several area locations, including the **Amelia Island Charter Boat Association** in Fernandina Beach (☎ 904-261-2870) and **Sea Lovers Marina** in St. Augustine (☎ 904-824-3328). **Fort Clinch State Park**, ☎ 904-261-4212, has a 2,200-foot pier, and the **Jacksonville Beach Pier**, ☎ 904-246-6001, is 1,000 feet. Local bait-and-tackle shops include **Atlantic Seafood**, ☎ 904-261-4302, in Fernandina, **Brown's**, ☎ 904-772-1046, in Jacksonville, **Beaches Bait & Tackle**, ☎ 904-223-3474, located on Jacksonville Beach, and **Hook, Line & Sinker**, ☎ 904-829-6073, St. Augustine.

Many fish camps provide a full line of services from ramps and boats to guides and fishing licenses. Among them are **Lake Crescent Resort**, ☎ 904-698-2485, on US 17 south of Palatka, **Camp Henry Resort and Marina**, ☎ 904-467-2282 (Lake George and St. Johns River) on County Road 309, just off US 17 south of Palatka, **Pacetti's Campground & Marina**, ☎ 904-284-5356 (St. Johns River and Trout Creek) on Highway 13 in northeast St. Johns County, **Gateway Fish Camp**, ☎ 904-467-2411 (St. Johns River) on Highway 309 off Highway 19 south of Palatka, and **Devil's Elbow Fish Camp**, ☎ 904-471-0398 (Intracoastal Waterway) off Highway 206 in St. Johns County.

Additionally, fishing is available at the following state parks, forests and conservation areas visited earlier in this chapter:

- **Anastasia Island State Recreation Area**, ☎ 904-461-2033.
- **Fort Clinch State Park**, ☎ 904-261-4212.
- **Jennings State Forest**, ☎ 904-693-5055.
- **Gold Head Branch State Park**, ☎ 904-473-4701.
- **Guana River State Park**, ☎ 904-825-5071.
- **St. Johns River Water Management District**, ☎ 904-329-4404, at the Bayard Point, Caravelle Ranch, Deep

Creek, Dunns Creek and Stokes Landing conservation areas, and the St. Marys River State Forest.

Don't forget to pick up a fishing license. Non-resident saltwater licenses range from $5 for three days to $30 per year. Non-resident freshwater licenses cost $15 for seven days and $30 for a year. Also, there are size and bag limits on many species. Information on these is available from bait-and-tackle shops, marinas, local guides, the **Florida Marine Patrol**, ☎ 904-359-6580, 2510 2nd Ave. N., Jacksonville Beach, FL 32250, and the **Florida Game & Fresh Water Fish Commission**, ☎ 904-758-0525, Route 7, Box 440, Lake City, FL 32055-8713.

In The Air

The up-up-and-away crowd can get a fix in two ways.

Balloon Adventures, ☎ 904-399-2882, lifts off from several locations in the Jacksonville area, depending on the winds. The hour-long flight includes views from treetop to 2,000 feet, including the St. Johns River, Atlantic Ocean and the Jacksonville skyline. Chilled champagne is served, but go easy – you don't want to tumble out of the gondola before the adventure is over. (Though the flight is an hour, plan to spend three to four hours on the adventure due to the time it takes to get to the rendezvous, load up, soar skyward, repack and return.)

If you want to skip the gondola, **Watersports of St. Augustine**, ☎ 904-829-0006, offers a bird's-eye view of the oldest city from a parasail. (The company also offers jet-skiing and other water sport adventures.)

Where To Stay & Eat

This is another area where there are literally tens of thousands of rooms available – from posh resorts and bed-and-breakfasts to lower-priced lodgings and campgrounds. You won't find a lack of places to eat, either. Reservations? They're generally not mandatory, but they're a smart idea to ensure your choice of room or dinner time.

Nassau County

The **Fairbanks House**, ☎ 800-261-4838 or 904-277-0500, in Fernandina Beach, is a beautifully restored house designed and built in 1885 by Robert S. Schuyler. Polished hardwood floors and 11 fireplaces complement nine guest rooms that are appointed with antiques, Oriental rugs and period furnishings. The rooms have four-poster or canopied king-size beds and private baths with your choice of jacuzzi, claw-foot tub or shower. If you get lonely for your canine companion left at home, Toby the cocker spaniel will soak up your attention.

The **Florida House Inn**, ☎ 800-258-3301, is the state's oldest surviving inn. Quilted beds, antique oak armoires and polished heart-pine floors decorate 11 guest rooms, some of which have accommodated Gen. Ulysses S. Grant and Cuban freedom fighter José Martí.

Amelia Island Plantation, ☎ 800-874-6878, is unique in that it was built around and over (rather than through) the area's dunes, marshes and savannas long before environmental fever caught on. The plantation stretches across 1,250 acres and provides 1,100 accommodations, ranging from suites to three-bedroom villas. The resort has 45 holes of golf, 27 tennis courts and a fitness center. The **Summer Beach Resort**, ☎ 800-772-3359, and the **Ritz Carlton**, ☎ 800-241-3333, have hundreds of additional guest rooms, suites and villas.

Sea Dunes rental unit, Amelia Island Plantation.

Amelia Island has several great restaurants to take care of your hunger pangs. The **Beech Street Grill**, ☎ 904-277-3662, specializes in exotic treats such as Mayport grouper macadamia, mahi-mahi with banana chutney and mango, and cioppino, a tasty blend of mussels, shrimp and fish over pasta. The **1878 Steak House & Seafood**, ☎ 904-261-4049, offers Black Angus steaks and local seafood. The **Florida House Inn** serves Southern cooking (fried chicken, meat loaf, pork chops, catfish, collard greens, blackeyed peas and mashed potatoes) boarding-house style (heaping platters and bowls). And don't miss at least one meal at the **Amelia Inn**, ☎ 904-261-6161, at Amelia Island Plantation. The Sunday brunch is a delicious belly-buster topped only by the inn's dinner menus: breast of pheasant on baby-leaf spinach with sun-dried tomatoes, grilled medallions of elk with risotto-stuffed mushrooms, buffalo strips with black-bean salsa and red snapper primavera, among others.

Jacksonville/Duval County

Being one of Florida's larger cities, Jacksonville has accommodations to suit any taste and wallet. Those on the higher end include the **Marriott**, ☎ 904-296-2222, the **Radisson Riverwalk**, ☎ 904-396-5100, and the **Omni**, ☎ 904-355-6664. At the moderate end, **Comfort Inn Oceanfront**, ☎ 904-241-2311, **Econo Lodge**, ☎ 904-737-1690 and the **Eastwinds Motel**, ☎ 904-249-3858, are the choices.

When it's time to put fuel in the furnace, **Juliette's** at the Omni, ☎ 904-355-7118, features pecan-crusted rack of lamb and pan-fried goat cheese; **Café St. Johns** in the Radisson, ☎ 904-396-5100, specializes in American-style seafood, steaks, chicken and pork; the **Island Grille**, ☎ 904-241-1881, serves mahi-mahi, tuna, salmon, grouper and other seafood; while **Harry's Oyster Bar**, ☎ 904-353-0444, has a raw bar to complement some warming Cajun entrées.

Putnam County

Welaka and Crescent City in Putnam County have some fishing resorts that go beyond the traditional rustic camps common along the St. Johns River, including the **Floridian Sports Club**, ☎ 904-467-2181 (a main lodge and cottages plus a casual dining room), **Riverbend Villas**, ☎ 904-467-2900 (72 villas that have kitchens and can accommodate up to six), **Bass Haven Lodge**, ☎ 904-467-8812 (a woodsy resort with four-poster beds and a riverview dining room), and **Acosta Creek Marina**, ☎ 904-467-2229 (a Victorian manor house set upon a hill overlooking the marina and the St. Johns).

Accommodations in Palatka include **Best Western**, ☎ 904-325-7800, **The Moorings**, ☎ 904-325-1055, **Azalea House Bed & Breakfast**, ☎ 904-325-4547, and **Holiday Inn**, ☎ 904-328-3481.

Some of the other restaurants are **Angler's Paradise**, ☎ 904-467-2000, in Crescent City; **Henri's Restaurant**, ☎ 904-328-5018, in Palatka, **Walt's Bar-B-Que**, ☎ 904-328-2784, in Palatka, and **Sprague House**, ☎ 904-698-2430, in Crescent City.

St. Augustine/St. Johns County

Ponte Vedra Beach, north of St. Augustine near the St. Johns and Duval County line, is a barrier island featuring three classy resorts set in a paradise for golfers (135 holes at seven courses) and tennis players (42 courts at four locations). **Ponte Vedra Inn and Club**, ☎ 800-234-7842 or 904-285-1111, has oceanfront rooms with patios or balconies and four restaurants; **Marriott at Sawgrass**, ☎ 904-285-7777, has rooms, suites and villas with three restaurants; and **The Lodge & Bath Club** at Ponte Vedra Beach has rooms and suites with three restaurants.

St. Augustine's accommodations include traditional motels such as the **Days Inn Historic**, ☎ 800-329-7566 or 904-829-6581, and **Quality Inn Alhambra**, ☎ 800-223-4153 or 904-824-2883. The **Conch House Marina Resort**, ☎ 800-940-6256 or 904-829-8646, has rooms and two-bedroom suites. On the bed-and-breakfast front, choose from the **Alexander Homestead**, ☎ 904-826-4147, a four-room Victorian home (1888) with private baths, fireplaces and private porches; **Casablanca**, ☎ 800-826-2626 or 904-829-0928, which has 10 suites (1914) with private baths (some with jacuzzis) and entrances; and **Penny Farthing Inn**, ☎ 904-824-2100, four rooms (1890) in the heart of the ancient city with private baths, porches and queen-size beds. Rental properties are available from companies such as **Livingston Resort Properties**, ☎ 800-727-4656, **Spyglass Resort Rental**, ☎ 904-461-4605, and **Cunningham Property Management**, ☎ 800-333-7335.

One of St. Augustine's best bets at mealtime is **The Columbia**, ☎ 800-227-1905 or 904-824-3341, where the specialties are Cuban and Spanish entrées, such as boliche with black beans and rice, paella and roast pork with rice. Other good spots to recharge batteries include the **Sunset Grille**, ☎ 904-471-5555 (fresh local seafood and hand-cut steaks in a Key West atmosphere), **Florida Cracker Café**, ☎ 904-829-0397 (seafood, steaks, chicken, pasta and a delicious key lime pie), **Zaharias**, ☎ 904-471-4799 (the place to go Greek), **Fiddler's Green**, ☎ 904-824-8897 (great Florida-style seafood, steaks and chicken), and the **Ragin Cajun**, ☎ 904-829-1005 (which has Louisiana – pronounce it, Looooooooosiana – treats such as jambalaya, gumbo, red beans and rice and blackened seafood).

Campgrounds

As always, options range from camping's five-star retreats to the "honey, what the hell was that?" primitive sites.

Jacksonville's **Flamingo Lake RV Resort**, ☎ 800-782-4323 or 904-766-0672, has 50 acres of pull-through sites, a 17-acre lake, recreation hall, cable and bath houses. **Bryn Mawr Ocean Resort**, ☎ 904-471-3353, in St. Augustine, has 250 sites, full hook-ups, free cable, a large swimming pool and tennis courts. **Ocean Grove RV Resort**, ☎ 800-342-4007 or 904-471-3414, in St. Augustine, offers 200 sites, a pool, heated and cooled bath houses, a recreation hall and a service center with on-site RV repairs. St. Augustine's **North Beach Camp Resort**, ☎ 800-542-8316 or 904-824-1806, has 120 heavily wooded sites stretching from the Atlantic to the Intracoastal Waterway, cable television, a pool with spa and a fishing dock.

If you want to rough it a little more, **Fort Clinch State Park**, ☎ 904-261-4212, **Gold Branch State Park**, ☎ 904-473-4701, and **Anastasia Island State Recreation Area**, ☎ 904-461-2033, have campsites available. (Anastasia is the largest of the three, with 139 sites, handicapped access, electric and water, a bath house and a dump station.)

Additionally, four St. Johns River Water Management District recreation areas feature campsites: **Bayard Point**, **Dunns Creek**, **Stokes Landing** and the **St. Marys River State Forest**. For information, call the district, ☎ 904-329-4404.

Wow, can you believe it's time to move on to a new adventuring hole?

Don't forget to call the boss and say you're taking a few extra days.

North-Central Florida

Wild Florida factoids, brought to you by Capt. Charlie Patrick, who runs a pontoon-boat tour on the picturesque Dora Canal in Lake County:

- Some folks get lucky and see an alligator sunning itself on a lake shore or river bank. But most gators seen in the wild are a little disappointing because they're in the water and mostly submerged. Unless you're submerged with them, that's the best way to view them – at a distance. The last thing you want is a landside rendezvous with a Stone-Age leftover that can outrun a quarterhorse in the 100 meters. Still, you came here for bragging rights in addition to adventure. If all you see are noses and eyes, what do you tell the folks back home who ask: How big was it? "Measure it from the tip of its nose to its eyes," Charlie says. "If it's six inches, he's six feet. If it's eight inches, he's eight feet," and so forth. Don't take that literally, Charlie says. Eyeball it, estimate it, lie if you have to, but keep your distance. Alligators may only need one big meal a year, but you don't want to become the annual banquet.

- From the what-they-won't-do-in-the-name-of-fashion category. You'll run into all makes and models of wading birds as you travel around Florida. Snowy-white egrets are among them. (These should not be confused with their cousins that sit atop cattle, looking for bug entrées.) The snowy white egret is somewhat rare, but this wasn't always the case. They were pretty abundant until the early part of this century when some French fashion designers went absolutely wonkers over what their plumes did for women's hats. "Each bird has 50 plumes," Charlie says. "They killed about 3 million birds. They almost wiped them out." Fortunately, the designers lost interest in plumage, becoming intrigued instead with fashion marvels like bikinis and Wonderbras – which so far haven't required any animal sacrifices.

❑ What is it about Spanish moss that catches people's interest – especially our northern visitors? Any Floridian will tell you nine out of every 10 people seen pulling this stuff off our trees is a Yankee. (The 10th is an entrepreneur who plans to sell it to a Yankee.) First thing, Charlie explains to his passengers, Spanish moss is neither Spanish nor moss. It's from the pineapple family. Second, and more important to your physical person should you insist on taking some home, it's usually the domicile of pesky little blighters called chiggers, tiny bugs with not-so-tiny teeth. They'll be glad to relocate to your house where there is plenty of human food. If you must take a handful of moss home, Charlie warns, "put it in a bag and cook it in a microwave oven for a minute." If you saw the movie "Gremlins," you have an idea of what a microwave does to chiggers, though because of their microscopic size it's far less messy than with Gremlins.

Leaving Charlie's neck of the woods for a little while, you'll find nature and natural history playing a large role in this region, which reaches from Flagler and Volusia counties on the Atlantic Coast inland to the scenic interior veins in Lake, Marion and Sumter counties.

Volusia County's name may not ring any bells, but say Daytona Beach, and most folks know what this place is all about – the five Bs: beaches, bikinis, bullet cars, bikers and (spring) break, not necessarily in that order. The anti-glitz crowd may want to steer clear of this landing site, at least the A1A/Atlantic Avenue strip where all the neon has managed to settle, but there are some nifty places to visit from touring and adventuring perspectives. For instance, there are more than 23 miles of beaches, in some cases 500 feet wide. Nine miles of them are open to traffic. The rest are closed because the sand is a nesting site for endangered sea turtles, including loggerheads. Speaking of the beach, it was the original Daytona International Speedway. In 1902 a car was clocked at 57 mph (a bit slower than some of you tackle the driveway), and 33 years later, Sir Malcolm Campbell rode his Bluebird V, equipped with an airplane engine, to the tune of 276 mph. Today, the speed merchants earn their reputations at Daytona International Speedway, which is a couple of miles inland, far from the turtles and tides.

Elsewhere in the region, away from the tourist destinations, you're going to find boulder-strewn beaches at Washington Oaks

State Gardens, ruins of an old plantation, scenic dunes, pelicans gliding on air draughts, tidal pools where little anemones and starfish camp out, coastal hammocks, hickories and magnolias. When you ride into Marion County you're going to find some of the most beautiful countryside and horse pastures this side of Lexington, Kentucky, as well as one of the most pristine rivers (and canoe trails) in Florida, including the spring-fed Rainbow River, which has the clarity of a swimming pool.

Adventures are pretty wide-ranging. Lake County is home to three world-class water-ski schools. You can go for a flight in a seaplane, biplane or glider; go ballooning, parasailing or sky diving; rent a jet-ski or waverunner and skim the surface like a flat rock. Divers and snorkelers get a taste of two worlds here. There are some nice spring and cave dives in the inland areas near Ocala and some good saltwater dives off Daytona Beach, including wreckage of a Liberty Ship and two torpedo bombers. Paddlers, peddlers and hikers can expect a lot of good opportunities in the area's five designated canoe trails, eight state parks and forests, and several tracts managed by two water management districts. Just in case that's not enough, the 378,178-acre Ocala National Forest cuts through the heart of the region, offering plenty of additional adventure.

But enough of a teaser. Let's get into the lay of the land and its roots.

Geography & History

Mount Dora? Aw, it's another Florida fake. A beautiful place but hardly Fuji or McKinley. At low tide, it might measure 300 feet or so above sea level.

Geographically, North Central Florida is very similar to the Northeast. The interior region has rolling hills, farms, timberlands, hardwood hammocks and an abundance of springs. The limestone-rich soil feeds lush pastures, which is what attracted the horse crowd to Ocala, starting with Carl Rose in 1937. These days, there are 400 farms. Coastal areas range from the man-made beaches such as Daytona and Ormond to more primitive ones carved by erosion.

Prehistoric Indians inhabited the region as far back as 12,000 years ago, and the Timucuans came at least as early as 500 B.C.

There was little European contact during the age of colonization, except for Hernando de Soto, who visited the Ocala-Marion County area in 1546. Seminole Indians migrated to the region from Alabama and Georgia in the mid-18th century. Plantations began to sprout about 75 years later, the same time the US Army built Fort King, which became the Seminole Indian War headquarters for Gen. Zachary Taylor.

Stay tuned for more recent history in the touring part of this chapter.

Getting Around

Daytona International Airport, ☎ 904-248-8069, is the region's commercial hub, served by four major carriers and a half-dozen regional ones. To the north, **Jacksonville International Airport**, ☎ 904-741-4902, offers eight major airlines and four regionals, while **Gainesville Regional Airport**, ☎ 352-373-0249, to the west, is served by two commercial carriers and four commuter airlines.

Interstate 95 and US 1 are the major north-south thoroughfares through the coastal areas of Flagler and Volusia counties. Interstate 75 is a north-south route on the western fringe, running through Marion and Sumter counties. Back on the coast, A1A is the primary beach road, varying from two to four lanes. It's scenic in some areas, especially in Flagler County where there are no highrise hotels obstructing your view on the ocean side. But A1A is often congested, so don't be in a hurry if you choose it. There are just two east-west, direct routes in the region – Highway 40, from Ocala to Ormond Beach, and Highway 42, from Pedro (south of Ocala) to Deland – and both are two lanes. Highway 40 is the more heavily traveled, but it has periodic passing lanes. There are some other secondary roads you'll be using once we start touring.

The weather generally is a shade warmer, both winter and summer, than what you've encountered in the last few chapters. The summer average is 84 to 86°, with the eastern portions of Flagler and Volusia counties cooled by sea breezes, while Marion, Lake and Sumter, in the interior, are usually a couple of degrees warmer on average. The interior may see a dozen high-humidity, high-90s days and two or three where the temps climb to the century mark. The winter average is 54 to 56°, with perhaps two to four days in the high teens to low twenties.

Getting Around 233

INFORMATION SOURCES

Daytona Beach Area Convention & Visitors Bureau, ☎ 800-854-1234 or 904-255-0415, 126 E. Orange Ave., Daytona Beach, FL 32114.
East Central Tourism Bureau (New Smyrna Beach, Edgewater and Oak Hill), ☎ 800-541-9621 or 904-428-2449, 115 Canal St., New Smyrna Beach, FL 32168.
Flagler County Tourist Development Council, ☎ 800-881-1022, 1200 E. Moody Blvd., Bunnell, FL 32110.
Lake County Convention & Visitors Bureau, ☎ 800-798-1071 or 352-429-3673, 20763 US 27, Groveland, FL 34736.
West Volusia Tourism Advertising Authority, ☎ 800-749-4350 or 904-734-4331, 336 N. Woodland Blvd., Deland, FL 32720.
Belleview/South Marion Chamber of Commerce, ☎ 352-245-2178, 5301 S.E. Abshier Blvd., Belleview, FL 34420.
Clermont Area Chamber of Commerce, ☎ 352-394-4191, 691 W. Monroe St., Clermont, FL 34711.
Daytona Beach/Halifax Area Chamber of Commerce, ☎ 904-255-0981, P.O. Box 2475, Daytona Beach, FL 32115.
Daytona Beach Shores Chamber of Commerce, ☎904-761-7163, 3048 S. Atlantic Ave., Daytona Beach Shores, FL 32118.
Deland Area Chamber of Commerce, ☎ 800-749-4350 or 904-734-4331, 336 N. Woodland Blvd., Deland, FL 32720.
Flagler Beach Chamber of Commerce, ☎ 904-439-0995, P.O. Box 5, Flagler Beach, FL 32136.
Flagler County Chamber of Commerce, ☎ 800-881-1022 or 904-437-0106, Star Route Box 18-N, Bunnell, FL 32110.
Greater Eustis Area Chamber of Commerce, ☎ 352-357-3434, 1 W. Orange Ave., Eustis, FL 32726.
Groveland/Mascotte Chamber of Commerce, ☎ 352-429-3678, P.O. Box 115, Groveland, FL 34736.
Holly Hill Chamber of Commerce, ☎ 904-255-7311, 1056 Ridgewood Ave., Holly Hill, FL 32117.
Greater Orange City Area Chamber of Commerce, ☎ 904-775-2793, 520 N. Volusia Ave., Orange City, FL 32763.
Lake County Chamber of Commerce, ☎ 352-383-8801, 31336 County Road 437, Sorrento, FL 32776.
Lake Weir Chamber of Commerce, ☎ 352-288-3751, P.O. Box 817, Oklawaha, FL 32679.
Leesburg Area Chamber of Commerce, ☎ 352-787-2131, P.O. Box 490309, Leesburg, FL 34749-0309.
Mount Dora Area Chamber of Commerce, ☎ 352-383-2165, P.O. Box 196, Mount Dora, FL 32757.
Ocala/Marion County Chamber of Commerce, ☎ 352-629-8051, 110 E. Silver Springs Blvd., Ocala, FL 34470.
Ormond Beach Chamber of Commerce, ☎ 904-677-3454, P.O. Box 874, Ormond Beach, FL 32175.

Port Orange/South Daytona Chamber of Commerce, ☎ 904-761-1601, 3431 Ridgewood Ave., Port Orange, FL 32119-3532.
Sumter County Chamber of Commerce, ☎ 352-793-3099, 223 N. Main St., Bushnell, FL 33513-0550.
Tavares Chamber of Commerce, ☎ 352-343-2531, P.O. Box 697, Tavares, FL 32778.
Umatilla Chamber of Commerce, ☎ 352-669-3511, P.O. Box 300, Umatilla, FL 32784.

Touring

Flagler County

You're going to follow the sometimes scenic though more congested A1A route for starters. From Daytona International Airport, take Highway 92 east four miles to A1A (Atlantic Avenue), turn left (north) and set the trip meter for a 21-mile spin and a trio of stops along the coast. If you're following a chapter-by-chapter itinerary, the tour begins 36 miles south of St. Augustine (64 miles south of Jacksonville Beach). If you flew into Gainesville, you might prefer to begin the tour in Marion County and travel in a different order. Otherwise, it's about a 93-mile drive from Gainesville to Flagler Beach (Highway 26 to Highway 100, for a brief period merging with US 17, before splitting east and hitting the beach).

At **Bulow Plantation State Historic Site,** ☎ 904-439-2219, Maj. Charles Wilhelm Bulow built a plantation in 1821 where slaves grew cotton, sugarcane, rice and indigo. When Bulow died, his son John returned from Paris and production really prospered, until the younger Bulow made a serious tactical error. Disagreeing with the federal government's plan to send Seminole Indians to reservations west of the Mississippi River, thereby draining his slave pool, he unloaded a cannon at state militia members as they entered the plantation to take custody of the Indians. Bulow went to the hoosegow briefly. The Seminoles weren't much happier than the militia with the young Mr. Bulow. Being the kind of guy who trusted his gut instincts and, sensing the growing hostility, he tucked his tail between his legs and followed the militia out. Shortly

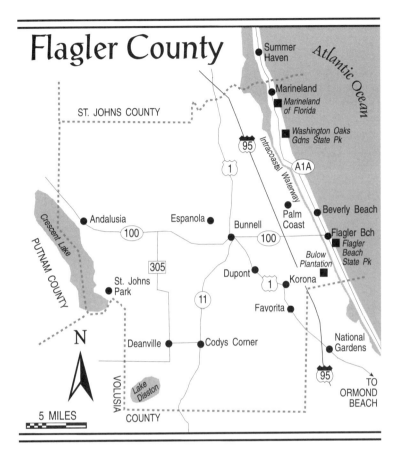

thereafter, in 1836, the Indians who remained free burned "Bulowville." All that remains of this once-thriving plantation are the coquina rock ruins of a sugar mill, some wells, a spring house and the crumbling foundations of a Colonial-style mansion and 46 slave cabins. Its once-cleared fields have been reclaimed by forest. There is an interpretive center that recounts the rise and fall of Bulowville. To reach the park from A1A and Flagler Beach, take Highway 100 west 2½ miles, then go left (south) on Highway 5-A (South Old Kings Road) and continue three miles to the entrance.

To get to **Washington Oaks State Gardens**, ☎ 904-445-3161, reverse your course from Bulow, taking Highway 5-A back to Highway 100, turning right and returning to A1A, then left (north) and drive 14 miles to the 400-acre site, which stretches from the Atlantic Ocean to the Matanzas River. The ocean side of the tract has a picturesque, boulder-strewn beach created by waves that have eroded the sand and exposed the underlying coquina rock. At low tide, you can watch anemones, starfish and crabs doing their things in tidal pools and mussels clinging to the rocks. Moving inland, dunes give way to huge live oaks, hickories and magnolias. The tract is part of a plantation once owned by a Seminole Indian War general. The gardens that are among the featured attractions today were planted by Owen Young, former chairman of General Electric, and his wife beginning in 1936. The centerpieces include azaleas, camellias and roses, as well as exotic plants that are displayed along footpaths and pools. The site's interpretive center, called "Young House," contains exhibits of the region's natural and cultural history. Washington Oaks is also home for the Florida scrub jay, which is threatened elsewhere due to a loss of habitat. You'll return to Bulow and Washington Oaks when we go adventuring.

One more stop before you head south to Daytona Beach: **Marineland of Florida**, ☎ 904-471-1111, opened its doors in 1938. It's a traditional marine park with high-jumping dolphins, aquariums and a wildlife preserve, located four miles north of Washington Oaks on A1A.

Daytona Beach/Volusia County

There are still pockets where you can drive on the hard-packed beaches, including the north end of Volusia County at Ormond Beach – where yesterday's daredevils tackled a natural speedway. You won't get close. Today's speed limit is 10 mph, and it's strictly enforced. Nearly two-thirds of the beach is closed as a result of environmental sanctions imposed to protect the rare nesting turtles and their offspring. Frankly, beach driving isn't that wonderful. The salt wreaks havoc on the paint job, and some people park, get out to sunbathe and fall asleep, forgetting a natural phenomenon called... the tides. If you're a victim, it can be an expensive contribution to Daytona's artificial reefs. Besides, you can rent a bike or moped and save the wear and tear on the family bus.

Speed has been one of the big drawing cards since that first beach race back in 1902. Sure, the seashore is what lured Louis Chevrolet and Henry Ford here, but one gander at that hard-packed sand gave them thoughts about doing more than just relaxing. **Daytona International Speedway**, ☎ 904-254-2700, about four miles east of A1A on Highway 92, is one of the biggest magnets other than the beach. Built in 1959, it's home to the Daytona 500 and

Speed Weeks every February, motorcycle racing's Biketoberfest in October, as well as several other events throughout the year. Even when there isn't a major event, the speedway's World Center of Racing Visitors Center offers 30-minute guided track tours, early films of beach racing and track action, and the Gallery of Legends photographic collection.

Daytona has two other attractions related to speed and the automobile. Mark Martin's **Klassix Auto Museum**, ☎ 904-252-3800, around a mile west of the speedway on Highway 92 (West International Speedway Boulevard), has more than 40 vintage motorcycles and a nifty collection of Corvettes from every year since 1953. There are also some race cars on display and the history of auto racing along the beaches, but those have been overshadowed a little by the summer 1996 opening of **Daytona USA**, ☎ 904-947-6800, which is located at the speedway. This state-of-the-art interactive attraction gives you a chance to beat the pros' record at a NASCAR Winston Cup pit stop, design and test

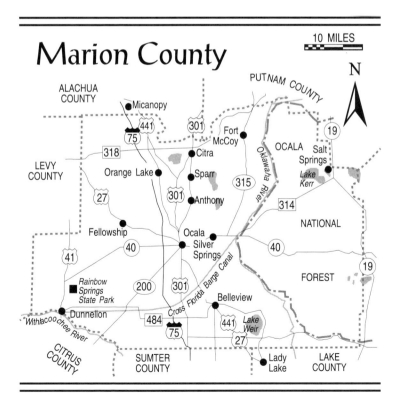

your own race car, compete with other race aficionados in a trivia game and call the final laps of a race from a broadcast booth. There also are several car displays, including Sir Malcolm Campbell's Bluebird V, the 30-foot, five-ton monster that set the land speed record on the beach back in 1935, and a more modern Jeff Gordon car that comes apart section-by-section to show how a race car is built.

The pace is a little slower, but certainly no less educational, at this area's museums. **The Casements,** ☎ 904-676-3216, 25 Riverside Drive, Ormond Beach, earned its claim to fame when billionaire John D. Rockefeller discovered he was being charged more than the other guests at the old Ormond Hotel. He checked out of the hotel for good, bought a home on the Halifax River, and ever after was known to the townies as "Neighbor John." Today, his restored home is a cultural center that includes art exhibits, a museum of the city, a Rockefeller period room and Boy Scout exhibits. **Bethune-Cookman College,** ☎ 904-255-1401, offers a pair of exhibits. The two-story frame house (1914) of civil rights leader, educator and college founder Dr. Mary McLeod Bethune contains photographs and artifacts of the college's history and the guest bedroom where one of her friends, First Lady Eleanor Roosevelt, often stayed. The "New Deal" Permanent Exhibit, in the Carl S. Swisher Library on campus, was established by the Smithsonian Institute to detail Bethune's involvement in FDR's "Black Cabinet." The campus is two blocks west of US 1 on Dr. Mary McLeod Bethune Boulevard.

The **Museum of Arts & Sciences,** ☎ 904-255-0285, 1040 Museum Blvd. in Daytona Beach, is just south of Highway 92 and Nova Road. Among its calling cards is the skeleton of a giant ground sloth that once stomped around this part of the planet. Unlike our mastodon buddy Herman back in Tallahassee, this one isn't named, but he's almost 11 times older (at 130,000 on his last birthday) and four feet taller (at 13 feet) than Hermie. The museum's Dow Gallery of American Art has a large collection of paintings, sculptures, crystal, silver and glass dating to 1640. The **Cuban Museum** spotlights Latin culture from 1759 to 1959. The African wing contains 165 objects from 30 cultures, and the main gallery has a permanent collection, as well as changing exhibits that include Russian and Greek icons, pre-Columbian artifacts and European art works.

One last stop before you aim the starship west.

The **Ponce Inlet Lighthouse and Museum,** ☎ 904-761-1821, is one of only a handful in Northwest and North Florida that has managed to keep its brick torso. Built in 1887, it stayed in service for 83 years, then was reactivated by the Coast Guard in 1982. The 175-foot sentinel features a panoramic view of the tiny town of Ponce Inlet if you're up for the climb – 203 steps. The lightkeeper's house has been turned into a museum, and his assistant's is restored as it would have been around 1890. The site also has a lens exhibit, a display of lights from around the world and the "F.D. Russell," a 46-foot tugboat that was built in 1938 and served until a few years ago. There are two rustic bar and grills in the area in case you find the need to regain your energy after the climb. The lighthouse and museum are located at the southernmost tip of the Ormond-Daytona Beach peninsula.

Now, off to the land of lakes.

Lake County

Step back into an older, more natural Florida. An aerial view (you'll get to them once you start adventuring) shows just how wet this area is. Literally 200 of its 1,200 square miles are lakes. That snippet should whet your appetite for the water adventures that await, but there are plenty more for sky and landlubbers. A brief stop now and a longer one later.

To get here, take Highway 92 east-southeast of Daytona Beach 22 miles to Deland, take a short jog left (south) on US 17 and go right (east) on Highway 44 for the 36-mile sprint to Eustis. Then turn left (south) on Highway 19 for a fast hop to US 441 and turn right (east) to Tavares, where you can choose from two peaceful boat tours. Capt. Charlie Patrick, whom you met earlier in this chapter, guides the *Miss Dora*, ☎ 352-343-0200, along the Dora Canal, which the famed sportswriter Grantland Rice in the 1930s described as "the most beautiful half-mile of water in the world." This link between lakes Eustis and Dora is literally overstocked with wildlife (eagles, ospreys, snowy-white egrets, raccoons and alligators), and the shorelines are thick with banana trees, giant bamboos and cypresses that are hundreds of years old. Capt. Vince McCarthy cruises Lake Harris in *La Reina*, ☎ 352-324-3101. This stately craft, built of mahogany, heart pine and cypress, began life in the 1930s and served such notables as Jimmy Stewart, Gary Cooper, Babe Ruth and some of the Roosevelts. She has been refurbished and carries up to 49 passengers on tours of the lake region.

From Tavares, continue west on US 441 around 12 miles to US 27 at Leesburg, turn left (south) and go 22 miles south to Clermont, where three local attractions are worth noting. The **Florida Citrus Tower**, ☎ 352-394-8585, offers a panoramic view of the Central Florida citrus region, tours of a packing plant and a 10-acre grove where most kinds of citrus grow. The **House of Presidents Wax Museum**, ☎ 352-394-2836, displays the presidents in period settings as well as an assortment of presidential memorabilia. There's also a 1/12th scale model of the White House where the light bulbs are the size of a grain of rice. Six miles north of Clermont on US 27, **Lakeridge Winery**, ☎ 904-394-8627, is the state's largest,

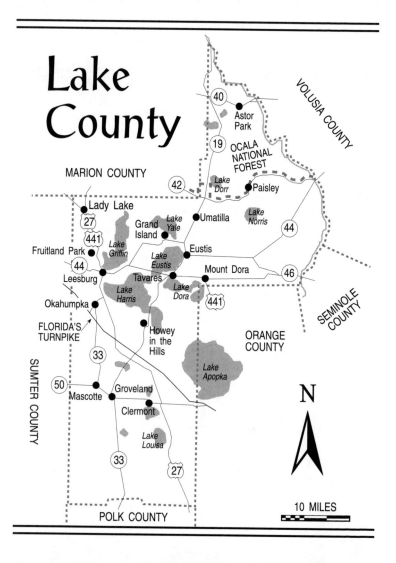

capable of up to 1,250 cases a day. While Florida is the birthplace of American wines (thank the Spanish for that), today it pales in comparison to places such as California, mainly due to climate conditions that restrict the crop to a variety of hybrids and muscadines. The winery, in a beautiful Spanish-style building and surrounded by 35 acres of grapevines, offers hour-long tours and tastings.

Marion County

Ocala is 49 miles north of Clermont on US 27.

Whether you're a rider or not, one of the true passive pleasures here is a tour of the area's horse farms. Since Carl Rose started the industry in 1937 and Bonnie Heath put Ocala on the thoroughbred map with a 1956 Kentucky Derby winner named "Needles," the business has grown to 400 farms raising, training, racing and showing virtually all breeds of horses. If you visit in October, the

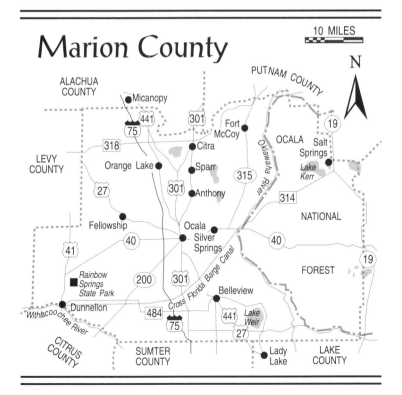

two-day **Florida Horse and Agriculture Festival**, ☎ 352-629-8051, is a good way to get a look at all of them, including the battle of the breeds, where horses of all sizes, shapes and colors compete in an equine decathlon.

Group or individual farm tours can be taken via **Lorna Hagemeyer Farm Tours**, ☎ 352-351-5524, **Eileen Scott Tours**, ☎ 352-624-9191, and Mary Thomas at **Temporary Horse Care**, ☎ 352-622-2040. Most last up to three hours. If you're not in the mood for multiple farm tours, you can make single pit stops at **Ocala Stud** (thoroughbred), ☎ 352-237-2171, **Young's Paso Finos**, ☎ 352-867-5305, or **Hooper Farm** (thoroughbred), ☎ 352-237-2104. The latter farm is owned by Fred Hooper, the grand old man of racing and owner of 1945 Derby winner, "Hoop Jr." Tours at Hooper Farm are on Friday afternoons only.

The **Brick City Center for the Arts**, ☎ 352-840-9521, features modern fine and performing arts in the center of downtown on Silver Springs Boulevard (Highway 40). The mix includes concerts, dramatic readings, photography and paintings. The **Appleton Museum of Art**, ☎ 352-236-5050, about five miles further east on the boulevard, has an older collection that allows you to see the beauty of European paintings and sculpture, the spiritual power of West African art, as well as the mysteries of the Orient. The museum is an affiliate of Florida State University and Central Florida Community College.

Silver Springs, ☎ 352-236-2121, is another four miles east on Highway 40. This attraction combines the natural beauty of Florida's largest artesian spring with modern features such as jungle cruises, Jeep safaris, exotic wildlife and a glass-bottom boat ride that gives you a clear view of a spring that attracted film crews for the early Tarzan movies and the *Sea Hunt* television series.

One more idyllic stop before you burn off some energy.

Take Highway 40 nine miles west to US 441/301 and turn right (north), traveling 20 miles north to the quiet village of **McIntosh**. (Note: 11 miles north of Ocala the two federal highways split. Make sure you follow US

Silver Springs.

441.) This burg is a lot like Micanopy, visited earlier. It's a turn-of-the-century village that's brimming with antique and curio shops, museums and more. The **McIntosh Ice House Gallery**, ☎ 352-591-1300, has an art gallery featuring the work of regional artists; **Tinker's Forge**, ☎ 352-591-1085, has custom and artistic blacksmithing; **Lambert's Clock Shop**, ☎ 352-591-2378, has vintage timepieces; while **Bob & Helene's at Harvest Village**, ☎ 352-591-1053, specializes in pottery, china, oak, glassware and various other collectibles. The **McIntosh Carriage House**, ☎ 352-591-1300, has a museum of yesterday's horse-drawn carriages, and the **Fort McIntosh Armory**, ☎ 904-591-2378, is a museum of Civil War-era military items.

Now, it's time for action.

Adventures

On Foot

The hands-down winner in the marathon category is the 66-mile section of the orange-blazed **Florida National Scenic Trail** that cuts through the heart of the **Ocala National Forest**, ☎ 352-625-7470. You find a trail entrance near the visitors' center, which is located about four miles east of the Silver Springs attraction (13 miles east of US 441/301 in downtown Ocala). The trail moves through typical Florida uplands where you might encounter deer, foxes, raccoons and squirrels. The trail is bordered by oaks, magnolias and black tupelos and, at some points, comes upon invigorating (70° worth of invigorating) springs.

The forest also offers three short trails:

- ❑ **Salt Springs**, a 2.1-mile trail (just before the visitors' center on Highway 40 turn left or north on Highway 314, go 18 miles, then left again at Highway 19 and drive a quarter-mile to the campground entrance).
- ❑ **Lake Eaton Sinkhole Trail**, 2.2 miles, and **Lake Eaton Loop Trail**, 1.8 miles (east of the visitors' center about three miles to Highway 314-A, go left or north for five miles, then right on Forest Road 96 for one-half mile,

then left onto Forest Road 96-A and continue approximately one mile).

State parks and forests throughout the region offer scenic trails. The 29.2-mile **Gen. James A. Van Fleet State Trail**, ☎ 352-447-1633 or, if you don't mind an answering machine, ☎ 352-394-2280, is an excellent choice for hikers willing to share the path with bikers. There is a parallel trail that's for horsemen and women. The hiking trail is paved except for the southernmost 2.8 miles and a 5.2-mile stretch in the northern one-third. There are restrooms, benches, covered shelters and two picnic areas along the way. From Clermont, follow Highway 50 about 12 miles west to tiny Mabel and the entrance. You can get additional information by writing the trail's office at 12549 State Park Drive, Clermont, FL 34711.

Washington Oaks State Gardens, ☎ 904-445-3161, has .4- , .5- and 1.2-mile trails plus a ranger-guided option on the Matanzas River side that allow views of the ornamental gardens. The park is located 14 miles north of Flagler Beach on A1A. **Bulow Plantation State Historic Site**, ☎ 904-439-2219, offers a .4-mile trail that ends at the ruins of the sugar mill and spring house and includes a spur that leads to the ruins of the slave cabins. To reach the site from Flagler Beach, take Highway 100 west 2½ miles from A1A, turn left (south) on Highway 5-A (or South Old Kings Road), then continue three miles to the entrance. The **Tiger Bay State Forest**, ☎ 904-226-0250, has a 2½-mile trail that borders the Dukes Island Canal, going through wetlands and pine islands to Rattlesnake Pond, which is normally lacking its namesakes. The forest is on Highway 92, 10 miles west of Daytona.

DeLeon Springs State Recreation Area, ☎ 904-985-4212, offers a one-mile round-trip trail that meanders through a flood plain forest at an old plantation site. The park is located on Highway 3, which is off US 17 about three miles south of Barberville in west Volusia County. **Hontoon Island State Park**, ☎ 904-736-5309, is unique in that it's an island park accessible only by ferry or private boat. Located on the St. Johns River and Lake Beresford, its calling cards include the 1.6-mile trail that passes marshes and a lagoon and leads to an Indian shell mound and a replica of a 600-year-old owl totem discovered here in 1955. There's also an 80-foot observation tower on one of the trail spurs. From DeLeon Springs, take US 17 south seven miles to Highway 15-A, turn right and go to Highway 44, go right again and follow the signs. **Blue Spring State Park**, ☎ 904-775-3663, is eight miles south of Deland on US 17 near Orange City. It features a four-mile hiking trail through

Adventures 245

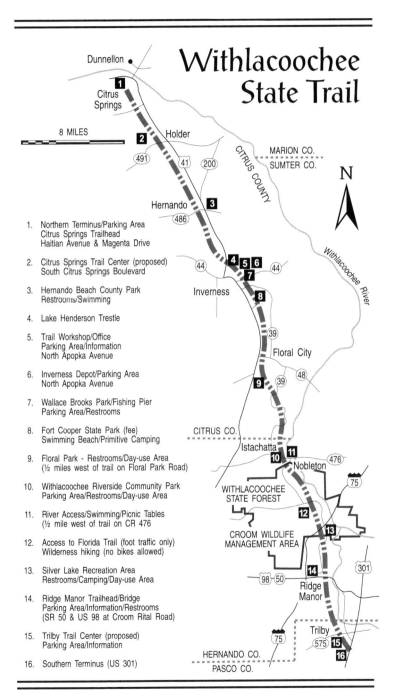

shaded hammocks and open flatwoods at a park that also includes a spring run, part of the St. Johns River and a lagoon.

Before you get into the water management district trails scattered across the region, there's one more option that provides up to a 47-mile route one-way: the **Withlacoochee State Trail**, accessible on its southern end by slipping just a tad out of the district. This one requires a long trip to hear the starter's gun, but it passes through scenic woodlands in west Sumter County, then goes into Citrus County, which you'll meet in the next chapter. From Ocala, follow US 301 south 57 miles to Trilby and the starting blocks. The trail, ☎ 352-796-5650, is part of the Florida Rails to Trails program. Most of it is paved, but some areas are graded. Much of it runs along uplands but there are wetland areas. Indigenous critters? Everything from otters and turkeys to deer and feral hogs. (Be careful if you run across the latter. They can't outrun a quarterhorse, but they can outrun you, and a feral hog can leave a nasty impression about shin or calf level.) There are a lot of additional access points that allow for shorter courses and pit stops where you can cool those tootsies. You can get a map, which shows the additional access points, by writing the trail office at 12549 State Park Drive, Clermont, FL 34711.

The **St. Johns River Water Management District**, ☎ 904-329-4404, will be happy to send you a handy-dandy little guidebook if you call or write to P.O. Box 1429, Palatka, FL 32178-1429. Among the more attractive hikes are:

- ❑ **Emeralda Marsh Recreation Area**, ☎ 407-897-4311, 16 miles of weaving trails along Lake Yale and Lake Griffin, where you might see snowy-white egrets, bald eagles, wood storks, limpkins, wood ducks, hooded mergansers and, during the winter months, sandhill cranes. From Ocala, follow US 27/301/441 south to Belleview, where US 301 splits away. Continue south on US 27/441 five miles to Highway 42, turn left (east) and go 13 miles to Highway 452. Turn right (south) for a three-mile dash to the entrance.

- ❑ **Kratzert Conservation Area**, ☎ 407-897-4311, offers 3½ miles of trails that go through wetlands, the St. Johns River and Lake Monroe. From Daytona, drive west on Highway 92 five miles to Highway 415, turn left and go 25 miles, then through Osteen one mile to the entrance.

- ❑ **Ocklawaha Prairie Restoration Area**, ☎ 904-329-4404, provides 10 miles of trails along the Kyle Young Canal, Ocklawaha River Channel and some pretty extensive wetlands. To reach it from Ocala, follow Highway 40 about 13 miles east of US 301 to Highway 314-A, go right (south) to the sign at the entrance.

- **Sunnyhill Restoration Area**, ☎ 352-821-1489, has 20 miles of hiking trails along a US Army Corps of Engineers canal and dike, the Ocklawaha River and a series of wetlands, where overhead you're likely to observe tri-colored herons, white ibises, red-tailed and red-shouldered hawks, several owl species and, in winter, sandhill cranes. To get to the site from Ocala, follow US 27/441 south 18 miles to Highway 42, turn left (east), go eight miles (through Weirsdale) to Forest Road 8 (S.E. 182nd Avenue Road) and turn left (north) one mile to the entrance.
- **Turnbull Hammock Conservation Area**, ☎ 407-984-4940, gives you nearly nine miles of trails through densely vegetated wetlands that are home to several bird species. From Daytona Beach, follow US 1 south 15 miles, through New Smyrna Beach, and follow the signs right on Halifax Road.

The **Southwest Florida Water Management District** will be equally happy to mail you its recreational guide if you call ☎ 800-423-1476 or 352-796-7211, or write the district at 2379 Broad St., Brooksville, FL 34609-6899. Its hiking trails include the following:

- The **Green Swamp** has 20 miles of trails that occasionally come across the Withlacoochee River and wetlands. To reach it from Ocala, take Interstate 75 south to the Bushnell exit (Highway 48) and turn left (east) six miles to Highway 471, then right (south) 18 miles to the site.
- The **Green Swamp Hiking Trail**, not to be confused with where you've just been, is 20.3 miles of off-road routes, broken into a 13.6-mile overnight trail and a 7.7-mile day-tripper. Orange blazes mark the main trail, blue blazes a side trail and double blazes warn you of a sharp turn – not that you're going to be hoofing it fast enough to skid on a sharp turn. From Ocala, take US 301 south 27 miles through Wildwood to Coleman and Highway 471, turn left and go 22 miles into the Richloam region of the Withlacoochee State Forest. Look for the signs directing you to the tract. (Warning:

This one's a little tricky to find and there's no site attendant. Call the water management district for specific directions or write for the guidebook.)
- **Little Withlacoochee Flood Detention Area**, ☎ 352-629-8162. Yes, most places call it a flood retention area. Detention sounds as if you're being made to stay after school. That aside, there are 30 miles of trails waiting, so maybe you don't mind being kept after. The trails saunter through flatwoods, swampy stands of cypress, bayheads and hammocks in a spring region that is a vital recharge zone for the Floridan aquifer, the main drinking water supply for folks in Central Florida. The trails, mainly across forest land but at one point crossing the Little Withlacoochee River, start on Highway 471 (see the directions to the Green Swamp Hiking Trail in the previous paragraph and look for the signs to the Little Withlacoochee area before you reach the Green Swamp).

Remember, when it comes to water management districts, conservation areas and forests, check in advance to make sure you're not planning on hiking when gun- or even bow-toting hunters are in the area.

If your appetite for hiking isn't satisfied, there are always the beaches – 23 miles in Daytona Beach/Ormond Beach and 18 miles at Flagler Beach.

INFORMATION SOURCES

Florida Trail Association, ☎ 800-343-1882 (in Florida) or 352-378-8823, P.O. Box 13708, Gainesville, FL 32604.
Office of Greenways & Trails, ☎ 904-487-4784, Mail Station 795, 3900 Commonwealth Boulevard, Tallahassee, FL 32399-3000.

GOLF COURSES

- **Bella Vista Golf & Country Club,** ☎ 352-324-3233, Highway 48, Howey-In-The-Hills, FL 34737, 18 holes, driving range, lessons, PGA rating R-67.1.
- **Clerbrook Resort,** ☎ 352-394-6165, 20005 US Hwy. 27, Clermont, FL 34711, 18 holes, driving range, lessons, R-63.

- **Continental Country Club**, ☎ 352-748-3293, Highway 44, Wildwood, FL 32785, 18 holes, driving range, lessons, R-68.1.
- **Country Club of Lady Lakes**, ☎ 352-733-4848, Rolling Acres Road, Lady Lakes, FL 32159, 18 holes, R-69.9.
- **Country Club of Mount Dora**, ☎ 352-735-2263, 1900 Country Club Blvd., Mount Dora, FL 32757, 18 holes, driving range, lessons, R-71.5.
- **Country Club at Silver Springs Shores**, ☎ 352-687-2828, 565 Silver Road, Ocala, FL 34472, 18 holes, R-69.5.
- **Cypress Knolls**, ☎ 904-437-5807, 1 Corporate Drive, Palm Coast, FL 32051, driving range, lessons, R-70.
- **Daytona Beach Golf & Country Club**, ☎ 904-258-3119, 600 Wilder Blvd., Daytona Beach, FL 32114, 36 holes, driving range, lessons, R-69 and 68.6.
- **Deltona Hills Golf & Country Club**, ☎ 904-789-4911, 1120 Elkham Road, Deltona, FL 32735, 18 holes, driving range, lessons, R-72.6.
- **Fairgreen Golf Club**, ☎ 904-427-4138, 35 Fairgreen Ave., New Smyrna Beach, FL 32075, 18 holes, no rating.
- **Golf Club at Cypress Head**, ☎ 904-756-5449, 6231 Palm Vista St., Port Orange, FL 32124, 18 holes, driving range, lessons, R-66.9.
- **Green Valley Country Club**, ☎ 352-394-2133, Highway 50 West, Clermont, FL 34712, 18 holes, driving range, lessons, no rating.
- **Hacienda Hills Golf & Country Club**, ☎ 352-753-5155, 1200 Avenida Central, Lady Lake, FL 32159, 18 holes, driving range, lessons, R-70.4.
- **Halifax Plantation**, ☎ 904-676-9600, 4000 Old Dixie Highway, Ormond Beach, FL 32174, 18 holes, driving range, lessons, R-73.9.
- **Harbor Hills Golf & Country Club**, ☎ 352-753-7000, 6538 Lake Griffin Road, Lady Lake, FL 32159, 18 holes, driving range, lessons, R-68.8.
- **Huntington Golf Club**, ☎ 352-347-3333, 14525 S.W. 67th Ave., Ocala, FL 34473, 18 holes, driving range, lessons, no rating.
- **Indigo Lakes Golf Club**, ☎ 904-254-3607, 312 Indigo Drive, Daytona Beach, FL 32114, 18 holes, driving range, lessons, R-73.5.

North-Central Florida

- **LPGA International**, ☎ 904-374-3880, I-95 & Highway 92, Daytona Beach, FL 32114, 18 holes, driving range, lessons, R-70.1.
- **Marion Oaks Country Club**, ☎ 352-347-1271, 4260 S.W. 162nd Street Road, Ocala, FL 32673, 36 holes, driving range, R-70.6.
- **Matanzas Woods Golf Club**, ☎ 904-446-6330, 398 Lakeview Blvd., Palm Coast, FL 32151, 18 holes, driving range, lessons, R-71.1.
- **Monastery Golf Club**, ☎ 904-774-2714, 1717 Monastery Road, Orange City, FL 32763, 18 holes, driving range, lessons, R-69.1.
- **Mount Dora Golf Club**, ☎ 352-383-3954, 1100 South Highland, Mount Dora, FL 32757, 18 holes, R-66.8.
- **New Smyrna Beach Municipal Golf Course**, ☎ 904-424-2192, 1000 Wayne Ave., New Smyrna Beach, FL 32168, 18 holes, driving range, lessons, R-70.2.
- **Ocala Golf Club**, ☎ 352-622-6198, 3130 E. Silver Springs Blvd., Ocala, FL 32670, 18 holes, lessons, R-71.1.
- **Ocean Palm Golf Club**, ☎ 904-439-2477, 3600 S. Central Ave., Flagler Beach, FL 32036, nine holes, driving range, lessons, R-62.2.
- **Palisades Country Club**, ☎ 352-394-0085, 16510 Palisades, Clermont, FL 34711, 18 holes, driving range, lessons, R-69.6.
- **Palm Harbor Golf Club**, ☎ 904-445-2686, Casper Road, Palm Coast, FL 32151, 18 holes, driving range, lessons, no rating.
- **Pelican Bay Golf & Country Club South**, ☎ 904-756-0034, 350 Pelican Bay Drive, Daytona Beach, FL 32019, 36 holes, lessons, no rating.
- **Pine Lakes Country Club**, ☎ 904-445-0852, 400 Pine Lakes Parkway, Palm Coast, FL 32051, 18 holes, driving range, lessons, R-69.3.
- **Pine Oaks of Ocala**, ☎ 352-867-7961, 2001 N.W. 21st St., Ocala, FL 32671, 27 holes, driving range, lessons, R-68.2.
- **River Bend Golf Club**, ☎ 904-673-6000, 730 Airport Road, Ormond Beach, FL 32174, 18 holes driving range, lessons, R-70.1.
- **Southridge Golf Club**, ☎ 904-736-0560, 800 East Euclid Ave., Deland, FL 32721, 18 holes, R-67.8.

- **Sheraton Palm Coast Resort**, ☎ 904-445-3000, 300 Clubhouse Drive, Palm Coast, FL 32137, 90 holes, driving range, lessons, R-71.1 to 73.5.
- **Spruce Creek Golf & Racquet Club**, ☎ 904-756-6114, 1900 Country Club Drive, Daytona Beach, FL 33124, 18 holes, driving range, lessons, R-69.5.
- **Sugar Mill Country Club**, ☎ 904-426-5200, 100 Clubhouse Circle, New Smyrna Beach, FL 32069, 27 holes, no rating.
- **Tomoka Oaks Golf & Country Club**, ☎ 904-677-7117, 20 Tomoka Oaks Blvd., Ormond Beach, FL 32174, 18 holes, driving range, lessons, R-72.1.
- **Village Green Golf Club**, ☎ 352-343-7770, Shirley Shores Drive, Tavares, FL 32778, 18 holes, no rating.
- **Water Oak Golf Club**, ☎ 352-753-3905, 106 Evergreen Lane, Lady Lake, FL 32159, 18 holes, R-67.4.

On Horseback

The **Ocala National Forest**, ☎ 352-669-3153, provides 134 miles of riding trails in four sections. Three of them have the same launch pad: the **Flatwoods Trail**, 40 miles, marked with red blazes; the **Prairie Trail**, 40 miles, marked with white blazes; and the **Baptist Lake Trail**, 20 miles, marked with blue blazes. To reach them from downtown Ocala, take Highway 40 (Silver Springs Boulevard) 31 miles east to Highway 19, turn right (south) and drive 12 miles to Lake Dorr Road and the starting point. The **Lake/Alachua/Marion Horse Trail** is 34 miles, marked with yellow blazes. The access point is at the Doe Lake Organizational Camp. From Ocala, take US 27/301/441 south – stick with US 27/441 when US 301 slips away – for 18 miles to Highway 42 and turn left (east), travel 11 miles to County Road 210-A, turn left (north) for four miles and then right on Forest Road 573. The trail begins three-quarters of a mile after the last turn. The scenery on all four trails includes oaks, magnolias and black tupelos, with the common assortment of native Florida varmints.

The 47-mile **Withlacoochee State Trail**, ☎ 352-796-5650, is part of Florida's Rails to Trails program, and it's open to horsemen and women. You can reach its southern end from Ocala by taking US 301 south 57 miles to Trilby and the trail entrance. Riding is not allowed on the pavement. Bridle paths are designated to keep you clear of hikers and bikers. The trail is mainly through uplands. You can get a map, which shows additional access points, by writing to the trail office at 12549 State Park Drive, Clermont, FL 34711.

The 29.2-mile **Gen. James A. Van Fleet State Trail**, ☎ 352-447-1633 (or, if you don't mind a taped message, ☎ 352-394-2280), is a nice route for riders. The Van Fleet trail is paved, except for the southernmost 2.8 miles and the 5.2-mile stretch located in the northern third. It has restrooms, benches, covered shelters and two picnic areas along the way. From Clermont, take Highway 50 about 12 miles west to a radar blip called Mabel and the trail entrance. You can get more information by writing to 12549 State Park Drive, Clermont, FL 34711.

The 2½-mile **Dukes Island hiking trail** at **Tiger Bay State Forest**, ☎ 904-226-0250, is open to riders as well. This part of the forest includes wetlands and pine islands leading to a small pond. The trail's entrance is on Highway 92, about 10 miles west of Daytona Beach.

The **St. Johns River Water Management District**, ☎ 904-329-4404, permits riding at three of its properties. You can get a guidebook by calling or writing to P.O. Box 1429, Palatka, FL 32178-1429.

- ❏ The **Lake George Conservation Area** has more than 20 miles of trails bordering the lake, hardwood swamps and pine flatwoods. Fox squirrels, owls, bald eagles, herons, ospreys, hawks, deer and otters are common to the area. From Ormond Beach, follow Highway 40 west 24 miles to Barberville and US 17, turning right (north) for a nine-mile drive to Seville and the tract's entrance.

- ❏ The **Emeralda Marsh Recreation Area**, ☎ 407-897-4311, offers about 15 miles of trails through upland areas near Lake Griffin. Snowy-white egrets, bald eagles, wood storks, limpkins, wood ducks, hooded mergansers and, during the winter months, sandhill cranes inhabit this area. From Ocala, take US 27 south to Belleview, where it splits with US 301, and continue on US 441 south about five miles to Highway 42, turn left (east) and go 13 miles to Highway 452, then turn right (south) for three miles to the entrance.

- ❏ **Kratzert Conservation Area**, ☎ 407-897-4311, offers 3½ miles of trails that go through wetlands, the St. Johns River and Lake Monroe. From Daytona, drive west on Highway 92 five miles to Highway 415, turn left and go 25 miles, through Osteen one mile, to the entrance.

The **Southwest Florida Water Management District**, ☎ 800-423-1476 or 352-796-7211, allows riding at its Little Withlacoochee River Flood Detention Area. It has 30 miles of trails through flatwoods, swampy cypress stands, bayheads and hammocks. From Ocala, take US 301 south 27 miles to Coleman and Highway 471, turn left and continue 22 miles to the Richloam region of the Withlacoochee State Forest, looking for the signs directing you to the tract. (As mentioned under the hiking adventures, this one's a bit tricky. Call or write the water management district – there's no site attendant – for specific directions.)

Two riding options are available if you don't bring a horse.

Fiddler's Green Ranch, ☎ 800-947-2624 or 352-669-7111, is on the edge of the Ocala National Forest and specializes in short and long trail rides. The ranch also has accommodations. It's located on Highway 19, at the southern tip of the forest in Altoona. **Young's Paso Fino Ranch**, ☎ 352-867-5305, which is located on Highway 326 in Ocala, also offers trail rides.

If you're bringing horses to Florida, don't forget a negative Coggins.

On Wheels

Peddlers won't find many bicycle trails in this region, but there are a handful that provide scenic workouts.

The 47-mile **Withlacoochee State Trail**, ☎ 352-796-5650, part of the Rails to Trails program, is open to cyclists. Most of it is paved, but some parts are graded. From Ocala, take US 301 south 57 miles to Trilby and the entrance. The trail is mostly through uplands. To get a map, which shows other access points, call or write the trail office at 12549 State Park Drive, Clermont, FL 34711.

The 29.2-mile **Gen. James A. Van Fleet State Trail**, ☎ 352-447-1633, or for a recording, 352-394-2280, is another nice route for peddlers. It has restrooms, benches, picnic areas and covered shelters. To get there from Clermont, follow Highway 50 about 12 miles west to Mabel and the trail's entrance. You can get additional information by writing the office at 12549 State Park Drive, Clermont, FL 34711.

The 2½-mile **Dukes Island Hiking Trail** at **Tiger Bay State Forest**, ☎ 904-226-0250, is open to bicyclists as well. This part of the forest includes wetlands and pine islands leading to a small pond.

The trail entrance is on Highway 92, about 10 miles west of Daytona Beach.

Additionally, Lake County has become a favorite spot for groups that put on organized rides. More than 20 are staged annually, including the **Mount Dora Bike Fest**, a 22-year-old, three-day event that draws 2,000 riders each October. One of the best routes includes climbing Sugarloaf Mountain. It's a mountain by Florida standards anyway: 320 feet above sea level, the second highest place in the state. You can chart your own course to it. From Ocala, follow US 27/301/441 south – stay on US 27/441 when US 301 slips away – 26 miles to Leesburg and stick with US 441 when it splits left (east) from US 27; continue east six miles to Tavares and Highway 19. You can begin your ride where Highway 561 begins. It's a nine-mile peddle to one of the most scenic lookout points in the state. For more information on regional touring options and events, ☎ 352-343-9655 or the Florida Freewheelers Club, ☎ 407-788-3446.

The **St. Johns River Water Management District**, ☎ 904-329-4404, permits cycling at four of its properties.

- ❏ The **Lake George Conservation Area** has a nine-mile trail one-way that ends at the lake. Fox squirrels, owls, bald eagles, herons, ospreys, hawks, deer and river otters inhabit the area. From Ormond Beach, follow Highway 40 west 24 miles to Barberville and US 17, turning right (north) for a nine-mile drive to Seville and the tract's entrance.
- ❏ The **Emeralda Marsh Conservation Area** offers a six-mile trail, one-way, that runs along Emeralda Island Road, across the Yale-Griffin canal and borders Lake Griffin. Snowy-white egrets, bald eagles, wood storks and wood ducks are pretty abundant. From Ocala, take US 27 south to Belleview where it splits with US 301 and continue on US 441 south about five miles to Highway 42, turn left (east) and go 13 miles to Highway 452, then turn right (south) for three miles to the entrance.
- ❏ The **Kratzert Conservation Area** provides a five-mile trail one way along Reed Ellis Road and bordering Lake Bethel. From Daytona Beach, go west on Highway 92 about five miles to Highway 415, turn left and go 25 miles, through Osteen, then one mile to the entrance.
- ❏ The **Turnbull Hammock Conservation Area** has a six-mile, one-way trail on Maytown Road through dense wetlands that are habitats of ospreys, roseate spoon-

bills, snowy egrets, ibises and other bird species. From Daytona Beach, travel US 1 south 15 miles, through New Smyrna Beach, and follow the signs right on Halifax Road.

For a guide, call or write to P.O. Box 1429, Palatka, FL 32178-1429.

The **Southwest Florida Water Management District**, ☎ 800-423-1476 or 352-796-7211, has cycling trails at two sites.

- The **Green Swamp tract** has more than 30 miles of graded trails that go across the Withlacoochee River and border wetlands. To get there from Ocala, follow Interstate 75 south to the Bushnell exit (Highway 48) and go left (east) six miles to Highway 471 and right (south) 18 miles to the site.

- **Little Withlacoochee Flood Detention Area**, ☎ 352-629-8162, has another 30 miles of graded trails through flatwoods, swampy cypress stands, bayheads and hammocks in a spring region. The trails mainly cut through forest but at one point you cross the Little Withlacoochee River. From Ocala, take US 301 south 27 miles to Coleman and Highway 471, turn left and go 22 miles to the Richloam region of the Withlacoochee State Forest, looking for the signs to the tract.

For a guide, call or write to 2379 Broad St., Brooksville, FL 34609-6899.

INFORMATION SOURCES

Office of Greenways & Trails, ☎ 904-487-4784, 325 John Knox Road, Building 500, Tallahassee, FL 32303-4124.

Florida Department of Transportation, ☎ 904-487-9220, Mail Station 82, 605 Suwanee St., Tallahassee, FL 32399-0450.

On Water

CANOEING

You can wear out a paddle in this region, which is one of the most prolific in Florida when it comes to canoe options. There are six designated state trails and several places to improvise, so bring plenty of Absorbine Jr.

The **Pellicer Creek Canoe Trail** is a four-mile run with virtually no current (zero-one mph). It winds through a tidal marsh where canoeists usually see wading birds, waterfowl, alligators, otters and raccoons. Bald eagles also nest in the area. The current is slow enough so you can paddle upstream for a round-trip. From Ormond Beach, travel US 1 north 31 miles to the Pellicer Creek bridge.

The **Bulow Creek Canoe Trail** in Flagler County begins at the plantation's ruins, ☎ 904-439-2219. It leads upstream and back, then heads downstream to the Intracoastal Waterway. The 13-mile trail passes grassy coastal marsh, and you're very likely to see ospreys and maybe an alligator and wild hog or two. This one's rated beginning in skill and easy-to-moderate in difficulty with a zero-one mph current. For the full run, drive Highway 100 2½ miles west of Flagler Beach, then turn left (south) onto Highway 5-A (South Old Kings Road) and continue three miles to the site's entrance. For a short course (six miles), take Highway 100 1½ miles west of A1A at Flagler Beach and go left (south) on Highway 201 for four miles to the Walter Boardman Bridge. Note: Wind and waves are possible on this run.

The **Tomoka River Canoe Trail** in Volusia County is another 13-miler that carries a beginner-to-intermediate skill rating and an easy-to-moderate difficulty factor. The trail twists around cypress knees before heading into coastal marsh habitats. It starts narrow and widens downstream before ending at the site of an ancient Timucuan Indian village known as Nocoroco. The full route begins at the Highway 40 bridge, four miles west of US 1 in Ormond Beach. A shorter, nine-mile option begins at the US 1 bridge, 2½ miles north of Highway 40. Current: zero-one mph.

The **Spruce Creek Canoe Trail**, also in Volusia, is 14 miles and rates as beginner and easy with a zero-one mph current. The trail goes upstream, then returns downstream to the same access point. You'll pass dense hardwood forests and coastal marshes. Egrets, ospreys and brown pelicans are abundant. From A1A in South

Daytona, travel Highway 421 (Taylor Road) four miles. Just beyond the Interstate 95 interchange (about 600 feet), turn left (south) on Airport Road and continue about a mile to Moody Bridge.

The **Econlockhatchee** (looks like someone scattered a bunch of vowels and consonants on the page, doesn't it?) **River Canoe Trail** is 19 miles soup to nuts. It's rated beginner and easy with a two-three mph current. Shallow and narrow at first, the river twists through oak and palm hammocks before it widens midway down and begins passing high, sandy banks. This puppy ends at the St. Johns River – watch for motorboats if you venture into it. You have to book it out of the region for the starting line, but you'll finish in Volusia. From New Smyrna Beach, take Highway 44 west four miles to I-95 and follow the interstate south 34 miles to the Highway 50 exit, turn right (west) and go 19 miles to Highway 419. Turn right (north) and go 8.2 miles to the bridge.

The **Wekiva River/Rock Springs Run Canoe Trail** is the region's longest, at 27 miles. This option is rated intermediate and moderate with parts packing currents in excess of three mph. It includes the Rock Springs Run and a jaunt along the Wekiva River. The trail passes sand pine scrub, pine flatwoods, hammocks and swamps. There are several islands, tributaries and lagoons that provide a lot of opportunities for side trips and camping. For the full trail, start at Tavares and travel US 441 southeast 25 miles to Apopka and Highway 435, going left (north) six miles to Kelly Park Road, turning right (east) .3 mile to Baptist Camp Road and heading left (north) .7 mile to Kings Landing. A short seven-mile run can be reached by driving US 441 from Tavares east eight miles to Highway 46, turning left and going 22 miles to Wekiva River Road, then right and going 1.4 miles to Wekiva Falls Resort.

The **Rainbow River** is next up. While it's not a designated trail, it's a hard one to pass up. The Rainbow really is one of the most beautiful rivers in Florida, primarily because it's spring-fed and virtually crystal clear the entire course. The output at the head spring is 250 million gallons a day. There are a lot of springs to tempt snorkelers and swimmers along the five-mile run and, if you're up for a longer voyage, it empties into the Withlacoochee River 22 miles before it winds its way to the Gulf of Mexico. Marion County operates the canoe concession at the state-owned **Rainbow Springs State Campground**. To get to the camp from Ocala, drive Highway 40 west 16 miles from downtown, turn left (south) on S.W. 180th Avenue (watch for signs to the spring and Dunnellon High School) and go 2½ miles to the entrance on the right. This camp, ☎ 352-489-5201, is a mile from the main spring, but the current is mild. Most paddlers don't find it difficult going upstream.

Three other state areas in the region have modest canoeing venues:

- **Hontoon Island State Park**, ☎ 904-736-5309, lets you paddle the St. Johns and Dead rivers, a lagoon and Lake Beresford. From DeLeon Springs, take US 17 south seven miles to Highway 15-A, turn right, drive to Highway 44, turn right again and follow the signs.
- **Blue Spring State Park**, ☎ 904-775-3663, has canoeing on the St. Johns River and a lagoon. It's eight miles south of Deland on US 17 near Orange City.
- **Lake Griffin State Recreation Area**, ☎ 352-787-7402, offers canoeing on its namesake lake. From Ocala, follow US 27 south to Belleview, where it splits from US 301 and continues with US 441. Go south five miles to Highway 42, turn left (east) and go 13 miles to Highway 452, then right (south) for three miles to the entrance.

Juniper Springs Recreation Area in the Ocala National Forest, ☎ 352-625-2808, features a seven-mile trail down Juniper Creek and a rental concession. The run is dotted with hammocks, springs and wildlife. From Ocala, point your Pontiac east on Highway 40 and drive 28 miles to the entrance on the left.

Four **St. Johns Water Management District** sites, ☎ 904-329-4404, or P.O. Box 1429, Palatka, FL 32178-1429, offer opportunities for canoeists:

- The **Lake George Conservation Area**, located in Volusia County west of US 17 on Highway 305, on its namesake lake.
- The **Emeralda Marsh Conservation Area**, in Lake and Marion counties between Highways 42 and 44, on Lake Griffin.
- The **Ocklawaha Prairie Restoration Area**, south of Highway 40, west of Highway 314-A in the Ocala National Forest (Marion County), on the Kyle Young Canal and Ocklawaha River.
- The **Sunnyhill Restoration Area**, just off Highway 42, southwest of Ocala and west of Weirsdale (Marion County), on canals and levées.

INFORMATION SOURCES & ADDITIONAL OUTFITTERS

For designated trail maps, write to the **Office of Greenways and Trails**, ☎ 904-487-4784, 325 John Knox Road, Bldg. 500, Tallahassee, FL 32303-4124.
Florida Association of Canoe Liveries & Outfitters, ☎ 941-494-1215, P.O. Box 1764, Arcadia, FL 33821.
Juniper Springs Canoe Rentals, ☎ 352-625-2808, 24860 N.E. 147th Place, Fort McCoy, FL 32134.
Ocklawaha Outpost, ☎ 352-236-4606, 15250 N.E. 152nd Place, Fort McCoy, FL 32134.
Florida Pack & Paddle, 10705 S.E. 151st St., Summerfield, FL 34491.

DIVING & SNORKELING

Whether your choice is on or below the surface, there's a nice assortment of freshwater and saltwater sites in the region.

Some of the aesthetics at **Devil's Sink** are above the water line – 75-foot bluffs towering over the dive. The sink is an 80-foot hole with a big room not very far beneath the surface. To get there from Ocala, take Highway 40 east 11 miles to Highway 315, turn left (north) and put it on cruise control for 34 miles until you reach Highway 20, then turn left (west) and go about four miles to a dirt road that is opposite a lake and turn right. (Note: If you reach Highway 21 you've gone two miles too far west.) One hundred yards in, take one of the two sand roads going in on the left to the sink. **Silver Glen Springs** is a snorkel-only site that features a challenge for free divers: At eight feet there's an entrance to a cave and a depth of 42 feet. There's also a spring run where fish are abundant. To find Silver Glen from Ocala, follow Highway 40 east 38 miles to Highway 19, turn left (north) and go 6½ miles to a dirt road on the right that runs under a wooden arch to the site. **Blue Spring** in Orange City is a magnet for cave divers and manatee lovers. The mammals come into the 72° spring during the winter months, but the park rangers are very protective of the critters. Underwater, you're not allowed to get closer than 50 feet, but that's near enough for a good view. The cave starts in 10 feet of water, drops to 60 feet, then angles to 120 feet and a strong flow. Cave certification is required. From Deland, go south on US 17 six miles to Orange City, turn left (west) onto West French Avenue and continue 3.2 miles. Turn left at the first dirt road past a railroad overpass to the check-in station.

Offshore, there are three dandy wreck sites to explore. The **Liberty Ship *Mindanao*** is a 446-footer resting at 80 feet, about 12 miles off Ponce Inlet and New Smyrna Beach. The top deck is 50 feet down, and there are large holes in the hull and compartments for adventurers and marine life. Around 18 miles off the inlet, a pair of **torpedo bombers** lie where they crashed during World War II. They are in 71 feet of water, about 200 yards apart. This is a good spearfishing site; it's usually loaded with snapper and sheepshead. **Twelve-Mile Wreck**, also 12 miles from the inlet, is thought to be the remains of a Spanish-American War-era gunrunner (the evidence is Gatling ammunition found around it). Big jewfish, amberjacks and spadefish haunt this site. **East Eleven** is a good reef to explore in this area. It's about 21 miles east of Ponce Inlet, with depths to 75 feet. This dive has large numbers of fish and some lobster. It's a good place for shelling and tropical fish collecting.

INFORMATION SOURCES

Florida Association of Dive Operators, ☎ 305-451-3020, 51 Garden Cove Drive, Key Largo, FL 33037.

US Coast Guard, Mayport, ☎ 904-246-7315.

Florida Marine Patrol, ☎ 904-359-6580, 2510 Second Ave. N., Jacksonville Beach, FL 32250.

Ned DeLoach's Diving Guide to Underwater Florida, ☎ 904-737-6558, New World Publications, 1861 Cornell Road, Jacksonville, FL 32207.

Bahama Island Adventures, ☎ 800-329-1337, 250 S. Beach St., #202, Daytona Beach, FL 32114.

Discover Scuba Diving, ☎ 904-677-2133, 1650 San Jose Blvd., Holly Hill, FL 32117.

Advanced Dive Center, ☎ 904-426-1442, 111 N. Riverside Drive, New Smyrna Beach, FL 32168.

Scuba Outfitters, ☎ 352-351-8099, 2023 E. Silver Springs Blvd., #302, Ocala, FL 34470.

Ocala Dive Center, ☎ 352-732-9779, 500 S.W. 10th St., #305, Ocala, FL 34474.

Crazy Dog Scuba, ☎ 352-357-5888, 4950 N. Highway 19, Mount Dora, FL 32757.

Underwater Adventures, ☎ 352-787-0760, 400 West Magnolia, Leesburg, FL 34748.

SALTWATER & FRESHWATER FISHING

Hang onto your rod. King mackerel are almost as common off Flagler and Volusia County beaches as they are off St. Augustine. The summer brings 50- to 60-pound heavyweights. Dolphins, blue marlins, swordfish and wahoos are other summer favorites well offshore. Closer to shore, you can fish for flounder, snook, sheepshead and mangrove snapper at the mouth of Ponce Inlet in summer and redfish and sea trout during winter. Sharks also are popular trophies in summer. For landlubbers, surf fishing is good almost anywhere you can get to the beach.

The region claims four state saltwater records: A 19½-pound hogfish that was landed off Daytona Beach, a 50½-pound African pompano also off Daytona Beach, an 8-pound, 1-ounce Florida pompano caught off Flagler Beach and a 190-pound spinner shark off Flagler Beach.

Charter and head boat operators include **Critter Fleet**, ☎ 904-767-7676, at Ponce Inlet, and **Fishin' Cove**, ☎ 904-428-6781, at New Smyrna Beach. Folks who prefer pier fishing can choose among the 1,009-foot **Ocean Pier**, ☎ 904-253-1212, in Daytona Beach, the 1,000-foot **Sunglow Fishing Pier**, ☎ 904-756-4219, located at Ormond Beach, and a 600-footer at Ponce Inlet (no telephone). Area bait-and-tackle shops include **Fishin' Hole**, ☎ 904-252-9804, on Daytona Beach, **Mike and Krims**, ☎ 904-439-3842, on Flagler Beach, and **Ormond Bait and Tackle**, ☎ 904-677-9636, in Holly Hill.

Freshwater anglers find **Lake Mineola** in Clermont on Highway 50 to be a productive bass, bluegill and shellcracker hole. There are a lot of channel catfish, and 20-pounders are not uncommon. **Lake Griffin**, which is accessible from US 441 in Leesburg, has water quality and habitat problems that make bass fishing poor. But the black crappie fishing is great from November through April, while shellcracker and bluegill are good targets in April and May. **Lake Weir** in Marion County has attractors that make it another good shellcracker spot in March and April. It's located north of Highway 42 and east of US27/441, 15 miles south of Ocala. The **Ocklawaha River**, which you can reach from Highway 40, nine miles east of Ocala, is a good bass spot in virtually all areas, especially from February through April. Redbreast and spotted sunfish also are found on the river. Sumter County's **Lake Panasoffkee** is most noted for shellcracker, but bass is another good prey. It's located on Highway 470 off Highway 44, about six miles west of Interstate 75. The **Withlacoochee River**, also accessible off Highway 44 a little west of Highway 470, has a range of fish, from largemouth, bluegill and redear sunfish to channel catfish and warmouth. Last, but not least, **Lake George** over in Volusia County is known as the best bass fishing lake in Central Florida. The lake has extensive vegetation that also makes it a good fishing spot for bream. Striped bass catches are good October through April, sunshine bass is best in the spring and fall and stripers are common May through September. The lake is accessible off Highway 40 in eastern Volusia.

Three state freshwater records have been set in the area: a 44½-pound channel catfish in Lake Bluff in Lake County, an 18.88-pound white catfish from the Withlacoochee River in Marion County and a 5.19-pound American shad in Volusia County's portion of the St. Johns River.

Many fish camps provide a full line of services, from ramps and boats to guides and fishing licenses. These include **Pine Island**, ☎ 352-753-2972, on Lake Griffin, **Blue Heron Cove**, ☎ 352-821-3701, on the Ocklawaha River, **Pana Vista Lodge**, ☎ 352-793-2061, on Lake Panasoffkee and the Withlacoochee River, and **Highbanks Marina and Camp**, ☎ 407-668-4491, on the St. Johns River in Volusia County.

Two state parks have popular fishing spots: **Lake Griffin State Recreation Area**, ☎ 352-787-7402, on US 27/441, is known for largemouth bass, bluegill and speckled perch, while **Washington Oaks State Gardens** in Flagler County, ☎ 904-445-3161, on A1A north of Flagler Beach, doubles the pleasure with surf fishing in the Atlantic (whiting, redfish, bluefish and pompano) and shore fishing in the Matanzas River.

You can drop a line at four **St. Johns River Water Management District** sites (the **Lake George, Emeralda Marsh** and **Kratzert conservation areas** and **Sunnyhill Restoration Area**). Guidebooks can be obtained by calling ☎ 904-329-4404 or writing the district at P.O. Box 1429, Palatka, FL 32178-1429. Further south and east, the **Southwest Florida Water Management District** has fishing holes at another four tracts (**Carlton Tract, Green Swamp, Lake Panasoffkee**, and **Little Withlacoochee River Flood Detention Area**). Call ☎ 800-423-1476 or write to 2379 Broad St., Brooksville, FL 34609-6899, for a guidebook.

Don't forget to pick up a fishing license. Non-resident saltwater licenses range from $5 for three days to $30 per year. Non-resident freshwater licenses cost $15 for seven days and $30 for a year. Also, there are size and bag limits on many species. Information on these is available from bait-and-tackle shops, marinas, local guides, the **Florida Marine Patrol**, ☎ 407-383-2740, 1 Max Brewer Memorial

Parkway, Titusville, FL 32796, and the **Florida Game & Fresh Water Fish Commission,** ☎ 352-732-1225, 1239 S.W. 10th St., Ocala, FL 34474-2797.

On Water II

Windsurfers, rowers and water skiers aren't left out in the North-Central region. **Sandy Point Sports Shop,** ☎ 904-756-7564, serves as a headquarters for windsurfers, who can choose between the Halifax River or the Atlantic Ocean. One of the best spots is Ponce Inlet, just north of New Smyrna Beach, which is noted for a variety of wave breaks. The Halifax River also is gaining popularity among the rowing and sculling crowd. There's even free instruction available from the **Halifax Rowing Association,** ☎ 904-257-5332, every Saturday morning. Water skiers find dozens of Lake County lakes that are good for skiing and this area also features three world-class ski schools: **Sunset Lakes,** ☎ 352-429-9027, in Okahumpka, **Benzel Skiing Center,** ☎ 352-429-3574, in Groveland, and **Swiss Ski School** ☎ 352-429-2178, in Clermont.

In The Air

Jumping out of an airplane isn't for everyone. Look at what happened 20 years ago when D.B. Cooper hijacked an airliner, collected a ransom and then rocketed (down, not up) into the ever after. If you're a little more skilled than old D.B., **Skydive Deland,** ☎ 904-738-3539, is a popular liftoff point 20 miles east of Daytona Beach, and **Paragators,** ☎ 352-669-9044, shuttles skydivers from Umatilla in Lake County.

Additionally, you can hitch a glider ride or get instruction at the **Seminole-Lake Gliderport,** ☎ 352-394-5450, in Clermont; seaplane rides and instruction from **Florida Seaplanes,** ☎ 352-343-2024, in Tavares; or biplane, glider and helicopter rides from **Thorpe Aviation,** ☎ 352-589-0767, near Eustis. **Graybird Airsports,** ☎ 352-245-8263, at Summerfield in Marion County provides hang gliding and ultralight flights.

Hot-air adventures? Bill Folkert's place (**Wet Willie's Balloon Team**), ☎ 352-481-3626, is based in Hawthorne (see page 187), but most of his lift-offs are from Ocala, with some in the Gainesville area. The 60-to 90-minute flights in the Ocala area give adventurers a bird's-eye view of the area's beautiful horse farms and forests. It's not unusual to see deer from treetop level. On clear days he'll shoot to 3,000 feet, where you can see the Atlantic Ocean and the Gulf of Mexico. **Cloud Encounters**, ☎ 352-237-4030, also provides hour-long balloon tours of the Ocala area.

Where To Stay & Eat

As through much of North and Northwest Florida, rooms and restaurants are, in general, plentiful enough that reservations are not mandatory, but consider the same caveat here as in other chapters. To ensure your first choice of dinnertime or accommodations, make them anyway, especially if you're coming to the Daytona Beach area during any of the frenzy periods, such as Bike Week or the Daytona 500.

Flagler County

On the upscale side, the **Palm Coast Resort**, ☎ 800-564-6538 or 904-445-3000, is a full service pit stop (golf, tennis, fishing, cycling, restaurant and more), four miles north of Flagler Beach. **Quality Inn Marineland**, ☎ 800-228-5151 or 904-471-1222, is located on the Atlantic. It has tennis courts and a restaurant and is a little more moderately priced. The county also has several smaller motels, such as the **Blue Atlantic Motel**, ☎ 904-439-1311, in Flagler Beach, the **Mil-Ton Motel** in Bunnell, ☎ 904-437-3801, and **Shire House Bed and Breakfast**, ☎ 904-445-8877, in Palm Coast. In addition to the usual chains, area restaurants include the **Dolphin Restaurant**, ☎ 904-471-1234, at Marineland, **Raymond's**, ☎ 904-446-2433, in Palm Coast, and the **Topaz Café**, ☎ 904-439-3275, at Flagler Beach.

Volusia County

Choices in the Daytona and Ormond Beach area include the **Adams Mark Daytona Beach Resort**, ☎ 800-872-9269 or

904-254-8200, the **Victorian Coquina Inn Bed and Breakfast**, ☎ 800-805-7533 or 904-254-4969, **Ramada Inn Speedway**, ☎ 800-353-2722 or 904-255-2422, **The Granada Inn**, ☎ 800-228-8089, **Best Western La Playa Resort**, ☎ 800-874-6996 or 904-672-0990, and the **Atlantic Waves Motel**, ☎ 800-881-2786 or 904-253-7186. When your hunger alarm starts screaming, the options are almost limitless. Consider just a few: **The English Rose Tea Room** in Ormond Beach, ☎ 904-672-7673, the **Crazy Horse Saloon**, ☎ 904-767-6022, located in Daytona Beach Shores, **The Oyster Club**, ☎ 904-672-8510, (home of the 25¢ oyster) in Ormond Beach, and **Teauila's Hawaii**, Daytona Beach, ☎ 904-672-3770, if you're in the mood for a luau.

Lake County

The area has several cozy room-and-restaurant combinations, including the **Citrus Sun Club**, ☎ 352-429-4111, in Clermont, the **Mission Inn Golf & Tennis Resort**, ☎ 352-324-3101, in Howey-in-the-Hills, **Marietta Park**, ☎ 352-323-0055, in Leesburg, **Lakeside Inn**, ☎ 800-556-5016 or 352-383-4101, in Mount Dora, and **Budget Inn Suites**, ☎ 352-343-4666, in Tavares. The **Lake Mineola Inn**, ☎ 352-394-2232, in Clermont, is a 90-year-old, old Florida-style bed-and-breakfast, while **Darst Victorian Manor**, ☎ 904-383-4050, sits above Lake Dora in Mount Dora.

Marion County

If you're into horses and are looking for a slightly different kind of resort, **Continental Acres**, ☎ 352-750-5500, in Weirsdale, combines down-on-the-farm charm with the sports of combined and pleasure carriage driving. In addition to cottage rentals and camping, Continental Acres has stables, training and a big community hall.

The Ocala area also has more traditional accommodations ranging from the **Hilton**, ☎ 352-854-1400, and **Marriott Courtyard**, ☎ 352-237-8000, to the **Seven Sisters Inn Bed and Breakfast**, ☎ 352-867-1170, to **Budget Host**, ☎ 352-732-6940, and **Days Inn East**, ☎ 352-236-2891. For a reasonably small city, Ocala has a mix of notable restaurants, including: **Carmichael's** (American specialties), ☎ 352-622-3636, **Victorian Gardens** (French and American gourmet), ☎ 352-867-5980, **Bella Luna** (Italian), ☎ 352-237-9155, and **Harry's** (seafood and steaks), ☎ 352-840-0900.

Campgrounds

North-Central Florida can accommodate any taste, from those who prefer the comfort of a heavily mortgaged Winnebago to the Happy Trails types whose only requirements are a sleeping bag, tent and six feet of soft turf.

The region has no shortage of commercial campgrounds.

In the coastal region, **Daytona Beach Campground**, ☎ 904-761-2663, offers 30 and 50 amp service, a heated pool, modern restrooms and other amenities. **Flagler by the Sea**, ☎ 800-434-2124, is on the ocean side of A1A, with free cable, pull-through sites, a café, store and more. **On Ocean Seaside RV & Trailer Park**, ☎ 904-441-0900, in Ormond Beach, is another oceanfront camp that's set among the beach's condominiums.

Inland, **Clerbrook Resort**, ☎ 800-440-3801, near Clermont, has hundreds of full hook-ups, an 18-hole golf course with driving range, fishing ponds, a heated pool and spa and activity directors. **Holiday Travel Resort**, ☎ 800-428-5334, which is in Leesburg, offers two recreation halls, an adult indoor heated pool and spa, as well as a family pool, mini-golf, a marina and tennis courts. **Thousand Trails**, ☎ 800-723-1217, in Clermont, has 734 full hook-ups, two pools, two lodges, mini-golf, tennis and more. The **Ocala/Silver Springs KOA**, ☎ 800-562-7798, sits amid oak and magnolia trees. Amenities include a large pool, hot tub, sauna, cable television, a playground and shuffleboard (it's Florida's state sport!) courts. Over in Sumter County, **Idlewild Lodge & RV Park**, ☎ 352-793-7057, is located on Lake Panasoffkee and provides boat rentals, a ramp, fishing pier, solar-heated pool, showers, rental efficiencies and large lots with concrete pads.

If you're among the grab-the-mosquito-net set, the five counties have a strong menu of campsites brought to you by the folks at our state parks, forests and water management districts.

Hontoon Island State Park, ☎ 904-736-5309, near Deland provides six rustic cabins and tent campsites around the St. Johns River. **Blue Spring State Park**, ☎ 904-775-3663, in Orange City, also has six rental cabins and primitive camping along the St. Johns. **Lake Griffin State Recreation Area**, ☎ 352-787-7402, offers a modern campground in a live-oak hammock near Fruitland Park. At the **Juniper Springs Recreation Area** in the Ocala National Forest, ☎ 352-625-2808, a 78-unit campground is just off Juniper Creek.

The **St. Johns Water Management District** permits camping at two tracts: the **Lake George Conservation Area** in western Volusia County and the **Kratzert Conservation Area** in southwest Volusia County. For a guidebook that includes maps and additional information, ☎ 904-329-4404 or write to P.O. Box 1429, Palatka, FL 32178-1429. Camping is permitted at the **Southwest Florida Water Management District's Green Swamp** site. For a guidebook, ☎ 800-423-1476 or 352-796-7211 or write to 2379 Broad St., Brooksville, FL 34609-6899.

Next up, your last dance, but what a dance: Manatee Central and the rest of The Nature Coast and the southern end of the Big Bend.

The Nature Coast & Big Bend

Hippopotamus husbandry learned the hard way:

"Lucifer the Rotund One" landed at a privately run tourist attraction, now the Homosassa Springs State Wildlife Park, in 1964, after a stellar career at Ivan Tors' Studio. (If you saw "Daktari" you saw Big Lu at his finest.)

J.P. Garner landed there a decade later.

Trouble was, J.P., an outdoors sort who had a natural way with wildlife, never had an experience with a two-ton animal that was vulnerable to stress and prone to eating anything that got in his way – which quickly led to two problems:

1) How do you hurricane-proof a hippo? The townies get nervous anytime flood waters start rising around their homesteads. They get even more nervous knowing Lu gets antsy when the rising Homosassa River threatens his own condo. Imagine two tons of non-indigenous bulk floating free, then running amok in your subdivision. "I've spent many a night down there with him," J.P. says in a velvety drawl, similar to Tom T. Hall's. "All ya gotta do is rub his gums and feed him a watermelon. He calms right down."

2) What if he eats something he's not meant to eat and gets constipated? "One time he swallowed one of those orange plastic sippers. Y'know, those little plastic things with a straw they sell juice in. He didn't have a bowel movement for three days so I mixed five gallons of mineral oil and got it into him." Well, nothing happened that night, but by the next morning Lucifer had worked things out in the trees and all over the walls of his home. "That orange sipper was in the next county."

Bedda-bing, bedda-bang, bedda-boom.

You won't find wild hippos in this part of Florida, but most of the critters in the park, and in the wild, were here hundreds, if not thousands, of years ago. The same thing goes for the land and water. This is nature's bedroom.

You can let the wind whip through your hair as you skim across pristine rivers in an airboat, languish in blissful silence as you paddle a canoe deeper into a landscape that remains as it was three centuries ago or dive into warm-water springs and watch a one-ton manatee glide by with her newborn calf.

The Nature Coast and Big Bend are two of the more popular names for this area. No signs proclaim where either begins or ends, but the four counties featured in this chapter – Citrus, Levy, Dixie and Taylor – are the heart of both. They form a back-to-nature paradise far from the glitter and crowds.

The headliner is a town of 4,000 named **Crystal River** – that pretty much summarizes the aesthetics. To passersby, it looks like many of the small towns along this stretch of US 19, which snakes along the coast. Small commercial and retail centers on the highway give little clue to the treasures that are within Citrus County.

Too bad for the passersby. Those who take the time to explore, like the first inhabitants, find a spring-fed river that holds the key to this natural wonder. Bald eagles, great blue herons, river otters and countless species of fish thrive here. Much of the reason is that more than 152,000 acres of coastal land have been set aside as refuges and preserves for wildlife and the environment. Record numbers of endangered West Indian manatees have been spending their winters in Crystal River and Kings Bay since the US Fish & Wildlife Service established refuges here.

Like the Crystal River, the Homosassa and Chassahowitzka rivers a few miles south have become favored haunts of scuba divers, snorkelers, canoeists and water skiers. Fishermen find these rivers and the connecting Gulf of Mexico rich with species ranging from black grouper, redfish and wahoo to cobia, trout and mangrove snapper. During spring and early summer, the Homosassa River is a hot spot for tarpon.

The adventure doesn't stop inland. More preserved land means additional chances to enjoy nature and outdoor activities. The 83-mile Withlacoochee River – called "long and winding water" by Native Americans – is a designated canoe trail. It's challenging enough so that the Canadian Olympic canoe team trained on it for several years. Gliding along the river or its feeder creeks, paddlers see hardwood forests and cypress swamps that remain undisturbed.

Speaking of forests, the 43,000-acre **Withlacoochee State Forest** and the 47-mile Withlacoochee State Trail, built on an abandoned railroad route, feature a variety of natural trails for hikers, horse-back riders and bicyclists. The forest is thick with scrub oaks, pines, sandhills and hammocks. If you're lucky, you'll bump into some of its many white-tail deer along the way.

The eastern side of the county, with more than 19,000 acres of lakes, is a bass fisherman's paradise. The **Tsala Apopka** chain of lakes has an abundance of largemouth bass as well as bream and crappie. The lakes are favorite areas for canoeists and kayakers, too.

One of the most astonishing things about this area of the state is that it's relatively undiscovered. More so the deeper you travel.

Moving north on US 19, Levy, Dixie and Taylor counties have vast tracts of timberland and game preserves dotted with glimpses of Old Florida. An artist painting a portrait of the region would include Cracker-style buildings, rivers and wetlands brimming with fish and wildlife, locals who smile and wave at strangers and, in the upper reaches, sweet corn, hay and peanuts planted on rolling hills.

Cedar Key on the Gulf Coast in Levy County is an island sanctuary where the old ways mingle with the new. It's surrounded by more than 100,000 acres of refuges and sanctuaries, including the Cedar Key National Wildlife Refuge and a scattering of restricted-access islands in the Gulf of Mexico that are havens for a number of rare bird species (roseate spoonbills, rare white pelicans and more). The historic Island Hotel, built in 1859, is a great spot to park yourself in a rocker and watch the world go by. And at launch points called Kiss-Me-Quick and Hug-Me-Tight, you can watch fishermen go to work as their forefathers did a century ago or, with camera in tow, capture marsh life or one of the spectacular coastal sunsets.

Dixie and Levy counties share a common boundary and the last leg of the historic Suwannee River before it empties into the Gulf of Mexico off Hog Island. The river is a popular place for houseboating and canoeing. (More on these when you start your adventures.) From the Dixie County side of the river near Old Town, a short jog up US 19, you can see one of the last reminders of the Suwannee's 19th-century steamboat past. The remains of the *City of Hawkinsville*, a steamer that worked the river a century ago, are a shallow-water archaeological site. It's a nostalgic dive, but one where care should be taken to preserve it for those who come after you. The banks throughout this 50-mile run are virtually undeveloped. To the north, the Steinhatchee River forms a boundary between Dixie and Taylor counties. It's dotted with rustic villages and weathered fishing boats, particularly at the mouth where it makes its final run by idyllic burgs such as Tenmile, Clara and Jena before disappearing into the Gulf.

The ads say the 19th century has returned to Steinhatchee, on the Taylor County side of the river. But most who have been here would argue it never left. The "old" part of the equation is represented by a more-than-century-old village that's reluctant to accept 21st-century ways. The new, well, that's part of the old, too.

Steinhatchee Landing.

Steinhatchee Landing is as modern as things get around here. A Georgia native, Dean Fowler, built the Cracker-style resort several years ago. While the interiors are definitely upscale, the exteriors are a blend of vintage homesteads carefully moved to the site and new buildings that keep the Cracker-esque flair. His backyard is the Steinhatchee River, where moss-heavy oaks bend over the water, cypress knees grow from the banks and the nights are filled with nothing noisier than nature breathing. A series of Old Florida beaches, such as Keaton, Jug Island, Dekle and Adams, are up the coast. At the north end of this area the Econfina River provides a more primitive getaway (an occasional fish camp separated by thousands of acres of preserves) for fishermen, canoeists, campers and assorted other adventurers.

Geography & History

State parks herald much of the region's history.

(And none claim to have a fountain of youth!)

The **Crystal River State Archaeological Site** is a six-mound camp built by a cultural group known as the pre-Columbian mound-builders. They were part of the Deptford culture. This riverfront camp is considered to be one of the longest continuously occupied sites in Florida. Now a 14-acre park, it was a ceremonial center for 1,600 years. Native Americans came from far away to bury their dead at the site and trade goods. It's believed as many as 7,500 traveled here yearly. The culture disappeared, perhaps merging with others, two centuries before the first voyage of Columbus. They left behind burial and midden mounds, the latter composed of oyster shells that are visible when touring the grounds. There is a small museum at the site with a display of pottery shards and arrowpoints found when the area was excavated several decades ago, ☎ 352-795-3827.

Fort Cooper State Park, ☎ 352-726-0315, and Lake Holathikaka likely were welcome sights for troops looking for a camp during the Second Seminole Indian War. The spring-fed lake was a source of good water and the woods were full of tasty game. Unfortunately, they were full of Seminoles, too. Maj. Francis L. Dade and 108 of his troops marched into the Wahoo Swamp on December 28, 1835. When the battle was over, only three soldiers remained alive. The war lasted until 1842, but much of the fight was taken out of the Seminoles when two of their leaders – Osceola and Coacoochee – were lured to "peace" talks, where they were captured and imprisoned at St. Augustine.

The **Yulee Sugar Mill Ruins State Historic Site**, ☎ 352-795-3817, recalls the area's limited involvement in the Civil War. Part of a 5,100-acre sugar plantation operated by 1,000 slaves, the mill was owned by David Levy Yulee, a member of Congress before the War Between the States. The mill supplied sugar products to Confederate troops. Poor Yulee, betting the farm on the wrong team, was left penniless following the war.

Public land is what saves nature in Citrus County. Of its 661 square miles, 46% is owned by federal, state and local government. In addition to more than 19,000 acres of lakes, the county has 52 miles of Gulf Coast and 106 miles of rivers. Its landscape performs a chameleon routine, changing from salt marshes and wetlands to uplands and native forests within a handful of miles.

The **Cedar Key State Museum**, ☎ 352-543-5350, heralds the time when the completion of the cross-state railroad (1861) made this island city an important port for overland shipments of cotton, lumber and turpentine to Fernandina and Jacksonville on the northeast coast. **Atsena Otie Key**, just offshore, had both a fort during the Seminole Indian wars and a flourishing lumber mill/pencil factory in the late 19th century. Hurricanes wiped out the fort and the mill, but remnants include a small cemetery. The key came under public ownership in late 1996.

One other historical note: While there are no longer visible reminders, the Suwannee River served as the boundary line between two once-common tribes. The Apalachee lived north of the river. They were fierce fighters whose rumored gold lured the Spanish conquistadors to the areas further north. (You may recall from earlier chapters that they often got gold confused with copper. And it's safe to assume the Spanish kings had no sense of humor when one of their conquistadors returned with a galleon-load of the raw materials for indoor plumbing and electrical wiring. After all, loos and light bulbs weren't invented for another 300 years.) Anyway, the Timucuan Indians controlled the areas to the south of the Suwannee River. Since they were less fierce and had no copper, they were often enslaved by the Spanish.

Getting Around

There are no commercial airports in this region. Locals, at least, consider it a blessing. The good news for visitors: All destinations in the Nature Coast-Big Bend area are 90 minutes (or less) from airports. That's how far Citrus County is from **Orlando**, ☎ 407-825-2352, and **Tampa**, ☎ 800-767-8882, **international airports**. Both are served by nine major carriers and several commuters. Levy and Dixie are an hour from **Gainesville Regional Airport**, ☎ 352-373-0249, which has a pair of major airlines and four commuters. Taylor County is located an hour from **Tallahassee Regional Airport**, ☎ 904-891-7800, a destination for two commercial carriers and six commuters. For private pilots or travelers who want to hitch a ride on a small plane, **Crystal River Airport**, ☎ 352-795-6868, and **Cross City Airport**, ☎ 352-498-3072, are fixed-base operations with 5,000-foot runways. (If you choose Cross City, make sure someone introduces you to the mascot, Airport Charlie. He's a 600-pound tame boar who loves to drink long-neck Budweisers and, when he escapes his pen, do the two-step in the airport's dance hall.)

If you're coming from Orlando or Tampa airports, the best way is to catch Highway 50 east of Brooksville, switch north of town to US 98 and draw a bead on US 19 in southwest Citrus County. US 19 is a four-lane, north-south feeder throughout the four-county area. If you're going from Gainesville to Levy County, Highway 24, which runs in front of the airport, makes a straight shot into US 19 at Otter Creek and continues into Cedar Key. From Gainesville to Dixie County, follow Highway 24 from the airport to Highway 26 (six miles) and take 26 east to US 19 at Fanning Springs. From the Tallahassee airport, take Highway 319 as it runs south around town, then connects with US 27. Fifteen miles east of town it merges with US 19 and you're on your way to Taylor County.

Specific routes will be covered in the touring section of this chapter.

For the most part, the four-county region is a year-round destination. The weather is seldom a long-term inhibitor. Winters are mild with the exception of a few days in the high teens or low 20s. Summers and autumns are occasionally, though briefly, interrupted by bad-tempered blights called hurricanes. But, keep heat and humidity in mind. High-humidity, high-90s days are common from mid-June into September. So pace yourself and dress accordingly.

INFORMATION SOURCES

Citrus County Tourist Development Council, ☎ 800-587-6667 or 352-746-4223, 1300 South Lecanto Hwy., Lecanto, FL 34461.
Levy County Development Authority, ☎ 352-486-3006, P.O. Box 1112, Bronson, FL 32621.
Original Florida, ☎ 904-758-1555, P.O. Box 1300, Lake City, FL 32056-1300 (Dixie and Taylor counties).
Bronson Chamber of Commerce, ☎ 352-486-1003, P.O. Box 1450, Bronson, FL 32621.
Cedar Key Chamber of Commerce, ☎ 352-543-5600, P.O. Box 610, Cedar Key, FL 32625.
Citrus County Chamber of Commerce, ☎ 352-726-2801, 208 W. Main St., Inverness, FL 34450.
Greater Chiefland Area Chamber of Commerce,
☎ 352-493-1849, P.O. Box 1397, Chiefland, FL 32644.
Dixie County Chamber of Commerce, ☎ 352-498-5454, P.O. Box 547, Cross City, FL 32628.
Homosassa Springs Area Chamber of Commerce, ☎ 352-628-2666. P.O. Box 709, Homosassa Springs, FL 34447-0709.
Nature Coast Chamber of Commerce, ☎ 352-795-3149, 28 N.W. Highway 19, Crystal River, FL 34428-3900.
Perry-Taylor County Chamber of Commerce, ☎ 904-584-5366, P.O. Box 892, Perry, FL 32347.
Taylor County Coastal Association, ☎ 352-498-3513, Route 2, Box 130, Keaton Beach, FL 32347.
Williston Area Chamber of Commerce, ☎ 352-528-5552, 19 N.E. 1st St., Williston, FL 32696.
Withlacoochee Area Chamber of Commerce, ☎ 352-447-3383, P.O. Box 427, Inglis, FL 34449-0427.

Citrus County

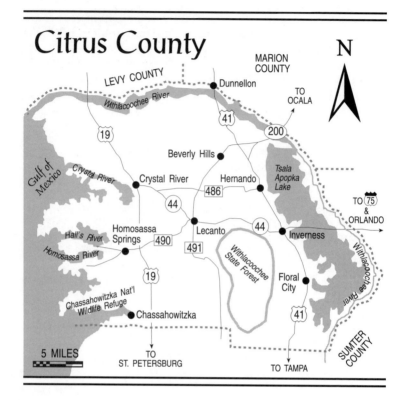

Touring

Citrus County

Chassahowitchka.

Say it fast, "Chass-a-whis-ka." The "how" is silent. Or, "Chass-a-whiskey." That's what the old-timers call it. Either way, it's a land that time forgot, part fishing village, part retirement camp settled by escape artists, all free of traditional markings such as seawalls, fancy houses, shopping centers and exhaust fumes. This is a place where great blue herons clip the tops of the sawgrass with their wings, otters perform aquatic ballets and black bears fish for bass with lightning-quick paws. The townspeople – even the newcomers – seem content to leave things alone.

That's no small blessing.

Chassahowitzka is a one blinker-light town. From US 98, cross US 19 onto what becomes County Road 480, also known as Miss Maggie Drive. Then just stay on the pavement and enjoy nature, much of it thanks to the 30,500-acre **Chassahowitzka National Wildlife Refuge**. Although it's not generally accessible to the public, the refuge is a haven to bears, alligators, wild pigs and an assortment of migratory water birds. On the short drive in, you'll pass **Jim Bob's Gas & Shrimp** ($1 long necks are the "gas" part – the shrimp speaks for itself). At two stories, it's the closest thing to a highrise in town and one of the few stops in this neck of the woods where you can get a good meal. But fishing and other water sports are the main reason to come. The No. 1 place for those is the **Chassahowitzka River Campground**, ☎ 352-382-2200. It points the way to one of the most pristine rivers in Florida. Rent a canoe or put in your boat at the public ramps and travel a six-mile river that's virtually devoid of signs of civilization. Or, if the mood strikes you, kick back on the dock and watch the Mullet Olympics in the morning or ask an attendant to fetch Claudine and her brood. The resident raccoons are happy to drop in and chatter for a peanut or cracker handout.

Chassahowitzka River Campground.

Double back to US 19 and drive north about 10 miles to one of the most unusual parks in Florida. The **Homosassa Springs State Wildlife Park**, ☎ 352-628-2311, once was home to a 1950s-era tourist attraction. Bought by the state, it was converted into a wildlife park and a captive-manatee habitat and recovery area. The park, located at the headwaters of the Homosassa River, has an underwater observatory with a panoramic view of thousands of fish and manatees munching lunch in a 45-foot spring. Nature trails wind through a lush umbrella of trees and plants. The residents include permanently injured eagles, bobcats, black bears, a cougar, owls, red-tail hawks and otters. The park rangers conduct educational programs on the importance of protecting wildlife and their habitats. It's a great place to learn the rules about snorkeling or diving with manatees before you have your first encounter,

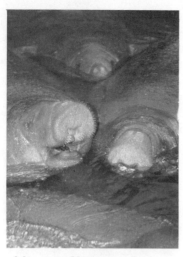

Manatees, Homosassa Springs.

although area dive shops are required to tell you the basics about contact with the endangered critters. The park also is where you'll run into Lucifer the hippo, with his cute little up-turned tusk (just one).

From the park's main entrance on US 19, head north one block and turn left (west) at the stoplight on CR 490-A. A quarter-mile in, Fishbowl Drive bears left at a convenience store. Follow it five miles along a scenic and winding path, stopping by the **Yulee Sugar Mill** for a history lesson. About .3 mile further, there is a modest colony of local artists, including **Riverworks Gallery**, ☎ 352-628-0822, where marine-life themes are done in copper. Here, Fishbowl Drive yields to its new name, Yulee Drive, a one-mile path that ends at the riverfront village of **Old Homosassa**, which is an excellent spot to engage in more water sports. Charter boats and rentals are available to fish the friendly Homosassa River and Gulf of Mexico, to dive or snorkel some of the lesser-known and less-crowded springs, to rent a jet-ski or waverunner, or to observe nature by boat, canoe or airboat. You'll learn more about these activities in the "On Water" part of this chapter.

Crystal River is nine miles north of Homosassa Springs on US 19. Most of its accommodations and restaurants are along or just off the highway.

The launch points for most water adventures also are on, or virtually within a stone's throw of, US 19, primarily because the river and Kings Bay just about kiss the pavement at several places through town.

The city's theme and the main attraction, at least from November through March, are the endangered West Indian manatees, whose population in Florida is estimated at 2,500. Every winter, this distant relative of the elephant migrates to Crystal River and Kings Bay to escape the chilly waters of the Gulf of Mexico. Their return makes the bay area heaven for snorkelers and divers. Seven areas of the river and bay are included in a wildlife refuge, the only federal ones in the state specifically protecting manatees, and motorboat speed limits imposed by the state further protect these slow-moving creatures, whose greatest enemies can be man and boat propellers. The seven sanctuaries, which are off-limits to people, and the speed restrictions have made the Crystal River a winter haven for one of the largest herds of manatees in the United States. Some 350 spend the coldest nights and mornings of the year in or around Kings Spring, the bay's 54-foot main spring, which has a year-round temperature of 72°. These gentle giant vegetarians are usually outgoing and inquisitive by nature. Don't be surprised when one rolls over before you, begging to have its belly rubbed. But a word of caution: Manatees are protected under federal and state endangered species acts. It's a crime to harass them, and sometimes "harassment" is in the eyes of the wildlife officer watching you. Area dive shops and marinas are filled with printed information as well as operators who can give you a crash course in what you can, and can't, do around the manatees. Be smart. That means don't chase them, let them come to you, and touch with one hand only.

While you're out of the water, there are two stops worth your time.

Wildlife artist **Don Mayo's Gallery**, ☎ 352-795-3825, 275 N.E. Highway 19, has an exciting selection of paintings and sculptings of native species, including manatees. Marie Bienkowski's **Manatee Toy Company**, ☎ 352-795-6126, 631 N. Citrus Ave. (CR 495 in the center of town), is a great place to browse through an assortment of manatee souvenirs and art work. (Attention parrotheads: There is some Jimmy Buffett stuff here. Jimmy loves manatees.) Those who come here in February also won't want to miss the Florida Manatee Festival, a two-day event featuring arts and crafts, local seafood and seminars on the marine mammals.

From Crystal River, Inverness is a 17-mile jaunt across Highway 44-East (watch for **Fat Boy's Barbecue** on the far right corner). **Inverness** is a small town, 4,300 people. Its calling cards include a 1912 courthouse, which is listed on the National Register of Historic Places, the rambling **Tsala Apopka** chain of lakes, the **Withlacoochee State Trail** and the **Withlacoochee River**. The lakes, trail and river are bases for hiking, biking and water activities to be discussed deeper in this chapter. Additionally, the adjoining **Withlacoochee State Forest**, which runs south from Highway 44 into three other counties, has plenty of wildlife, including turkeys, deer, fox squirrels, hawks, armadillos and (be careful) skunks. Its trees and plants range from wild dogwood, maple and oak varieties to golden aster, lavender deer tongue and dollar weed.

From Inverness and Highway 44, go south five miles on US 41 to **Floral City**, a sleepy little burg reminiscent of 1930s Florida. Once

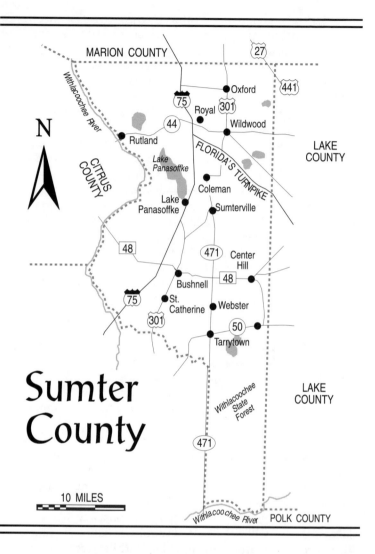

the western point of the Orange State Canal and a reasonably flourishing citrus industry, today it has two notable attractions. One, **Fort Cooper State Park**, will be revisited under the canoeing and hiking adventures later in this chapter. It's about three miles north of Floral City on US 41. The other is Floral City's picturesque **Avenue of Trees**, located on Orange Avenue (Highway 48). Two blocks east of US 41, this rural highway is canopied by a majestic, moss-laden umbrella of more than 100-year-old live oaks. It's one of the most photographed roads in Florida.

One other worthwhile attraction before heading north is the **Ted Williams Museum & Hitters' Hall of Fame**, ☎ 352-527-6566, 2455 N. Citrus Hills Boulevard, Citrus Hills. This is not only a step back into baseball's past, but America's, too. You can relive some of baseball's most glorious days, see game footage of the Red Sox hall of famer at bat and in the field, marvel at the delightful collection of memorabilia and even get a military history lesson: Williams was a Marine pilot in World War II. There are eight galleries of dreams, and the museum, built in the shape of a baseball diamond and colored in Fenway green, is filled with limited-edition art work. The Hitters' Hall honors some of the greats, inducted annually, 20 at a time. From Highway 44 at the courthouse, travel one-half mile to US 41 and turn right (north), go about seven miles to the Highway 486 stoplight and go four miles to the museum on the left.

OK, ladies and gentlemen, start your engines. It's 14 miles from the Ted Williams Museum (left from the parking lot) on Highway 486 to Highway 44 and then steer the wagon right again to begin our journey north.

Levy, Dixie & Taylor Counties

Once you hit US 19, turn right and enjoy the scenery (yes, there are a lot of palmettos and ugly cows in this part of Florida) for about 10 miles. You'll pass over the Cross Florida Barge Canal's hump-back bridge, then a flat bridge over the Withlacoochee River to the stoplight at Highway 40. Turn left for the pathway to the sleepy villages of Inglis and Yankeetown. The route takes you past the historic **Yankeetown School**, a rock structure dating to 1936, a few storefronts, some bait shops and a honky-tonk or two, before ending at a public boat ramp, where you can fish or watch the fishermen leaving the Yankeetown pass into the Gulf at dawn. But there is a more visual turnoff, which makes for a better trip. On 40, look for the huge Saxon Oil drums on the left and take any road thereafter left to Riverside Drive, a narrow, though scenic, road that runs on the north shore of the Withlacoochee River, which makes its final run to the Gulf. You can continue on Riverside (or, if you decide not to leave Highway 40, simply proceed to the stop sign and go left) to find Izaak's, the five-star eatery that also offers lodgings and river excursions. More on **Izaak's**, ☎ 352-447-2311, its cats and its cuisine later in this chapter.

Cedar Key? Back out to US 19, turn left (north) and travel 45 minutes to Otter Creek and Highway 24, turn left (west) for an

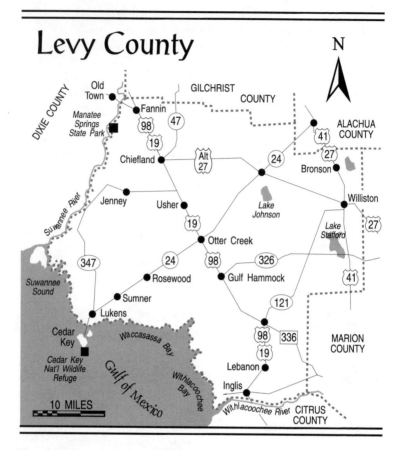

18-mile trip, which is lacking scenery except for woodlands and wildlife preserves. You'll know you're getting close when you start seeing salt marshes and bridges. You'll know you're there when you see a series of dry spots barely above the water line.

There's no fancy stuff on the outskirts. Just sawgrass, run-aground boats, crab shacks, mom-and-pop inns, fish houses, marinas and lots of pickup trucks. When you reach a stop sign and public-service-announcement pedestal planted in the middle of the road you're on Second Street. (Cedar Key has one cop and no traffic, but obey the law: You don't want to know the fine or see the jail.)

For a small town there's plenty of activity. There are no fewer than 18 gift shops, art galleries and crafts stores (with its natural beauty, this is a grand place for visual artists, photographers and craftsmen), many on the main drag (**D Street Gallery**, ☎ 352-543-6731, **Fanta Sea Fashions**, ☎ 352-543-9318, and the

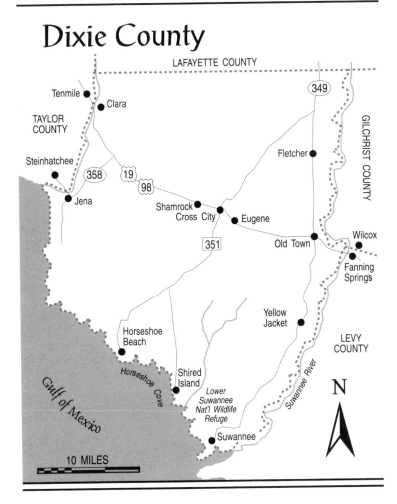

Dixie County

Susan Dauphinee Studio, ☎ 352-543-9509). While you might not spend the night or eat dinner, at least sneak a peek, maybe have a whistle wetter, at the **Island Hotel** on the corner of Second and B streets. It's like stepping into yesterday, as are many of the storefronts in this compact town. First Street is one block west, parallel to the Gulf, while C Street loops into it and forms a small stilt village that includes restaurant row, a fishing pier and City Dock. There are two annual festivals: the quarter-century-old **Cedar Key Sidewalk Art Show** attracts 75,000 people for a two-day bash in April and the **Cedar Key Seafood Festival** in mid-October

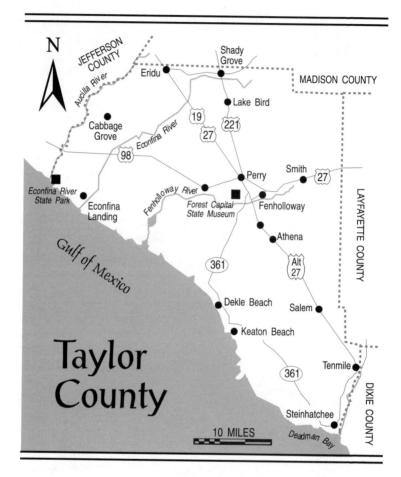

is every bit as popular. You'll learn more about the area restaurants, lodging, fishing and other adventures later in the chapter.

Return on Highway 24 to US 19, then north 23 miles through Chiefland to the town of **Fanning Springs**, where there's one final stop before leaving Levy County. The **Fanning Springs State Recreation Area** on the Suwannee River is on the left. It's a small wayside park with a few hiking trails, picnic areas and a steel section of the old Suwannee River bridge replaced a decade ago.

From Fanning Springs, follow US 19 north 26 miles to Highway 51 and turn left for a scenic route that leads into Steinhatchee, then skirts the coastline through time warps called Fish Creek, Keaton Beach, Jug Island, Dekle Beach and Adams Beach. As noted earlier, these are old Florida beaches devoid of the commercialization found in the tourist hot spots, but there are several places to grab a bite or enjoy water sports, as you'll discover later. Continue on Highway 361 as it returns to US 19, turning left for the six-mile drive to **Perry**. Your nose will tell you this is lumber country. The pulp smell from the local mills permeates the air. The **Forest Capital Museum**, ☎ 904-584-3227, tells the industry's heritage from humble beginnings 150 years ago to a $3.7-billion business (today it's the state's third largest). The museum has photographs of early lumber operations, as well as exhibits on turpentine production, state-of-the-art forestry techniques and more than 5,000 products made from the long-leaf pines. For kids, there's Terry the Talking Tree, which at the push of his buttons explains the life cycle of local trees. The grounds also include a life-size cypress swamp and hardwood hammock that include birds and other animals inhabiting these communities. The **Cracker Homestead** has an interpretive center using the Whiddon House, built in 1864 and moved here in 1972, to let you see what Florida life was like around the Civil War. In addition to the main house, it includes a kitchen, syrup kettle, smokehouse, cane grinder and barn. There's even an outhouse (but – please – don't try to use it).

Adventures

On Foot

If you've been following the plan, you don't need the "F" word beaten into your brain any longer. This one's flatter than any other region covered in this guide. But there are plenty of hiking venues, passing through sandhills, prairies, coastal scrubs, hydric swamps, hardwood hammocks and a nice assortment of other upland areas.

The **Withlacoochee State Trail**, ☎ 352-796-5650, is one of Citrus County's better-known trails. It's part of the Florida's Rails to Trails program under which the state bought rights to an abandoned railroad right-of-way, then paved a 47-mile stretch from county line to county line with recycled rubber. It goes through parts of the Withlacoochee State Forest and parallels US 41 and the Withlacoochee River. The central entry-exit point is at North Apopka Avenue in Inverness. North Apopka intersects Highway 44-East (Main Street) in downtown Inverness at the historic courthouse. It's a bit tricky skirting the courthouse and managing to stay on North Apopka, but not impossible. From the stoplight at the courthouse, turn north, toward the three-story structure. Go one block and turn left. Go another block and, at the stop sign, turn right. The trail entrance is two blocks away and it has a designated parking area. In addition to the natural points of interest in the forest and along the river, the trail passes Fort Cooper State Park (two miles south of the entrance), the Floral City railroad depot (five miles south) and the Istachatta railroad depot (10 miles south).

Additional hiking trails in the region include:

- **Withlacoochee State Forest, Citrus Hiking Trail**, ☎ 352-754-6777, 46.7 miles. From the courthouse in Inverness, drive west about 1.2 mile to Highway 581, turn left (south) and continue 2½ miles to the trail entrance. You'll pass the Holder Mine Recreation Area at the two-mile mark. This is a mainly uplands trail, through scrub oaks and pine lands, that in most areas is paved and skirts US 41, but most of it is far enough removed from the highway to keep you clear of an exhaust-fume overdose.

- **Pott's Preserve**, ☎ 800-423-1476, 24 miles of trails including a boardwalk through hammocks, wetlands and marshes. The trails are within 20,000 acres of land owned by the Southwest Florida Water Management District. The preserve is about five miles north of Highway 44 in Inverness on Highway 581, also called Turner Camp Road.

- **Flying Eagle Tract**, ☎ 800-423-1476, another water district site, offers 15 miles of trails that pass through a mosaic of small lakes, marshes, swamps and upland forests. From Inverness, go three miles south on US 41 to Eden Drive, turn left (east) and travel to the gate. Call or write the district at 2379 Broad St., Brooksville, FL 34609-6899 for a guide booklet that includes more information on Pott's Preserve, Flying Eagle and other district properties.

- **Fort Cooper State Park**, ☎ 352-726-0315, two miles of trails that include interpretive plaques explaining the fort's importance during the Second Seminole Indian War. It's two miles south of Inverness on US 41.

Manatee Springs State Park near Chiefland, ☎ 352-493-6072, features 8½ miles of designated hiking trails, as well as a boardwalk and dock that reach into the Suwannee River. The main attraction is a first-magnitude spring (117 million gallons of water per day). With a 1,200-foot run to the river, the park is a scuba divers' and snorkelers' favorite. The spring was described by William Bartram in his 1774 writings. The park property has cypress, gum, maple, ash and sandhill. Otters, raccoons, wading birds and other small mammals live here.

Manatees make occasional appearances, too.

INFORMATION SOURCES

Florida Trail Association, ☎ 800-343-1882 (in Florida) or 352-378-8823, P.O. Box 13708, Gainesville, FL 32604.
Office of Greenways & Trails, ☎ 904-487-4784, Mail Station 795, 3900 Commonwealth Blvd., Tallahassee, FL 32399-3000.

Golf Courses

- **Citrus Hills Golf Club**, ☎ 352-746-4425, 509 E. Hartford St., Hernando, FL 34442, 36 holes, driving range, lessons, PGA rating R-69.7.
- **Citrus Springs Country Club**, ☎ 352-489-5045, 8690 Golfview Drive, Dunnellon, FL 34434, 18 holes, driving range, lessons, R-70.1.
- **Lakeside Golf Club**, ☎ 352-726-1461, 4555 E. Windmill Drive, Inverness, FL 34450, 18 holes, lessons, R-69.0.
- **Pine Ridge Country Club**, ☎ 352-746-6177, 5600 Elkan Blvd., Beverly Hills, FL 34465, 18 holes, driving range, lessons, R-68.6.
- **Plantation Inn & Golf Resort**, ☎ 352-795-4211, 9301 W. Fort Island Trail (CR 44-West), Crystal River, FL 34423, 27 holes, driving range, R-70.1
- **Twisted Oaks Golf Club**, ☎ 352-746-6257, 4801 N. Forest Ridge Blvd., Beverly Hills, FL 34465, 18 holes, driving range, lessons, R-66.7.

On Horseback

Neighboring Marion County is the heart of Florida's horse country. It's the core of a thoroughbred industry that's second only to Kentucky's. Citrus County's love-affair with nature provides plenty of places for riding, especially on the trail. Many of the earlier-mentioned sites available to hikers accommodate horsemen and women who come with their own mounts.

The **Citrus tract of the Withlacoochee State Forest**, offers a 20-stall stable and a 37-site camping area at **Tillis Hill**, ☎ 352-754-6777. The campground serves as a starting point for a 14-mile, one-day ride and a 24-mile, two-day ride. To get to Tillis Hill from Inverness, follow Highway 44-East to Highway 581, and then go south seven miles to Highway 480 and turn right. (The entrance to Tillis Hill is on the right about two miles from Highway 480.)

The **Southwest Florida Water Management District**, ☎ 800-423-1476, offers riding trails at two sites. **Pott's Preserve** has 12 miles of equestrian trails through marshes and oak hammocks. The site has a small number of stalls and it's open to horse-drawn carriages, but you need to get a carriage permit in advance. The preserve is five miles north of Highway 44 in Inverness on Highway 581, which is also called Turner Camp Road. The **Flying Eagle Tract** offers nine miles of horse trails through swamps, marshes and uplands. From Inverness, travel south three miles on US 41 to Eden Drive, turn left (east) and drive to the gate. Call or write the district at 2379 Broad St., Brooksville, FL 34609-6899 for more information, permits or a guidebook on these and other district properties.

Part of the Rails to Trails in Citrus County.

The **Withlacoochee State Trail**, extends for 47 miles and also allows riders on designated bridal paths. It's part of Florida's Rails to Trails program in which the state bought rights to an abandoned railroad right-of-way, then paved most of the trail with recycled rubber.

The trail goes through parts of the same-named state forest and parallels US 41 and the river. A central entry-exit point is at North Apopka Avenue in Inverness. North Apopka intersects with Highway 44-East (Main Street) in downtown Inverness at the historic courthouse. Again, it's tricky skirting the courthouse and managing to stay on North Apopka, but not impossible. From the stoplight at the courthouse, turn north at the three-story structure. Travel one block and turn left; go another block and turn right. Its entrance is two blocks away at a parking area. In addition to its natural points of interest in the forest and along the river, this trail passes Fort Cooper State Park (two miles south of town), the Floral City railroad depot (five miles south) and the Istachatta railroad depot (10 miles south). ☎ 352-394-2280 or 352-796-5650.

Have your own horses? Bring proof of a negative Coggins test. Again, it's mandatory in Florida.

INFORMATION SOURCES

Office of Greenways & Trails, ☎ 904-487-4784, 325 John Knox Road, Building 500, Tallahassee, FL 32303-4124.
Florida Department of Transportation, ☎ 904-487-9220, Mail Station 82, 605 Suwanee St., Tallahassee, FL 32399-0450.

On Wheels

Cyclists have three options: On- and off-road trails inside Citrus County and, for those with stout hearts and a willingness to travel 75 minutes north (but still within the region), the torturous lure of that six-day, 327-mile Florida Springs Bicycle Tour through some of the prettiest, most historic land in North Florida.

The **Withlacoochee State Trail**, ☎ 352-796-5650 (see the "On Foot" section of the chapter), has 16 miles of paved trails that welcome cyclists. The North Apopka Avenue starting point is ideal because it has a lot of parking and can be used for a northerly or southerly course. Adventurers who forget (or don't want to pack) their bikes can rent them at **Chain Reaction**, ☎ 352-637-5757, located at the trail's entrance. North Apopka intersects Highway 44-East (Main Street) in downtown Inverness at the courthouse. From the courthouse stoplight, turn north, go a block and turn left, go another block and turn right. The entrance to the trail is two blocks away.

A more scenic route is the 38-mile round-trip ride along **Pleasant Grove Road** (Highway 581), which begins 1.2 miles west of the courthouse (watch for the ABC Liquor Store and turn left, then just punch those peddles down). **Stage Coach Road** (Highway 480) is another favorite of cyclists. Its mid-section is 10 miles south of Highway 44 on Highway 581. You can catch its east boundary at US 41 six miles south of Inverness or its western boundary on US 19, eight miles south of Homosassa Springs. Both also are 38 miles round-trip.

The length and energy levels needed for the area's two off-road trails are pretty much at your discretion. The **Withlacoochee State Forest**, ☎ 352-796-5650, has numerous dirt trails, the most convenient of which is off Highway 44-East, around three miles west of the courthouse (.2 mile from a Golden Corral Steakhouse on the right, the entrance is on the left). **Pott's Preserve**, ☎ 800-423-1476, has existing dirt trails as well as an invitation to make your own, without destroying the preserve, of course. It's located five miles north of Highway 44-East in Inverness on Highway 581, which is also Turner Camp Road.

Hardcores might want to do "spring training" on some or all of these trails before setting their sights on the **Florida Springs Bicycle Tour**, ☎ 904-487-4784. A six-day, 327-mile odyssey, the tour takes you over rural back roads to turquoise-blue springs, Stephen Foster's celebrated Suwannee River, and the rustic home of Pulitzer Prize-winning writer Marjorie Kinnan Rawlings, author of *The Yearling*. You go through 10 state parks, including Florida's only major Civil War battlefield at Olustee, before ending at **Manatee Springs State Park**. It can be accessed in this region by taking US 19 one mile north of Chiefland to Highway 320, turning left (west) and going five miles to the park. As noted in other chapters, the springs tour can be tackled as a whole or in individual legs: Manatee Springs to Paynes Prairie State Preserve (63 miles), Paynes Prairie to Gold Head Branch State Park (63 miles), Gold Head to the Olustee Battlefield Historic Site (67 miles), Olustee to Stephen Foster State Folk Culture Center (30 miles), Stephen Foster to O'Leno State Park (47 miles) and O'Leno to Manatee Springs (58 miles). You can get a detailed itinerary of each of the legs by calling or writing the Office of Greenways & Trails listed under information sources.

INFORMATION SOURCES

Office of Greenways & Trails, ☎ 904-487-4784, 325 John Knox Road, Building 500, Tallahassee, FL 32303-4124.
Florida Department of Transportation, ☎ 904-487-9220, Mail Station 82, 605 Suwanee St., Tallahassee, FL 32399-0450.

On Water

In counties bounded by water on three sides and blessed with numerous interior lakes and rivers, water activities rule. Scuba diving, snorkeling, fishing, canoeing and other water sports bring more people to Citrus County than any other activities. Three tips to make your trip as enjoyable as possible:

1) If seeing the manatees is one of your main goals, the best time to see them in the Crystal and Homosassa rivers is from mid-December to late March. Manatees can be seen in much smaller concentrations other times of year near the mouths of the rivers and in the Gulf of Mexico, but divers and snorkelers find observation far superior in the winter near Citrus County's springs.

2) Early spring through late fall is the best time for fishing, swimming and boating, although, like most of Florida, this is a year-round destination where the winter weather remains, for the most part, mild.

3) You will find the rivers and springs less crowded on weekdays. During weekends, particularly during manatee season and summer, waterways can get more crowded, though it's less of a concern in Levy, Dixie and Taylor counties.

AIRBOATING

The folks at **Wild Bill's Airboat Tours**, ☎ 352-726-6060, east of Inverness, take you for a ride on the wild side along the Withlacoochee River. Here you'll catch a glimpse of one of Florida's most beautiful rivers, wildlife ranging from alligators and turtles to ospreys and bald eagles, and the charm of fish camps dotting the river banks. Some of the cypress trees at the water's edge are as much as 1,000 years old. From the courthouse in Inverness, travel east to the next traffic light and go left following Highway 44-East nine miles to Wild Bill's doorstep on the right.

HOUSEBOATING

Never piloted a houseboat?

In an hour or two Bill Miller at **Miller's Marina**, ☎ 800-458-2628 or 352-542-7349, in the village of Suwannee, will have you confident and comfortable. Miller gives customers a detailed course and short check-out cruise before sending them on their way to explore 70 miles of the Suwannee River, from the mouth north to Branford, that are accessible by houseboat. His boats, all at least 43 feet long and 14 feet wide, have everything – hot and cold water, full kitchens, refrigerators, dining rooms, sun decks, showers, full-size beds, furnaces, gas grills and flush toilets. (It's a good idea to rent a skiff and tow it along to check out the many creeks and lagoons off the Suwannee). The reward for your bold adventure: This section of the river has 20 or more clear springs for diving and snorkeling, incredible fishing holes (redfish, trout, Suwannee River bass, even scallops at East Pass near the Gulf) and virtually no development –making it great for romantics or folks just trying to get away from the world. The scenery includes swamps, red-clay bluffs and limestone deposits reaching high above the water. To find Miller's (P.O. Box 280, Suwannee, FL 32692), take US 19 north through Levy County, crossing the Suwannee River and, after two miles, turn left at Highway 349 at Old Town. Follow it to the town of Suwannee.

CANOEING

Trust the Canadian Olympic team.

They found one of the best smooth-water canoe treasures in Florida, not to mention one of the most scenic. The **Withlacoochee River**'s chocolate brown color isn't from pollution but from the magnificent cypress trees lining its banks. Paddling its waters can't help but give you the sense of awe the American Indians must have felt when they used it as a major highway centuries ago. Along your way, you'll see many species of turtles, some anhingas and maybe an alligator sunning on the water's edge (remember Capt. Charlie's warnings from the last chapter). Don't forget to pack your camera, but memories are certainly a close second on these soothing excursions.

The region has two designated trails beginning with the Withlacoochee.

The river has six small trails in Citrus County that snake through cypress swamps, hardwood forests and freshwater marshes that are virtually untouched by civilization, ☎ 904-487-4784. All of those in Citrus are rated for beginners, with currents usually two-three mph and, in a couple of places, three-plus. The southernmost trail is a nine-mile route that starts at the State Road 48 bridge, just east of Floral City. (This is also the starting point for the more ambitious canoeists who want to try the entire 55-mile course through the county). From the courthouse in Inverness, follow US 41 south five miles to Highway 48 and turn left, traveling eight miles to the bridge and the entry point. Carlson Landing is an 11-mile run accessible from Highway 44-East. Follow it 14 miles east from the courthouse to Highway 470, then proceed two miles right (south). Go one-half mile and turn right (west) at Gator Lodge and continue to the ramp. For the Highway 44 bridge entrance and its four-mile course, follow Highway 44-East from the courthouse 12 miles, launching at the boat ramp located on the far side of the Withlacoochee River. The Highway 581 course, a six-mile stretch, isn't far from downtown Inverness. Take Highway 44-East west to US 41 (it's .8 mile) and turn right. Just past the Circle K convenience store turn right and go to the stop sign, then turn left and drive eight miles to the ramp. The Highway 200 bridge is a 10-mile course near the county's northern end. From the Highway 44-US 41 intersection, take US 41 six miles to Hernando, going through a traffic light. Two blocks north of the light veer right onto Highway 200, then go 6½ miles to a wayside park. The northernmost starting point in Citrus County is at the US 41 bridge, which is a 15-mile run. From the Hernando traffic light, drive two blocks north and veer left onto US 41, then go 13 miles to the ramp.

The **Aucilla River Canoe Trail** is a pristine, though difficult, 19-mile course that begins just north of the four-county area. With its swift (three-plus mph) current, this trail is rated intermediate to technical. (At times it's strenuous.) The Aucilla River rushes across shoals and the remains of two rock dams that help make this one challenging, especially at low water. High limestone banks frame the river, which flows through cypress-gum swamps inhabited by river otters, hawks and various wading birds. To reach the entrance, drive US 19 north of Perry 24 miles to the US 19/27 bridge, one mile before Lamont. Then hop in.

But there is one more that awaits – an open-water course where canoes usually will suffice, but kayaks are recommended. The saltwater run starts at the end of Highway 349 in the town of Suwannee and follows the coast 91½ miles to St. Marks in Wakulla County. Water conditions usually are mild, but waves can be two to four feet in exposed bays and a few miles offshore. You may *need* to be a few miles offshore at times because at low tide there may be only a few inches of water closer in. This is a route recommended for the most experienced paddlers. Shorter courses from Suwannee include exit points at Steinhatchee (32 miles) and Keaton Beach (51½ miles). Additional information and access points can be obtained from the Office of Greenways and Trails listed below.

Additionally, there are limited canoeing opportunities at the **Fort Cooper State Park, Chassahowitzka River Campground** and **Pott's Preserve** sites that were mentioned earlier in this chapter.

INFORMATION & RENTAL SOURCES

For designated trail maps, write to the **Office of Greenways and Trails**, ☎ 904-487-4784, 325 John Knox Road, Bldg. 500, Tallahassee, FL 32303-4124.
Florida Association of Canoe Liveries and Outfitters, ☎ 941-494-1215, P.O. Box 1764, Arcadia, FL 33821.
Citrus Paddling Club, Route 1, Box 415, Floral City, FL 32636.
Angler's Resort, ☎ 352-489-2397, 12189 S. Williams St., Dunnellon, FL 34432.
KOA Campground, ☎ 352-542-7636, P.O. Box 460, Old Town, FL 32680.
Manatee Springs State Park, ☎ 352-493-9726 or 493-9740, Route 2, Box 617, Chiefland, FL 32626.
Turner's Camp, ☎ 352-726-2685, 3033 Hooty Point, Inverness, FL 32650.

DIVING & SNORKELING

There's only one way to describe the experience: Wow!

The dive sites may be more alluring in other parts of Florida, but you can't match the winter manatee encounters, particularly in Crystal River. But one blunt fact can't be stressed too much: These lovable Pillsbury Doughboys and girls of the sea are walking a tightrope. Their survival depends on humans giving them space. Two decades ago, marina operators, fishermen and boaters bristled at the first suggestion that sanctuaries were necessary to save the manatees, but these restrictions are what has caused their ranks locally to grow nearly tenfold. So when diving in manatee waters make sure you know the rules. These gentle giants are protected by the Endangered Species Act and the Marine Mammal Protection Act. Both can be a little vague about what is, and isn't, harassment. There are a few rules of thumb to avoid being cited and to protect these throw-backs to another time. Never feed them. Never chase them. Never hitch a ride. And never reach for a manatee that approaches you with more than one open hand. Any reputable dive-shop owner in the area will tell you in detail what you can and can't do around the manatees. And if you want to be on the safe side, call or stop at the **US Fish & Wildlife Service** office, ☎ 352-563-2088, 1502 SE Kings Bay Drive, for information.

One of the best manatee starting points is the **Plantation Inn Marina**, ☎ 352-795-5797, located on Highway 44-West on the southside of Crystal River, a half-mile west of US 19. This shop, operated by Crystal River native Sam Lyons, is two minutes by rented motorboat or tour boat (and four minutes by canoe) from Manatee Central in winter: **Kings Spring**. While the Crystal River is translucent, the big spring is crystal clear and turquoise blue. *Rodale's*, a scuba magazine, rates this the best spot in the country to see large marine animals – large meaning up to 2,000 pounds.

Down under, you'll find a main spring that is 75 feet across. At a depth of 30 feet, there are two entrances to a cave that reaches a depth of about 54 feet. This is a wide open cave that doesn't require special certification. Once inside, you'll have a breathtaking view, especially on sunny days when the crevices and other divers are silhouetted. It's one of the most photographed underwater spots in Central Florida. In addition to your fellow divers and the manatees, you'll have plenty of company – mullet, redfish and red snapper that, on the cold days, are thick enough to form a wall. But don't bring a speargun. Spearfishing is illegal.

The bay area has several other springs to dive. **Grand Canyon**, located just west of Kings Spring, is a 35-foot crevice in the rock that has a depth of 25 feet. **Gator Hole**, in a canal system on the east side of the bay, has an entrance area at a depth of 35 feet. This is another good manatee observation area and one that's not as crowded as the main spring. **Mullet's Gullet**, just east of Kings Spring, is another area where the flow comes from crevices in the rock bottom. This one's a shallow dive, about 20 feet, and very clear, which makes it another favorite spot of marine-life photographers. You can pick up a map of the area's sites at any dive shop in town.

Sam Lyons' dive shop is far from the only show in town. It's just one of the more convenient ones to the main spring, as is **Port Paradise Dive Shop**, ☎ 352-795-7234. The access road to Port Paradise is Paradise Point Road, a block north of Highway 44-West on US 19. (Turn west and follow the road .8 mile to Port Paradise, which is on a narrow pass 50 yards behind Banana Island. The island forms a cup around the main spring.) **Crystal Lodge Dive Center**, ☎ 352-795-3171, is on the river near the north end of the city. From the Highway 44-East and US 19 intersection, follow US 19 north .9 mile. Crystal Lodge is adjacent to a Best Western on the left.

No matter where you choose to start your diving or snorkeling expedition, local shops rent all of the gear needed – from masks, fins and snorkels to tanks, regulators and BCs. During the winter, wet suits are recommended, not because of the water temperature – which stays constant year-round – but because of the air temperature, which, even in Florida, can turn your skin blue when you're wet and leaving the water. The suits also are a blessing for children or others who aren't good swimmers: The neoprene suits make you so buoyant that without a set of weights it's virtually impossible to sink.

There is one other site worth exploring in this region, at **Manatee Springs State Park**, ☎ 352-493-6062. To get there, follow US 19 into Chiefland, then take Highway 320 (it's well-marked with brown Manatee Springs signs) left about five miles to the park. But don't arrive unprepared. There isn't a dive shop on the site, so make sure you get your tanks filled or rent your gear at some of the locations listed in Crystal River, if you're coming from that far south, or at those listed in the Information & Rental Section.

You learned earlier this is a first-magnitude spring with a force that spits out 81,280 gallons of crystal clear water every minute – substantially more than your kitchen faucet. It's also more than enough to give snorkelers a lot of thrust from the spring head 1,200 feet into the Suwannee River. At the spring's head, divers and snorkelers find a 30-foot clear drop to the entrance of a cave, where cave-diving certification is required. If you don't have one, expect the rangers to confiscate any underwater lights you may have with you. If you're a cave diver, you may be disappointed in this system; it's very silty and not complex. If cave diving is your game, Branford (which was covered on page 152) offers some of the best cave sites in Florida, and they're just beyond this area.

A wet suit? You decide.

The water temperature is four degrees colder, at 68, than at Crystal River and Kings Spring.

INFORMATION & ADDITIONAL RENTAL SOURCES

Florida Association of Dive Operators, ☎ 305-451-3020, 51 Garden Cove Drive, Key Largo, FL 33037.
US Fish & Wildlife Service, ☎ 352-563-2088, 1502 S.E. Kings Bay Drive, Crystal River, FL 34429.
Florida Marine Patrol, ☎ 352-447-1633 or 800-342-5367.
US Coast Guard, ☎ 352-447-6900.
Ned DeLoach's Diving Guide to Underwater Florida, ☎ 904-737-6558, New World Publications, 1861 Cornell Road, Jacksonville, FL 32207.
Cedar Key Scuba, ☎ 352-543-8002, 509 Third St., Cedar Key, FL 32625.
Aztec Dive Center, ☎ 352-493-9656, P.O. Box 1600, Chiefland, FL 32626.

SALTWATER & FRESHWATER FISHING

This region is a fisherman's (or woman's) nirvana.

Bounded on three sides by water and dotted with thousands of acres of lakes, Citrus County's second biggest attraction is its catch-it-yourself seafood.

On the freshwater side there is an abundance of bass, largemouth and spotted to striped and sunshine, not to mention bluegill, crappie and panfish. Where the species aren't abundant, the Florida Game and Fresh Water Fish Commission stocks the lakes and rivers with fish raised in hatcheries.

Marshes and the Gulf are noted for the popular saltwater species, from sport fish such as tarpon – the whoppers that migrate into the area each spring reach 150 pounds – and snook, to incredible edibles such as grouper, red snapper and redfish. Fishing guides say there isn't a bad time to fish in this region, but spring, summer and autumn are the best times to catch most of the area's saltwater species.

Make sure to get a fishing license. On the saltwater side, a non-resident license ranges from $5 for three days to $30 for a year. Non-resident freshwater licenses are $15 for seven days and $30 for one year. Florida also has size and bag limits on many species. Information on these can be obtained at area bait-and-tackle shops, marinas or by contacting the **Florida Marine Patrol**, ☎ 352-447-1633, P.O. Box 5124, Homosassa Springs, FL 32647-5124 for saltwater or the **Florida Game and Fresh Water Fish**

Commission, ☎ 352-732-1225, 1239 S.W. 10th St., Ocala, FL 34474-2797 for freshwater.

Fishing records? On the saltwater side a 15-pound, 2-ounce sheepshead was hooked off Homosassa. While there are no tarpon records by gross weight, several caught with fly rods in the region, particularly off Homosassa, set records based on weight and line test. Still, that gross-weight monster is lurking in these parts. You just need to land it. Tarpon season runs May through July. In addition to **Homosassa**, good places to go looking include **Chassahowitzka, Cedar Key** and **Steinhatchee** on the flats. Redfish are eager any time the Gulf temperature is more than 68°, and the fishing is that much better if you can find some of the state's vanishing mangroves.

The calendar? Go after barracuda every season but fall, redfish any time except winter, grouper in spring and summer and amberjack in the hot months.

Is freshwater your preference? Look to the **Tsala Apopka** chain of lakes, the **Withlacoochee River** or the **Steinhatchee, Aucilla, Suwannee** and **Econfina** rivers. Fallen trees, such as those along the Withlacoochee and its backwaters at **Lake Rousseau**, are good places to hunt for redbreast and spotted sunfish. The lily pads on the Lake Tsala Apopka chain are ideal for crappie and the full menu of bass. The Suwannee, Steinhatchee, Aucilla and Econfina rivers also are hangouts for largemouth bass, bluegill and channel catfish.

Fishermen who bring their own boats will find numerous ramps, including those at most area marinas. There also are several public ramps, three of them with access to the 19,111-acre Tsala Apopka chain of lakes. To get to the ramp for the **Hernando Pool**, go west of the Inverness courthouse .8 mile, and then go north on US 41 six miles to where US 41 and Highway 200 meet. The ramp is .3 mile east. For the **Inverness Pool** ramp, travel on Highway 44-East .2 mile to the stoplight, turning left. The ramp is a half-mile on the left. To reach the **Floral City Pool** ramp, follow US 41 south of Inverness five miles to Floral City. Turn left at Highway 48 and go one mile to Duval Island Road, then turn left again and drive a half-mile. **Crystal River** has a public ramp right across US 19 from City Hall while **Chassahowitzka**'s ramps are at the namesake campground, four miles west of US 19 and 98 on Miss Maggie Drive. All of the areas have public access for fishing along the banks.

Crystal River has the area's only large party boat, *The Apollo*, ☎ 352-795-3757. Capt. Fred Standard offers day charters into the Gulf of Mexico. Smaller charters are run by dozens of other guides. **Mike Locklear**, ☎ 352-628-4207, and **Tim Slaght**, ☎ 352-628-5222, operate out of Homosassa. **Bill Hampton**, ☎ 352-795-6765, and **Donald Watkins**, ☎ 352-795-1812, guide from Crystal River, while **Bud Andrews**, ☎ 352-726-1272, is master of Citrus County's lakes and rivers region on the east side of the county. **Lloyd Collins**, ☎ 352-543-9102, and **Bill Roberts**, ☎ 352-542-5690, launch from Cedar Key. (Collins, Roberts and other guides are more than happy to take you island-hopping in the national wildlife refuge.) **Gil Parker**, ☎ 352-498-0709, guides out of the River Haven Marina in Steinhatchee, while **Pat McGriff**, ☎ 352-578-2699, sets sail out of beautiful downtown Keaton Beach.

Want to rent your own boat and guide yourself? There are plenty of spots to rent small john boats with outboards or larger craft. The **Plantation Inn Marina**, ☎ 352-795-5797, **Crystal Lodge Dive Center**, ☎ 352-795-6798, and **Port Paradise Marina**, ☎ 352-795-7234, have boats for fishing or scuba trips in Crystal River. In Homosassa, **Nature's Resort Marina**, ☎ 352-628-4344, **MacRae's of Homosassa**, ☎ 352-628-2922, and **River Safaris**, ☎ 352-628-5222, rent boats. Rental locations in east Citrus County include **Bud Andrews' Cypress Lodge** in Inverness, ☎ 352-726-6593, **Trail's End Fish Camp** near Floral City, ☎ 352-726-3699, and **Watson's Fish Camp** in Hernando, ☎ 352-726-2225. Rentals are available in Cedar Key at **Willis Marina**, ☎ 352-543-6148, and in Steinhatchee at **Westwinds**, ☎ 904-498-5254.

Many of the marinas and camps offer bait and tackle, but larger selections are available at **Happy's Bait & Tackle**, ☎ 352-726-2281, just south of Inverness on US 41, **Skidmore's Sports Supply**, ☎ 352-795-4033, near US 19 on Highway 44 in Crystal River, **Cypress Station**, ☎ 352-543-5862, on Highway 24 at Shiloh Road in Cedar Key, **Dockside Marina**, ☎ 352-498-5768, on Highway 351 in Horseshoe Beach, and **Sportsman's**, ☎ 904-498-5800, on Riverside Drive in Steinhatchee.

In The Air

Tom Davis is a career Navy pilot who retired and took over operation of the Crystal River Airport. His **Crystal Aero Group**, ☎ 352-795-6868, provides two great aerial treats. One is a 20-minute glider ride that combines the adventures of motorless flight with the thrills of an amusement park ride. The other is a 25-minute air tour of the area. During the winter months, this gives you a different perspective of the Crystal River area's manatees and plentiful springs. A good option here if you're looking for a burst of personality with your aerial tour: Ask for Gudi Lashbrook to take you up. She's a delight.

Where To Stay & Eat

One of the blessings of the area is that it truly hasn't been discovered by the masses. While reservations are suggested at motels, inns and restaurants just to be safe, there isn't a time of year or even an event, including the manatee season, when every place in the region is sold out. Keep in mind that weekends everywhere, including The Nature Coast/Big Bend, can become a little crowded, so the travelers who come to town without reservations may not always get their first choice of lodging and may have to wait up to an hour for a dinner table.

Generally, though, that isn't the case.

The few chain motels that have come into the area are on Citrus County's west side. The **Best Western**, ☎ 352-795-3171, is on US 19, three blocks north of city hall and just off the river. The **Days Inn**, ☎ 352-795-2111, is 1.3 miles north, at the intersection of US 19 and State Park Drive, the access road to the Crystal River State Archaeological Site. **Comfort Inn**, ☎ 352-563-1500, is one more mile north on US 19.

Those looking for non-chain accommodations should consider the **Plantation Inn Resort**, ☎ 352-795-4211, which overlooks Kings Spring and features patio rooms, suites and villas, along with golf and tennis. At **Citrus Hills** in Hernando, ☎ 352-746-6121, condominiums and townhouses are available for rent. Amenities include tennis, golf and the Ted Williams Museum.

MacRae's of Homosassa, ☎ 352-628-2802, provides rustic, log-cabin-style rooms accompanied by a picturesque view of the Homosassa River and nearby Monkey Island (if you go boating, be careful – the monkeys bite). In Inverness, the **El Rancho Motel**, ☎ 352-726-4744, and the **Central Motel**, ☎ 352-726-4515, are on US 41, just a few blocks off Highway 44. Cedar Key has the wonderfully rustic **Island Hotel**, ☎ 352-543-5111; **Old Fenimore Mill**, ☎ 800-767-8354, which features one- to three-bedroom condominiums that overlook nature's wonders; and the live-oak-surrounded **Cedar Key Bed & Breakfast**, ☎ 800-453-5051, which was built during the 1880s. In Taylor County, **Econfina on the Gulf**, ☎ 904-584-5811, has a mixture of condominiums, motel rooms, cottages and camping sites surrounded by a massive state refuge. Saving the best for last: **Steinhatchee Landing**, ☎ 352-498-3513, is a special place for the Old Florida purists, combining nature with creature comforts and a backyard on its namesake river.

At dinnertime, call it a toss up for the best bet.

Izaak's, ☎ 352-447-2311, in Yankeetown, is one of the best refueling stops around. Maybe it's because the owners refuse to buy freezers, so everything is fresh. Or, maybe it's a menu rich in exotically prepared local seafood (snapper Monte Carlo, pan-fried grouper and shellfish with angel-hair pasta) or a variety of game, including venison. Or, maybe it's the view of the Withlacoochee River, which rushes through woodlands on its way to the Gulf. Make sure you save a few scraps for the resident cats that frequent the grounds.

The other half of the toss-up? **The Landings Restaurant** at Steinhatchee Landing, ☎ 904-498-5313. The chef will lead you through blackened shrimp and lump crab cakes for starters, pecan-encrusted grouper and tender filet mignon for the main course and incredible chocolate desserts (with too many calories) for closers that will force you into calorie burning adventures the next morning.

In Crystal River, **Oyster's Restaurant**, ☎ 352-795-2633, serves local seafood prepared the Old Florida way, while the **Boathouse**, ☎ 352-795-4454, blends fresh seafood with Italian specialties. If you're in the mood for some tempting Chinese vittles try **Mr. Wang's**, ☎ 352-628-6366. You can order from the menu or take your catch from the fishing expedition and ask them, giving a little time, to prepare it for your dinner.

In Hernando's Citrus Hills, there are two good choices. **Andre's**, ☎ 352-746-6855, offers a menu that relies heavily on New England favorites, while **Sergio's**, ☎ 352-746-7676, features classic Italian cuisine from pizza to veal marsala.

Where's Lecanto? It's about midway between Crystal River and Inverness on Highway 44. Stop at the **Country Oaks Tea Room**, ☎ 352-746-3335. It's a century-old home that's part Cracker and part Victorian. Best bet: any of the Black Angus beef offerings.

When it comes to local seafood, Cracker-style (stone crabs, soft shells, clams, oysters and blue-crab fingers), few prepare it better than the restaurants at Cedar Key. Three out on the stilt pier

(**Captains Table**, ☎ 352-543-5441, **Brown Pelican**, ☎ 352-543-5428, and the **Seabreeze**, ☎ 352-543-5738, specialize in belly-busting platters, mullet dip and delightful hearts of palm salads.

Campgrounds

Forget all those creature comforts? You want the outdoors?

Great, there are plenty of campgrounds, ranging from primitive sites to the ones where you can berth a 50-foot Winnebago. As is the case with area motels, reservations are a smart idea if you want your first choice.

The **Chassahowitzka River Campground**, ☎ 352-382-2200, in southeastern Citrus has 52 RV sites and 30 tent sites, some on the pristine river. If cabins are more to your liking the **B&L Resort**, ☎ 352-382-5218, in Chassahowitzka, has some quaint ones that fit the mood of the area.

Crystal Isle RV Resort, ☎ 352-795-3774, is a large campground (25 tent and 250 RV sites) located on a canal that leads to the Crystal River. The **Quail Roost Campground**, ☎ 352-563-0404, has 43 RV sites three miles east of US 19.

Riverside Lodge, ☎ 352-726-2002, has 11 RV sites and nine cabins along the Withlacoochee River. **Trail's End Camp**, ☎ 352-726-3699, also is on the river, near Floral City. It has 20 RV sites, five cabins and a trio of honeymoon suites equipped with jacuzzis.

Cedar Key RV Park, ☎ 352-543-5150, on a bluff overlooking the Gulf, has 30 sites, full hook-ups and cable. **Miller's Marine Campground** in Suwannee, ☎ 800-458-2628, has canal-front campsites, semi-luxury cabins and tree houses, while the **Suwannee River KOA** in Old Town, ☎ 352-542-7636, has shady pull-throughs on the river, cable, boat rentals, a dock and a ramp.

Primitive camping along the Withlacoochee River and the Tsala Apopka chain of lakes is allowed in **Pott's Preserve**, ☎ 800-423-1476, the **Withlacoochee State Forest**, ☎ 352-754-6777, and **Fort Cooper State Park**, ☎ 352-726-0315.

Index

Adventures, 5-6, 8-13; *in air, 12; Central Panhandle, 72-85; Eastern Panhandle, 113-124; eco-travel excursions, 12-13; on foot, 8-9; on horseback, 9-10; Nature Coast, 285-300; North-Central Florida, 243-264; Northeast Florida, 211-224; Northern Heartland, 175-188; Suwannee Region, 142-155; on water, 11-12; Western Panhandle, 40-52; on wheels, 10-11*
In air, 12; *Central Panhandle, 85; Nature Coast, 299-300; North-Central Florida, 263-264; Northeast Florida, 224; Northern Heartland, 188; Western Panhandle, 51-52*
Airboating, 291
Alachua County, 167-172, 188-190
Alfred B. Maclay State Gardens, 111; *on foot, 114-115; on horseback, 116; on wheels, 116-117*
Amelia Island, 194, 200-201; *fishing, 222; on foot, 212; on horseback, 217; where to stay and eat, 225-226*
American Beach, 194, 201
Anastasia Island, 209, 211
Apalachicola, 102, 104
Apalachicola Bluffs and Ravines Preserve, 99-100
Apalachicola National Estuarine Research Reserve, 104
Apalachicola National Forest: *on foot, 113; on horseback, 116; on wheels, 117*

Baker County, 174-175
Ballooning, see *In air*
Bayard Point Conservation Area: *on horseback, 216; on wheels, 218*
Bay County, 62-65
Big Gum Swamp Wilderness Area, 143, 178
Big Lagoon State Recreation Area, 33
Big Talbot Island State Park, 194, 203; *on foot, 212*
Biking, see *On wheels*
Black Heritage Trail, 201

Blackwater River State Forest, 34; *canoeing, 45-48; on foot, 40-41; on horseback, 43-44; on wheels, 44-45*
Blue Spring State Park, *on foot, 244-245*
Bradford County, 172-173, 190
Bulow Plantation State Historic Site, 234-235; *on foot, 244*

Calhoun County, 88
Campgrounds: *Central Panhandle, 89; Eastern Panhandle, 126-127; Nature Coast, 302; North-Central Florida, 266-267; Northeast Florida, 228; Northern Heartland, 190-191; Suwannee Region, 158-159; Western Panhandle, 56*
Camping tips, 20-21
Canoeing: *Central Panhandle, 77-79; Eastern Panhandle, 118-120; Nature Coast, 292-294; North-Central Florida, 256-259; Northeast Florida, 219-220; Northern Heartland, 183-184; Suwannee Region, 150-152; Western Panhandle, 45-48*
Cape San Blas, 58, 69, 71
Caravelle Ranch Conservation Area, *on horseback, 216*
Carrabelle, 105
Cary State Forest: *on foot, 212; on horseback, 216*
Cedar Key, 271, 273, 281-284
Central Panhandle, 57-89; *adventures, 72-85; campgrounds, 89; geography and history, 59-60; getting around, 60-62; information sources, 61-62; touring, 62-72; where to stay and eat, 85-89*
Chassahowitzka, 276-277, 302
Chipley, 65-67, 87
Citrus County, 276-281
Clay County, 202-206
Climate, 18
Clothing and gear, 19-20
Coldwater Recreation Area: *on foot, 41; on horseback, 44*

Columbia County, *137-140, 158*
Crystal River, *270, 272-273, 278-279*
Cumberland Island, *193-194*
Cycling, see *On wheels*
Cypress Springs, *81*

Daytona Beach, *230, 236-239, 264-265*
Daytona International Speedway, *236-237*
Dead Lakes State Recreation Area, *69*; fishing, *83*
DeLeon Springs State Recreation Area, *on foot, 244*
Destin, *36-37, 54*
Diving/snorkeling: *Central Panhandle, 80-82; Eastern Panhandle, 120-122; Nature Coast, 294-297; North-Central Florida, 259-260; Northeast Florida, 220-222; Northern Heartland, 184-185; Suwannee Region, 152-154; Western Panhandle, 48-49*
Dixie County, *281-285*
Dog Island, *106*
Dunes, *precautions, 14*
Dunns Creek Conservation Area, *on wheels, 218*
Duval County, *202-206, 226*

Eastern Panhandle, *91-127; adventures, 113-124; campgrounds, 126-127; geography and history, 93-94; getting around, 95-96; informatios, 96; touring, 96-113; where to stay and eat, 124-127*
Eastpoint, *104-105*
Eco-travel excursions, *12-13; Central Panhandle, 85; Eastern Panhandle, 123; Western Panhandle, 52*
Eden State Gardens and Wesley Mansion, *27, 39*
Elinor Klapp-Phipps Park, *115, 116*
Escambia County, *29-40, 52-53*

Falling Waters Recreation Area, *58, 66-67; on foot, 73*
Fanning Springs State Recreation Area, *166-167, 284-285*
Fires, *precautions, 14*
Fishing: *Central Panhandle, 82-85; Eastern Panhandle, 122-123; licenses, 84-85; Nature Coast, 297-299; North-Central Florida, 261-263;* Northeast Florida, 222-224; Northern Heartland, 186-187; Suwannee Region, 154-155; Western Panhandle, 50-51
Flagler County, *234-235, 264*
Floral City, *279-280*
Florida Caverns State Park, *57, 68-69; on foot, 73; on horseback, 76*
Florida National Scenic Trail, *113-114, 142, 178, 243-244*
Florida Springs Bicycle Tour, *148, 181, 217*
On foot, *8-9; Central Panhandle, 72-75; Eastern Panhandle, 113-116; Nature Coast, 285-287; North-Central Florida, 243-251; Northeast Florida, 211-216; Northern Heartland, 175-188; Suwannee Region, 142-145; Western Panhandle, 40-52*
Forest Capital Museum, *285*
Fort Clinch, *194, 199-200*
Fort Cooper State Park, *273, 280*
Fort Gadsden State Historic Site, *102*
Fort Gates Ferry, *195, 207*
Fort George Island State Cultural Site, *203-204; on foot, 212-213*
Fort Pickens, *30*
Fort Walton, *36-37*
Fort Walton Beach, *54*
Frangista, *37*
Frank Hawley's Drag School, *182-183*
Franklin County, *102-106, 125*
Freshwater fishing, see *Fishing*

Gadsden County, *96-99, 124-125*
Gainesville, *on wheels, 182*
Gear and clothing, *19-20*
Geography and history, *3-5; Central Panhandle, 59-60; Eastern Panhandle, 93-94; Nature Coast, 272-274; North-Central Florida, 231-232; Northeast Florida, 196-197; Northern Heartland, 164; Suwannee Region, 131-132; Western Panhandle, 26-27*
Gilchrist County, *166-167, 188-190*
Gold Head Branch State Park: *on foot, 213; on wheels, 217*
Golf: *Central Panhandle, 75; Eastern Panhandle, 115-116; Nature Coast, 287; North-Central Florida, 248-251; Northeast Florida, 214-216; Northern Heartland, 179; Suwannee Region, 145; Western Panhandle, 41-43*

Index 305

Grayton Beach, 25
Grayton Beach State Recreation Area, 39
Guana River State Park, 211; *on foot,* 213; *on wheels,* 217
Gulfarium, 36-37
Gulf Breeze, 33-34
Gulf Coast Triathlon, 64
Gulf County, 69-72, 88-89
Gulf Islands Nat'l Seashore, 27, 40
Gulf Specimen Marine Laboratory, 92, 106, 108
Gulf World, 64

Hamilton County, 135-137, 156
Henderson Beach State Recreation Area, 37
High Springs, 171-172
Holmes County, 67-68, 87
Homosassa Springs State Wildlife Park, 277-278
Hontoon Island State Park, 244
On horseback, 9-10; *Central Panhandle,* 75-76; *Eastern Panhandle,* 116; *Nature Coast,* 288-289; *North-Central Florida,* 251-253; *Northeast Florida,* 216-217; *Northern Heartland,* 179-181; *Suwannee Region,* 146-147; *Western Panhandle,* 43-44
Houseboating, 292

Ichetucknee Springs State Park, 140, 144, 153, 183
Indian Temple Mound Museum, 26, 36
Insects and wildlife, 15-18

Jackson County, 68-69, 87-88
Jacksonville, 202-206, 226; *fishing,* 222-223
Jefferson County, 113
Jennings State Forest: *canoeing,* 220; *on foot,* 213; *on horseback,* 217; *on wheels,* 218

Kanapaha Botanical Gardens, 169-170

Lafayette County, 158
Lake Butler, 173-174
Lake County, 239-241, 265
Lakeridge Winery, 240-241

Lake Talquin State Forest: *on foot,* 115; *on horseback,* 116
Leon County, 109-111, 126
Levy County, 281-285
Liberty County, 99-102
Little Talbot Island State Park, 203
Lochloosa Wildlife Conservation Area: *canoeing,* 184; *fishing,* 187; *on horseback,* 180; *on wheels,* 182
Lyme disease, 17

McIntosh, 242-243
Madison County, 133-135, 156
Manatees, 278-279
Manatee Springs State Park, 286-287, 296
Maps, source for, 115 ; *counties,* 6; *Northern Florida Trail sections,* 7; *Pensacola,* 30; *Escambia County,* 31; *Santa Rosa County,* 32; *Okaloosa County,* 35; *Walton County,* 38; *Bay County,* 63; *Washington County,* 65; *Holmes County,* 67; *Jackson County,* 68; *Gulf County,* 70; *Calhoun County,* 71; *Gadsden County,* 98; *Torreya State Park,* 100; *Liberty County,* 101; *Franklin County,* 103; *Wakulla County,* 107; *Tallahassee,* 109; *Leon County,* 110; *Jefferson County,* 112; *Madison County,* 134; *Hamilton County,* 135; *Ichetucknee Springs State Park,* 138; *Columbia County,* 139; *Suwannee County,* 141; *Suwannee River State Park,* 142; *Lafayette County,* 157; *Gainesville,* 163; *Gilchrist County,* 167; *Alachua County,* 168; *Bradford County,* 173; *Union County,* 174; *Baker County,* 175; *Nassau County,* 200; *Duval County,* 202; *Clay County,* 203; *Jacksonville & Vicinity,* 204; *St. Johns County,* 206; *Putnam County* 208; *Gold Head Branch State Park,* 212; *Flagler County,* 235; *Volusia County,* 237; *Lake County,* 240; *Marion County,* 241; *Withlacoochee State Trail,* 245; *Citrus County,* 276; *Sumter County,* 280; *Levy County,* 282; *Dixie County,* 283; *Taylor County,* 284
Marion County, 241-243, 265-266
Mayport, 194, 205

Mexico Beach, *64-65*
Micanopy, *169*
Milton, *34, 53-54;* canoeing, *45-48*
Museum of Man in the Sea, *62-63*

Nassau County, *199-202, 225-226*
National Museum of Naval Aviation, *29*
Natural Bridge, *94, 108*
Nature Coast and Big Bend, *269-302;* adventures, *285-300;* campgrounds, *302;* geography and history, *272-274;* getting around, *274-275;* information sources, *275;* touring, *276-285;* where to stay and eat, *300-302*
North-Central Florida, *230-267;* adventures, *243-264;* campgrounds, *266-267;* geography and history, *231-232;* getting around, *232-234;* information, *233-234;* touring, *234-243;* where to stay and eat, *264-267*
Northeast Florida, *193-228;* adventures, *211-224;* campgrounds, *228;* geography and history, *196-197;* getting around, *198-199;* information sources, *198-199;* touring, *199-211;* where to stay and eat, *224-228*
Northern Florida: adventures, *5-6, 8-13;* Central Panhandle, *57-89;* Eastern Panhandle, *91-127;* geography and history, *3-5;* Nature Coast and Big Bend, *269-302;* North-Central Florida, *230-267;* Northeast Florida, *193-228;* Northern Heartland, *161-191;* Suwannee Region, *129-159;* travel tips, *13-21;* Western Panhandle, *23-56;* where to stay and eat, *13*
Northern Heartland, *161-191;* adventures, *175-188;* campgrounds, *190-191;* geography and history, *164;* getting around, *165-166;* informatios, *165-166;* touring, *166-175;* where to stay and eat, *188-191*
Northwest Florida Water Management District, *41;* on foot, *74, 114;* on horseback, *76*

Ocala National Forest, *251*
O'Leno State Park, *180*
Olustee Battlefield Historic Site, *132, 138, 140, 174-175*

Osceola National Forest: fishing, *155;* on foot, *142, 178, 243-244;* on horseback, *147, 180-181*

Panama City Beach, *62-65, 86-87;* fishing, *82-83*
Payne's Prairie State Preserve, *164;* campgrounds, *191;* fishing, *187;* on foot, *176;* on horseback, *179-180;* on wheels, *181-182*
Peacock Springs State Park, *153*
Pensacola, *24, 26, 29-40, 52-53*
Perdido Key Recreation Area, *29-30*
Plants, precautions, *14, 17-18*
Ponce de Leon Springs State Recreation Area, *67;* on foot, *73;* snorkeling, *81-82*
Ponce Inlet Lighthouse and Museum, *238-239*
Putnam County, *207-211, 226-227*
Ravine State Gardens, *207*
Rowing, *263*

St. Andrews State Recreation Area, *62*
St. Augustine, *193, 207-211;* fishing, *222;* where to stay and eat, *227-228*
St. George Island State Park, *106*
St. Johns County, *207-211, 227-228*
St. Johns River, *195;* fishing, *222*
St. Johns River Water Management District: canoeing, *220, 258;* on foot, *213-214, 246-247;* on horseback, *252-253;* on wheels, *218, 254-255*
St. Joseph Peninsula, *69, 71;* on wheels, *76-77*
St. Joseph State Park, *71-72;* canoeing, *79;* on foot, *73-74*
St. Marks Lighthouse, *108*
St. Marks National Wildlife Refuge, *108;* on foot, *114*
St. Marys River State Forest, *214;* on horseback, *216-217;* on wheels, *218*
St. Vincent Island, *105*
Saltwater fishing, see *Fishing*
San Felasco Hammock State Preserve, *180*
San Marcos de Apalache, *94, 108*
Santa Rosa County, *53-54*
Seaside, *24-25, 39-40*
Seven Hills to the Sea Bike Tour, *77, 117-118*

Index 307

Shell Island, *64*
Snorkeling, see *Diving/snorkeling*
South Walton, *37-40, 55-56*
Southwest Florida Water Management District: *on foot, 247-248; on horseback, 253, 288; on wheels, 255*
Spanish moss, *230*
Steinhatchee, *271-272*
Stephen Foster State Folk Culture Center, *129, 137, 144, 147, 155*
Suwannee County, *140-141, 156-157*
Suwannee Region, *129-159; adventures, 142-155; campgrounds, 158-159; geography and history, 131-132; getting around, 132-133; information sources, 133; touring, 133-141; where to stay and eat, 156-159*
Suwannee River State Park, *144, 155*
Suwannee River Water Management District: *campgrounds, 191; canoeing, 183; fishing, 187; on foot, 144-145, 178; on horseback, 146-147, 180; on wheels, 148-149, 182*

Tallahassee, *92-93*
Tallahassee-to-St. Marks Historic State Trail: *on foot, 114; on horseback, 116; on wheels, 117*
Taylor County, 281-285
Ted Williams Museum and Hitters' Hall of Fame, *281*
Three Rivers State Recreation Area, *69; canoeing, 79; fishing, 83; on foot, 73*
Tiger Bay State Forest: *on foot, 244; on horseback, 252; on wheels, 253-254*
Torreya State Park, *92, 100, 102; on foot, 114*
Touring: *Central Panhandle, 62-72; Eastern Panhandle, 96-113; Nature Coast, 276-285; North-Central Florida, 234-243; Northeast Florida, 199-211; Northern Heartland, 166-175; Suwannee Region, 133-141; Western Panhandle, 29-40*
Travel tips, *13-21; camping, 20-21; climate, 18; clothing and gear, 19-20; driving and road conditions, 20; information sources, 21; precautions, 14; wildlife and insects, 15-18*

Tsala Apopka lakes, *270-271, 279*
Twin Rivers State Forest, *147, 155*
Tyndall Air Force Base: *on foot, 74; on horseback, 76; on wheels, 77*

Union County, *173-174*

Van Fleet State Trail: *on horseback, 252; on wheels, 253*
Volusia County, *236-239, 264-265*
Vortex Spring, *67-68, 81*

Wakulla County, *106-109, 125-126*
Wakulla Springs State Park, *117, 120*
Walton County, *23*
Washington County, *65-67, 87*
Washington Oaks State Gardens, *231-232, 235-236; on foot, 244*
On water, *11-12; Central Panhandle, 77-85; Eastern Panhandle, 118-123; Nature Coast, 291-299; North-Central Florida, 256-263; Northeast Florida, 219-224; Northern Heartland, 183-187; Suwannee Region, 150-155; Western Panhandle, 45-51*
Water skiing, *187, 263*
Welaka State Forest: *on foot, 213; on horseback, 216*
Western Panhandle, *23-56; adventures, 40-52; campgrounds, 56; geography and history, 26-27; getting around, 27-29; information sources, 28-29; touring, 29-40; where to stay and eat, 52-56*
On wheels, *10-11; Central Panhandle, 76-77; Eastern Panhandle, 116-118; Nature Coast, 289-291; North-Central Florida, 253-255; Northeast Florida, 217-218; Northern Heartland, 181-183; Suwannee Region, 147-149; Western Panhandle, 44-45*
Where to stay and eat, *13; Central Panhandle, 85-89; Eastern Panhandle, 124-127; Nature Coast, 300-302; North-Central Florida, 264-267; Northeast Florida, 224-228; Northern Heartland, 188-191; Suwannee Region, 156-159; Western Panhandle, 52-56*
Wildlife and insects, *15-18*
Windsurfing, *263*

Withlacoochee State Trail, 279; *on foot,*
246, 285-286; on horseback, 251-252,
288-289; on wheels, 253, 289-291

Yulee Sugar Mill Ruins, 273, 278